图书策划委员会

主任　俞敏洪

委员　（按姓氏笔划为序）

王　强　　王文山

包凡一　　仲晓红

李　杜　　邱政政

沙云龙　　汪海涛

陈向东　　周成刚

徐小平　　窦中川

前　言

　　本书毫无保留地汇集了我在北京新东方学校讲授 GRE 句子填空题型三年以来的全部心得体会。我希望本书不仅能够成为新东方学员备考 GRE 句子填空的补充和提高材料，而且能为更多的 GRE 考生提供一份全面系统的学习材料。我深知本书的读者是 GRE 考生，需要的是简洁高效的作战技巧，实实在在的考分。因此，在编写本书的过程中，我追求最大限度地贴近 GRE 考生实际学习过程，充分注意了如下三个方面：

　　1. 翻译例句时尽量体现原文的结构，以便考生能对照原文体会句子结构的特征，从而领会结构与答案选项之间的关系，这才是填空题的解题精华。由于 GRE 句子填空的例句选自各自然、人文学科的专业期刊论文，逻辑结构往往复杂晦涩，但其表达结构却总是万变不离其宗。GRE 句子填空考查你是否能够从句子的表达中学习新的逻辑思想，考查你阅读中的逻辑推理能力，考查你是否是一个积极的阅读者。从句子的表达结构到逻辑结构，乃至分析填空选项的逻辑结构，你都需要一个非常清晰的头脑。这正是你与众不同之处，也是欧美研究生院录取你并给你高额奖学金的原因之一。然而对于英语为非母语的考生而言，连对句子的表达结构都未必熟悉，所以，考生需要强化训练，让自己主动适应这些表达结构，并进而能使用这些表达结构进行积极的逻辑思考。

　　2. 解题指导强化从句子的表达结构到逻辑结构的清晰分析，强化从逻辑结构到填空选项的清晰分析。填空考的是逻辑，阅读中的逻辑。广大考生往往有很好的数理逻辑思维，也有很高的文学修养，却缺少边阅读边批判思考的习惯，而这却恰恰是欧美研究生院异常重视的素质之一。本书除了训练考生在阅读中的逻辑思维外，还提供了大量经验层面的实战技巧。有些技巧的思路类似于见红花就选绿叶，这看上去有悖于培养清晰阅读逻辑的宗旨，也不宜过度渲染，但考场上偶尔能用一两句，颇有快感。

　　3. 难词注释中的选词并非电脑统计结果，全部是根据我三年以来的教学经验所做的判断。由于近几年填空题对中级词汇的深入理解以及熟词僻义提出了更高的要求，所以书中加大了对中级词汇的注释。这些注释中，绝大多数（尤其是动词和形容词）都是中英文注释，因为通过英文注释更能精确把握词汇的真实含义。众多考生在最后向更高的考分冲刺时都会发现"词汇修养"是难以越过的障碍。词汇修养，其中包含词义的辨析和词义的转化，并非一朝一夕之功，需要考生在长期的磨练中去领会。很多考生往往是到了复习的最后阶段才认识到这一点，但为时已晚。在教学过程中，我发现尽管许多学生都知道这一道理，却很少去注意培养。问及原因，他们要么没有时间去查阅英文词典，要么不知道哪些词该通过英文注释精确掌握含义,哪些只要背中文释义即可;另外一个原因是有些英文注释本身过于复杂,难以理解。基于上述原因考虑,本书对 GRE 句子填空中需精确掌握的词汇做了一个总结。每个词均斟酌再三,从众多词典的众多释义中选出需要 GRE 考生掌握的词义,并配以最恰当的英文解释。很可惜的是当初促使我写这本书,并且迫切希望得到帮助的考生都已经考完了 GRE,再也不能从本书中获得帮助。惟希望后来者受益,认真对待每一个注释,认真揣摩每个单词的各个义项之间的转化关系。

感谢俞敏洪老师为本书的整体结构提出的中肯建议。

感谢北京大学的高洁同学,她为本书的校稿付出了大量的时间和精力;感谢北京师范大学的陈大铭同学和孟德宏同学,没有他们的帮助本书不可能顺利地完稿。

出国留学对于大多数考生而言是一条人生"绿色通道",往往会导引 GRE 考生们到一个全新的境界。与它需要付出的巨大努力相比,它的回报更加惊人。我衷心地希望我的努力能给广大考生带来帮助,因为我也曾经在这条道路上奋斗过,因为我敬佩所有在这条道路上奋斗的人!

陈圣元
于北京新东方学校

使 用 建 议

过去几十年来,GRE 考题的一个语文 SECTION 有 7 道填空题,本书收集了 100 个语文 SECTION 的 700 道题。

对于参加新东方培训的学生而言,本书可应用于三个环节:

首先,每节课的复习阶段。新东方的课堂讲课速度远远超过了正常的理解速度。在课程设计中从未奢望学生能在课堂上当场理解。按照经验,2.5 小时的课堂内容必须当天在课下复习 2.5 小时。否则时过境迁,仅凭记忆或简略的笔记很难回忆起当天的全部课程内容。本书里的讲解不仅比课堂讲解更详细,而且书里的单词注释本应是课下自行钻研的内容,在短短的课堂时间里无法深究词汇。因此,每一个渴望获得 GRE 高分,走向哈佛、耶鲁、斯坦福的学子必须在课下付出额外的努力!

其次,总复习提高阶段。若干道考题的解题分析的末尾都给出了索引,指向同类思路的考题。在总复习阶段,这些索引能帮助考生融会贯通。

最后,考前的冲刺阶段。SECTION 79 至 SECTION 88 的考题无论从风格上,从解题思路上,还是从用词习惯上,都非常典范,对考生在考场上激发思路,形成有益的联想很有帮助。建议考生保留这些考题到应考前一周做适应性练习。

对未参加新东方 GRE 培训课程的学生而言,除了需要充分注意上文涉及的几点外,还需注意如下几点:

首先,熟读本书的第一部分,熟悉每一个概念,并且尽量在解题中运用。 几乎所有的初学者都会不由自主地放弃这些概念,仍回到自己熟悉的精读的解题方法上去。这是可以理解的,谁都希望彻底读懂面前的句子,这几乎是本能! 但问题是在考场时间紧迫,不允许慢条斯理,需要快速熟练、准确到位的逻辑推理。几乎没有人可以在考场上彻底读懂那些过于抽象、压缩、晦涩的学究式难句。凭借本书的这些概念和技巧可以更快地解题,或者置晦涩句意于不顾而直接得出答案。尽管每个 SECTION 的前 4 道考题往往可以凭阅读的功底对付,但后 3 道往往需要这些技巧,所以请熟练掌握这些概念。

其次,在练习 SECTION 42 之前的题目时,不要控制解题时间。 将重心放在句子结构分析和具体的技巧运用上,多研究,多揣摩。在 SECTION 43 之后,注意控制做题时间,尽量在 7 分钟内做完一个 SECTION,最终应能在 5~6 分钟之间做完一个 SECTION。如果到后期能在此规定时间做完,并且稳定在大多数的 SECTION 答对 5 道题以上,或半数以上的 SECTION 能做对 6 道或 7 道题,那么,你已经跨进了最优秀考生的行列之中!

最后,请记住 GRE 考试的最大特点就是高度模式化。 熟悉全部考题几乎就可以保证考场上的成功。所以,请反复练习各套考题,做 5 遍是我对新东方学生的要求。

在整个出国留学的奋斗过程中攻克 GRE 是最花精力的一步,也是最有决定意义的一步,也是完全靠个人努力即可成功的一步! 我深深希望本书能为广大考生艰苦的奋斗贡献一点绵薄之力。祝成功!

陈圣元
于北京新东方学校

目　　录

第一部分 解题指导

第一章 解题方法综述

第一节 背后的法则

句子填空思路独特,与正常的阅读迥然不同,它是一种文字与文字之间,概念与概念之间的逆向推理游戏,是众多考生望而生畏,觉得捉摸不透的题型之一。

中国考生往往对数理逻辑的正向逆向推理轻车熟路,而对文字内部的逆向推理则非常陌生。很多考生上了考场仍然误以为"读懂就行"。试想,如果连句子主干的谓语动词都是一个空格,怎么可能阅读呢? 中国考生过去经常做的政治、历史等学科的填空题是一种知识性填空题,比如要填入攻陷巴士底狱的时间,或是萨拉热窝事件中被谋杀的公爵的名字等等。这种考题考查考生的记忆能力,答案是上考场前记忆下来带到考场上去的。而即将面对的 GRE 填空考题却是 GRE General Test 的一部分。这些题目针对二十多个专业的考生,题目本身不能涉及任何专业知识,否则对其他考生都是一种极大的不公平。那么,句子填空中空格的信息从何而来呢? 永远不会来源于专业知识的忆记,永远都来自于题目内部。总之,答案都会在原句中重复。考生需要做的只是在原句中寻找答案。

第二节 重复的基本规律

既然空格的信息会在原文中重复,重复的方式就成为被关注的焦点,试比较下面两个例句。(本章中所有例句都已被简化,从而降低初学者的难度,并非真实考题。)

例句 1:Joshin was in his private life a _____ man: he lived in rented room, ate little, wore drab clothes.

    (A) simple   (B) sordid   (C) foolish   (D) miserly   (E) ascetic

例句 2:Though his political writing was often flamboyant, he was in his private life a surprisingly _____ man.

    (A) simple   (B) sordid   (C) foolish   (D) miserly   (E) ascetic

这两个例句典型体现了不同的重复方式,第一个例句用了冒号后的整整一句话来描述 Joshin 的性格,要求考生自行归纳,总结出一个形容词填到空格中去。第二个例句由转折关系及 surprisingly 一词明确规定出空格处词义应与 flamboyant 相反。

第一个例句的出题方式几乎不会在 GRE 的填空中出现。因为归纳这种思路本身与考生的背景文化、专业知识相关。比如该句中"住在租来的房子里,吃得很少,穿着颜色暗淡的衣服"究竟应该归纳为哪一种人呢? 在一个崇尚消费的社会中,此种行为会被认为是吝啬,从而选选项 D;而在一个崇尚简朴的社会里,这种行为又会被认为是节俭朴素,从而选选项 A;甚至可能在一个具有某种宗教信仰的考生的思想中,该行为又会被认为是一种节欲苦行,从而选选项 E。众说纷纭,莫衷一是。但在第二个例句中就不会出现这种情况,句中的转折结构及 surprising 都非常明确地规定了空格应为 flamboyant 的反义词,答案只能是 A。

　　如果将一个句子形象地看成一条线段,每个单词就是其上的一点。第一个例句用冒号后的一个句子重复空格这一个词,我们将之称为"线对点";第二个例句用 flamboyant 这个词重复空格这个词,我们将之称为"点对点"。GRE 句子填空的重复方式为点对点。

　　每个空格在原句中都会有一个词或词组与之重复,我们称这个词为中心词。这种重复可能是同义词直接重复,也可能如本例一样为反义重复。这种中心词和空格之间的逻辑关系往往都非常明确,很多时候都简单到同义词或反义词。一言以蔽之,解题就是要找对中心词及其与空格的逻辑关系。

第三节　攻其一点,不及其余

　　考生可以根据句子提供的逻辑关系进行推理,比如由转折关系知前后为反义词,并列关系知前后为同义词。一个句子往往会有很多层逻辑关系,考生要抓准空格所在的那层逻辑关系。其他层面的逻辑关系有可能会更精彩,用词更生僻,却纯属陷阱。

　　比如,一个句子可能会有很多定语从句结构,而空格出现在定语从句内部的 and 所引导的并列结构中,and 左边有一空格,句子其他位置上还有一个空格。此时能满足 and 前后同义词关系的选项有几个呢? 你可能会发现只有一个,此时实在没有必要再去反复阅读、理解句子其他部分。因为保证从句正确的只有一个答案,要使得全句都正确就首先必须使每一个分句先正确,而使得 and 前后关系正确的只有一个答案,当然没有必要再看句子的其他部分;考生也可能发现满足该 and 并列结构的有 A 和 D 两个选项,这时才需要去阅读句子的其他部分,看 A 和 D 两个选项哪一个正确。

例句 3: Yellow fever, the disease that killed 4,000 Philadelphians in 1793, and so ＿＿ Memphis, Tennessee, that the city lost its charter, has reappeared after nearly two decades in ＿＿ in the western Hemisphere.

　　(A) terrorized. . contention　　(B) ravaged. . secret　　(C) disabled. . quarantine

　　(D) corrupted. . quiescence　　(E) decimated. . abeyance

　　此句主干为"黄热病重新出现",句意非常简洁。第二个空格要求填出黄热病重新出现之前的 20 年处于何种状态。重新出现之前当然就是不出现的状态,所以空格应填上"未发生疾病的状态"。五个选项中只有选项 E 的 abeyance 为"中止,搁置,不发生"之义。至于 secret, quarantine(隔离检疫期),quiescence 都是针对存在的情况做的描述,因为对于一个根本不存在的事物,既不能用"安静",也不可能用"不安静"去形容它。答案可确定为 E。此时考生如果尚未阅读主语 Yellow fever 至谓语动词之间的一段文字,在考场上也千万不要去阅读它,不但浪费时间,而且反而增加很多疑惑,比如其中的 charter 作何种含义解释才说得通呢? 事实上 charter 共有 25 个词义,本句中的含义为"君主或者立法机构批准成立自治市或自治州的特许状"。若要成为一个自治市,一定数量的人口是个必要因素,结果突如其来的一场传染病却杀死了田纳西州曼菲斯这个城市的大批人口,所以这个城市就丧失了它成立自治市的资格,这就是 charter 在此句中的含义,恐怕要让人大跌眼镜。

根据经验,最难的单词永远都出现在不需要阅读的部分。解题时只关心空格所在的逻辑结构即可。解题时切记"攻其一点,不及其余"。

第四节　读题干的策略

在上节的讲解中,直至做完答案都未涉及主语和谓语之外的部分,考生在做句子填空时应养成这样的好习惯:先读主干,再读分隔。这就是读题干的策略。

所谓分隔即是指主干之外的一切成分,如定语从句、同位语从句、分词短语作修饰语、长的介词短语作修饰语等等。这些都是考生阅读时需跳过去的部分。有时候一个句子中这些成分多达几个,这更是阅读时的障碍,此时应该毫不犹豫地跳过去,先提炼出句子的主干。这种能力是解 GRE 句子填空题的基础。

例句 4：The disjunction between educational objectives that stress independence and individuality and those that emphasize obedience to rules and cooperation with others reflects a _____ that arises from the values on which these objectives are based.

　　(A) conflict　　(B) redundancy　　(C) gain　　(D) predictability　　(E) wisdom

此句的主干简化后为"The disjunction reflects a"考生以后再见到 reflect 或 represent 这两个动词时可以将主语和宾语等同起来,此句中的空格可以填上 disjunction 的同义词,答案为(A)conflict。此句的其他部分都是冗余信息。考生可自行将 disjunction 之后的 between. . .and 所连接的两件事物换成不同的人生观、不同的历史观、不同的世界观。只要是不同的价值观所能导致的一切不同观点均可。你会发现题目的答案根本不会受任何影响,可见这些部分的确是冗余信息。请考生仔细揣摩思考。

例句 5：Conceptually, it is hard to reconcile a defense attorney's _____ to ensure that false testimony is not knowingly put forward with the attorney's mandate to mount the most _____ defense conceivable for the client.

　　(A) efforts. . cautious　　(B) duty. . powerful　　(C) inability. . eloquence
　　(D) failure. . diversified　　(E) promise. . informed

这种先读句子主干,后读分隔的读题策略在近几年考题中尤为重要,例句 5 实际上就是国内题 1999 年 4 月 SECTION 5 第 3 道题。请考生尽量去分清句子主干并解题,详细解答请参阅 SECTION 88 的第 3 道题相应解答。

这种读题的策略是由基本解题思路决定的。既然解题是通过逻辑推理,而逻辑推理每次只能进行一步,所以相应地考生在读句子时,每次只读一个逻辑层面。

第五节　分析的策略

分析的目的只是为了找出中心词和逻辑关系,因为这才是解题的依据。找出中心词和逻辑关系并不依赖于对全句的理解,而来源于句子结构特征,尽管句子的内容可能天文地理无所不包,但表达结构却只有几种。

相应地解题步骤应为四步:第一步,分析句子结构;第二步,根据句子结构特征定位中心词和确定逻辑关系;第三步,选词;第四步,理解句意。

但是,在考场上第四步是可做可不做的,这已在第四节中做了充分的解释。第三步(选词)一定要注意是在第二步之后进行,即推理出空格的含义之后再去选词。千万不要在尚未根据原句推知空格信息,在仍然对空格一头雾水的情况下去看选项,许多考生很容易不由自主地先瞄一眼选项,想看看哪一个选项代回原句中感觉更通畅,这实际上是一种思维中懒惰的表现。一定要强迫自己对原文做一个主动的逻辑推理,推知空格的信息后再去看选项。否则极易掉进那些本来就是故意设计的似是而非的各种陷阱中去。第二步要求根据句子结构特征进行中心词定位和逻辑推理。句子结构特征将在下一节中详细讲述,第一步分析句子结构是和上一节的阅读的方法密不可分的。

第二章 各种具体的解题方法——分隔与粘连

各种具体的解题方法实际上就是针对英文这种语言可能出现的重复信息的方式——列举。大致可分为两类:分隔和粘连。

分隔这种提供重复信息的方式出现在分隔成分和主干的关系中。比如空格要求填一名词,其后又出现一同位语从句,考生不难想像该如何解题,并且由衷地感慨这的确只是一种文字游戏而已。

粘连这种提供重复信息的方式出现在上下两句中,或者只是一个句子内部直接、简单的重复。所谓上下两句,通常是用分号或冒号分开的两个完整的句子(当然很多时候也用逗号)。所谓句子内部直接的重复,如指示代词和指代对象的重复等等。

分隔提供答案的方式在难题中出现较多,而粘连出现得比较普遍。

第一节 分隔结构

句子中充当分隔结构的通常为定语从句、同位语从句、分词结构、大的介词短语结构,对于这四种结构考生要烂熟于胸,因为 40% 的答案都在这些结构中。分隔结构一旦出现则成为其前空格的答案;或者这些分隔中本身具有空格,则应从分隔前的结构中找寻信息。

请注意分隔前的结构指主干的一个句子成分,比如一个宾语,一个谓语,而不是指单一的词。

例句 1: The state is a network of exchanged benefits and beliefs, ____ between rulers and citizens based on those laws and procedures that are ____ to the maintenance of community.

(A) a compromise. . inimical   (B) an interdependence. . subsidiary   (C) a counterpoint. . incidental   (D) an equivalence. . prerequisite   (E) a reciprocity. . conducive

　　此句主干甚为简单，"The state is a network of exchanged benefits and beliefs"。其后全部为分隔结构。主干之外全部是分隔，用这种简单的判定规则，避开繁琐的语法分析，是为了更快地分析解决问题，考生在解题时也应采取这一判断方法。第一空格应直接重复"a network of exchanged benefits and beliefs"。请注意领会上一段所述的"重复前文主干中的一个结构，而不是一个单词"的含义，此处重复的是上文的宾语，答案可据此直接选 E。此句的其他部分详述请参阅 SECTION 6 的第 5 题。

例句 2：It has been argued that politics as ＿＿，whatever its transcendental claims, has always been the systematic organization of common hatreds.　憎恨

　　　　(A) a theory　　　(B) an ideal　　　(C) a practice　　　(D) a contest　　　(E) an enigma

　　此句主语为 politics，谓语动词为 has always been，所以中间的一段为主干之外的成分为分隔，分隔与空格的关系由 whatever 指明，空格应与 transcendental claims 构成反义，答案为 C，具体分析请参阅 SECTION 30 的第 4 题。　　（似乎）超越经验的 / 理论的（答案）

例句 3：In a most impressive demonstration, Pavarotti sailed through Verdi's "Celeste Aida", normally a tenor's ＿＿，with the casual enthusiasm of a folk singer performing one of his favorite ＿＿.　轻快地通过，轻而易举的获得成功

　　　　(A) pitfall . . recitals　　　　(B) glory . . chorales　　　　(C) nightmare . . ballads

　　　　(D) delight . . chanteys　　　(E) routine . . composers

　　此句尽管难点甚多，但简单分隔才是应注意的目标。句中的 a folk singer 之后出现了分词短语构成的分隔，其中空格的信息应由 a folk singer 提供，可直接得答案 C 的 ballads。其他部分的具体分析请参阅 SECTION 17 的第 2 题。　民谣歌手　　　　民谣

　　以上三个例句的分隔在解题中都起到了举足轻重的作用。原因是分隔结构中，或分隔结构前的主干中出现了一个空格。如果分隔中或分隔前均无空格出现，这个分隔就是一个无用的分隔，一个冗余信息，阅读时跳过去就再也不用理会，考生读题干的策略是先读主干，后读分隔。这时需进一步强调，不需再读这种无效的分隔。

例句 4：The valedictory address, as it has developed in American colleges and universities over the years, has become a very strict form, a literary ＿＿ that permits very little ＿＿.

　　　　(A) text . . clarity　　　　(B) work . . tradition　　　　(C) genre . . deviation　偏离

　　　　(D) oration . . grandiloquence　　　(E) achievement . . rigidity　（文学）类型

　　此句甚典型，主语之后的分隔中无空格，分隔前的成分中也无空格，故此分隔完全不需理会，句末出现的分隔中却有空格存在，所以解题的关键在于此分隔。详细解答请参阅 SECTION 49 第 3 题。

　　有时候分隔结构会出现在主从句中，比如因果句的 because 之后为逗号，不直接出现原因从句，而先出现分隔；或者 although 之后先出现分隔，然后再出现真正的转折从句等等。这种情况下，一律先跳过分隔，将真正的因果、转折、并列等主干逻辑关系找出来。

例句 5：Eric was frustrated because, although he was adept at making lies sound ＿＿，when telling the truth, he ＿＿ the power to make himself believed.

　　　　(A) plausible . . lacked　　　　(B) convincing . . held　　　　(C) honest . . found

　　　　(D) truea . . acquired　　　(E) logical . . claimed

　　此句主干为因果关系，而 because 之后出现了分隔，先跳过去处理真正的原因从句，由"Eric was frustrated because he ＿＿ the power to make himself believed"这样的简单的因果句不难看

出选项 A 为正确答案,详细解答请参阅 SECTION 46 第 2 题。

第二节　粘连中的上下句结构

粘连方法中的上下句重复指以分号、逗号或冒号分开的上下两句中的直接同义重复、双重否定与肯定句的重复、主动句与被动句的重复、逆否命题重复、比较句的重复、手段目的句的重复、特殊并列句的重复、时间对比句的重复。大多数 GRE 的句子填空都可看成上下两句。读下句时主动地寻找与上半句的重复之处。

例句 1:Natural selection tends to eliminate genes that cause inherited diseases, acting most strongly against the most severe disease; Consequently, hereditary diseases that are ＿＿＿ would be expected to be very ＿＿＿, but, surprisingly, they are not. (直接同义重复)

    (A) lethal.. rare   (B) untreated.. dangerous   (C) unusualr.. refractory

    (D) new.. perplexing   (E) widespread.. acute

此句分号后的下半句中要求填一形容词修饰 hereditary diseases,这个形容词当然不应凭空创造,应由分号句的上半句提供,而分号句上半句提供的修饰 hereditary diseases 的形容词只有 most severe,所以空格填之即可,A 为正确答案。详细解答请参阅 SECTION 5 的第 2 题。

例句 2:Parts of seventeenth-century Chinese pleasure gardens were not necessarily intended to look ＿＿＿; they were designed expressly to evoke the agreeable melancholy resulting from a sense of the ＿＿＿ of natural beauty and human glory. (双重否定句与肯定句)

    (A) beautiful.. immutability   (B) cheerful.. transitoriness

    (C) colorful.. abstractness   (D) luxuriant.. simplicity

    (E) conventional.. wildness

此分号上下句的主语相同,谓语动词"were intended to"与"were designed to"在此句中也同义,只不过上半句为否定形式,下半句为肯定形式,为了保证上下句重复,即不冲突,第一个空格里应填 the agreeable melancholy 的反义词,故答案为 B。详细解答请参阅 SECTION 7 的第 7 题。

例句 3:The struggle of the generation is one of the obvious constants of human affairs; therefore, it may be presumptuous to suggest that the rivalry batten young and old in western society during the current decade is ＿＿＿ critical. (双重否定与肯定)

    (A) perennially   (B) disturbingly   (C) uniquely   (D) archetypal   (E) cautiously

此句的分号上下又构成了一肯定与双重否定的重复,尤其是下句的句型请考生熟记,它往往就是双重否定转换的标识。"It's wrong to say that." 当然,wrong 可以换成 foolish,也可换成此句的 presumptuous。由双重否定句可知,上句称"the struggle of generation"为"constant",则下句应称"the rivalry between young and old"也为"constant",双重否定句中空格处应填"非 constant",即答案 C 的 uniquely。详细解答请参阅 SECTION 13 的第 5 题。

例句 4:An investigation that is ＿＿＿ can occasionally yield new facts, even notable ones; typically the appearance of such facts is the result of a search in a definite direction. (主动与被动)

    (A) timely   (B) unguided   (C) consistent   (D) uncomplicated   (E) subjective

此句中分号上下句存在明显的重复,下句的 search 重复上句的 investigation。两者各有一个定语,一个为定语从句,一个为介词短语,通常主动句变被动句的结构为 A→B;B→by A。或者 by 可以由下列三个短语代替:is the result of, is the outgrowth of, is the product of。此句在此基础略加变化而成为非 A→非 B;B→by A。不难得知空格应与"in a definite direction"构成反义词,正确答案为 B。详细解答请参阅 SECTION 4 的第 5 题。

例句 5: Any population increase beyond a certain level necessitate greater ＿＿ vegetable foods; thus, the ability of a society to choose meat over cereals always arises, in part, from ＿＿ the number of people. (逆否命题)

　　(A) reliance on. . replenishing　(B) production of. . estimating　(C) spending on. . concealing　(D) recourse to. . limiting　(E) attention to. . varying

此句为一难句。首先可以明确的是上下句发生了重复,因为这是一个分号句。上句为 P 增→V 增,即人口的上升必然导致素食的上升,而下句的阅读时,就应该主动地寻找重复,可看出空格后的"the number of people"重复上文的 population,而 cereals 为上文 vegetable food 的下义词,也即包含于 vegetable food 概念中的一个词,所以下句可简单地看成,V 减与人口 P 的关系。由 P 增→V 增:则 V 减→P(?),这样的关系不难判断为 P 增→V 增;V 减→P 减。所以第二个空格应该填一个表示人口下降的词,只有 D 的 limiting 正确。此句运用了一个典型的逆否命题的思路,此句的详细解答请参阅 SECTION 46 的第 6 题。

当然,逆否命题的思路对于很多考生而言是难于掌握的,很多考生认为"我在解题时思路怎么可能想到逆否命题呢?"事实上,解题时,如果上下句出现了 A→B;B→A 这种将两个事物颠倒叙述的结构,可以认定此句属于被动句转换,或双重否定句转换之一。进一步的区分就是看一下句中有无 by, is the result of, is the outgrowth of, is the product of 这几个表被动的短语。如果有则该句为被动句转换;如果没有,必是逆否命题。

例句 6: Although some consider forcefulness and ＿＿ to be two traits desirable to the same degree, I think that making a violent effort is much less useful than maintaining a steady one. (比较句的重复)

　　(A) promptness　(B) persistence　(C) aggression　(D) skillfulness　(E) lucidity

比较句的重复是最简单的,上下两句均为比较句,则两个比较句的比较的双方根本不会发生转变,相应地填到空格中即可。如本句的上半句为一比较句,当然这是一个同级比较,to the same degree 就表示比较的结果是两者相同。表示同级比较还可以用 as. . .as. . . 结构,或者 matter neither more nor less than 结构。本句的下半句又为一比较结构,比较双方为"making a violent effort"和"maintaining a steady one"。上句要求填一比较的事物,而且已知"forcefulness"与"making a violet effort"同义,所以空格应与"maintaining a steady one"同义,答案为 B 的 persistence。本题的全部详细解答请参阅 SECTION 69 的第 5 题。

当然,这只是比较句的一种考法,其中出现了上下两个比较句。比较句的另外一种考法是只出现一个比较结构,仍然要求填出比较的一方,这时解题更简单,因为比较的双方不能存在概念的交叉,否则就是概念不清,如"高大的人"只能和"矮小的人"作比较,而不能和"肥胖的人"构成一对比较。所以此时考生只需要让比较双方构成一组反义词即可,见下例。

例句 7: Although scientists claim that the seemingly ＿＿ language of their reports is more precise than the figurative language of fiction, the language of science, like all language, is inherently ＿＿. (比较句)

(A) ornamental. . subtle　　(B) unidimensional. . unintelligible　　(C). symbolic. . complex　　(D) literal. . allusive　　(E) subjective. . metaphorical

此句中出现了一个比较句,显然是比较双方应该构成对比,空格里应该填上 figurative 的反义词即可,答案为 D。Literal 词义的解释请参阅 SECTION 30 的第 6 题。宗教生活

例句 8：In most native American cultures, an article used in prayer or ritual is made with extra-ordinary attention to and richness of details: it is decorated more ____ than a similar article intended for ____ use.（比较句）

(A) delicately. . vocational　　(B) colorfully. . festive　　(C) creatively. . religious

(D) subtly. . commercial　　(E) lavishly. . everyday　　lavish 浪费的,丰富的

此句中又出现一个比较结构,比较双方为 it 和 article intended foruse。将 it 还原为其指代的对象,即 article used in prayer and ritual。可见被比较双方的区别在于其用途上。与宗教生活中(in prayer and ritual)的用途相对比的当然是在世俗生活中的用途。选项 E 为正确答案,其他文字部分的解答请参阅 SECTION 18 的第 2 题。

例句 9：Social tensions among adult factions can be ____ by politics, but adolescents and children have no such ____ for resolving their conflict with the exclusive world of adults.（手段目的句重复）

(A) intensified. . attitude　　(B) complicated. . relief　　(C) frustrated. . justification

(D) adjusted. . mechanism　　(E) revealed. . opportunity

此句中上句由 by 表现了一组手段目的关系,下句用 for 表现了手段目的关系,所以上下句重复点一目了然。第一个空格应该填 resolve 的同义词,第二个空格填 politics 的同义词,答案为 D。需要强调的是 D 答案的 mechanism 并非 politics 的同义词,而是上义词,即能包含politics 的一个概念,因为政治是一种社会机制,一种解决方案,所以 politics 和 mechanisms 构成了上下义关系。在解题的第二个步骤,考生推出了一个词义,第三步除了选这个词义的同义词外,还可以选这个词义的上义词,这是希望考生注意的,而千万不能选下义词,相关解释请参阅 SECTION 6 的第 4 题。

By 和 for 的对称出现是手段目的句的外部特征,当然有时候题目会简单地用两次 by,也重复了手段和目的的关系。用两次 by 时往往比较直接、简单,不再举例。By 也可被 in terms of 这个短语代替。

更有趣的是有时句中只出现一次 by,也要求填出手段或目的,这时候更简单,因为此时给出的手段往往是动词的变化形式,如动名词或其抽象名词,此时直接将目的部分填成这个动词即可。反过来,已知目的填手段时,采取同样的方法即可。见下例。

例句 10：The natural balance between prey and predator is increasingly ____, most frequently by human intervention.（手段目的句）

(A) celebrated　　(B) predicted　　(C) observed　　(D) disturbed　　(E) questioned

此句 by 后出现的手段 intervention 为动词 intervene 的抽象名词,所以前面的空格只需填上 intervene 的同义词即可,答案为 D 选项的 disturbed。

例句 11：The poet W. H. Auden believed that the greatest poets of his age were almost necessari-ly irresponsible, that the possession of great gifts ____ the ____ to abuse them.（特殊并列句）　不可靠,不负责任的

(A) negate. . temptation　　(B) controls. . resolution　　(C) engenders. . propensity

产生　　嗜好,习性

　　(D) tempers. . proclivity　　(E) obviates⋯inclination

　　此句句子结构特征是 believe 的宾语从句有两个,包含两个并列关系从句的句式为特殊并列句。它不单单指宾语从句的并列,还包括诸如原因从句、同位语从句等一切从句的并列。只要存在两个从句同时担当句子的一个成分的情况,就会出现特殊并列句。此时解题应在两个并列从句之间进行推理,不必考虑从句与主句的关系,在此情况下,从句与主句之间的关系或者无关痛痒,或者晦涩难懂,都不必去理解。

　　本句两个从句的重复关系是非常明显的。The greatest poets of his age 与 the possession of great gifts 重复;irresponsible 与 to abuse them 重复;下句的两个空格应与上句的 were almost necessarily 重复,表示一种必然性、倾向性。五个选项中,C 为正确答案,详细的分析请参阅 SECTION 24 的第 6 题。

例句 12：Regardless of what ____ theories of politics may propound, there is nothing that requires daily politics to be clear, thorough, and consistent ~~and~~ nothing, that is, that requires reality to conform to theory. (特殊并列句)

　　(A) vague　　　(B) assertive　　　(C) casual　　　(D) vicious　　　(E) tidy　整齐的　整洁的

　　此句的句式仍为特殊并列句,分析思路与上文一致,答案为 E。具体分析请参阅 SECTION 21 的第 6 题。

例句 13：Before about 1960, virtually all accounts of evolution assumed most adaptation to be a product of selection at the level of populations; recent studies of evolution, however, have found no ____ this ____ view of selection. (时间对比型)

　　(A) departures from. . controversial　　　　(B) basis for. . pervasive　普遍深入

　　(C) bias toward. . unchallenged　　　　　　(D) precursors of. . innovative

　　(E) criticisms of. . renowned

　　此句句首的 before about 1960 就标志着时间对比题题型的出现。考生以后读题干时需养成一个好习惯,所有标志时间的词都随手标记出来。这些词中包括：once, formerly, initial pristine, erstwhile, hereto, hitherto, now, future 或者 begin, start, create 或者 until, no longer 等。时间相反,一切对称成分相反,比如说相反的时间会有相反的动作、目的、原因、状态、观点等等。此句的分号又出现"recent",这就进一步明确了时间对比。This 所指代的当然是上文的,也即过去的事物,所以第一个空格中应填现在的动作会反对它,驳斥它,时间相反一切相反,当然也会持不同的态度,五个选项中表反对和驳斥的只有选项 B。具体分析请参阅 SECTION 25 的第 4 题。

　　时间对比型被运用得非常广泛,一个句子内部只要出现时间对比也可以同样处理。当然,另外一点要指出的是,如果时间相同,则对称状态应相同。现各举一例如下。

例句 14：Having fully embraced the belief that government by persuasion is preferable to government by ____, the leaders of the movement have recently ____ most of their previous statements supporting totalitarianism. totalitarian 极权主义的

　　(A) intimidation. . issued　　　(B) participation. . moderated　　　(C) proclamation. . codified　　　(D) demonstration. . deliberated　　　(E) coercion. . repudiated　高压统治　coerce 强制 高压 威胁

　　此句的第二个空格填一现在的动作,而宾语是一过去的观点,所以可以毫不犹豫地填上"反对"、"驳斥"一类词即可,答案为 E 的 repudiated。详细解答请参阅 SECTION 15 的第 4 题。

例句 15：While she initially suffered the fate of many pioneers —— the in comprehension's of her

octogenarian
80至89岁的人

colleagues —— octogenarian Nobel laureate Barbara Mcclintoch has lived to ＿＿ the triumph of her once ＿＿ scientific theories.

(A) descry. . innovative　　(B) regret. . insignificant　　(C) perpetuate. . tentative

(D) enjoy. . authoritative　　(E) savor. . heterodox **异端的，非正统的，**

此句中的 initial 和 once 都指过去，所以第二空格中应填上表示过去的状态，即"不被同僚接受的"，从而选答案 E 的 heterodox，更详细的分析请参阅 SECTION 18 的第 5 题。

在时间对比型中尤其要强调两个极易出错的词 no longer 与 until。No longer 只能修饰过去的某动作或状态，表示其不再发生，所以 no longer 所修饰限定的对象一定是过去的那个动作和状态。Until 单独使用等同于 before，但 until 强调之前之后的截然对比，也即反义词，各举例如下。

例句 16：No longer ＿＿ by the belief that the world around us was expressly designed for humanity, many people try to find intellectual ＿＿ for that lost certainty in astrology and in mysticism.（no longer 时间对比句）

(A) satisfied. . reasons　　(B) sustained. . substitutes　　(C) eassured. . justifications

(D) hampered. . equivalents　　(E) restricted. . parallels

此句中的 that lost certainty 中的 certainty 指代上文的 belief，从而可知我们不再相信这个信仰，第一个空格填什么动词可以表示出这个含义呢？请仔细思考 B、D 和 E 三个选项的区别，事实上这三个选项的第二个词的同义词都为"代替物"之意，区别在于 B 的 sustained 是指过去的动作，也即当初我们相信这个信仰时，信仰支撑(sustain)了我们。而 D 和 E 的第一个词尽管用中文去字面翻译非常正确，但却违背了 no longer 的用法，因为当初我们相信这个信仰时，信仰对我们并非"hamper"或"restrict"的动作，尽管 no longer 与中文的"不再"语义类似，但用法却不一样，这是需要考生注意领会的，此题的详解请参阅 SECTION 11 第 6 题。

例句 17：Until the current warming trend exceeds the range of normal climatic fluctuations, there will be, among scientists, considerable ＿＿ the possibility that increasing levels of atmospheric CO_2 can cause long-term warming effects.（时间对比型 until）

(A) interest in　　(B) uncertainty about　　(C) enthusiasm for

(D) worry about　　(E) experiment on

此句中出现了 until，主句表 until 这个时间之前发生的动作。而 until 后的时间状语从句表示温室效应真正发生的那一刻，所以，在这个时间之后，科学家对温室效应的可能性，当然会持确信无疑的态度，已经发生的事情的 possibility 当然是 100%。那么，由于 until 强调前后的对比，所以主句中科学家的态度就应和确凿无疑相反，应该为"不确信"的态度，答案为 B 的 uncertainty about。不少考生误选 D。选项 D 的含义是：科学家在温室效应发生前忧心忡忡，而温室效应发生后科学家们反而高枕无忧了！更详细的解题请参阅 SECTION 16 的第 6 题。

第三节　粘连的小连接结构

句子中会出现各种连词：and, but, rather than, even, as. . .as. . .，so. . .as to. . .等等，这些都是需关注的对象。因为这些连词已经解决了明确逻辑关系这一要求，而中心词的定位则会在小连接结构中异常简单,在大连接中则无法完成,所以只将小连接作为一解题方法。所谓小连接是指连词的两端为对称的两个形容词、动词、副词或不定式结构,而大连接中的连词都是连接了两个句子,此时只能知道两个句子之间的逻辑关系,却难于知晓究竟哪两个词之间发生了重复关系,故无法直接解题。小连接都非常简单,可直接利用连词两端进行推理。

例句1:Even though formidable winters are the norm in Dakotas, many people wee unprepared for the ____ of the blizzard of 1888. (大连接)

    (A) inevitability   (B) ferocity   (C) importance   (D) probability   (E) mildness

此句的连词 even though 连接了两个句子,所以即使我们知道上下句为递进转折关系也无法由 even though 得知究竟哪一个词与空格构成此递进转折关系,有不少考生会误以为是“norm”,但实际上是“formidable”,答案为 formidable 的递进词,故选 B“ferocity”。

例句2:Although ancient tools were ____ preserved, enough have survived to allow us to demonstrate an occasionally interrupted by generally ____ process through prehistory. (小连接:连接形容词)

    (A) partially..noticeable   (B) superficially..necessary   (C) unwittingly..documented   (D) rarely..continual   (E) needlessly..incessant

此句中的 although 为大连接,而 but 为小连接,but 前后连接了两个形容词,所以不难判断 but 之后的空格应为“interrupted”的反义词,从而非常明确地选出 D 和 E 的 continual 与 incessant,而 D 和 E 的第一词则不难辨别,应为 D。

例句3:The new biological psychiatry does not deny the contributing role of psychological factors in mental illness, but posits that these factors may act as a catalyst on existing physiological conditions and ____ such illness. (小连接:连接动词)

    (A) disguise   (B)impede   (C)constrain   (D)precipitate   (E) consummate

此句中的 and 为小连接,连接两个动词,and 作小连接可以表示并列、时间的顺承以及因果。此句 and 前后简化后即为 act as a catalyst andsuch illness。催化剂的作用当然是加快反应速度,此句的 and 表示因果,所以可直接选答案 D 的 precipitate。更具体详细的解答请参阅 SECTION 25 的第 5 题。(化学系的学生,请忘掉你的专业!虽然有些催化剂的作用是减速,但 GRE 的句子填空只需要常识,千万不要用专业的但与常识有出入的知识来理解。)

例句4:The technical know-how, if not the political ____, appears already at hand to feed the world's exploding population and so to ____ at last the ancient famine. (小连接:连接动词不定式)

    (A) will..weaken   (B) expertise..articulate   (C) doubt..banish

    (D) power..denounce   (E) commitment..eradicate

此句中虽然出现了一些生僻的单词,但那些都不是需要阅读的部分。文中的 and 为一小连接,连接了两个动词不定式,所以只需要在这两个动词不定式之间做一推理即可。而这个推理是如此简单,“喂饱了全世界膨胀的人口,因此就____彻底地自古以来就有的大饥荒和营养不良。显然“喂饱了”就等同于“消除了饥饿”,所以直接选答案 E 的 eradicate。本文其他部分的详细解答请参阅 SECTION 62 的第 2 题。

    大连接中也有特例,比如在大连接的一端为一判断句,另外一端出现空格,此时也可认定空格与判断词互相重复。

例句5:Although the minuet appeared simple, its ____ steps had to be studied very carefully, before they could be gracefully _____ in public.

(A) progressive. . revealed   (B) intricate. . executed   (C) rudimentary. . allowed

(D) minute. . discussed   (E) entertaining. . stylized

该句中的 simple 为判断词,可直接在第一空格中填其反义词即可,答案为 B,更具体的解释请参阅 SECTION 2 的第 1 题。

第四节 粘连中的照应结构

所谓照应就是指句子行文中直接点明的重复手法,如人称代词,指示代词,定冠词。此时将重复部分填回空格即可,考生需要练习的是以后在读题干时随手将这些照应词标记出来,便于思考分析。

例句 1: Though extremely _____ about his own plans, the man allowed his associates no such privacy and was constantly _____ information about what they intended to do next. (照应:指示代词)

privacy
独处而不受干扰
秘密

(A) idiosyncratic. . altering   (B) guarded. . eschewing   (C) candid. . uncovering

solicit
恳求,教唆

(D) reticent. . soliciting   (E) fastidious. . ruining

此句中的 such privacy 指明上句曾出现过 privacy。而上句出现过的单词没有一个表现出 privacy 的含义,所以只有空格表示这个含义才行,故选 D 的 reticent。具体分析请见 SECTION 69 的第 7 题。 *沉默不语*

例句 2: Londale and stern discovered that mitochondria and chloroplasts _____ a long, identifiable sequence of DNA; such a coincidence could be _____ only by the transfer of DNA between the two systems. (照应:指示代词)

(A) manufacture. . accomplished   (B) reveal. . repeated   (C) exhibit. . determined

(D) share. . explained   (E) maintain. . contradicted

此句中的 such a coincidence 表明上句曾出现过一次"重复,重合,巧合",但细读上文却并无此意,所以上句的空格必须表明此含义,因而选 D 的 share。具体分析请参阅 SECTION 16 的第 5 题。

例句 3: Doreen justifiably felt she deserved recognition for the fact that the research institute had been _____ a position of preeminence, since it was she who had _____ the transformation. (照应:定冠词)

(A) reduced to. . controlled   (B) raised to. . deserved   (C) mired in. . imagined

(D) maintained in. . created   (E) returned to. . directed

此句中的 for 引导了一段原因解释主句,而 since 也引导了一段原因解释主句,故实际上两者是重复关系。所以第二个空格后的 the transformation 为定冠词结构,应该是对上文某处的重复,而上文已有的单词都没有 transformation 的含义,所以空格应有此含义,具体分析请见 SECTION 70 的第 2 题。

例句 4: At several points in his discussion, Graves, in effect, _____ evidence when it does not support his argument, tailoring it to his needs. (照应:人称代词)

(A) addresses   (B) creates ·   (C) alters   (D) suppresses   (E) substitutes

此句中的代词 it 显然是重复上文的 evidence。而 evidence 之前要求填一动词,当然就将 it 之前的动词填过去即可。答案为 C,具体分析请参阅 SECTION 21 的第 5 题。

第五节　粘连中的主体词汇

主体词汇是指一个句中起到题眼作用的词,在此讲述三种:主体动词,表人物身分的名词,描述人或事物性质或特征动作的词。

例句1: The First World War began in a context of jargon and verbal delicacy and continued in a
　　　 cloud of ____ as ____ as language and literature, skillfully used, could make it. (主体动
　　　 词)

　　　 (A) circumlocution. . literal 　　 (B) cliche. . lucid 　　 (C) euphemism. . impenetrable
　　　 (D) particularity. . deliberate 　　 (E) subjectivity. . enthralling

此句中的动词 continue 为主体动词,不难理解,既然是 continue 就应前后一致,所以第一空格中应该填上"jargon and verbal delicacy",答案为 C,句子其他部分的更详细解释请参阅 SECTION 25 第 7 题。continue, remain 都有相同的考法,一旦出现后,前后保持同义即可。当然 continue 也有另外一种考法。如下例:

例句2: Opponents of the expansion of the market economy, although in ____, continued to con-
　　　 stitute ____ political force throughout the century. (主体动词)

　　　 (A) error. . an inconsequential 　　 (B) retreat. . a powerful 　　 (C) disarray. . a disci-
　　　 plined 　　 (D) jeopardy. . an ineffective 　　 (E) command. . a viable

此句中又出现 continue,但未出现过去的状态,如何填 continue 之后的状态呢? 请注意 continue 之前出现了一个转折,既然状态会 continue,所以这个转折就不可能是对立面转折,而只能是一个程度转折,并且程度上升通常用递进结构表达,所以此处的只能是程度下降的转折,应先在转折句的空格中填一表示程度下降的词,这是这一种 continue, remain 考法的解题关键,此题可直接根据此规律选 B,更详细的解释请参阅 SECTION 19 的第 4 题。

与主体动词 continue, remain 相对的主体动词则为 shift from. . . to, oscillate between. . . and, turn to, reconcile. . . and. . . 等这些表示反面转折的动词,不再举例,在相应题目中自有分析。

表示人物身分的名词在解题中也有直接提示作用。如果要填一个 critics 的动作,只能在 judge, evaluate, praise, criticize, assail 几个词当中选择:而医生的动作永远都是恢复健康,salvage;企业家考虑问题的角度永远都是是否盈利;下级对上级的指令也会永远服从,这些原则都是可以直接运用而不需要考虑原文含义的,在相应的题目中会有解释。在此恕不举例。

描述人或事物性质和特征动作的主体词在句子填空中尤为重要,因为 ETS 是个很愿意对人或事做出评价的机构,并且往往观点新颖,与通常观点相反,描述人或事物性质和特征动作的方式有四种:

1. 判断句:如"The minuet appeared simple."
2. 词组:regard. . . as. . . 或者 view / consider / label / portray. . . as. . .
　　 如"We label him as a novice musician."
3. 物主代词加特征性格或特征动作,如"his intransigence"。

4. of 结构作后置定语,如"a critic of vanity"。

对于这些描述人或物的特征性格或特征动作的词有两种考法。第一种考法就是将其置于一个复杂的主从句中,此时要记住,不管是发生何种逻辑关系都是针对主体词而来的。第二种考法是这四种表达结构在上下句中重复出现,来描述人或物的性格或动作。考生只需辨认出来并填回正确的位置即可,分别举例如下:

例句3: Foucault's rejection of the concept of continuity in western thought, though radical, was not unique; he had ＿＿＿ in the United States who, without knowledge of his work, developed parallel ideas. (主体词汇)

(A) critics　　　(B) counterparts　　　(C) disciples　　　(D) readers　　　(E) publishers

此句中的冒号前为一判断句,主体词为 not unique,这就是对福柯的概括,所以下文发生重复也必然是重复主体词,空格里应填"非独有的"也即"相同的人",故答案为 B,更详细的解释请参阅 SECTION 59 第 3 题。

例句4: It is ironic that a critic of such overwhelming vanity now suffers from a measure of the oblivion to which he was forever ＿＿＿ others; in the end, all his ＿＿＿ has only worked against him.

(A) dedicating. . self-possession　　　(B) leading. . self-righteousness　　　(C) consigning. . self-adulation　　　(D) relegating. . self-sacrifice　　　(E) condemning. . self-analysis

此句分号上下文的重复用了明确的提示,上句用了描述人或物特征性格的第四种方法,而分号后出现的 his 加空格结构,又明显是第三种方法,所以空格里直接填上 vanity 即可,答案为 C 的 self-adulation。更详细的解答请参阅 SECTION 9 的第 6 题。

例句5: Ever prey to vagrant impulses that impelled him to ＿＿＿ his talents on a host of unworthy projects, his very ＿＿＿ nonetheless enhanced his reputation, for the sheer energy of his extravagance dazzled observers. (主体词汇)

(A) undermine. . enthusiasm　　　(B) isolate. . selectiveness　　　(C) display. . affability (D) squander. . dissipation　　　(E) implicate…genius

此句的第二个空格出现在 his 之后,故可断定为是描述他的特征性格的一个词,所以接着就应该在原文中寻找描写特征性格或特征动作的四种方式之一,果然在其后不远便有 his dissipation 表达出现,所以第二个空格填 dissipation 即可,答案为 D。更详细的解答请参阅 SECTION 33 的第 7 题。

第二部分　填空题解答

11 min

SECTION 1

1. Hydrogen is the ____ element of the universe in that it provides the building blocks from which the other elements are produced.
   (A) steadiest
   (B) expendable
   (C) lightest
   (D) final
   (E) fundamental

2. Few of us take the pains to study our cherished convictions; indeed, we almost have a natural ____ doing so.
   (A) aptitude for
   (B) repugnance to
   (C) interest in
   (D) ignorance of
   (E) reaction after

3. It is his dubious distinction to have proved what nobody would think of denying, that Romero at the age of sixty-four writes with all the characteristics of ____.
   (A) maturity
   (B) fiction
   (C) inventiveness
   (D) art
   (E) brilliance

4. The primary criterion for ____ a school is its recent performance: critics are ____ to extend credit for earlier victories.
   (A) evaluating. . prone
   (B) investigating. . hesitant
   (C) judging. . reluctant
   (D) improving. . eager
   (E) administering. . persuaded

5. Number theory is rich in problems of an especially ____ sort: they are tantalizingly simple to state but ____ difficult to solve.
   (A) cryptic. . deceptively
   (B) spurious. . equally
   (C) abstruse. . ostensibly
   (D) elegant. . rarely
   (E) vexing. . notoriously

6. In failing to see that the justice's pronouncement merely ____ previous decisions rather than actually establishing a precedent, the novice law clerk ____ the scope of the justice's judgment.
   (A) synthesized. . limited
   (B) overturned. . misunderstood
   (C) endorsed. . nullified
   (D) qualified. . overemphasized
   (E) recapitulated. . defined

7. When theories formerly considered to be ____ in their scientific objectivity are found

instead to reflect a consistent observational and evaluative bias, then the presumed neutrality of science gives way to the recognition that categories of knowledge are human ____.

(A) disinterested. . constructions
(B) callous. . errors
(C) verifiable. . prejudices
(D) convincing. . imperatives
(E) unassailable. . fantasies

SECTION 1 解答

1. 【正确答案】E
   【中文释义】氢元素是宇宙中的基本元素,因为它提供了生产其他元素的建筑构件。
   【解题分析】由因果关系不难得知氢是构成其他元素的元素,可知其为 primary 或 formative,这正是 fundamental 的第一含义。
   【重点词条】**fundamental** *adj* . ①基本的,基本构成物的 (primary, formative)
   ②基础的(underlying, basic)
   ③重要的,必要的(indispensable, irreducible)

2. 【正确答案】B
   【中文释义】我们当中很少有人费力去研究我们早就喜爱的信仰;事实上,我们对这种做法几乎有一种本能的厌恶反感。
   【解题分析】分号下句表重复,而 indeed 又提出了递进关系,比上文不愿意更递进一步的为"厌恶",需要强调的是 indeed 的用语,都是表递进,进一步的肯定。尽管其中文翻译与 in fact 相同,但却永远只表递进。并且本句的选项 E 是一个语法上错误的选项,正确的说法应该是 reaction to。但这只是一个特例。以后大家做 GRE 句子填空时不需要考虑其选项语法上是否正确。只需要考虑其语义逻辑是否正确,这一点上,TOEFL 的句子填空截然相反。
   【重点词条】**take pains to do sth** 尽力去做某事

3. 【正确答案】A
   【中文释义】这是他令人感到怀疑的独特贡献:证明了没有人会想到否定的事物,也就是证明了罗曼罗在 64 岁时的写作带有所有成熟的特征。
   【解题分析】该句的句子结构比较独特,prove 的从句出现两个,一个是 what 从句,另一个是随后的 that 从句。我们将这种情况称之为特殊并列句题型:两个从句同时担当一个语法成分,比如该句中 what 从句和 that 从句都担当 prove 的宾语从句,其他类型的从句在 GRE 填空中都出现了类似的用法。此时两个从句之间为同位重复关系,所以应在这两个从句之间做出推理,而不应该做主句和从句之间的推理,比如一个原因从句被重复了一次,这时我们通常在两个原因从句之间寻找重复,而原因从句和主句之间尽管也有因果逻辑关系,但在特殊并列句这种题型中,因果关系肯定是晦涩的,无法推理。该句中空格所填的事物应该从"没有任何人会怀疑"这个角度去思考,很容易得出结论,64 岁的人所具有的毫无疑问的特征当然是"成熟",正确答案 A。需要指出的是,文中的 his 指一个评论家,而不是作家 Romero,his 的指代对象在原文中并未明确指出,这也是一个特例,这种情况在 NO 题中出现过两次,而在国内考题中从未出现过。

【重点词条】fiction *n*. ①虚构物,小说

②假设(an assumption of a possibility as a fact irrespective of the question of its truth)

③想象(a useful illusion or pretense)

④欺骗,捏造(the action of feigning or of creating with the imagination)

4.【正确答案】C

【中文释义】评价学校的主要标准是它最近的表现:评论家们不愿意因其过去的成就增加赞誉。

【解题分析】由分析句子结构可知,第一个空格所填的动名词的逻辑主语为 critics。评论家这样的特征人所做的动作只可能是"评价,赞扬或批评"三种方式,故可选 A 和 C。A 和 C 的第二词成为一对反义词,由时间对比"recent"和"earlier"可知评论家们必然不愿意承认早期的成就,故选 C。

【重点词条】credit *n*. 优点,赞誉

5.【正确答案】D E

【中文释义】数论中充满了特别令人恼火的问题,这些问题表述起来诱人地简单,但却众所周知难以解决。

【解题分析】上文需填一个空格表示这些问题属于哪些类型。而冒号后直截了当地表达了他们是"说起来简单而解决起来困难",故可直接选词 C 和 E。Tantalizingly 修饰 simple 强调"非常简单",所以对称地第二个空格应强调"非常困难",C 的第二个词 ostensibly 解释为"表面的",故反而成了不困难了。正确答案为 E。

【重点词条】tantalizing *adj*. ①吸引人的(possessing a quality that arouses or stimulates desire or interest)

②可望而不可及的(mockingly or teasingly out of reach)

notorious *adj*. ①闻名的(generally known and talked of)

②臭名远扬的(widely and unfavorably known syn see famous)

ostensible *adj*. ①用于公开的(intended for display, open to view)

vex: *vt*. 使烦恼,使恼火   ②表面上的,假装的(being such in appearance: plausible rather than demonstrably true or real) 例 the～purpose for the trip

6.【正确答案】D

【中文释义】没有看到法官的判决只不过是引用了以前的先例而非真正地建立先例,所以这个初等的法律簿记员夸大了法官判决的重要性。

【解题分析】由 rather than 可知前后应为反义,且 precious decisions 与 precedent 构成同义,故空格应与 establish 构成反义,由美国的特殊司法制度可知对于法官而言,或

依照先例判决,或自创先例,所以应选 D, qualify 表"引用"。

【重点词条】**qualify** *v*. ①限定(to reduce from a general to a particular or restricted form)

②缓和(to make less harsh or strict, moderate)

③修正(to limit or modify the meaning of)

④使胜任(to fit by training, skill, or ability for a special purpose)

⑤证明合格(to declare competent or adequate, certify)

qualified *adj*. ①有限制的

②合格的

unqualified *adj*. ①无限制的,无条件的　例 ~acceptance

②不合格的

scope *n*. ①范围,重要性

②眼界,见识,理解范围

③活动余地,机会

7.【正确答案】A

【中文释义】当过去被认为科学、客观、公正无私的理论,现在却被发现反映了一个永恒的观察和解释上的偏见时,过去认为科学所具有的客观公正性就让位于一个新的认识,即所有学科知识都是人类主观创造之物。

【解题分析】此题的解题点甚多。第一种解法:第三个单词 formerly 已经在提示这是一个时间对比型题目。所以思路正常发展就是寻找现在对 theories 的判断。由 theories are found to... 这个主干指现在理论被认为是 bias,故过去就应被看成是"不偏不倚的看法、公正无私的看法"。五个选项中 A 正确。第二种解法:第一个空格后紧跟着介词短语,分隔的四种形态之一。故可认定空格的信息可由介词短语提供。"in their scientific objectivety"翻译为"在科学客观公正性方面",故空格里只能填上"客观"或者"非客观",五个选项中只有 A 正确。第三种解法:bias 之后为下半句,应该重复上半句,而 presumed 即为上文的 formerly considered。故可直接将 neutrality 变为形容词 neutral 填回上文空格,得答案 A。

　　并且此句的意思是一个固定观点,即科学(家)过去被认为是客观的,而现在则认为其是非客观的。这个观点屡次重考,从未变化,我们将这种观点称为固定观点。其他固定观点句将在以后的练习中涉及。

【重点词条】**construction** *n*. ①人的思维产物(result of construing, interpreting, or explaining)

②建筑或建筑业(the construction industry)

③创作(the arrangement and connection of words or groups of words in a sentence)

bias *n*. ①偏见(a personal and sometimes unreasoned judgment, prejudice)

②偏差(deviation of the expected value of a statistical estimate from the quantity it estimates)

SECTION 2

1. Although the minuet appeared simple, its
   ____ steps had to be studied very carefully
   before they could be gracefully ____ in pub-
   lic.
   (A) progressive. . revealed
   (B) intricate. . executed
   (C) rudimentary. . allowed
   (D) minute. . discussed
   (E) entertaining. . stylized

2. The results of the experiments performed by
   Elizabeth Hazen and Rachel Brown were
   ____ not only because these results chal-
   lenged old assumptions but also because they
   called the ____ methodology into question.
   (A) provocative. . prevailing
   (B) predictable. . contemporary
   (C) inconclusive. . traditional
   (D) intriguing. . projected
   (E) specious. . original

3. Despite the ____ of many of their col-
   leagues, some scholars have begun to em-
   phasize "pop culture" as a key for ____ the
   myths, hopes, and fears of contemporary
   society.
   (A) antipathy. . entangling
   (B) discernment. . evaluating
   (C) pedantry. . reinstating
   (D) skepticism. . deciphering
   (E) enthusiasm. . symbolizing

4. In the seventeenth century, direct flouting of a
   generally accepted system of values was regarded

as ____ , even as a sign of madness,
   (A) adventurous
   (B) frivolous
   (C) willful
   (D) impermissible
   (E) irrational

5. Queen Elizabeth I has quite correctly been
   called a ____ of the arts, because many
   young artists received her patronage.
   (A) connoisseur 行家
   (B) critic
   (C) friend
   (D) scourge 鞭苔, 磨难 .
   (E) judge

6. Because outlaws were denied ____ under me-
   dieval law, anyone could raise a hand against
   them with legal ____ .
   (A) propriety. . authority
   (B) protection. . impunity
   (C) collusion. . consent
   (D) rights. . collaboration
   (E) provisions. . validity

7. Rather than enhancing a country's security,
   the successful development of nuclear
   weapons could serve at first to increase that
   country's ____ .
   (A) boldness
   (B) influence
   (C) responsibility
   (D) moderation
   (E) vulnerability

SECTION 2 解答

1. 【正确答案】B
   【中文释义】尽管小步舞显得简单,但在公众面前优雅地表演之前,它复杂的步法却必须被仔细地研究。
   【解题分析】Appear 为系动词,故 simple 即为主体词汇,所以下文的转折必然是与之转折,可知空格填"复杂"得答案 B。
   【重点词条】minute *adj*.①细小的
   　　　　　　　　　　　②详细的
   　　　　　　　　　　　③琐碎的
   　　　　　　stylized *adj*.①程式化的(to conform to a conventional style)
   　　　　　　　　　　　②风格化的(to represent or design according to a style or stylistic pattern rather than according to nature or tradition)

2. 【正确答案】A
   【中文释义】由伊丽莎白·海斯和罗歇尔·布朗所做的实验结果是挑战性的,不仅仅因为这些结果挑战了基本假设,而且因为它们质疑了主体方法论。
   【解题分析】因果句的原因从句中反复提及这些实验结果挑战别的事物(challenge 与 call…into question),故可直接得结论。这些结果是 challenging。请注意这种思路,下句重复上句的信息时,采用了间性转换的方法。这种情况也是频繁出现的。
   【重点词条】provocative *adj*.挑衅的,激动人心的,发人深思的,引起讨论的(serving or tending to provoke, excite, or stimulate)
   　　　　　　intriguing *adj*.吸引人的(engaging the interest to a marked degree, fascinating)

3. 【正确答案】D
   【中文释义】尽管他们的很多同僚表示怀疑,一些学者已经开始强调通俗文化是解释当代社会的神话、害怕和希望的一个关键。
   【解题分析】由转折关系可知第一空格应填"反对",可选 A 和 D。而第二个空格动名词的逻辑主语为学者,故 A 的第二个词 entangling 不正确,学者的特征动作为 D 的第二词 deciphering。学者的任务是解释这个社会。
   【重点词条】entangle *v*.①编织(to wrap or twist together, interweave)
   　　　　　　　　　　　②纠缠,使牵累(involve in a perplexing or troublesome situation)
   　　　　　　　　　　　例 became entangled in a lawsuit
   　　　　　　　　　　　③复杂化(to make complicated)
   　　　　　　reinstate *v*.①重新放置(to place again, as in possession or in a former position)
   　　　　　　　　　　　②恢复(to restore to a previous effective state)

4.【正确答案】E

【中文释义】在 17 世纪,直接嘲弄被普遍接受的价值观被看成不理智,甚至是疯狂的标志。

【解题分析】由空格后的 even 可知,空格应填一个比 madness 程度轻一些的词,得答案 E。请注意 A 的 adventurous 为褒义词,这是一种美国人很欣赏的品性。

【重点词条】**impermissible** *adj*. 不允许的(not permissible)

frivolous *adj*. ①不重要的(of little weight or importance)

②事实上或法律上无根据的(having no sound basis〔as in fact or law〕)

③琐碎的,无意义的(lacking in seriousness)

④轻浮的(marked by unbecoming levity)

5.【正确答案】C

【中文释义】伊丽莎白女王一世被非常恰当地称为艺术的朋友,因为很多年轻的艺术家收到了她的捐赠。

【重点词条】**connoisseur** *n*. 鉴赏家,行家

6.【正确答案】B

【中文释义】因为在中世纪法律中罪犯被剥夺了保护权,所以任何人都可以举起手来痛揍他们而同时获得法律的豁免。

【解题分析】第一个空格后的介词短语提供了线索。首先法律所剥夺犯人的只能是 B 和 D,其次"中世纪"这个具有时间色彩的单词又提示我们做一个时间对比,在今天的法律下,只有执法机关才能惩罚罪犯,而在中世纪的法律下,的确是任何人都可以惩罚。由此对比可知 B 和 D 中只能选 B。

【重点词条】**impunity** *n*. ①(惩罚,伤害,损失的)免除(exemption or freedom from punishment, harm, or loss)

②特指法律的豁免权

7.【正确答案】E

【中文释义】成功地发展核武器非但没有增加一个国家的安全性,反而一开始就起到增加这个国家的易受攻击的作用。

【解题分析】句末的 that country 指代句首的 a country,而 enhance 与 increase 又是同义,故可知空格与 security 构成粘连成分。由 rather than 可知其关系为反义,故可选 E。

【重点词条】**vulnerability** *n*. ①脆弱(capable of being physically wounded)

②易受攻击性(open to attack or damage, assailable)

SECTION 3

1. Physicists rejected the innovative experimental technique because, although it ____ some problems, it also produced new ____.
   (A) clarified. . data
   (B) eased. . interpretations
   (C) resolved. . complications
   (D) caused. . hypotheses
   (E) revealed. . inconsistencies

2. During a period of protracted illness, the sick can become infirm, ____ both the strength to work and many of the specific skills they once possessed.
   (A) regaining
   (B) denying
   (C) pursuing
   (D) insuring
   (E) losing

3. The pressure of population on available resources is the key to understanding history; consequently, any historical writing that takes no cognizance of ____ facts is ____ flawed.
   (A) demographic. . intrinsically
   (B) ecological. . marginally
   (C) cultural. . substantively
   (D) psychological. . philosophically
   (E) political. . demonstratively

4. It is puzzling to observe that Jones's novel has recently been criticized for its ____ structure, since commentators have traditionally argued that its most obvious ____ is its relentlessly rigid, indeed schematic, framework.

   (A) attention to. . preoccupation
   (B) speculation about. . characteristic
   (C) parody of. . disparity
   (D) violation of. . contradiction
   (E) lack of. . flaw

5. It comes as no surprise that societies have codes of behavior; the character of the codes, on the other hand, can often be ____.
   (A) predictable
   (B) unexpected
   (C) admirable
   (D) explicit
   (E) confusing

6. The characterization of historical analysis as a form of fiction is not likely to be received ____ by either historians or literary critics, who agree that history and fiction deal with ____ orders of experience.
   (A) quietly. . significant
   (B) enthusiastically. . shifting
   (C) passively. . unusual
   (D) sympathetically. . distinct
   (E) contentiously. . realistic

7. For some time now, ____ has been presumed not to exist: the cynical conviction that everybody has an angle is considered wisdom.
   (A) rationality
   (B) flexibility
   (C) diffidence
   (D) disinterestedness
   (E) insincerity

SECTION 3 解答

1. 【正确答案】C
   【中文释义】物理学家反对这个革新的实验技术,因为尽管它解决了一些问题,但也产生了新的不确定因素。
   【解题分析】Because 连接的原因从句为 it also produced new ____,故可知空格填上一个贬义词,得 C 和 E。而 although 又与其构成转折。可得 C。
   【重点词条】complication *n.* ①复杂,复杂化(complexity, intricacy; esp. a situation or a detail of character complicating the main thread of a plot)
   　　　　　　　　　　②不确定因素(a difficult factor or issue often appearing unexpectedly and changing existing plans, methods, or attitudes)
   　　　　　　　　　　③并发症(a secondary disease or condition developing in the course of a primary disease or condition)
   　　　　inconsistency *n.* ①前后矛盾,不一致(an instance of being inconsistent)
   　　　　　　　　　　②易变,反复无常(the quality or state of being inconsistent)

2. 【正确答案】E
   【中文释义】在延长的生病期间,病人会变得虚弱,既失去工作的力量,又失去他们曾经拥有的许多专业技巧。
   【解题分析】空格为一个分隔,重复前文的 infirm,可得答案 E。

3. 【正确答案】A
   【中文释义】人口对有限资源的压力是理解历史的关键;随之而来,任何没有注意到人口统计事实的历史作品本质上都是有缺陷的。
   【解题分析】分号下句重复上句,显然 historical writing 是重复上文的 understanding history,因为任何历史著作都必然反映作者对历史的理解。第一个空格的信息只能重复上句的主语,应与人口相关,五个选项中能构成重复的为 A。A 的第二个词 intrinsically 可由上句的 key 来理解。
   【重点词条】demographic *adj.* ①人口统计学的(of or relating to demography or demographics)
   　　　　　　　　　　②人口学的(relating to the dynamic balance of a population esp. with regard to density and capacity for expansion or decline)
   　　　　marginal *adj.* ①边缘的,边界的(of, relating to, or situated at a margin or border)
   　　　　　　　　　　②不重要的(not of central importance) 例 regards violence as a ~ rather than a central problem
   　　　　　　　　　　③边缘人的,边缘文化的(characterized by the incorporation of

habits and values from two divergent cultures and by incomplete assimilation in either）例 the ~ cultural habits of new immigrant groups

④被主流社会或主流思想所排斥的（excluded from or existing outside the mainstream of society, a group, or a school of thought）

substantive *adj*. ①实际的（real rather than apparent, firm, also, permanent, enduring）

②大量的（considerable in amount or numbers, substantial）

demonstrative *adj*. ①示范（demonstrating as real or true）

②感情外露的（inclined to display feelings openly）

4. 【正确答案】E

【中文释义】令人惊奇的是琼的小说最近因其缺乏结构而受到了批评，因为评论家们过去指出他的小说的最明显的缺陷是它的彻底僵化、事实上刻板的结构。

【解题分析】文中的 puzzling 提示上下句之间会出现反义词，而 recently 与 traditionally 再次提醒这一点。上句为批评它的某个不优秀的结构，而下句也是在指明它的不优秀的僵化结构，故上下句并非批评与表扬的转折。惟一可供转折的就是两个结构本身应该相反。能与僵化刻板的结构构成反义的为 E 的缺乏结构，也即结构松散。

【重点词条】parody of   拙劣地模仿

5. 【正确答案】B

【中文释义】每个社会都有其行为规则，这一点不会让任何人感到惊奇；相反，规则的具体内容却通常是出乎人们意料的。

【解题分析】分号句上下句构成反义重复。on the other hand 在通常文体中并不一定表对立面转折，但在 GRE 句子的两极思维模式下，却始终是反义关系。空格填上 no surprise 的反义词，故选 B。

【重点词条】code *n*. 规则

character *n*. 内容，特征

6. 【正确答案】D

【中文释义】将历史分析作品描绘成小说的形式不会被历史学家和文学家同时接受。他们一致认为历史和文学处理着截然不同的经验类型。

【解题分析】第一个空格填副词，这种情况下我们通常将副词忽略不计而将上句当成完整句来理解，故可知上句的含义为历史和文学相互表达是不被接受的，从而推知下句应该强调历史和文学的不同性。因为如果下句欲强调两者相当的话，那么上句也应重复两者的共性，事实上上句是在谈两者的不同性。五个选项中只有 D 的第二个词表达了两者的不同性，其他几个选项都是表达两者共同一致的某种属性，故答案为 D。

并且请大家注意下句表达的特殊性。主语为并列主语,所以其表语可分为两类:相同和不同。并且只有 different, distinct, antithetical, irreconcilable 可表达出不同性,其他形容词作并列主语的表语只能表达出两者相同这个概念,以后见到并列主语填表语的情况,首先考虑两者应该是相同还是不同,而考过的题目中,都是填不同,可作一种经验指导以后的解题。

【重点词条】sympathetically *adv.* ①同情地,共鸣地
　　　　　　　　　　　　　②同时地

shifting *adj.* ①移动的
　　　　　　　②相互转换的

7.【正确答案】D

【中文释义】现在有一段时间,大公无私被认为是不可能存在的:认为每个人都有私心的愤世嫉俗的信仰被认为是一种智慧的见解。

【解题分析】冒号前后表解释,也即重复,既然冒号后认为每个人都有私心,故冒号前当然可推知没有私心的人不存在,一种双重否定的转换。文中的短语 everybody has an angle 是一俚语。但这是一种特殊例子。国内考题中从不出美国俚语短语考题。

【重点词条】cynical *adj.* ①愤世嫉俗的,对人性怀疑的,悲观的
　　　　　　　　　　②挑剔挖苦的,冷嘲热讽的
　　　　　　　　　　③犬儒主义的(活跃于公元前 4 世纪的哲学流派,以最简陋的生活,无欲无求的境界和对高尚德行的追求而获得尊敬,犬儒主义者往往极端地嘲讽世人的欲望)

SECTION 4

1. The ____ of mass literacy coincided with the first industrial revolution; in turn, the new expansion in literacy, as well as cheaper printing, helped to nurture the ____ of popular literature.

(A) building. . mistrust
(B) reappearance. . display
(C) receipt. . source
(D) selection. . influence
(E) emergence. . rise

2. Although ancient tools were ____ preserved, enough have survived to allow us to demonstrate an occasionally interrupted but gener-

ally ____ progress through prehistory.

(A) partially. . noticeable
(B) superficially. . necessary
(C) unwittingly. . documented
(D) rarely. . continual
(E) needlessly. . incessant

3. In parts of the Arctic, the land grades into the landfast ice so ____ that you can walk off the coast and not know you are over the hidden sea.

(A) permanently
(B) imperceptibly
(C) irregularly

(D) precariously

(E) slightly

4. Kagan maintains that an infant's reactions to its first stressful experiences are part of a natural process of development, not harbingers of childhood unhappiness or ____ signs of adolescent anxiety.

(A) prophetic

(B) normal

(C) monotonous

(D) virtual

(E) typical

5. An investigation that is ____ can occasionally yield new facts, even notable ones, but typically the appearance of such facts is the result of a search in a definite direction.

(A) timely

(B) unguided

(C) consistent

(D) uncomplicated

(E) subjective

6. Like many eighteenth-century scholars who lived by cultivating those in power, Winckelmann neglected to neutralize, by some ____ gesture of comradeship, the resentment his peers were bound to feel because of his ____ the high and mighty.

(A) quixotic. . intrigue with

(B) enigmatic. . familiarity with

(C) propitiatory. . involvement with

(D) salutary. . questioning of

(E) unfeigned. . sympathy for

7. In a ____ society that worships efficiency, it is difficult for a sensitive and idealistic person to make the kinds of ____ decisions that alone spell success as it is defined by such a society.

(A) bureaucratic. . edifying

(B) pragmatic. . hardheaded

(C) rational. . well-intentioned

(D) competitive. . evenhanded

(E) modern. . dysfunctional

SECTION 4 解答

1. 【正确答案】E

【中文释义】广大群众识字状态的出现与第一次工业革命同时发生;作为结果,这种新出现的识字人数变多,与更便宜的印刷一起有助于培养通俗文学的上升。

【解题分析】分号上下句重复,分号下句的 the new expansion in literacy 显然是重复上文的 mass literacy 一段,故第一空格填完后应表达出识字人数变多这个概念。五个中 E 正确。B 是一些同学误选的选项,事实上 B 的含义是非常荒谬的。因为大规模群众识字的状态不可能逆转,也即群众由识字退回到不识字的状态,因而当然谈不上"再出现"reappearance。

【重点词条】literacy *n*. 有修养的状态(the quality or state of being literate)

emengency 紧急事件
emengence 出现

visual literacy 视觉艺术方面的修养(the ability to recognize and understand ideas conveyed through visible actions or images)

literal *adj*. ①真实的,就其本质而言的(adhering to fact or to the ordinary construction or primary meaning of a term or expression, actual) 例

liberty in the~sense is impossible——B. N. Cardozo

②毫无夸张的(free from exaggeration or embellishment) 例 the～
  truth
③实事求是的(characterized by a concern mainly with facts) 例 a
  very～man
④文字的(of, relating to, or expressed in letters)
⑤逐字逐句的(reproduced word for word, exact, verbatim) 例 a
  ～translation

2. 【正确答案】D
   【中文释义】尽管古代的工具很少被保存下来,但仍有足够多的流传下来使我们可能揭示
           出一个偶尔被打断但是总体上却连贯的贯穿史前时期的发展过程。
   【解题分析】第二个空格出现在一个 but 构成的小连接当中,很容易推知空格应该填上 in-
           terrupted 的反义词,可知 D 和 E 应候选,D 的第一个词符合上句的转折关系,
           故选 D。
   【重点词条】noticeable adj. ①值得注意的(worthy of notice)
                      ②能够被注意到的(capable of being noticed)
           partially adv. ①部分地,不完全地
                      ②偏袒地,偏心地

3. 【正确答案】B
   【中文释义】在南极的部分地区,陆地逐渐变化为与陆地紧紧相连的冰,这种变化如此无法
           察觉以致于你可以走出海岸线,而不知道你已经在隐藏的海洋之上。
   【解题分析】文中的空格出现在 so...that... 的因果结构中,故我们应努力地从 that 构成的
           结果从句中推知 so 后的空格。很显然结果中强调了 not know,故上文的原因
           应为 B 的 imperceptibly,等于是 not known 的同义词,思路与 SECTION 2 的第
           2 题几乎一模一样。有些同学会错误地选择 E 的 slightly,事实上选 E 的同学
           可能自己都未认识到自己的思路是由 slightly 推知未察觉(imperceptibly)进而
           推出结果 not know ,所以仍然用了中间步骤 imperceptibly,如果 slightly 正确,
           imperceptibly 就先正确。大家以后在思考句子填空的推理时一定要注意它的
           思路是非常严密的,必须是直接推理,通常表现为直接重复,不会存在模糊的,
           需要假想的中间步骤才能完成的推理。句子填空中,重复才是永远正确无可
           驳斥的推理。
   【重点词条】landfast n. 牢固粘在岸边的(fast on the shore)
           fast adj. ①牢固的(firmly fixed)
                    ②牢固地附着的(adhering firmly)
           precarious adj. ①取决于别人的(depending on the will or pleasure of another)
                        ②不可靠的,值得怀疑的(dependent on uncertain premises, dubious)
                        ③缺乏安全或稳定性的(characterized by a lack of security or stabili-
                          ty that threatens with danger)

4.【正确答案】A

　【中文释义】凯根坚持认为婴儿对它第一次痛苦经验的反应是一个自然的成长过程的一部分,并不是童年忧郁症的先兆,也不是青春期焦虑症的预先的标志。

　【解题分析】文末的 not...or...构成了一个小连接,or 单独使用可以连接同义词或反义词,但当 or 与 not 或 without 连用时,一般都连接同义词,故答案为 A,harbinger 与 prophetic sign 构成同义重复。

　【重点词条】**harbinger** *n*. ①先驱者(one that pioneers in or initiates a major change, precursor)

②预兆,先兆(one that presages or foreshadows what is to come)

prophetic *adj*. 预言的,预兆的,先知的(of, relating to, or characteristic of a prophet or prophecy)

5.【正确答案】B

　【中文释义】一个没有明确导向的研究很少能够产生新的结果,即便是那些显而易见的结果,但是典型地说来这种结果的出现是一个有明确方向的研究的结果。

　【解题分析】上句的 investigation 与下文的 search 为同义重复,相应的 investigation 的定语从句应与 search 的介词短语构成重复,由 but 关系知其为反义重复,故选 B。

　　　　　　并且请大家注意这种表达 An investigation that is unguided 是不够简洁的,更好的表达是 An unguided investigation,填空题之所以这样写作完全是为了增加句子结构的复杂程度,强调定语从句与后置的形容词性介词短语在表达上有相同的功能,如此而已。在 GMAT 的句子语法改错中,An investigation that is unguided 干脆被认为是错误的,但在 GRE 中又被 ETS 煞费苦心地炮制出来。我们付之一笑,出题的人远比考题的人痛苦得多:即要将答案在短短的一句中重复出来,又不能太明显,所以只好变换表达结构,变换同、反义词,变换句型来隐藏,而这些方法又是如此地明显易辨,以至于这么多年的考题看上去一样,简直让人怀疑 ETS 明年还能干些什么。

　【重点词条】**timely** *adj*. 及时的,恰当的(in time, opportunely) 例 the question was not...~ raised in the state court

6.【正确答案】C

　【中文释义】正如很多 18 世纪的通过奉迎讨好那些有权势的人来谋生的学者一样,威克尔曼忽略了来通过一些谋求别人好感的友爱姿态来缓和他的同僚因其与有权势的人过于接近而必然产生的憎恨情绪。

　【解题分析】上文的 those in power 与下文的 the high and mighty 重复,故第二个空格应与 cultivating 构成重复,或者由第二个空格前的 his 可知空格应填威克尔曼的特征性格特征动作,同样应填 cultivating,可得答案 B 和 C。B 和 C 的第一个词是很好区分的,能缓和憎恨情绪的当然是 C 的 propitiatory 的态度,而不可能是 B 的 enigmatic 的态度。

　【重点词条】**propitiatory** *adj*. 劝慰的,谋求别人好感的(intended to propitiate, expiatory)

propitiate *v*. 劝慰,劝人息怒,抚慰(to gain or regain the favor or goodwill of, appease, conciliate)

cultivate *v*. ①种植,培养

②教育(to improve by labor, care, or study, refine)

③交友(to seek the society of, make friends with)

7.【正确答案】B

【中文释义】在一个崇尚效率的实用主义社会,一个敏感而且理想主义的人难以做出精明的决策,这种决策自身就要保证被这个社会所定义的成功。

【解题分析】第一个空格后的定语从句就提供了这个空格形容词的信息,如果熟悉句子填空的简单思维的原则就可以直接选 B。因为 pragmatic 本身的含义就是强调实际功效。D 和 E 也会被一些同学误选,这两个词并不能直接推知 worships efficiency。所以相比之下,越是直接重复的选项越可能正确。当然如果思路还没有养成 GRE 的这种简单思路,第一个空格可候选 B、D、E,接着从第二个空格的角度判断。由于 success 是由 such a society 所定义的,所以必然是一个具有实际功效的 success,那么保证这种成功的决策也应该是具有实际功效的决策,故 B 的第二个词正确,D 的第二个词 evenhanded 与 efficiency 构成了反义词,即公平与效率为学者们所认为反义词,这一点请切记。

【重点词条】spell *v*. 保证

n. 一段时间

hardheaded *adj*. ①顽固的(stubborn)

②精明的(practical, realistic)

SECTION 5

1. Her _____ should not be confused with miserliness; as long as I have known her, she has always been willing to assist those who are in need.

(A) intemperance

(B) intolerance

(C) apprehension

(D) diffidence

(E) frugality

2. Natural selection tends to eliminate genes that cause inherited diseases, acting most strongly against the most severe diseases; consequently, hereditary diseases that are _____ would be expected to be very _____,

but, surprisingly, they are not.

(A) lethal..rare

(B) untreated..dangerous

(C) unusual..refractory

(D) new..perplexing

(E) widespread..acute

3. Unfortunately, his damaging attacks on the ramifications of the economic policy have been _____ by his wholehearted acceptance of that policy's underlying assumptions.

(A) supplemented

(B) undermined

(C) wasted

(D) diverted

(E) redeemed

4. During the opera's most famous aria the tempo chosen by the orchestra's conductor seemed ____, without necessary relation to what had gone before.

　(A) tedious

　(B) melodious

　(C) capricious

　(D) compelling

　(E) cautious

5. In the machinelike world of classical physics, the human intellect appears ____, since the mechanical nature of classical physics does not ____ creative reasoning, the very ability that had made the formulation of classical principles possible.

　(A) anomalous. . allow for

　(B) abstract. . speak to

　(C) anachronistic. . deny

　(D) enduring. . value

　(E) contradictory. . exclude

6. During the 1960's assessments of the family shifted remarkably, from general endorsement of it as a worthwhile, stable institution to widespread ____ it as an oppressive and bankrupt one whose ____ was both imminent and welcome.

　(A) flight from. . restitution

　(B) fascination with. . corruption

　(C) rejection of. . vogue

　(D) censure of. . dissolution

　(E) relinquishment of. . ascent

7. Documenting science's ____ philosophy would be ____, since it is almost axiomatic that many philosophers use scientific concepts as the foundations for their speculations.

　(A) distrust of. . elementary

　(B) influence on. . superfluous

　(C) reliance on. . inappropriate

　(D) dependence on. . difficult

　(E) differences from. . impossible

SECTION 5 解答

1.【正确答案】E

　【中文释义】她的节俭不该被混淆为吝啬;据我对她的了解,她总是愿意帮助那些有需要的人。

　【解题分析】此句在校大学生恐怕会深有感触,虽然吝啬和节俭都是不爱花钱,但区别在于究竟在什么方面节省,如果能帮助别人,而对自己生活节省,则为节俭;如果每逢捐款或集体活动时高举节省的牌子,而个人生活却又并非如此节省,这才是吝啬。

　【重点词条】intemperance *n*. 无节制,放纵(lack of moderation; esp: habitual or excessive drinking of intoxicants)

2.【正确答案】A

　【中文释义】自然选择倾向于消除会导致遗传疾病的基因,对最严重的疾病其抵制力度也最强有力;相应地,那些致命的遗传疾病可预期会变得非常稀少,但是让人惊奇的是,这些疾病并没有变少。

【解题分析】分号下句重复上句,上句关于遗传疾病的形容词只有一个 most severe,故可直接选 A。

【重点词条】**untreated** *adj*. 未治疗过的

        untreatable *adj*. 不可能治愈的

        acute *adj*. ①剧烈的(characterized by sharpness or severity) 例 ~pain

           ②急性的(having a sudden onset, sharp rise, and short course) 例 ~disease

           ③锐角的(composed of acute angles) 例 ~triangle

           ④敏锐的,具有洞察力的(marked by keen discernment or intellectual perception esp. of subtle distinctions, penetrating) 例 an ~thinker

           ⑤严重的(felt, perceived, or experienced intensely) 例 ~distress

3.【正确答案】B

【中文释义】不幸的是,他对经济政策细节条款的强劲攻击被他的全心全意接受那个政策的根本前提所削弱了。

【解题分析】句首状语修饰主句的谓语动词,unfortunately 可修饰的只有 B 的 undermined。D 的 wasted 勉强可候选,再结合 by 短语可明确正确答案为 B。

【重点词条】**underlying** *adj*. ①下面的

           ②基础的(basic, fundamental)

           ③隐含的(evident only on close inspection, implicit)

           ④提前声明的(anterior and prior in claim) 例 ~mortgage

           ⑤理论或学说的深层结构的(of or being present in deep structure)

        ramification *n*. ①分支,分流(branch, offshoot)

           ②后果,派生影响(consequence, outgrowth) 例 the ~s of a problem

4.【正确答案】C

【中文释义】在这个歌剧最著名的咏调当中,由乐团指挥所选择的速度看上去多变任意,与刚刚演奏过的部分没有必然的联系。

【解题分析】空格后的分隔明确提示出速度前后不连贯,且变化得毫无规律和联系,故可得 C。

【重点词条】**caprice** *adj*. ①变化无常的(a sudden, impulsive, and seemingly unmotivated notion or action)

           ②任性的(a disposition to do things impulsively)

        compelling *adj*. ①强制性的,强迫性的

           ②吸引人的(demanding attention)

           ③令人信服的(convincing)

5. 【正确答案】A

   【中文释义】在经典物理学机械一般的世界里,人的智商显得反常。因为经典物理学机械的本性不容忍任何创造性推理,而恰恰是这种能力使得经典物理学原则的形成成为可能。

   【解题分析】请注意 the very ability 中的 ability 即指代前文的 creative reasoning,而 very 在此处并非副词,它表示了一种强烈的转折语气,故前后欲构成转折关系的话,可选 A 和 D,而第一个空格选词必须与其后文构成因果关系,只能选 A。

   【重点词条】speak to ①对…说话

   ②责备(scold or reproach someone with a view to change his conduct for the better) 例 You must speak to the children, Henry, they never listen to a word I say.

   ③证明(speak in confirmation of) 例 Can anyone speak to having seen him here yesterday?

   ④引起…的好感或同情(appeal to) 例 Great music speak directly to the emotion. / I am afraid this kind of art doesn't speak to me.

   enduring *adj*. 耐久的(lasting, durable)

6. 【正确答案】D

   【中文释义】在 20 世纪 60 年代,对家庭的评价改变得非常显著,从普遍地认可其为一个有价值的、稳定的机构到广为传播的将其责难为一个令人压抑的、毫无价值的机构,并且家庭的解体被认为迫在眉睫且大受欢迎。

   【解题分析】文中的短语 shift from...to... 表明了中心词位置和反义逻辑关系。第一空格应与上文的 endorsment 构成反义,第二个空格可由其前的 bankrupt and oppressive 得到思路,可得答案 D。

   【重点词条】bankrupt *adj*. ①破产的

   censure 指责,非难

   蔑 *endorse* v. 认可,赞同.
   endorsement n.

   ②无价值的(exhausted of valuable qualities, sterile) 例 a~old culture

   ③贫乏的,一无所有的(destitute) 例 ~of all merciful feelings

   restitution *n*. ①恢复原状,复职,复位

   ②归还,赔偿

   dissolution *n*. 溶解,分解,解体,解散

7. 【正确答案】B

   【中文释义】证明科学影响哲学是多余的,因为这一点几乎成为不需要证明的公理,即许多哲学家使用科学的观点作为他们哲学思考的基础。

   【解题分析】熟悉句子填空出题思路重复的考生不难看出下文的 that 从句重复上文的主语 documenting science's influence on philosophy,故可直接得知,下句认为 that 从句是不需证明的,所以上句的主语也是不需要的,空格里直接填上 B 即可。

   【重点词条】axiomatic *adj*. ①不证自明的(taken for granted, self-evident)

   ②公理的(based on or involving an axiom or system of axioms)

SECTION 6

1. The spellings of many Old English words have been _____ in the living language, although their pronunciations have changed.
   (A) preserved
   (B) shortened
   (C) preempted
   (D) revised
   (E) improved

2. The sheer diversity of tropical plants represents a seemingly _____ source of raw materials, of which only a few have been utilized.
   (A) exploited
   (B) quantifiable
   (C) controversial
   (D) inexhaustible
   (E) remarkable

3. For centuries animals have been used as _____ for people in experiments to assess the effects of therapeutic and other agents that might later be used in humans.
   (A) benefactors
   (B) companions
   (C) examples
   (D) precedents
   (E) surrogates

4. Social tensions among adult factions can be _____ by politics, but adolescents and children have no such _____ for resolving their conflict with the exclusive world of adults.
   (A) intensified. . attitude
   (B) complicated. . relief
   (C) frustrated. . justification

   (D) adjusted. . mechanism
   (E) revealed. . opportunity

5. The state is a network of exchanged benefits and beliefs, _____ between rulers and citizens based on those laws and procedures that are _____ to the maintenance of community.
   (A) a compromise. . inimical
   (B) an interdependence. . subsidiary
   (C) a counterpoint. . incidental
   (D) an equivalence. . prerequisite
   (E) a reciprocity. . conducive

6. Far from viewing Jefferson as a skeptical but enlightened intellectual, historians of the 1960's portrayed him as _____ thinker, eager to fill the young with his political orthodoxy while censoring ideas he did not like.
   (A) an adventurous
   (B) a doctrinaire
   (C) an eclectic
   (D) a judicious
   (E) a cynical

7. To have true disciples, a thinker must not be too _____: any effective intellectual leader depends on the ability of other people to _____ thought processes that did not originate with them.
   (A) popular. . dismiss
   (B) methodical. . interpret
   (C) idiosyncratic. . reenact
   (D) self-confident. . revitalize
   (E) pragmatic. . discourage

SECTION 6 解答

1.【正确答案】A
　【中文释义】许多老英语单词的拼写在今天使用的语言中保存下来,尽管它们的发音改变了。
　【解题分析】空格应与下文的 changed 构成反义,选 A
　【重点词条】**preempt** *v.* ①抢先占有,取得优先购买权
　　　　　　　　　　　　 ②预先制止

2.【正确答案】D
　【中文释义】热带植物的绝对多量性代表了一个看上去取之不尽的原材料资源,在这当中只有少部分被使用了。
　【解题分析】由 diversity 可直接推知空格应填上"数量多"这个词义,空格后的一段分隔也强调只有少量被使用,也即"数量很多的"的可使用,故选 D。
　【重点词条】**quantifiable** *adj.* ①用数量表达的,测量的
　　　　　　　　　　　　　　　 ②量化的
　　　　　　　inexhaustible *adj.* ①取之不尽,用之不竭的(incapable of being used up)
　　　　　　　　　　　　　　　 ②永不疲倦的(incapable of being wearied or worn out)
　　　　　　　　　　　　　　　 例 an～hiker

3.【正确答案】E
　【中文释义】几个世纪以来,动物在实验中被当作人的代替物来评估以后可能会用于人类的治疗术以及其他的因素的效果。
　【解题分析】由文中的 later 可知以后用于人类,也即现在都没有用于人类而用于动物身上,所以动物是成了试验品,代替人来测试疗效,选 E。有些同学误选 D 的 precedent,而 precedent 的含义是"榜样先例",显然在做动物药理实验时所采取的残酷的方案,如用药过量等等都不会成为对人用药的榜样。
　【重点词条】**precedent** *n.* 先例,前例,榜样,法律的判例
　　　　　　　benefactor *n.* 捐助人,施主,主动行善的人(one that confers a benefit; esp. one that makes a gift or bequest)

4.【正确答案】D
　【中文释义】成年人派系之间的社会冲突可以被政治解决,但青少年和儿童却没有这样的机制来解决他们与成年人排外世界之间的冲突。
　【解题分析】文中的 such 后应重复上文的 politics。五个选项中并没有 politics 的同义词,此时我们应该找 politics 的上义词,答案为 D。选词时应选推出来的词义的同义词或上义词。另一种解决是由 by 与 for 得知的,by 和 for 连接的均为一组手段和目的的关系,故第一个空格应直接填上后文的 resolving,可得答案 D。
　【重点词条】**frustrate** *v.* ①挫败(to balk or defeat in an endeavor)

②使人沮丧(to induce feelings of discouragement in)

adjust *v*. 调节,调解(to bring to a more satisfactory state)

5. 【正确答案】E

【中文释义】国家是一个由共同利益和共同信仰构成的体系,也就是一个统治者和市民之间的互惠体系,这个体系建立在那些有助于国家稳定的法律和法规基础之上。

【解题分析】第一个空格是分隔结构重复前文的 a network of exchanged benefits and beliefs,最直接重复的为 E 答案的 reciprocity。

另外一种解法是,先做第二个空格,前文提及的法律和国家之间的关系只有一个词 based on,故可得知法律对国家起到了"基础性的支持作用",五个选项中无此意项的同义词,但 E 答案的 conducive 与之构成了上义词,故正确。

【重点词条】counterpoint *n*. ①对比法

②补充物,对比物,相互作用

inimical *adj*. ①有害的(being adverse often by reason of hostility or malevolence)

②敌意的,不友好的(having the disposition of an enemy, hostile)

conducive *adj*. 有帮助的(tending to promote or assist) 例 an atmosphere～to education

6. 【正确答案】B

【中文释义】20 世纪 60 年代的历史学家并不将杰弗逊看成一个具有怀疑主义和启蒙精神的知识分子,而将他描写成了一个教条思想家,一个热衷于给年轻人灌输他正位的政治思想,并同时禁止一切他不喜欢的思想的人。

【解题分析】空格后为分隔成分,由此不难推知答案为 B。另外一种解法是分析 far from 结构,应与下文构成相反的观点,动词 view...as...与 portray...as 是同义词组,故空格应与 a skeptical but enlightened intellectual 构成反义,请注意这个特殊的表达结构,它表示 intellectual 同时具有 skeptical 与 enlightened 的性质,并且强调了 enlightened 这个性质,所以与这个词组反义就是与 enlightened 构成反义,答案为 B。

如果填空中出现两个形容词同时修饰一个名词并且用 but 连接两个形容词的话,请注意选词时的细节,这两个形容词应该满足如下三个条件①构成转折;②不能是对立面反义词;③通常两词应为褒贬转折关系。如"a ____ but enervating place"的五个选项:frantic, naive, ignorant, intrusive, placid 中只能选 placid。

【重点词条】enlightened *adj*. ①受过教育的,文明的,有教养的(freed from ignorance and misinformation)

②有深刻了解的(based on full comprehension of the problems involved 例 issued an～ruling

7. 【正确答案】C

【中文释义】为了拥有真正的信徒,一个思想家就不能太偏执,任何有效的精神领袖有赖于其他人的能力来重复本来并不是由他们自己所产生的思想过程。

【解题分析】句首状语提示我们第一空格应填贬义词,因为若希望拥有信徒,思想家必须优秀,也即不能"不优秀",满足第一空格为贬义的选项只有 C。故得正确答案为C,有些同学将 D 错选出来,认为 too self-confident 即是"自负",请注意 too 的用法只等同于 very,只有在 too...to 结构中才表示"过分"的意思。

      另外一种解法由冒号前后重复得知。intellectual leader 即指前文的 think,而 effective 只能指 to have true disciple,对于一个思想家而言是否有效只看他能否将自己的思想传播出去,也即有信徒。other peope 重复上文的 disciple,而第二个空格后的 thought process 显然是指思想家的思维过程,故第二个空格就应填上一个学生对老师思想的典型动作,当然是 C 的 reenact,也即学生能在自己的大脑中重复老师的思想,即学习。

【重点词条】**reenact** *v.* ①重新颁布(to enact〔as a law〕again)

            ②重新表演(to act or perform again)

            ③再次展现(to repeat the actions of an earlier event or incident)

          idiosyncratic *adj.* ①个人习惯的(a peculiarity of constitution or temperament, an individualizing characteristic or quality)

             ②个人癖好的(individual hypersensitiveness, as to a drug or food)

             ②偏执的,古怪的(eccentricity)

          revitalize *v.* 复兴,复生(to give new life or vigor to)

SECTION 7

1. Clearly refuting sceptics, researchers have ____ not only that gravitational radiation exists but that it also does exactly what theory____ it should do.

   (A) doubted..warranted

   (B) estimated..accepted

   (C) demonstrated..predicted

   (D) assumed..deduced

   (E) supposed..asserted

2. Sponsors of the bill were ____ because there was no opposition to it within the legislature until after the measure had been signed into law.

   (A) unreliable

   (B) well-intentioned

   (C) persistent

   (D) relieved

   (E) detained

3. The paradoxical aspect of the myths about Demeter, when we consider the predominant image of her as a tranquil and serene goddess, is her ____ search for her daughter.

   (A) extended

   (B) agitated

   (C) comprehensive

   (D) motiveless

   (E) heartless

4. Yellow fever, the disease that killed 4,000 Philadelphians in 1793, and so ____ Memphis, Tennessee, that the city lost its charter, has reappeared after nearly two decades in ____ in the Western Hemisphere.

(A) terrorized. . contention

(B) ravaged. . secret

(C) disabled. . quarantine

(D) corrupted. . quiescence

(E) decimated. . abeyance

5. Although ____, almost self-effacing in his private life, he displays in his plays and essays a strong ____ publicity and controversy.

(A) conventional. . interest in

(B) monotonous. . reliance on

(C) shy. . aversion toward

(D) retiring. . penchant for

(E) evasive. . impatience with

6. Comparatively few rock musicians are willing to laugh at themselves, although a hint of ____ can boost sales of video clips very nicely.

(A) self-deprecation

(B) congeniality

(C) cynicism

(D) embarrassment

(E) self-doubt

7. Parts of seventeenth-century Chinese pleasure gardens were not necessarily intended to look ____; they were designed expressly to evoke the agreeable melancholy resulting from a sense of the ____ of natural beauty and human glory.

(A) beautiful. . immutability

(B) cheerful. . transitoriness

(C) colorful. . abstractness

(D) luxuriant. . simplicity

(E) conventional. . wildness

SECTION 7 解答

1. 【正确答案】C

【中文释义】清楚地驳斥了怀疑的人,研究者们不但证明了重力的辐射作用存在,而且证明了重力辐射作用正如理论推测的那样做它应该做的事情。

【解题分析】句首状语修饰主句的谓语动词,故第一空格应能够驳斥怀疑的人,五个选项中只有 C 正确。

【重点词条】**warrant** v. ①授权,批准(sanction, authorization; also: evidence for or token of authorization)

②证明(confirm, proof)

③保证

2. 【正确答案】D

【中文释义】这个议案的提案人心情放松下来了,因为一直到这个提案被签署生效为法律之前都没有任何反对。

【解题分析】文中的 the bill, it, the measure 指的是同一事物,均为提案人支持的议案,既然议案顺利通过,他们的努力就没有泡汤,所以当然应该高兴,D 为正确答案,需要指出的是本句中的 until 并不与前面的 no 构成 not…until… 的结构,首先是 no 是修饰 opposition 的,其次 until 后跟的并不是一个明确的时间点,而是一个模糊的概念(before)。而 not…until… 中的 until 之后必须跟一个明确的时间概念。如果理解成 not…until… 此句的解法就大为不同。not…until… 强调的是之后的状态,此句就会强调议案通过之后有很多人反对它。而单独用 until 只表示 before,强调的是议案通过之前没有人反对它。故切不可混淆两者,当然 until 本身也意味着之前之后的截然对比。在有些填空题中 until 的出现本身就意味着时间对比题型的出现,应该使两段时间的动作对立起来,如 SECTION 16 第 6 题。

【重点词条】detain v. ①留住,耽搁(to hold or keep in or as if in custody, or to keep back, withhold)

②约束,阻止(restrain esp. from proceeding, stop)

relieved adj. 宽心的,宽慰的(experiencing or showing relief esp. from anxiety or pent-up emotions)

3. 【正确答案】B

【中文释义】狄美特女神(注:古希腊中的农业女神)的神话中相互矛盾的方面是她狂躁不安地寻找她的女儿(作者注:被森林大王抢走),而我们却认为她的主体形象是一个宁静安详的女神。

【解题分析】文中的 paradoxical 意味着一组反义词的出现,类似功能的词为 ironically, puzzling, surperising。文中的 consider…as… 短语是描述人或事物主体特征的一个典型短语,类似的短语如 view…as…,portray…as…,label…as… 等,故 tranquil and serene 为主体词汇。反义词就应与之反义,故空格里填上 tranquil and serene 的反义词即可,答案为 B。

【重点词条】agitate v. ①搅动(to give motion to sb, to move with an irregular, rapid, or violent action) 例 the storm agitated the sea

②纷扰,使不安(to excite and often trouble the mind or feelings of, disturb)

predominant adj. ①占主导地位的(having superior strength, influence, or authority, prevailing)

②主要的,普遍的(being most frequent or common)

4. 【正确答案】E

【中文释义】黄热病,这一种病曾在 1793 年夺去 4,000 个费城人的生命,并且曾大批杀死田纳西州曼菲斯这个城市的人口以至于这个城市丧失其自治市资格,这种疾病在西北半球近 20 年销声匿迹之后又重新出现了。

【解题分析】句子主干即可解题。reappear 之前的时间当然应该是疾病未发作的时间,故可直接选第二个空格为 E。

【重点词条】quarantine n. 隔离检疫期; v. 隔离,封锁

5.【正确答案】D

　　【中文释义】尽管不爱与人交往,几乎在个人生活中从不抛头露面,但他却在戏剧和散文作品中表现出一种强烈的爱出风头、爱与人争吵的倾向。

　　【解题分析】有两种解法。首先第一个空格后的分隔就是直接重复空格的,可得答案 D 或 C,再由上下句的转折关系得 D。或者由上下句的转折关系知,第一空格只能填上 publicity and controversy 的同义或反义词,可候选的为 C 和 D,再由转折关系得 D。事实上两种解法大同小异,但都有一个难点即 retiring 词义的推测,由于此处用了它的一个生僻义项。retiring 的第一含义是退休的,而退休的生活是孤独的,如同隐居一样,隐居的人当然就是不愿与世人交往的人,孤独的、隐居的、不愿与人交往的就是 retiring 的另外三个义项。大家平时应该多查阅英英词典,并且仔细揣摩词义之间的转换衍生关系,这种水滴石穿的积累是英文学习的大补。

　　【重点词条】**retiring** *adj*. ①退休的

　　　　　　　　　　　　②隐居的

　　　　　　　　　　　　③沉默寡言的

　　　　　　　　　　　　④不爱与人交往的,害羞的(reserved, shy)

　　　　　　　publicity *n*. ①公众的注意力,名声(the quality or state of being public)

　　　　　　　　　　　　②宣传,吸引注意力(an act or device designed to attract public interest; specif. information with news value issued as a means of gaining public attention or support)

　　　　　　　　　　　　③广告,宣传品

　　　　　　　evasive *adj*. 支支吾吾的(tending or intended to evade, equivocal)

6.【正确答案】A

　　【中文释义】比较而言很少有摇滚乐手愿意嘲笑他们自己,尽管一些自我贬低可以非常好地推动唱碟的销售。

　　【解题分析】由转折关系可知上句为不愿意嘲笑自己,下句应为愿意嘲笑自己,所以下句至少会出现自嘲的同义或反义词,只有 A。含义是卖唱碟是摇滚乐手们最愿意干的事情,而自嘲又可以推动唱碟的销售,但他们偏偏不愿意这么做。

　　【重点词条】**congenial** *adj*. ①和谐一致的(having the same nature, disposition, or tastes, kindred , or existing or associated together harmoniously)

　　　　　　　　　　　　②高兴的, 相宜的(pleasant; esp. agreeably suited to one's nature, tastes, or outlook)

7.【正确答案】B

　　【中文释义】17 世纪中国乐园的某些部分并不是必然意在看上去显得快乐的,他们被专门设计来激发出一个令人愉快的忧伤情绪,这种情绪是由一种大自然的美和人类的光辉转眼即逝的感觉导致的。

　　【解题分析】此句有三种解法。第一种解法:分号前后构成了肯定句与双重否定句的转换。分号前后的 were intended to look 与 were designed to evoke 几乎同义,相应的情绪应为反义,故空格与 agreeable melancholy 构成反义,得答案 B。第二种解法:melancholy 后的 resulting from 为分隔结构,其中空格应由 melancholy 推出,五个选项中能导致忧伤这种感觉的只有 B,这是一种中国人特别熟悉的感春伤秋的情怀。第三种解法不太常用。上半句出现了否定,这是比较奇怪的,因为否定必须有所指,否定的对象只能出现在否定词之前,not 之前能否定的只有 pleasure,故可直接选第一空格为 B。

【重点词条】**transitory** *adj*. 短暂的,稍纵即逝的

SECTION 8

1. Since it is now ＿＿ to build the complex central processing unit of a computer on a single silicon chip using photolithography and chemical etching, it seems plausible that other miniature structures might be fabricated in ＿＿ ways.

    (A) unprecedented. . undiscovered

    (B) difficult. . related

    (C) permitted. . unique

    (D) mandatory. . congruent

    (E) routine. . similar

2. Given the evidence of Egyptian and Babylonian ＿＿ later Greek civilization, it would be incorrect to view the work of Greek scientists as an entirely independent creation.

    (A) disdain for

    (B) imitation of

    (C) ambivalence about

    (D) deference to

    (E) influence on

3. Laws do not ensure social order since laws can always be ＿＿, which makes them ＿＿ unless the authorities have the will and the power to detect and punish wrongdoing.

    (A) contested. . provisional

    (B) circumvented. . antiquated

    (C) repealed. . vulnerable

    (D) violated. . ineffective

    (E) modified. . unstable

4. Since she believed him to be both candid and trustworthy, she refused to consider the possibility that his statement had been ＿＿.

    (A) irrelevant

    (B) facetious

    (C) mistaken

    (D) critical

    (E) insincere

5. Ironically, the party leaders encountered no greater ＿＿ their efforts to build a progressive party than the ＿＿ of the progressives already elected to the legislature.

    (A) support for. . advocacy

    (B) threat to. . promise

    (C) benefit from. . success

    (D) obstacle to. . resistance

    (E) praise for. . reputation

6. It is strange how words shape our thoughts and trap us at the bottom of deeply ＿＿ canyons of thinking, their imprisoning sides carved out by the ＿＿ of past usage.

    (A) cleaved. . eruptions

    (B) rooted. . flood

(C) incised. . river

(D) ridged. . ocean

(E) notched. . mountains

×. That his <u>intransigence</u> in making decisions _____ no open disagreement from any quarter was well known; thus, clever subordinates

learned the art of _____ their opinions in casual remarks.

(A) elicited. . quashing

(B) engendered. . recasting

(C) brooked. . intimating

(D) embodied. . instigating

(E) forbore. . emending

SECTION 8 解答

1. 【正确答案】E

   【中文释义】既然现在使用光石刻图法以及化学腐蚀的方法将复杂的计算机 CPU 制作在一个单硅晶片上已经是很常规的,看上去其他的微观结构以类似的方法制造也是行得通的。

   【解题分析】文中的 other miniature structure 照应上文的计算机的 CPU。有 other 必然有其对应的事物,这也是一种常见的照应,上下文的 build 与 fabricate 又是同义词,这些都在提示着第二个空格应填"相同,类似",可候选的为 B、D、E、再由因果关系可得 E 正确。

   【重点词条】**mandatory** *adj*. 强制性的(containing or constituting a command, obligatory) 例 ～retirement age

   routine *adj*. ①常规的,普遍的(of a commonplace or repetitive character, ordinary)

   ②例行公事的(of, relating to, or being in accordance with established procedure) 例 ～business

2. 【正确答案】E

   【中文释义】考虑到埃及和巴比伦对后来希腊文明影响的证据,将希腊科学家的成就看成完全独立的创造是不对的。

   【解题分析】文中的 later 告诉我们时间关系,而更早的埃及和巴比伦根本无从知晓后来会有希腊文明,故 A、B、C、D 都是荒谬的,正确答案为 E。或者由下文的 view. . . as. . .可知 independent 为主体词,故否定词 incorrect 否定的即为 independent,非独立的方式,也就是受到别人影响的方式,仍可推出答案 E。

   【重点词条】**ambivalence** *n*. ①矛盾情绪或态度(simultaneous and contradictory attitudes or feelings such as attraction and repulsion toward an object, person, or action)

   ②摇摆,举棋不定(continual fluctuation such as between one thing and its opposite)

3. 【正确答案】D

   【中文释义】法律不能保障社会秩序因为法律总是被违反,从而就使得法律失去效力,除非权威机构有意愿和能力来发现和惩罚犯罪分子。

【解题分析】此句是一个很典型的题目,很多同学由于分析句子结构的功夫欠火候而导致解题的失败。文中的 which 显然是指代前文全句,从而是指代前句的主句,由"laws do not ensure social order"所能推出的结论当然是法律未能尽到自己的职能,也即 ineffective。不少同学将 which 看成指代"laws can always be ____",从而该选 E。事实上从 unless 的分析也可以很好地解题,unless 之前就应该是法律权威机构能够惩罚犯罪分子,这就能说明法律的"有效"(ineffective 的反义词),而选 D 的含义成了法律"稳定不变"(unstable 的反义词),这与法律能惩罚犯罪分子一点关系都没有。

【重点词条】**repeal** *v.* ①撤消,废止(to rescind or annul by authoritative act; esp. to revoke or abrogate by legislative enactment)

②放弃,反对(abandon, renounce)

provisional *adj.* 短暂的(serving for the time being, temporary)

4.【正确答案】E

【中文释义】既然她认为他是坦诚并且值得信任的,所以她拒绝认为有这种可能性,即他的言论会是不真诚的。

【解题分析】此题中的 him 和 his statement 为同义重复,上句为 him 是 candid,故下句双重否定应为 his statement 不可能 insincere。此题虽然简单,但请注意这种同义词复述的方式:他和他的言行。作者与作者的书,科学家与科学家的时代,甚至是 we 与 our time 等等都是同义词关系,选词时应选同义词来描绘它们。

【重点词条】**facetious** *adj.* ①滑稽可笑的(joking or jesting often inappropriately, waggish)

②不严肃的(meant to be humorous or funny, not serious)

5.【正确答案】D

【中文释义】具有嘲讽意味的是,这个政党的领导人在他们建设一个激进党的努力中,最大的障碍来自于那些早就选入了立法机构的激进分子的抵抗。

【解题分析】首先请注意本句并不是比较结构,而是一种最高级结构,所以请不要套用比较结构的解题思路,文中的解题点实际上很明显,主体词汇 progressive 出现了两次,这就是我们思考的出发点,第二个空格要求填激进分子的动作或态度,而激进党领导人正努力力建设激进党,故正常的态度应为支持自己的党。文学的 ironically 提示我们一种反常情况的出现,故第二个空格反而应该填"反对",答案为 D。

【重点词条】**ironically** *adv.* 具有嘲讽意味地,出乎意料地,令人啼笑皆非地

6.【正确答案】C

【中文释义】非常奇怪的是语言如何塑造了我们的思想,并且将我们围捕在深不可测的被雕刻而成的思维峡谷的底部,这种思维峡谷禁锢的内壁是被语言的过往使用的河流雕刻而成的。

【解题分析】此句内容过于晦涩,国内真正考题很少出这种学术专业性太强的句子,当然解

题的思路仍然一样,第一个空格要求填一个形容词修饰思维峡谷,而随后的分隔成分完全表达出来:思维峡谷是被雕刻而成的,故可直接将 carved out 作过去分词修饰思维峡谷,直接选 C 即可。此句阐明了西方语言学的一个流行观点,即语言可以产生思想,语言是思想的最深层结构,语言的反复使用会在语言接受者的脑中形成一个难以摆脱的思想,并且进入到潜意识层面也即此句中的比喻物 bottom of deeply incised canyons of thinking。大众往往被围捕在精英们所创造的语言陷阱中,伪真理、伪道德的圈套里而无法摆脱,并且执迷不悟。所谓"谎言重复一千遍也成了真理"部分表达了这个含义。

【重点词条】ridged *adj*. 起皱的,成脊状的,像山脊一样隆起的

notch *n*. ①V 形的凹口(a V-shaped indentation)

②程度,等级

vt. ①开出 V 形的凹口(to cut or make a notch in)

②通过刻 V 形凹口来做标记(to mark or record by a notch)

③赢得,记录(score, achieve)

7.【正确答案】C

【中文释义】他做决策时的顽固性格不容忍任何方面来的公开不同意见是众所周知的,因此聪明的下属学会这种艺术的方式:在漫不经心的评价中暗示出自己的观点。

【解题分析】文中的 his intransigence 以物主代词加抽象名词的方式指明了人物的特征性格,故第一个空格可以由之直接推断出答案,因为顽固的概念本身就是"不接受人的意见",可直接选 C。选 E 是由于单词概念不清导致的,请参阅下面的注释。

【重点词条】elicit *v*. ①引出,引申出(to draw forth or bring out something latent or potential)例 hypnotism~ed his hidden fears

②导致,引发(to call forth or draw out as information or a response)例 her performance~ed wild applause

quash *v*. ①镇压,平息)(to suppress or extinguish summarily and completely)例 ~a rebellion

②废除,宣布无效(to nullify esp. by judicial action)例 ~an indictment

brook *v*. (只用于否定句)容忍,忍受,容许。另外请注意区分下列两组词:

①表示克制压抑自己的欲望:forbear doing sth;refrain from doing sth;abstain doing sth

②表示忍受别人的,或外界的不良刺激:brook, bear, endure, abide

emend *vt*. 修正,修订。另外请注意区分下列三组词:

①表示将错误的改成正确的:emend, rectify, redress, revise

②表示将正确的改成错误的:distort, deform, contort, warp

③只表示变化,不表明方向:transcribe, transform, transmute, convert, metamorphose, transmogrify

SECTION 9

1. Created to serve as perfectly as possible their workaday ____, the wooden storage boxes made in America's Shaker communities are now ____ for their beauty.
   (A) environment. . accepted
   (B) owners. . employed
   (C) function. . valued
   (D) reality. . transformed
   (E) image. . seen

2. In order to ____ her theory that the reactions are ____, the scientist conducted many experiments, all of which showed that the heat of the first reaction is more than twice that of the second.
   (A) support. . different
   (B) comprehend. . constant
   (C) evaluate. . concentrated
   (D) capture. . valuable
   (E) demonstrate. . problematic

3. The sheer bulk of data from the mass media seems to overpower us and drive us to ____ accounts for an easily and readily digestible portion of news.
   (A) insular
   (B) investigative
   (C) synoptic
   (D) subjective
   (E) sensational

4. William James lacked the usual ____ death; writing to his dying father, he spoke without ____ about the old man's impending death.
   (A) longing for. . regret
   (B) awe of. . inhibition
   (C) curiosity about. . rancor
   (D) apprehension of. . eloquence
   (E) anticipation of. . commiseration

5. Current data suggest that, although ____ states between fear and aggression exist, fear and aggression are as distinct physiologically as they are psychologically.
   (A) simultaneous
   (B) serious
   (C) exceptional
   (D) partial
   (E) transitional

6. It is ironic that a critic of such overwhelming vanity now suffers from a measure of the oblivion to which he was forever ____ others, in the end, all his ____ has only worked against him
   (A) dedicating. . self-procession
   (B) leading. . self-righteousness
   (C) consigning. . self-adulation
   (D) relegating. . self-sacrifice
   (E) condemning. . self-analysis

7. Famous among job seekers for its ____, the company, quite apart from generous salaries, bestowed on its executives annual bonuses and such ____ as low-interest home mortgages and company cars.
   (A) magnanimity. . reparations
   (B) inventiveness. . benefits
   (C) largesse. . perquisites
   (D) discernment. . prerogatives
   (E) altruism. . credits

SECTION 9 解答

1.【正确答案】C

【中文释义】当初被创造来尽可能地完美地实现它们工作日时的实用功效,这些在美国震颤派教区所制作出来的木质结构的储藏盒现在因为它们的美而受到珍视。

【解题分析】第二个空格前的 now 给出了充分的提示,一个典型的时间对比型,紧接着思路就是寻找过去的对比,不难发现第一行的 created 显然是指过去的时间,一个工具的两方面属性为美观和实用。故现在是为了美。过去当然是为了实用,所以第一个空格可得答案 C。

【重点词条】employ *v*. ①使用,利用

②使忙碌,使从事

③雇用

value *vt*. ①给…定价,估价(to estimate or assign the monetary worth of, appraise) 例 ~a necklace

②评价(to rate or scale in usefulness, importance, or general worth, evaluate)

③夸奖,尊重,珍视(to consider or rate highly, prize, esteem) 例 ~s your opinion

2.【正确答案】A

【中文释义】为了支持她的理论,即这些反应是不同的,这位科学家做了许多实验,所有这些实验都证明第一次反应的热量比第二次反应的热量的两倍还多。

【解题分析】第二个空格要求填词表示这些反应是什么样的,紧随其后的信息就告诉我们这些反应的热量是不一样的,所以当然选 A 的第二个词 different。该题不需要任何专业知识,有些同学经过深入地思考热量之间的关系后反而将答案做错了,一定要清醒地认识到这是一份 General Test,不会涉及任何专业知识,故任何时候都应以常识思维去理解句意,尤其是曾有过极个别的题目,如果用专业的观点去看居然与常识的观点去看不一样,这时应毫不犹豫地舍弃专业观点。当然,这种题是 ETS 的败笔,因为这种题目对于该专业的考生是很不公平的,有可能误导他们做过深的专业思考。所以近几年从出题的内容看,专业的知识涉及得越来越少。

【重点词条】problematic *adj*. ①难于解决或决策的(posing a problem, difficult to solve or decide)

②未解决的,不确定的(not definite or settled, uncertain) 例 their future remains~

3.【正确答案】C

【中文释义】大众传媒的绝对大量的信息看上去超过了我们的承受能力,并且驱使我们到那些摘要的文章上来获得一个容易的并让人欣然接受的好理解的那部

分信息。

【解题分析】该句中 and 前后可互相推理。And 之前称大量的信息超过承受能力,所以 and 之后当然是要求获得一个信息量少一些的文章 accounts,即 C 选项的 synoptic。当然由空格后的 for 引导的介词短语也可推知空格应为"好理解、简单的",而得答案 C。

【重点词条】insular *adj.* ①小岛的
　　　　　　　　　　②岛国狭隘心态的(characteristic of an isolated people; esp. be-ing, having, or reflecting a narrow provincial viewpoint)

　　　　　　synoptic *adj.* ①宏观的,整体上的(affording a general view of a whole)
　　　　　　　　　　②概要的,梗概的(manifesting or characterized by comprehen-siveness or breadth of view)

　　　　　　readily *adj.* ①准备好的,毫不犹豫的(in a ready manner, as a without hesita-ting, willingly) 例 ~accepted advice
　　　　　　　　　　②容易的(without much difficulty, easily) 例 for reasons that anyone could~understand

4. 【正确答案】B

【中文释义】威廉·詹姆斯缺乏通常对死亡的敬畏之情;当给他垂死的父亲写信的时候,他肆无忌惮地谈论这个老人日益逼近的死亡。

【解题分析】第一个空格前的 usual 是一个很受欢迎的词,它意味着我们可以纯粹从常识出发去考虑问题。可以候选 B 和 D。而分号下句显然可知,由于缺乏对死亡的恐惧,所以他说话时不带有忌讳,即 B 的 inhibition。

【重点词条】rancor *n.* 深仇大恨,积怨(bitter deep-seated ill will)

　　　　　　apprehension *n.* ①理解(the act or power of perceiving or comprehending) 例 a person of dull~
　　　　　　　　　　②逮捕(seizure by legal process, arrest)
　　　　　　　　　　③怀疑,恐惧(suspicion or fear esp. of future evil, forebod-ing)

　　　　　　commiseration *n.* 同情,怜悯,哀悼

5. 【正确答案】E

【中文释义】目前数据表明,尽管害怕和进攻之间存在过渡状态,但是害怕和进攻无论在心理上还是在生理上都是截然不同的。

【解题分析】句子结构非常简单,推理线索也很明确应为空格与 distinct 构成反义,但不少同学误选 A。实际上 A 的 simultaneous 的反义词只能是"不同时的,异步的",而 distinct 却没有这个义项。文中的害怕和进攻是指动物的行为,如一只猛兽见人之后的第一反应是害怕,随后它就会用进攻的方式来消除它的威胁物,而弱小的动物产生害怕情绪之后,会用逃跑来摆脱威胁物。害怕和进攻对身体的生理水平肯定是截然不同的,有不同的激素,不同的血压和脉搏,但两者之间都会有一个中间转变过程,这个转变过程就将两者有机结合起来,故选 E。

【重点词条】**distinct** *adj*. ①有区别的,不同种类或性质的(distinguishable to the eye or mind as discrete, separate) 例 a～cultural group/teaching is ～from research

②有特征,有特点的(presenting a clear unmistakable impression) 例 a neat～handwriting

③明显的(readily and unmistakably apprehended) 例 a～possibility of snow/a～British accent

exceptional *adj*. ①特例的,特殊的(forming an exception, rare) 例 an～number of rainy days

②杰出的(better than average, superior) 例 ～skill

③与众不同的(deviating from the norm, as a having above or below average intelligence)

④身体残疾的(physically handicapped)

exceptionable *adj*. 会引起反感的(being likely to cause objection, objectionable) 例 visitors even drink the～beer

unexceptionable *adj*. 无可指责的,无懈可击的(not open to objection or criticism, beyond reproach, unimpeachable)

6.【正确答案】C

【中文释义】具有讽刺意味的是一个具有如此强烈虚荣心的批评家现在遭到了一些被人遗忘的痛苦,而这种被人遗忘是他永远都力图赋予别人的;最终,所有他的自我吹嘘都对他起到了相反的作用。

【解题分析】文中的 a critic of such overwhelming vanity 是一个典型的表示人物特征性格的结构,该批评家的特征性格为 vanity。而分号下半句重复了这个特征性格,只不过换了一种语言表达方式,用 his 物主代词加空格的方式,故空格中应直接填上表示 vanity 性格的词即可。C 的 secf-adulation 即指 vanity,它不单单指行动上的自我吹嘘,同时指心理上的自大,这就是 vanity 的含义。另外原文中用了一个与中国人的表达相异的结构,consign others to oblivion。中国人谈及有虚荣心的人的特征动作通常描述为"自吹自擂,自我表现,使自己鹤立鸡群",而此时周围的人必然会黯然失色,被人遗忘,周围人被人遗忘由谁造成的呢?是由该有虚荣心的人的自我表演造成的。故英语中的表达虚荣心的特征动作可以说成"consign others to oblivion"。另外该句的分号句上下句也构成了完全的重复,请对照原文仔细体会。

【重点词条】**consign** *v*. 寄放,托管(to give, transfer, or deliver into the hands or control of another; also: to commit esp. to a final destination or fate) 例 a writer～ed to oblivion

self-adulation *n*. 自我吹嘘,自我吹捧,虚荣心

relegate *v*. ①流放(to send into exile, banish)

②降级,不重视(to assign to a place of insignificance or of oblivion, put out of sight or mind)

③归类(to assign to an appropriate place or situation on the basis of classification or appraisal)

7.【正确答案】C

【中文释义】在求职人员中由于其慷慨而知名,这家公司,除了有慷慨的薪水之外,还授予它的经理们年度分红以及诸如低息的房屋抵押金和公司公车等特殊津贴。

【解题分析】第一个空格在 its 之后,显然应该填特征性格或特征动作。而读至 quite apart from generos salaries 即可知该公司除了有慷慨的薪水之外,还有很多"慷慨的东西",故其特征性格即为"慷慨",可直接选出 C 答案。

【重点词条】magnanimity *adj.* 宽容的,从容的(the quality of being magnanimous, loftiness of spirit enabling one to bear trouble calmly, to disdain meanness and pettiness, and to display a noble generosity)

　　　　　　largesse *adj.* 慷慨大方的(liberal giving as of money to or as if to an inferior; also: something so given)

　　　　　　perquisites *n.* ①特殊待遇,特权
　　　　　　　　　　　　　②额外所得,津贴,外快

SECTION 10

1. There are no solitary, free-living creatures; every form of life is ____ other forms.

(A) segregated from

(B) parallel to

(C) dependent on

(D) overshadowed by

(E) mimicked by

2. The sale of Alaska was not so much an American coup as a matter of ____ for an imperial Russia that was short of cash and unable to ____ its own continental coastline.

(A) negligence..fortify

(B) custom..maintain

(C) convenience..stabilize

(D) expediency..defend

(E) exigency..reinforce

3. Despite assorted effusions to the contrary, there is no necessary link between scientific skill and humanism, and, quite possibly, there may be something of a ____ between them.

(A) generality

(B) fusion

(C) congruity

(D) dichotomy

(E) reciprocity

4. A common argument claims that in folk art, the artist's subordination of technical mastery to intense feeling ____ the direct communication of emotion to the viewer.

(A) facilitates

(B) averts

(C) neutralizes

(D) implies

(E) represses

5. While not completely nonplussed by the usu-
ally caustic responses from members of the
audience, the speaker was nonetheless visi-
bly ____ by their lively criticism.
(A) humiliated
(B) discomfited
(C) deluded
(D) disgraced
(E) tantalized

6. In eighth-century Japan, people who ____
wasteland were rewarded with official ranks
as part of an effort to overcome the shortage
of ____ fields.
(A) conserved. . forested

(B) reclaimed. . arable
(C) cultivated. . domestic
(D) irrigated. . accessible
(E) located. . desirable

7. If duty is the natural ____ of one's ____ the
course of future events, then people who are
powerful have duty placed on them whether
they like it or not.
(A) correlate. . understanding of
(B) outgrowth. . control over
(C) determinant. . involvement in
(D) mitigant. . preoccupation with
(E) arbiter. . responsibility for

SECTION 10 解答

1.【正确答案】C
　【中文释义】没有单独的、自由生活的动物;每种生命形式都依赖于其他生命形式。
　【解题分析】此句话很容易推理,需要注意的是 B 选项 parallel to,填回原文的含义是指在
　　　　　　　进化史上两种生命处于平行的发展阶段,所以并不吻合题意。
　【重点词条】**overshadow** $v.$ ①遮蔽(to cast a shadow over)
　　　　　　　　　　　②超过,胜过(to exceed in importance, outweigh)

2.【正确答案】D
　【中文释义】阿拉斯加的出售与其说是美国人成功的策略不如说是沙皇俄国的权宜之计,
　　　　　　　其时沙皇俄国缺少现金而无法保卫它自身的大陆海岸线。
　【解题分析】此句需重点理解一个连词短语"not so much. . .as. . .",对应的中文短语是"与
　　　　　　　其说是…不如说是…"这个短语表示从不同角度来看待同一个事物而得到截然
　　　　　　　不同的结论,故连接的两端应为反义词,比如一个邪恶的势力打赢了一场战争,
　　　　　　　评论家们会说"与其说它赢了,还不如说它输了,因为它的胜利促使了全世界正
　　　　　　　义力量的觉醒"。这就是典型的从不同角度看待问题得出不同结论的例子。
　　　　　　　　本句中的 not so much. . .as. . .,一句连接的是"美国主动的策略",所以另
　　　　　　　一方就应该是"俄国人主动的策略",从而选 D。全句强调了俄国人在出售阿
　　　　　　　拉斯加的生意中吃亏是俄国人早就意料之中的,而并非被美国人的策略所蒙
　　　　　　　蔽的。
　【重点词条】**fortify** $v.$ ①加强,巩固(to make strong, to strengthen and secure 〔as a town〕
　　　　　　　　　　by forts or batteries)
　　　　　　　　　　②鼓励,激励(to add mental or moral strength to, encourage)

$\boxed{例}$ fortified by prayer

③增加(to add material to for strengthening or enriching)

expediency *n.* ①适宜,合算(the quality or state of being suited to the end in view, suitability, fitness)

②权宜之计(adherence to expedient means and methods)

$\boxed{例}$ put more emphasis on~than on principle——W.H.Jones

3.【正确答案】D

【中文释义】尽管有各式各样的对反面观点的认同情绪,但是科学技巧和人文主义之间的确没有必然的联系,并且非常可能的是两者之间有着本质的对立。

【解题分析】文中 and 前后很容易推理,空格中应填上 no link 而 generality(A)表哲学中普遍联系性,fusion(B)表熔合混合,congruity(C)表完全一致,reciprocity(E)表互惠互利,都表达出了有联系的概念。D 的 dichotomy 有"二分法","本质对立"的两个义项,正确解释为"本质对立的"。

本句的意思是非常晦涩的,事实上它提出了一个与普遍信念相反的观点,我们通常会认为科学水平的提高会导致物质生活的提高,从而导致诸如偷窃、抢劫等等行为的消失,从而提高了人的精神道德。但西方社会的发展却表明,那些有很高科技水平、非常富有的国家,道德却面临着巨大的堕落,从而又有人提出本文的观点,即科技的发展是与人的道德背道而驰的。正应了老庄的一句话"绝圣弃智,大盗乃止"。法兰克福学派则认为,"科学规则和技术操作毁灭文化和人性。"

中国人引出一段会遭大家反对的话时会说"尽管我知道大家可能会不赞同我下面的观点,但是我仍要指出…"而英文中则用了本句的句套"Dispite assorted effusions to the contrary."

【重点词条】**effusion** *n.* ①(液体、气体)流出,溢出

②(思想感情)迸发,倾泻(unrestrained expression of words or feelings) $\boxed{例}$ greeted her with great~

③极度支持,热情支持

assorted *adj.* ①适合的,配对的(suited esp. by nature or character) $\boxed{例}$ an ill-assorted pair

②各种各样的(consisting of various kinds) $\boxed{例}$ ~chocolates

4.【正确答案】A

【中文释义】一个普遍的论点认为,在民间艺术中,艺术家使技术上的精湛技巧服从于强烈感情的做法有利于直接将情绪表达给观众。

【解题分析】文中 intense feeling 即为 emotion,"subordination of A to B"的含义为"使 A 屈从于 B"。故不难推知这种做法是对表达感情起到了正面作用,只有 A 的 facilitate 表达了这种正面作用。

【重点词条】**subordination** *n.* ①下级地位

②隶属,从属(to)

5. 【正确答案】B

【中文释义】尽管没有被来自某些观众的尖刻的反应导致彻底的狼狈不堪,但这位演说家仍然很明显地被他们鲜明的批评搞得灰心丧气。

【解题分析】上文否定的是 completely,所以下句应该表达出这个演说家"轻微的狼狈不堪",比 nonplussed 程度轻的态度为 B 的 discomfited。

【重点词条】**discomfit** *v*. ①挫败(to frustrate the plans of, thwart)

②使尴尬(to put into a state of perplexity and embarrassment, disconcert)

disgrace *v*. ①使丢脸,使受耻辱(to be a source of shame to) 例 your actions disgraced the family

②使失宠,使失去地位(to cause to lose favor or standing) 例 was disgraced by the hint of scandal

6. 【正确答案】B

【中文释义】在八世纪的日本,开垦荒地的人被授予了官衔来作为他们克服可耕地短缺的努力的一部分。

【解题分析】第一个空格的动作导致被授予官衔这样的奖励,故肯定为一有功劳的动作,可选 B 和 C。第二个空格是在重复上文,开垦荒地也即克服了可耕地的短缺,故答案为 B。

【重点词条】**reclaim** *v*. ①使改过,使感化

②开垦,开拓

③回收利用

7. 【正确答案】B

【中文释义】如果责任是指一个人控制未来事件发展方向的自然结果的话,那么有权力的人就应承担责任而不管他们是否喜欢。

【解题分析】一个典型的句子。这种上句两个空格,下句完整的句子解法与分号句完全一样,即上下句重复即可,下句明确表达出了权力产生责任的观点。而上句的主语为责任,所以与之发生关系的必然是权力,这样才能构成上下文的重复,第二个空格只有填 B 的 control over 才表示权力,故可直接选 B。此时结合第一个词可以看出此句是一个主动句与被动句之间的转换,通常如果上句为"A 推出 B"的句式,而下句变成"B 推出 A"的结构,也即主宾颠倒了次序时,会有两种情况,第一种是主动与被动的转换,这时的特征是会出现 by, though 或者 is the result of, is the outgrowth of, is the product of 这样的短语出现在下句中,如果没有上列短语单词,则可绝对认为上下句是逆否命题的关系。"A 增则推出 B 增;B 降则推出 A 降",主动被动转换与逆否命题转换之间的区别就在于上列的几个标志词,如果没有这些标志词,就可断定这种 A 推出 B;B 推出 A 的结构转换为逆否命题转换。这在许多难题中显得尤为重要。

【重点词条】mitigate *v*. ①中和,缓和(to cause to become less harsh or hostile, mollify) 例
　　　　　　　 aggressiveness may be mitigated or...channeled——Ashley Montagu
　　　　　　②减轻痛苦(to make less severe or painful, alleviate)
　　mitagant *n*. 缓和物(something mitigating)
　　arbiter *n*. ①仲裁人(a person with power to decide a dispute, judge)
　　　　　　②全权仲裁机构或仲裁人(a person or agency having the power of
　　　　　　deciding)

SECTION 11

1. By divesting himself of all regalities, the former king ____ the consideration that customarily protects monarchs.
   - (A) merited
   - (B) forfeited
   - (C) debased
   - (D) concealed
   - (E) extended

2. A perennial goal in zoology is to infer function from ____, relating the ____ of an organism to its physical form and cellular organization.
   - (A) age. . ancestry
   - (B) classification. . appearance
   - (C) size. . movement
   - (D) structure. . behavior
   - (E) location. . habitat

3. The sociologist responded to the charge that her new theory was ____ by pointing out that it did not in fact contradict accepted sociological principles.
   - (A) banal
   - (B) heretical
   - (C) unproven
   - (D) complex
   - (E) superficial

4. Industrialists seized economic power only after industry had ____ agriculture as the preeminent form of production; previously such power had ____ land ownership.
   - (A) sabotaged. . threatened
   - (B) overtaken. . produced
   - (C) toppled. . culminated in
   - (D) joined. . relied on
   - (E) supplanted. . resided in

5. Rumors, embroidered with detail, live on for years, neither denied nor confirmed, until they become accepted as fact even among people not known for their ____.
   - (A) insight
   - (B) obstinacy
   - (C) introspection
   - (D) tolerance
   - (E) credulity

6. No longer ____ by the belief that the world around us was expressly designed for humanity, many people try to find intellectual ____ for that lost certainty in astrology and in mysticism.
   - (A) satisfied. . reasons
   - (B) sustained. . substitutes
   - (C) reassured. . justifications
   - (D) hampered. . equivalents

(E) restricted. . parallels

(A) depraved . . hesitation

7. People should not be praised for their virtue if they lack the energy to be ____; in such cases, goodness is merely the effect of ____.

(B) cruel. . effortlessness
(C) wicked. . indolence
(D) unjust. . boredom
(E) iniquitous . . impiety

SECTION 11 解答

1.【正确答案】B

【中文释义】通过剥夺掉自己所有的主权,这个前国王失去了所有传统上保护君王的考虑因素。

【解题分析】事实上 consideration that customarily protects monarchs 即为上文的 regalities,故上下句的推理关系极为简洁,剥夺掉王权之后当然就不存在王权,正确答案为 B。

【重点词条】**divest(of)** *v.* ①使脱去,使卸下

②使摆脱

③迫使放弃,剥夺…的权利

forfeit *vt.* ①因为被惩罚而失去(to lose or lose the right to by some error, offense, or crime)

②充公(to subject to confiscation as a forfeit)

2.【正确答案】D

【中文释义】动物学的永久目标是从结构中推断功能,也即将一个生命体的行为和它的物理形式及细胞组织方式联系起来考虑。

【解题分析】第一个空格后为分隔结构,infer from 所联接的双方应与 relate. . .to. . .联接的双方相同,所以可推知第一个空格就填"physical form and cellular organization",第二个空格填出后应表达出"function"的概念。由第一个空格很容易推得答案为 D,生命体的功能 function 事实上也即生命体的行为 the behavior of an organism。

【重点词条】**relate(A) to(B)** 将 A 和 B 联系起来考虑

habitat *n.*(动植物的)栖息地

3.【正确答案】B

【中文释义】通过指明她的理论事实上并没有与广为接受的社会学原则相违背,这位社会学家对指责她的理论是异端学说的指控做出了反应。

【解题分析】The charge 之后的从句就是 charge 的具体内容,故必为贬义,并且可推知为"反对违背广为接受的原则",故可选 B。

【重点词条】**heretical** *adj.* 异教的,异端的(of, relating to, or characterized by departure from accepted beliefs or standards, unorthodox)

4.【正确答案】E

【中文释义】只有在工业取代了农业成为主要生产方式之后,工业家们才获得了经济权;在此之前,这种权力归属于土地所有权。

【解题分析】上句的 only after 与下句的 previously 相照应,故下句应表达出与上句相反的意思,即工业家没有获得经济权,由简单常识知工业社会之前为农业社会,其时工业家当然没有经济权,经济权为土地所拥有,归属于土地拥有者,这就是下句欲表达的内容,正确答案是 E 的 reside in,通常含义为"居住于…",但其在学术文章中往往是指"权力归属于…"或"性质存在于…"。

【重点词条】**sabotage** *v.* ①心怀不满的工人的蓄意破坏(destruction of an employer's property〔as tools or materials〕or the hindering of manufacturing by discontented workers)

②破坏战争(destructive or obstructive action carried on by a civilian or enemy agent to hinder a nation's war effort)

③故意破坏或阻止(an act or process tending to hamper or hurt)

　　　　　　overtake *v.* ①赶上或超过

②突然降临于

③(感情)压倒

　　　　　　topple *v.* 倒塌,推翻,颠覆(fall from or as if from being top-heavy)

5.【正确答案】E

【中文释义】谣言,装饰着细节,存在了好几年时间,既不被否定也不被肯定,直到它们被当成事实接受,甚至是被那些本来并不轻易上当的人所接受。

【解题分析】句中的 even 表示了转折关系,说明其后的 people 本来不该接受谣言,people 之后的过去分词修饰短语应该表达出这个意思,故选 E 的 credulity。

【重点词条】**introspection** *n.* 反省,内省(a reflective looking inward, an examination of one's own thoughts and feelings)

6.【正确答案】B

【中文释义】不再被这个信仰所支撑,这个信仰是指围绕着我们的世界是专门为人而设计的,许多人试图在占星术和神秘主义当中寻求精神的替代物来代替那个丢失的信仰。

【解题分析】文中的 thay lost certainty 只有可能指代上文的 believe,故我们可以直接得出结论,"我们不再有这样的信仰",即"我们不再相信这个信仰",而第一个空格要求填的是被动方式,即信仰对人的动作,那么"我们相信信仰"反过来说即是"信仰支撑我们",故应选 B。

　　　　此题颇具有迷惑性,不少同学选 D 或 E,并且如果将 D 和 E 翻译成中文的话,中文是正确的!问题就在于中文的"不再"和英文的"no longer"用法并不一样,英文的"no longer"只能否定过去的动作或状态,故填 no longer 之后的动词或形容词时很好操作,考虑一下过去的状态即可。而此句中,过去状态是我们相信信仰,信仰支撑我们,并不是信仰阻碍了我们,当翻译成缺乏时态感的中文后,D 和 E 这样的句子也正确了,但如果仔细思考会发现中文的这种用法中,"不再"之后的动词或形容词是用了现在时态。当然这就牵扯到了很多的概念和模糊的区分。大家在做题时只需考虑一点,no longer 之后填表示过去状态的动词或形容词。

【重点词条】 expressly *adv.* ①明显地,确切地

②特意地,特诚地

intellectual *adj.* ①知识的,智力的,理智的

②理解力强的

③头脑的,思想的

reassure *v.* 向…再保证,安慰,使放心,使消除疑虑

parallel *n.* ①平行,并列

②可相比拟的事物,相似之处

③比拟

sustain ①支撑,承受(to support the weight of, prop; also: to carry or withstand a weight or pressure)

②支持,给…以力量(to support as true, legal, or just)

③证实(to support by adequate proof, confirm) 例 testimony that～s our contention

7.【正确答案】C

【中文释义】人们不应该因为他们的德行受到表扬,如果他们缺乏能力来邪恶的话;在这种情况下,善仅仅是无能的作用而已。

【解题分析】分号句上下句重复,上句称某种条件下德行不应受表扬,下句的 goodness 显然重复上句的 virtue,在 effect of sth 的结构中 effect 表"结果、效果、作用",而 sth 就相应地表示导致这个 effect 的条件,故第二个空格应对应上文的条件句,C 的 indolence 很好地重复了上句条件句的 lack the energy。故选 C。

此句的观点非常深刻,值得每一个将自己的懦弱、胆怯粉饰成谦让美德的中国人时刻铭记。

【重点词条】 effortlessness *n.* 容易,不费吹灰之力,轻而易举

wicked *adj.* 坏的,邪恶的,缺德的

indolence *n.* 懒惰,懒散,惰性,无能

iniquitous *adj.* 邪恶的,罪恶的

SECTION 12

1. Animals that have tasted unpalatable plants tend to ____ them afterward on the basis of their most conspicuous features, such as their flowers.

(A) recognize

(B) hoard

(C) trample

(D) retrieve

(E) approach

2. As for the alleged value of expert opinion, one need only ＿＿＿ government records to see ＿＿＿ evidence of the failure of such opinions in many fields.

　(A) inspect. . questionable

　(B) retain. . circumstantial

　(C) distribute. . possible

　(D) consult. . strong

　(E) evaluate. . problematic

3. In scientific inquiry it becomes a matter of duty to expose a ＿＿＿ hypothesis to every possible kind of ＿＿＿.

　(A) tentative. . examination

　(B) debatable. . approximation

　(C) well-established. . rationalization

　(D) logical. . elaboration

　(E) suspect. . correlation

4. Charlotte Salomon's biography is a reminder that the currents of private life, however diverted, dislodged, or twisted by ＿＿＿ public events, retain their hold on the ＿＿＿ recording them.

　(A) transitory. . culture

　(B) dramatic. . majority

　(C) overpowering. . individual

　(D) conventional. . audience

　(E) relentless. . institution

5. Philosophical problems arise when people ask questions that, though very ＿＿＿, have certain characteristics in common.

　(A) relevant

　(B) elementary

　(C) abstract

　(D) diverse

　(E) controversial

6. Although Johnson ＿＿＿ great enthusiasm for his employees' project, in reality his interest in the project was so ＿＿＿ as to be almost nonexistent.

　(A) generated. . redundant

　(B) displayed. . preemptive

　(C) expected. . indiscriminate

　(D) feigned. . perfunctory

　(E) demanded. . dispassionate

7. Not all the indicators necessary to convey the effect of depth in a picture work simultaneously, the picture's illusion of ＿＿＿ three-dimensional appearance must therefore result from the viewer's integration of various indicators perceived ＿＿＿.

　(A) imitative. . coincidentally

　(B) uniform. . successively

　(C) temporary. . comprehensively

　(D) expressive. . sympathetically

　(E) schematic. . passively

SECTION 12 解答

1. 【正确答案】A

　【中文释义】那些尝过不可口植物的动物以后经由这些植物的最显眼的特征,比如花,来再认出它们。

　【解题分析】On the basis of 就是 through 的意思,而 conspicuous 指显眼的,故可推知通过显眼的特征当然是看出一个东西,故选 A。

　【重点词条】retrieve v. ①重新得到,收回

②使恢复

③挽救,纠正

conspicuous ①明显的(obvious to the eye or mind)

②引人注目的(attracting attention, striking)

2.【正确答案】D

【中文释义】谈到所谓的专家观点的价值,一个人只需要查阅政府的档案即可知这种观点在许多领域失败的强有力的证据。

【解题分析】文中 alleged 是个重点词汇,它表示"所谓的,值得怀疑的",用于引出一个批评的对象,故可知下文欲批判专家观点,而下文的例子又是专家观点失败的例子,故为正面证据。用于支持自己观点的例子当然应该明确有力,而不应该似是而非,故第二个空格可选 B 和 D。B 的第一词显然错误,句意不通,故选 D。

【重点词条】**consult** *v*. ①考虑(to have regard to, consider)

②向…咨询(to ask the advice or opinion of) 例 ~a doctor

③查阅(to refer to) 例 ~a dictionary

circumstantial *adj*. ①与环境相关的,由环境决定的(belonging to, consisting in, or dependent on circumstances)

②外围的,不重要的(pertinent but not essential, incidental)

③仔细的(marked by careful attention to detail, abounding in factual details) 例 a ~account of the fight

④隆重的,排场大的(ceremonial)

3.【正确答案】A

【中文释义】在科学的调查研究中,这已经成为一种责任来将一个尝试性的假设暴露于各种各样的可能的检验当中。

【解题分析】文中的 expose...to... 意为"将…暴露于(检查、核对)之下",故第一个空格内为需要检查的假设,可候选 A、B 和 E,而 B 的第二个词 approximation 为近似值检验,E 的第二个词 correlation 为相关性检验,都是一种特定的检验方法,上文都是泛指在科学的研究中,故不应选 B 和 E,应选 A。

【重点词条】**approximation** *n*. 近似值检验

correlation *n*. 相关性检验

elaboration *n*. ①精心制定,精心策划(planned or carried out with great care) 例 took~precautions

②精致,详尽(marked by complexity, fullness of detail, or ornateness) 例 ~prose

rationalize *v*. 合理化,理性化

4.【正确答案】C

【中文释义】夏洛特·沙尔门的结论作品是一个提示:个人生活的种种道路,尽管被过于强大的公众事件所转向、偏离或扭曲,但保留了对记录它们的人的影响力。

【解题分析】尽管该句的意思是比较晦涩的,但分析结构仍可知 retain 这个动词的主语是 currents of private life, retain 之后的 their 即指 currents of private life,而最后的 them 也是指 currents of private life。第二个空格后的分隔结构告诉我们即将填入空格的词记录了这些个人生活的种种道路,那么究竟是谁记录呢? 当然是传记传家! 故五个选项中找传记作家即可。结果只有 C 的 individual 是传记作家的上义词,故正确答案为 C。

　　此句的含义如下:一个传记作品的主人公必然为 public figure,其生平有两类事件:public events 和 currents of private life,在人们的记忆中,典籍的记载中显然 currents of private life 会被影响力过于强大的 public events 所淹没、隐藏,人们的回忆中更多的是充斥着 public events 的回忆。但是对于传记作家而言,currents of private life 仍有吸引力。他必须将主人公的生活琐事也挖掘出来,以全面展示作品主人公多面的人生。

【重点词条】**hold** *n*. 控制,影响,吸引

　　　　　　reminder *n*. 提醒者,提示物

　　　　　　current of life　人生方向,人生历程

　　　　　　disloge *v*. (从固定位置上)强行去除,(从躲藏处)把…逐出,离开原位

5.【正确答案】D

【中文释义】当人们问出尽管多样但却具有某种共同特征的问题时,哲学问题就产生了。

【解题分析】空格应与 in common 构成反义,故选 D。

【重点词条】**diverse** *adj*. ①不同(differing from one another, unlike)

　　　　　　　　　　　　②具有相异特征或构成的(composed of distinct or unlike elements or qualities)

6.【正确答案】D

【中文释义】尽管琼森对雇员的建议伪装出极大的热情,但现实中他对这建议的兴趣是如此敷衍了事以至于几乎等同于不存在。

【解题分析】文中的 so…as to… 构成了一个很简洁的推理线索,五个选项中合适的只有 D。

【重点词条】**redundant** *adj*. ①多余的,不必要的(exceeding what is necessary or normal, superfluous)

　　　　　　　　　　　　②千篇一律的(characterized by similarity or repetition) 例 a group of particularly～brick buildings

　　　　　　preemptive *adj*. ①有优先购买权的(having power to preempt)

　　　　　　　　　　　　②先发制人的,抢先的(marked by the seizing of the initiative, initiated by oneself) 例 a～attack

　　　　　　indiscriminate *adj*. ①没有区别的,不加区分的(not marked by careful distinction, deficient in discrimination and discernment)

例 ～reading habits／～mass destruction

②随便的,偶然的(haphazard, random) 例 ～application of a law

③毫无节制的(promiscuous, unrestrained) 例 ～sexual behavior

④各种各样的,纷繁复杂的(heterogeneous, motley)

例 an～collection

7.【正确答案】B

【中文释义】表达一幅画深度效果所必须的全部因素并非同时起作用;这幅画的整体三维形象的视觉图景必须由观众对相继观看的各个因素的综合才能达到。

【解题分析】本题典型解法有两种。第一种解法:分号句的上下句重复,而上半句只说了一个事物即 indicators 非同时地起作用,所以下半句只能重复这个信息。果然在文末又出现了 indicator,其后的过去分词作状语。需要填一个副词,很显然在重复上文,故填上一个表示"非同时"的副词即可,正确答案为 B。第二种解法:将下半句简化后成为 illusion must result from the integration。那么必须由综合"integration"才能导致的视觉景象当然是一个综合的景象,第一个空格的五个选项中只有 B 正确。

【重点词条】**convey** *v*.①传输(to bear from one place to another; esp. to move in a continuous stream or mass)

7②表达,交流(to impart or communicate by statement, suggestion, gesture, or appearance)

illusion *n*.①幻觉(the state or fact of being intellectually deceived or misled, misapprehension)

②致幻物(something that deceives or misleads intellectually)

③视网膜上物体的倒像

successively *adj*.①相继发生的(following in order, following each other without interruption)

②以序列为特征的(characterized by or produced in succession)

imitative *adj*.①模仿的(marked by imitation) 例 acting is an～art

②拟声的(reproducing or representing a natural sound, onomatopoeic) 例 "Hiss"is an～word.

③仿生的(exhibiting mimicry)

④伪造的(imitating something superior, counterfeit)

expressive *adj*.①表达的,表现的(of or relating to expression) 例 the～function of language

②富有表现力的(effectively conveying meaning or feeling)

例 an～silence／～line drawings

SECTION 13

1. The natural balance between prey and predator has been increasingly ____, most frequently by human intervention.
   (A) celebrated
   (B) predicted
   (C) observed
   (D) disturbed
   (E) questioned

2. There is some ____ the fact that the author of a book as sensitive and informed as Indian Artisans did not develop her interest in Native American art until adulthood, for she grew up in a region rich in American Indian culture.
   (A) irony in
   (B) satisfaction in
   (C) doubt about
   (D) concern about
   (E) presumptuousness in

3. Ecology, like economics, concerns itself with the movement of valuable ____ through a complex network of producers and consumers.
   (A) commodities
   (B) dividends
   (C) communications
   (D) nutrients
   (E) artifacts

4. Observable as a tendency of our culture is a ____ of ____ psychoanalysis: we no longer feel that it can solve our emotional problems.
   (A) divergence. . certainly about

(B) confrontation. . enigmas in
   (C) withdrawal. . belief in
   (D) defense. . weaknesses in
   (E) failure. . rigor in

5. The struggle of the generations is one of the obvious constants of human affairs; therefore, it may be presumptuous to suggest that the rivalry between young and old in Western society during the current decade is ____ critical.
   (A) perennially
   (B) disturbingly
   (C) uniquely
   (D) archetypally
   (E) captiously

6. Rhetoric often seems to ____ over reason in a heated debate, with both sides ____ in hyperbole.
   (A) cloud. . subsiding
   (B) prevail. . yielding
   (C) triumph. . engaging
   (D) reverberate. . clamoring
   (E) trample. . tangling

7. Melodramas, which presented stark oppositions between innocence and criminality, virtue and corruption, good and evil, were popular precisely because they offered the audience a world ____ of ____.
   (A) bereft. . theatricality
   (B) composed. . adversity
   (C) full. . circumstantiality
   (D) deprived. . polarity
   (E) devoid. . neutrality

SECTION 13 解答

1. 【正确答案】D

   【中文释义】捕食者和被捕食者之间的自然平衡已经越来越被干扰了,尤其非常频繁地被人干扰(所干扰)。

   【解题分析】一个很无聊的句子。以后再见到 by 后的单词为动名词,或动词的抽象名词,如 intervention(intervene), encouragement(encourage), criticizement(criticize), by 之前的动作即为此动词。或者 by 之前的动词已存在,by 之后需填空格时,直接将该动词改成动名词或抽象名词即可,与 by 同义的表达为:through, in terms of, on basis of。

2. 【正确答案】A

   【中文释义】这位写了像《印第安民间匠人们》一样细致入微并且见多识广的书的作者在成年之前,却没有发展出她对土著美洲文化的兴趣,这个事实当中是有一些矛盾的,因为作者生长在一个富于美洲印第安文化的地区。

   【解题分析】首先请注意全句的结构。由于 the fact 之后的冗长的同位语分隔,所以很多人没有看到主句为 There is some ＿＿＿ the fact, for she grow up in a region rich in American Indian Culture。不少同学错选 C,如果选 C,主句的含义就是"有人对这个事实产生了怀疑",那么这些人为什么怀疑呢? 这就应该是 for 引导的原因从句的内容,但显然文中的 for 引导的原因从句根本未涉及这个内容,正确答案为 A。

   　　作者是一个敏感的人,应该对周围的事物有着敏感的心灵,但她在成功之前没有发展出对美洲文化的兴趣,如果成年之前她的身边并没有出现美洲文化的话,这个事实就不足为奇,而原因从句偏偏强调她成年之前身边充斥着美洲印第安文化,故这个原因从句就解释了,为何主句中的事实是具有 irony 的,这个 irony 就是,像作者这样一个敏感的人成年之前生活在美洲印第安文化区,却对周边的事物熟视无睹,与她的敏感性格截然相反。

   【重点词条】informed *adj*. 消息灵通的,见多识广的(educated, knowledgeable) 例 what the～person should know

3. 【正确答案】A

   【中文释义】生态学正如经济学一样关心着有价值的商品在一个复杂的由生产者和消费者构成的网络中的运动。

   【解题分析】空格后出现一个介词短语,这是一种典型的分隔,由此可推知在生产者和消费者构成的网络中运行的当然是商品,答案为 A。实际上从句为比喻句,并且请注意 like economic 为状语修饰其后的主句的谓语,故整个谓语部分就应为喻体,而不是本体。此比喻句的本体是答案 D 的 nutrients。作者将养分在食物链中由初级光合作用生产者向各层次消费者的传递过程比喻成商业社会中的生产消费过程,有时同学过于细节地理解了全句而错选 D,实际上是由于未能理解 like economics 的语法作用,切记如果希望精读解题就一定要深度读懂,否则就采用经验的解法,分隔与粘连即可。

【重点词条】concern...with...　关心某事,从事于某事,忙于某事

　　　　　　dividents *n*. 股息,被除数

4. 【正确答案】C

【中文释义】我们文化生活的显而易见的一个趋势是从对心理分析学说的信仰的全面撤退:我们不再觉得它可以解决我们的情感问题。

【解题分析】冒号后表示对前文的解释重复,故冒号前应表示对心理分析学说的彻底不信任,A、B 和 E 都是部分的否定,如 E 答案表示心理分析学说在严谨性上(rigor in) 有失败之处,言外之意即为在其他方面,如科学性、前瞻性等等方面还是成功的。表示彻底反对的只有 C。这是一种习惯表达法,上句为倒装句,改成正常的句序为:A withdrawal of belief in psychoanalysis is as observable as a tendency of our culture. 为了强调 observable 而引起了倒装。

【重点词条】enigma *n*. ①难于理解的语言或字迹(an obscure speech or writing)

　　　　　　　　　　　②谜团(something hard to understand or explain)

　　　　　　　　　　　③神秘的人(an inscrutable or mysterious person)

　　　　　　rigor *n*. ①严肃(harsh inflexibility in opinion, temper, or judgment, severity)

　　　　　　　　　　②严格(the quality of being unyielding or inflexible, strictness)

　　　　　　　　　　③严谨朴素(severity of life, austerity)

　　　　　　　　　　④严谨(strict precision, exactness) 例 logical~

5. 【正确答案】C

【中文释义】一代人与一代人之间的冲突是人类事件中明显的恒定事件之一;因此,这样说就显得专横武断:西方社会近十年中年轻一代和年老一代之间的竞争是独一无二地重要的。

【解题分析】分号句的上下句表重复,尤其是看到下句的句型 It's presumptuous to suggest that... 时,我们可以断定该句是肯定句与双重否定句之间的重复。事实上表双重否定重复的方式也就两种。上句为 A is red,下句可以重复为 A is not black 或者 It's wrong to say that A is black,本题中用了第二种说法。上句的 struggle of generations 对应于下句的 the rivalry between young and old。空格应与上文的 constant 构成反义,故正确答案为 C。

【重点词条】constant *adj*. ①永恒不变的,统一的(invariable, uniform)

　　　　　　　　　　　　②持续不断的(continually occurring or recurring, regular)

　　　　　　　　　　n. ①永恒的事物

　　　　　　　　　　　　②常量

　　　　　　archetypal *n*. 原型或典型(the original pattern or model of which all things of the same type are representations or copies, prototype; also: a perfect example)

　　　　　　captious *adj*. ①吹毛求疵的(marked by an often ill-natured inclination to stress faults and raise objections)

②故意混淆的,抬杠的(calculated to confuse, entrap, or entangle in argument)

6.【正确答案】C

【中文释义】在热烈的辩论当中修辞看上去总是战胜严密的推理,因为辩论双方都致力于
夸张的手法之中。

【解题分析】此句具有一定的特殊性,第一空格后的 over 几乎已经将上半句的含义完全点
明了,事实上 A、B、C、E 与 over 搭配时均表示修辞战胜推理,而 D 语义根本不
通。故实际上该句是考查第二个空格。请注意 with 在之中的用法是表原因,
(with 和 without 可表原因,条件,伴随状态)。hyperbole 又指代上文的
rhetoric,故结论非常简单:当辩论双方都主动采取夸张时,修辞就战胜推理。
五个选项中,只有 C 的 engaging 表示双方努力主动地采取夸张的手法。

【重点词条】**subside** *v*.①下陷(to sink or fall to the bottom, settle)

②下降(to tend downward, descend; esp. to flatten out so as to
form a depression)

③坐下(to let oneself settle down, sink) 例 subsided into a chair

④平息(to become quiet or less) 例 as the fever～s/my anger subsided

reverberate *v*.①反射(reflect)

②反击(repel)

③回荡(echo)

7.【正确答案】E

【中文释义】善恶分明的轻松歌舞剧,总是表现出无辜和罪行,德行和腐败,善和恶之间的
尖锐对立,是非常受欢迎的,主要是因为它们给观众提供了一个避免了中立的
世界。

【解题分析】此句不难推理知此种歌舞剧提供了一个充满对立的世界,答案 E 为此推理结
果的双重否定说法,正确答案为 E。

【重点词条】**theatrical** *adj*.① 戏剧的(of or relating to the theater or the presentation of
plays) 例 a～costume

②不自然的(marked by pretense or artificiality of emotion)

③戏剧性的,戏剧化的(histrionic) 例 a～gesture

④夸大的,故意表演的(marked by extravagant display or exhi-
bitionism)

polarity *n*.①对立(the quality or condition inherent in a body that exhibits opposite properties or powers in opposite parts or directions or that
exhibits contrasted properties or powers in contrasted parts or directions, the condition of having poles)

②电极(the particular state either positive or negative with reference to the two poles or to electrification)

adversity *n*. ①厄运,灾难(a state or condition contrary to one of well-being)

②痛苦,不幸(an instance of adversity syn see misfortune)

circumstantial *adj*. ①与环境相关的,由环境决定的(belonging to, consisting in, or dependent on circumstances)

②外围的,不重要的(pertinent but not essential, incidental)

③仔细的(marked by careful attention to detail, abounding in factual details) 例 a～account of the fight

④隆重的,排场大的(ceremonial)

SECTION 14

1. In the current research program, new varieties of apple trees are evaluated under different agricultural _____ for tree size, bloom density, fruit size, _____ to various soils, and resistance to pests and disease.

   (A) circumstances. . proximity

   (B) regulations. . conformity

   (C) conditions. . adaptability

   (D) auspices. . susceptibility

   (E) configurations. . propensity

2. At first, I found her gravity rather intimidating; but, as I saw more of her, I found that _____ was very near the surface.

   (A) seriousness

   (B) confidence

   (C) laughter

   (D) poise 泰然自若,镇定

   (E) determination

3. Even though in today's Soviet Union the _____ the Muslim clergy have been accorded power and privileges, the Muslim laity and the rank-and-file clergy still have little _____ to practice their religion.

   (A) practitioners among. . opportunity

   (B) dissidents within. . obligation

   (C) adversaries of. . inclination

   (D) leaders of. . latitude

   (E) traditionalists among. . incentive

4. The proponents of recombinant DNA research have decided to _____ federal regulation of their work; they hope that by making this compromise they can forestall proposed state and local controls that might be even stiffer.

   (A) protest

   (B) institute

   (C) deny

   (D) encourage

   (E) disregard 消极,抵抗

5. It is to the novelist's credit that all of the episodes in her novel are presented realistically, without any _____ or playful supernatural tricks.

   (A) elucidation

   (B) discrimination

   (C) artlessness

   (D) authenticity

   (E) whimsy

6. Our new tools of systems analysis, powerful though they may be, lead to ____ theories, especially, and predictably, in economics and political science, where productive approaches have long been highly ____.

(A) pragmatic. . speculative

(B) inelegant. . efficacious

(C) explanatory. . intuitional

(D) wrongheaded. . convergent

(E) simplistic. . elusive   不存在，难逮的

elude v. 搞不清

7. Nineteenth-century scholars, by examining earlier geometric Greek art, found that classical Greek art was not a magical ____ or a brilliant ____ blending Egyptian and Assyrian art, but was independently evolved by Greeks in Greece.

(A) stratagem. . appropriation

(B) exemplar. . synthesis

(C) conversion. . annexation

(D) paradigm. . construct

(E) apparition. . amalgam

幽灵，神奇的现象.

SECTION 14 解答

1.【正确答案】C

【中文释义】在目前的研究项目中,苹果树的新品种在不同的农业条件下受到测评,来测评其果树大小、花蕾密度、果实大小、对不同土壤的适应能力以及对病害和虫害的抵制力。

【解题分析】此题非常常识化,第二空格显然应填对不同土壤的适应能力,答案为C。也有少部分同学理解了句意却选错了词,比如说E的 propensity,"propensity to which kind of soil"可以表示某一果树的土壤适应能力,但在原文中空格后的表达为 various soils,故E搭配并不正确。

【重点词条】auspices n. ①(以鸟的飞行和觅食活动为依据的) 占卜(observation by an augur esp. of the flight and feeding of birds to discover omens)

②赞助,支持(kindly patronage and guidance)

③预兆,先兆,尤其指吉兆(a prophetic sign; esp. a favorable sign)

configuration n. 布局,结构,外型

2.【正确答案】C   gravity   intimidating

【中文释义】起初,我发现她的严肃认真已经达到令人望而生畏的程度;但是,当我对她了解更多之后,我发现幽默才是真实的。

【解题分析】前后转折是很简单的,但此题别出心裁地考了两个形似短语 on the surface 和 near the surface,这两个短语正好反义,一个表示"表面上的,虚假的",另一个表示"真实的",故正确答案为C,而不是A,这种考法国内题中从未出现过。

【重点词条】near the surface   真实的

on the surface   表面上的

determination n. ①决定,确定(the act of deciding definitely and firmly; also: the result of such an act of decision)

②决断力,果断(the power or habit of deciding definitely and firmly)

③测量(a fixing or finding of the position, magnitude, value, or character of something)

3.【正确答案】D

【中文释义】在今天的苏维埃,即使穆斯林信徒的领导人已经被授予了权力和特权,穆斯林的俗家弟子和低级教徒仍然没有言行自由来实践他们的宗教。

【解题分析】下句的低级成员后的谓语动词为否定的形式,上句第一空格应与下句的低级成员构成反义,即高级成员,这样就构成了上下句的对称,五个选项中表示高级成员的是答案 D 的 leaders。

【重点词条】**laity** *n*. 俗家弟子(the mass of the people as distinguished from those of a particular profession or those specially skilled)

rank-and-file *adj*. 低级的

latitude *n*. ①纬度(distance north or south from the earth's equator measured through 90 degrees)

②言行自由(freedom of action or choice)

4.【正确答案】D

【中文释义】DNA 重组研究的支持者们决定支持联邦政府对他们工作的管制;他们希望通过做出这个妥协,他们可以阻止提议中的州和当地政府的可能更加严厉的控制。

【解题分析】分号下句重复上句,尤其是下句的 this compromise 更是指明上句的动词具有妥协意味,所以五个选项中能表示控制妥协的只有 D。A 和 C 是抵抗,E 是消极抵抗,B 不相关。

【重点词条】**institute** *v*. ①建立,设定(to establish in a position or office)

②开始,开创(to set going, inaugurate) 例 instituting an investigation of the charges

5.【正确答案】E

【中文释义】这归功于小说家:她的小说中的所有情节都非常现实地表现出来,没有任何古怪的表达方式,也没有任何戏谑的超自然的小花招。

【解题分析】Without...or...连接的为同义词,故选 E,均表示那种古里古怪的写作方法。

【重点词条】**whimsy** *n*. 古怪,异想天开的创造(尤其指文学或艺术作品)(a fanciful or fantastic device, object, or creation esp. in writing or art)

authenticity *n*. 可靠性,真实性,权威性

discrimination *n*. ①区别,鉴别(the act of discriminating, or the process by which two stimuli differing in some aspect are responded to differently, differentiation)

②鉴别力(the quality or power of finely distinguishing)

③偏见,歧视(prejudiced or prejudicial outlook, action, or treatment) 例 racial~

6.【正确答案】E

【中文释义】我们的新的系统分析工具,尽管它们可能是很强大的,却导致简化主义的理论学说,尤其并且可预料到会在经济学和政治学中如此,在这两个学科领域中富有成效的方法长期以来一直是非常难以得到的。

【解题分析】第一空格由转折关系可知选贬义词,候选 D、B 和 E,E 的 simplistic 是指简化主义,即头脑简单之义。接着原文中用了一种罕见的推理方式:经验推理。Predictably 一词实际上提示我们"过去在经济学和政治学领域有效的方法一直不存在,所以据此可预测现在这种尽管强大的工具,却不会有效"。这种经验模式的推理在全部填空题中只出现过一次,国内题从来未考过,故大家可浅尝辄止。B、D 和 E 的第二个词中表示"长期以来有效的方法不存在"的词为 E 的 elusive。

【重点词条】**wrongheaded** *adj*. 固执己见的,执迷不悟的(stubborn in adherence to wrong opinion or principles) 例 a~policy

simplistic *adj*. ①简单的(simple)
②简化主义的,过于简化的(of, relating to, or characterized by simplism, oversimple) 例 adequate, if occasionally ~, historical background

intutional *adj*. 直觉的

convergent *adj*. ①汇合的,会聚的(tending to move toward one point or to approach each other, converging) 例 ~lines
②显示会合趋向的(exhibiting convergence in form, function, or development) 例 ~evolution

7.【正确答案】E

【中文释义】19 世纪的学者们,通过检查早期的几何学风格的希腊艺术而发现古典希腊艺术并不是一个魔术般的幽灵之物,也不是一个辉煌的混合着古埃及和上述艺术的混合体,而是由希腊人在雅典独立地发展而成的。

【解题分析】第二空格后的分隔结构已经做了充分的提示,空格中应填一个表示"混合"概念的词,E 的 amalgam 是再恰当不过了。理解时请抓住转折句的转折点。转折句中的 independently 显然是针对上文的 amalgam 的转折;evolve 就是针对上文的 magical apparition 提出的转折,西方有很多学者非常认真地对待下文的观点:古代的那种灿烂得不可思议的文明绝不可能是当时的人类所创造的,是外星文明的遗留物或协作产物。这种观点即将古文明视为 magical apparition。而本句针锋相对地提出古文明是由古代人类自己创造(evolve)而来的。

【重点词条】**stratagem** *n*. 策略,计谋(an artifice or trick in war for deceiving and outwitting the enemy) exemplar *n*. 模范,典范(one that serves as a model or example, as an ideal model)

conversion *n*. ①转换,转化(the act of converting, the process of being converted)

②皈依

apparition *n*. ①超常现象(an unusual or unexpected sight, phenomenon)

②鬼怪,幻影(a ghostly figure)

SECTION 15

1. Dreams are _____ in and of themselves, but, when combined with other data, they can tell us much about the dreamer.

(A) uninformative

(B) startling

(C) harmless

(D) unregulated

(E) uncontrollable

2. The Muses are _____ deities: they avenge themselves without mercy on those who weary of their charms.

(A) rueful

(B) ingenuous

(C) solicitous

(D) vindictive

(E) dispassionate

3. Without the psychiatrist's promise of confidentiality, trust is _____ and the patient's communication limited; even though confidentiality can thus be seen to be precious in therapy, moral responsibility sometimes requires a willingness to _____ it.

(A) implicit. . extend

(B) ambiguous. . apply

(C) prevented. . uphold

(D) assumed. . examine

(E) impaired. . sacrifice

4. Having fully embraced the belief that government by persuasion is preferable to government by _____, the leaders of the movement have recently _____ most of their previous statements supporting totalitarianism.

(A) intimidation. . issued

(B) participation. . moderated

(C) proclamation. . codified

(D) demonstration. . deliberated

(E) coercion. . repudiated

5. The powers and satisfactions of primeval people, though few amd meager, were _____ their few and simple desires.

(A) simultaneous with

(B) commensurate with

(C) substantiated by

(D) circumscribed by

(E) ruined by

6. Some scientists argue that carbon compounds play such a central role in life on Earth because of the possibility of _____ resulting from the carbon atom's ability to form an unending series of different molecules.

(A) deviation

(B) stability

(C) reproduction

(D) variety

(E) invigoration

7. Whereas the art critic Vasari saw the painting entitled the Mona Lisa as an original and
   wonderful ____ feat, the reproduction of a
   natural object, the aesthetes saw it as ____

that required deciphering.

(A) collaborative. . an aberration

(B) historical. . a symbol

(C) technical. . a hieroglyph 象形文字.

(D) mechanical. . an imitation 展品.

(E) visual. . an illusion

SECTION 15 解答

1.【正确答案】A

　【中文释义】梦就其自身而言是没有信息的,但是当和其他数据结合起来,梦会告诉我们很
　　　　　　　多关于做梦者的信息。

　【解题分析】上文的 in and of themselves 与下文的 when combined with other findings 构成
　　　　　　　一对相反的副词,所以其各自修饰的对象也为反义词,空格与 can tell 构成反
　　　　　　　义,答案为 A。

　【重点词条】**startling** *adj*. 令人吃惊的(causing momentary fright, surprise, or astonish-
　　　　　　　ment)

2.【正确答案】D

　【中文释义】缪斯是报复性的神:她们毫不怜悯地报复那些对她们的魅力感到厌倦的人们。

　【解题分析】由冒号的短语 avenge oneself on sb 不难得出这些平时浪漫可爱的女神充满了
　　　　　　　报复心,希腊神话中的神都具有两面性,神性和人性,所以不管对他们做出何
　　　　　　　评价大家都不要吃惊,本题曾有文学青年考生拒而不选 D,问及原因,曰其最
　　　　　　　爱缪斯。

　【重点词条】**ingenuous** *adj*. 单纯的(showing innocent or childlike simplicity and candid-
　　　　　　　ness)

　　　　　　　solicitous *adj*. ①关心的(full of concern or fears, apprehensive) 例 ~about
　　　　　　　　　the future

　　　　　　　②极为小心的(meticulously careful) 例 ~in matters of dress
　　　　　　　③热切的,渴望的(full of desire, eager)

　　　　　　　dispassionate *adj*. 心平气和的,冷静的,不带偏见的(not influenced by
　　　　　　　　strong feeling; esp. not affected by personal or emotional
　　　　　　　　involvement) 例 a~critic/a~approach to an issue

3.【正确答案】E

　【中文释义】没有心理治疗医生保密的承诺,信任就受到了破坏并且病人的交流就受到了
　　　　　　　限制;即使保密因而可看成治疗中非常珍贵,道德责任感有时必然导致一个愿
　　　　　　　望来放弃它。

　【解题分析】分号句的下半句是个非常简单的转折句,因为转折句的主句是个判断句,主体词
　　　　　　　汇为 precious,转折句应与之构成转折,就填一个对"it"不良的动作,只能选 E。A、

B、C 都是好动作,D 的 examine 只指中性的检查,并不像"搜身"那样带有贬义,这个词是很多中国考生误解的词,要切记。道德责任感为何有时会导致放弃保密?事实上,有时候病人会向心理医生坦露一些对别人的生命,甚至是国家的安危都会有极大破坏的计划,此时心理医生就处于进退两难的境界,职业道德保密的要求和世俗道德相冲突,何去何从,完全看医生思想斗争的结果了。

【重点词条】**confidential** *n*.①亲密(marked by intimacy or willingness to confide) 例 a~
tone

②保密的(private, secret) 例 ~information

③可信的,可靠的(entrusted with confidences) 例 ~clerk

④机密的(containing information whose unauthorized disclosure could be prejudicial to the national interest)

require *v*.①要求

②必然导致

4.【正确答案】E

【中文释义】全面接受了这样的信仰,即劝说方法的政府比强迫压制方式的政府更可取,所以运动的领导人们最近驳斥了他们过去支持集权主义的那些声明。

【解题分析】主句中的 recently 明确提了一种时间对比题型,其后的 previous 与其构成对应,故空格里的动作表示最近的动作,当然应与以前的 statement 相反,反对它,驳斥它,可直接得答案 E。答案 E 的第一个词 coercion 实际上与原句的最后一个单词 totalitarianism 构成照应,仔细辨别不难发现,句首的 Having 构成的原因状语实际上与主句是重复,都是谈从过去的集权主义信仰转换到今天的民主的信仰。

【重点词条】**codify** *v*.①编码(to reduce to a code)

②系统化(systematize)

③整理(classify)

repudiate *v*.①拒绝,拒绝接受

②否认,批驳,驳斥

③声明与…脱离关系

totalitarianism *n*.极权主义

5.【正确答案】B

【中文释义】太古时期人的能力和满足尽管少而且简单,但却和他们少而且简单的欲望相称。

【解题分析】文中显然的一组同义词 few and meager 与 few and simple 已经明确地提示了答案。既然能力和欲望的定语相同义,所以两者当然是 commensurate。

【重点词条】**meager** *adj*.①(人)瘦弱的

②质量差的,粗劣的

③(文学作品或思想)贫乏的

commensurate *adj*.同样的,相称的,符合一致的

circumscribe *v.* 立界限于,约束,限制

6.【正确答案】D

【中文释义】有些科学家认为碳的化合物在地球生命中扮演一个中心角色,这是由于其变化的可能性所导致的,而这种变化的可能性又来源于碳原子形成无穷尽系列的不同分子的能力。

【解题分析】由空格后的分隔结构即可推知 D 的 variety 正确,也有部分同学误选 C 的 reproduction。虽然 reproduction 也可能生成无穷尽的分子,但它们都是相同的,与分隔中的 different 相违背。

【重点词条】invigorate *v.* ①增加精力(to give life and energy to, animate)
②鼓舞,激励(stimulate)

7.【正确答案】C

【中文释义】尽管文艺批评家瓦萨丽将标题为"蒙娜丽莎"的这幅画看成一个独创的并且辉煌的技艺的成就,是对自然对象的精确复制,但是审美学家将它看成一种类似于古埃及象形文字一样需要解释的事物。

【解题分析】首先我们来看一个错误的解法。由 whereas 可知上下文转折,上文将之看成一个 original 的事物,故第二个空格为下句的看法,应与 original 相反,故可直接选 D 的 imitation。该解法对句子的整体结构把握,以及对对应词的判断都是正确的,但致命的失误是对 whereas 的判断,whereas 与 while 一样表对照而不是转折,所以第二个空格只要与 original 不同即可,五个选项都正确。正确的解法是由分隔结构解题,第一空格和第二空格后均出现了分隔结构,尤其是第一个空格后的分隔,强调这幅画将自然对象,也即达芬奇创作时所面对的模特,佛罗伦萨古城中一个美丽的少妇,复制到了画布上,这种说法无非是强调画面形象与真人无差异。这是哪一种成就(feat)呢? 当然是画家作画技巧高超的表现,是技艺的成就,故选 C,E 答案的 visual feat 指能给人带来视觉上的享受,这种评价应该是审美学家的评论,而不应该是文艺批评家的评论,C 答案的第二个词强调这幅画难以理解,事实也是如此,蒙娜丽莎神秘莫测的永恒微笑究竟蕴含着什么? 这已是被无数个审美学家花了无数笔墨解释的对象。

【重点词条】collaborative *adj.* ①合作的(to work jointly with others or together esp. in an intellectual endeavor)
②通敌的(to cooperate with or willingly assist an enemy of one's country and esp. an occupying force)

decipher *v.* ①解码(decode)
②解释,诠释(to make out the meaning of despite indistinctness or obscurity)

hieroglyph *n.* ①象形字(符号)
②难以辨认的或难以理解的事物

visual *adj.* ①视力的,视觉的
②直观的,形象化的

SECTION 16

1. As late as 1891 a speaker assured his audience that since profitable farming was the result of natural ability rather than ____ , an education in agriculture was ____ .
   - (A) instruction. . vital
   - (B) effort. . difficult
   - (C) learning. . useless
   - (D) science. . intellectual
   - (E) luck. . senseless

2. In spite of the ____ nature of Scotland's terrain, its main roads are surprisingly free from severe ____ .
   - (A) rocky. . weather
   - (B) mountainous. . grades
   - (C) uncharted. . flooding
   - (D) unpredictable. . damage
   - (E) landlocked. . slipperiness

3. Walpole's art collection was huge and fascinating, and his novel The Castle of Otranto was never out of print; none of this mattered to the Victorians, who ____ him as, at best, ____ .
   - (A) dismissed. . insignificant
   - (B) judged. . worthwhile
   - (C) revered. . talented
   - (D) reviled. . meager
   - (E) taunted. . dangerous

4. Since the author frequently ____ other scholars, his objection to disputes is not only irrelevant but also ____ .
   - (A) supports. . overbearing
   - (B) provokes. . frightening
   - (C) quotes. . curious
   - (D) ignores. . peevish
   - (E) attacks. . surprising

5. Longdale and Stern discovered that mitochondria and chloroplasts ____ a long, identifiable sequence of DNA; such a coincidence could be ____ only by the transfer of DNA between the two systems.
   - (A) manufacture. . accomplished
   - (B) reveal. . repeated
   - (C) exhibit. . determined
   - (D) share. . explained
   - (E) maintain. . contradicted

6. Until the current warming trend exceeds the range of normal climatic fluctuations, there will be, among scientists, considerable ____ the possibility that increasing levels of atmospheric CO_2 can cause long-term warming effects.
   - (A) interest in
   - (B) uncertainty about
   - (C) enthusiasm for
   - (D) worry about
   - (E) experimentation on

7. Without seeming unworldly, William James appeared wholly removed from the ____ of society, the conventionality of academe.
   - (A) ethos
   - (B) idealism
   - (C) romance
   - (D) paradoxes
   - (E) commonplaces

SECTION 16 解答

1. 【正确答案】C

　　【中文释义】直到 1891 年一个演讲者仍力图使他的听众确信,既然有利可图的农业是自然能力,而不是学习的结果,那么农业上的教育是没有用的。

　　【解题分析】请注意 that 从句中的因果关系。既然因果句的结果是对 education 做出了判断,故原因从句中至少应就教育做出一个解释,所以第一个空格只能填教育,否则原因从句中就根本不会出现教育,无法构成因果关系,而判断出第一空格填"教育"之后,就可直接推知教育是"无用"的,答案为 C。

　　【重点词条】intellectual *adj*. ①知识的,理智的
　　　　　　　　　　　　　　　　②用脑的,需要智力的
　　　　　　　　　　　　　　　　③理解力强的

　　　　　　　senseless *adj*. ①失去知觉的(destitute of, deficient in, or contrary to sense; unconscious) 例 knocked～
　　　　　　　　　　　　　②愚蠢的(foolish, stupid) 例 it was some～practical joke
　　　　　　　　　　　　　③无意义的,无目的的(meaningless, purposeless) 例 a～mur-der

2. 【正确答案】B

　　【中文释义】尽管苏格兰的疆土的多山的性质,它的主要公路却是让人惊奇地摆脱了严重的陡坡。

　　【解题分析】下句的 its main road 与上文的 Scotland's terrain 保持同一属性,这是一种常规的判断。我们将作者和作者的书,科学家和科学家的实验,我们和我们的时代均列为同义词,因为这种词在上下文中均含有同样的性质。此句中不难判断出上下两个空格应为同义词,正确答案为 B。Mountainous 为"多山的",grade 为"山的斜坡"。

　　【重点词条】landlocked *adj*. ①内陆的(enclosed or nearly enclosed by land) 例 a～country
　　　　　　　　　　　　　②内陆水域的(confined to fresh water by some barrier) 例 ～salmon

　　　　　　　slipperiness *n*. ①光滑(causing or tending to cause something to slide or fall) 例 ～roads
　　　　　　　　　　　　②易移动的(tending to slip from the grasp)
　　　　　　　　　　　　③不稳定的(not firmly fixed, unstable)
　　　　　　　　　　　　④奸诈,狡猾的(not to be trusted, tricky)

3. 【正确答案】A

　　【中文释义】威尔柏的艺术收藏非常多,并且他的小说 The Castle of Otranto 一版再版;所有这些对维多利亚人均没有影响,他们忽略他,最多也只是认为他为无足轻

重之人。

【解题分析】文中的 at best 修饰一个轻微的贬义词,这是 at best 的固定用法,许多考题中均有涉及,五个选项中轻微的贬义只有 A 的 insignificant。D 的 meager 的含义为"思想贫乏的",这对作家而言是一种无以复加的批评。

【重点词条】**meager** *adj*. ①瘦弱的(having little flesh, thin)

　　　　　　　②可怜的(lacking desirable qualities, such as richness or strength)

　　　　　　　　例 leading a~life

　　　　　　　③贫乏的,缺乏的,数量不充分(deficient in quality or quantity)

　　　　　　　　例 a~diet

4.【正确答案】E

【中文释义】既然这位作者总是攻击别的学者,他反对互相驳斥就不但是不符合其性格的而且是让人吃惊的。

【解题分析】由 irrelevant 可知该作家总是干 dispute 的动作,这就是第一空格应该填的内容,正确答案为 E 的 attack。B 的 provoke 多指态度上的"激怒",而并非"驳斥"别人的观点。

【重点词条】**overbearing** *adj*. ①盛气凌人的(tending to overwhelm, overpowering)

　　　　　　　　　②专横的,傲慢的(harshly and haughtily arrogant)

5.【正确答案】D

【中文释义】蒙黛尔和史特发现线粒体和叶粒体共享着一种长的、可认为相同的 DNA 链条;这种重合只有通过两个系统之间 DNA 的转录才能解释。

【解题分析】分号下句重复上句,而 such 更是指明了这层关系。故上文应出现 coincidence(重合,巧合,重复)。上文已出现的单词中没有一个表示这种概念,故空格应表示出"重合"这种概念。五个选项中答案 D 的 share 为"共享"的含义。

【重点词条】**share** *v*. ①共享(a portion belonging to, due to, or contributed by an individual or group)

　　　　　　　②同时具有(the same thing or idea possessed by several people) 例 ~ an opinion

6.【正确答案】B

【中文释义】在目前变暖的趋势超过正常气候波动范围之前,科学家之间将会有相当程度的对下列可能性的不确定的态度,这种可能性就是指大气层中持续增加的二氧化碳能导致长期变暖的效果。

【解题分析】Untill 单独使用意为 before,并且强调之前与之后的对比。故本句 until 之后的时间为全球真正地变暖,也就是温室效应真地发生了。主句问及科学家在这一刻到来之前会对它发生的可能性持何种态度,这时我们应充分注意 until 前后截然相反这一属性,在这一事件真正发生之后,possibility 当然就是 100%,确凿无疑,故在这一时间之前,应该是"非确定无疑",即不确定的态度,B 为正确答案。

此题有若干同学错选,选答案 D 的同学尤其多。选 D 的言外之意即为:温室效应发生之前科学家很担忧,但温室效应发生之后科学家再也不担忧了!

【重点词条】uncertainty *n*. ①不确定,不确信(the quality or state of being uncertain, doubt)

②不确定的事物(something that is uncertain)

7.【正确答案】E

【中文释义】并没有显得惊世骇俗,威廉·詹姆斯显得完全摆脱了学术界的平庸之见,学术界的传统之见。

【解题分析】文末的短语 the conventionality of academe 显然是一分隔结构直接重复上文的短语。事实上 society 在此并不指"社会"而指"学术界",与分隔中的 academe 同义,空格应与 conventionality 同义。答案 E 为正确答案。

【重点词条】unworldly *adj*. ①非世俗的,精神上的,脱俗的(not of this world, unearthly; spiritual)

②天真的,不谙世故的(not wise in the ways of the world, naive)

remove from 摆脱,脱离

SECTION 17

1. Heavily perfumed white flowers, such as gardenias, were favorites with collectors in the eighteenth century, when _____ was valued much more highly than it is today.

   (A) scent 气味
   (B) beauty
   (C) elegance
   (D) color
   (E) variety

2. In a most impressive demonstration, Pavarotti <u>sailed</u> through Verdi's "Celeste Aida," normally a tenor's _____, with the casual enthusiasm of a folk singer performing one of his favorite _____.

   (A) pitfall. . recitals 朗诵
   (B) glory. . chorales 赞美诗
   (C) nightmare. . ballads
   (D) delight. . chanteys

   (E) routine. . composers

3. Dependence on foreign sources of heavy metals, though _____, remains _____ for United States foreign policy.

   (A) deepening. . a challenge
   (B) diminishing. . a problem
   (C) excessive. . a dilemma
   (D) debilitating. . an embarrassment
   (E) unavoidable. . a precedent

4. Cynics believe that people who _____ compliments do so in order to be praised twice.

   (A) bask in
   (B) give out
   (C) despair of
   (D) gloat over
   (E) shrug off

5. Although nothing could be further from the truth, freight railroads have been _____ of _____ the nation's shift from oil to coal by charging exorbitant fees to transport coal.

(A) accused. . impeding

(B) proud. . accelerating

(C) guilty. . delaying

(D) conscious. . contributing to

(E) wary. . interfering with

6. Although the revelation that one of the contestants was a friend left the judge open to charges of lack of _____, the judge remained adamant in her assertion that acquaintance did not necessarily imply _____.

(A) prudence. . tolerance

(B) detachment. . foreknowledge

(C) exoneration. . impropriety

(D) prejudice. . preference

(E) disinterestedness. . partiality

7. Within the next decade, sophisticated telescopes now orbiting the Earth will determine whether the continents really are moving, _____ the incipient _____ among geologists about the validity of the theory of continental drift.

(A) obviating. . consensus

(B) forestalling. . rift 裂隙，裂痕

(C) escalating. . debates

(D) engendering. . speculation

(E) resolving. . rumors

SECTION 17 解答

1.【正确答案】A

　　【中文释义】具有浓重香味的白色的花,比如栀子花,在 18 世纪的收藏者之间是非常受欢迎的,那时候香味比今天更受到高度重视。

　　【解题分析】此花受欢迎,而原文中说明了此花的两个特征:香味和白色。显然原文强调了香味,故空格里填香味。

　　【重点词条】perfumed *adj*. 芳香的(the scent of something sweet-smelling, a substance that emits a pleasant odor)

2.【正确答案】C

　　【中文释义】在一场极为感人的表演之中,帕瓦罗蒂以一个民谣歌手表演其最喜爱的民谣的那种随意挥洒的热情轻松地演唱着威尔第的"天堂阿依达",而这通常是一个男高音歌手的梦魇之物。

　　【解题分析】此句的文化背景虽然对中国学生而言比较陌生,但本文的分隔结构却是一种常见的提供答案的方法, a folk singer 后的分词结构充当了分隔,此分隔中的空格当然由 a folk singer 提供。民谣歌手表演其最喜爱的什么呢? 当然是民谣,故空格直接填"民谣"即可。C 为正确答案。文中的 Aida 为一著名的歌剧,尤其是以其高音而闻名于世,非常难于演唱,故文中称其通常为一男高音歌手的 nightmare。

　　【重点词条】pitfall *n*. ①陷阱(trap, snare, a pit flimsily covered or camouflaged and used to capture and hold animals or men)

②隐藏的危险,易犯的错误(a hidden or not easily recognized danger or difficulty)

sail through ①轻快地经过(move through without effort)

②轻而易举地获得成功(succeed easily in passing)

routine *n*. ①例行公事,日常工作(a regular course of procedure) 例 if resort to legal action becomes a campus~

②惯例(habitual or mechanical performance of an established procedure) 例 the~of factory work

③重复的话,老一套(a reiterated speech or formula) 例 the old "After you"~

3.【正确答案】B

【中文释义】对外国重金属资源的依赖尽管正在减少,但继续成为美国外交政策的一个问题。

【解题分析】此句是一个典型句。Remain 或 continue 是主体动词,有两种典型的考法。第一种考法是原文先出现当初的状态,continue 或 remain 之后出现空格要求填现在的状态,解法当然是昭然若揭的。如 SECTION 25 的第 7 题,第二种考法是先出现 though 或其他转折方式,然后接 continue。此种情况中并没有出现过去的状态,故 continue 的思路表面受阻,但细究一下不难发现,既然 continue,所以转折之中就不会对立面转折,而只能程度转折,程度上升通常用递进结构表达,故此种 continue 句型中的 although 只能是程度下降的转折。五个选项中 B 表示程度的下降,D 的 debilitate 表示使别人虚弱,并非自身变得虚弱之意。

【重点词条】**debilitate** *v*. 使衰弱,削弱…的力量(to impair the strength of)

4.【正确答案】E

【中文释义】犬儒主义者们认为那些拒绝表扬的人之所以这样做的目的是为了被表扬第二次。

【解题分析】犬儒主义者是非常有趣的人,其创造人 Antisthenes 为雅典人,古希腊哲学家,自称自己的生活像狗一样简陋,提倡"依德行而生活",Antisthenes 非常有智慧,往往观点都与平常的看法不一样!此文中空格里为平常人对表扬的态度,主句为犬儒主义者对这种态度的与众不同的认识。通常人对表扬的态度为谦虚、推辞,故应选答案 E。其他几个选项的含义都比较古怪,请看下文的单词注释。

【重点词条】**bask**(in)*v*. ①晒太阳

②承受别人的恩惠

give out 用光,消耗干尽

give off 放弃,拒绝

gloat(over)*v*. 对…幸灾乐祸

shrug off 故作姿态地耸肩,谦让,放弃,拒绝

5.【正确答案】A

【中文释义】尽管从这个事实中什么结论也得不出来,但是铁路货运部门被指责为由于其征收了过高的费用来运煤而阻碍了这个国家从油到煤的转变。

【解题分析】此句中 by 之后的动作为 freight railroad 所做,显然对于国家的转变无益。而文中第二个空格应填入现在分词结构,其逻辑主语也是 freight railroad。By 连接的正是这两个短语,构成了一组手段和结果的关系,故第二个空格应填表示有害的结果。可选 A、C。B 和 D 的第二个词显然是有益的作用,而 E 的 inter-fere 是没有明确含义,既不有益也不有害。请大家仔细体会填空题选项的这种典型设计。A 和 C 的第一个词的区分才是本题真正的难点。A 的 accused 放入第一空格后构成一被动句型,也即铁路货运部门被指责为阻碍了国家的转变。那么究竟是谁指责了铁路的货运部门呢? 至少可以肯定不是本句的作者。故 A 选项使原句成为一个简单的转折关系:尽管作者认为任何结论都得不出来,但别人却指责铁路的货运部门是有罪的,因而构成了对同一件事实,作者和别人分析的截然不同而 C 选项的 guilty 放回原文后,仍然为主动语态。此时,上句和下句都为作者自己的观点,却迥然不同,当然是一个错误的逻辑,故正确答案为 A。

【重点词条】be further from   进一步引申,推断

conscious *adj*. 有意识的,有知觉的,清醒的(perceiving, apprehending, or noticing with a degree of controlled thought or observation)

exorbitant *adj*. ①(收费)过高的,过高的
②不在法律范围内的

6.【正确答案】E

【中文释义】尽管有一个竞争队员是其朋友的消息走漏使得这个裁判公开面临缺乏公正性的指责,但这位裁判继续顽固地坚持她的断言,即熟悉并不必然意味着不公平。

【解题分析】下句的 acquaintance 重复上文的 that 引导的从句,故上句别人据此批评这位裁判,下句该裁判对别人的批判做出驳斥,所以上句的 lack of 加空格应该与下句的空格构成一组同义词,从而两个空格应为反义词,答案 E。

【重点词条】detachment *n*. 公开,公平,冷静,超然

impropriety *n*. ①不合适,不得体(an improper or indecorous act or remark, an unacceptable use of a word or of language)
②不合标准(the quality or state of being improper)

exoneration *n*. ①(义务等的)免除、解脱(to relieve of a responsibility, obligation, or hardship)
②证明无辜,免受指控(to clear from accusation or blame)

7.【正确答案】B

【中文释义】在未来的十年中,现在正围绕地球旋转的精密的望远镜将决定是否大陆真地在移动,阻止掉地质学家之间的初期的关于大陆漂移学说理论正确性的分歧。

【解题分析】文首的时间状语在明确提示着时间对比题型,果然在第一个空格后出现了一个 incipient,从而构成了将来和过去的对比。将来会决定这个理论的正确性,故初期是未确定的状态,第二个空格可选 B、C 和 D。显然 B 是最好的答案。那么第一个空格显然又是分隔结构重复前文,应表达出明确这个理论正确性这个概念,也即避免或消除或消除分歧就导致明确一个理论正确性,B、C、D 中显然是 B 的第一词 forestalling 为正确选择。

【重点词条】**incipient** *adj.* 刚开始(出现)的,早期的(beginning to come into being or to become apparent) 例 an~solar system/evidence of~racial tension

SECTION 18

1. The commissions criticized the legislature for making college attendance dependent on the ability to pay, charging that, as a result, hundreds of qualified young people would be _____ further education.
   (A) entitled to
   (B) striving for
   (C) deprived of
   (D) uninterested in
   (E) participating in

2. In most Native American cultures, an article used in prayer or ritual is made with extraordinary attention to and richness of detail: it is decorated more _____ than a similar article intended for _____ use.
   (A) delicately. . vocational
   (B) colorfully. . festive
   (C) creatively. . religious
   (D) subtly. . commercial
   (E) lavishly. . everyday

3. Having no sense of moral obligation, Shipler was as little subject to the _____ of conscience after he acted as he was motivated by its _____ before he acted.
   (A) rewards. . chastisement 惩罚
   (B) balm. . eloquence 雄辩, 口才
   香油

   (C) reproaches. . prompting 责备 刺激,鼓励
   (D) ridicule. . allure 嘲笑 诱惑力, 魅惑力
   (E) qualms. . atonement
   一阵眩晕, 眼花

4. Freud derived psychoanalytic knowledge of childhood indirectly: he _____ childhood processes from adult _____.
   (A) reconstructed. . memory
   (B) condoned. . experience 宽恕
   (C) incorporated. . behavior
   (D) released. . monotony
   (E) inferred. . anticipation

5. While she initially suffered the fate of many pioneers—the incomprehension of her colleagues—octogenarian Nobel laureate Barbara McClintock has lived to _____ the triumph of her once _____ scientific theories.
   (A) descry. . innovative
   (B) regret. . insignificant
   (C) perpetuate. . tentative
   (D) enjoy. . authoritative
   (E) savor. . heterodox 寻觅

6. Broadway audiences have become inured to 不屑于
   _____ and so _____ to be pleased as to make their ready ovations meaningless as an indicator of the quality of the production before them.

(A) sentimentality. . reluctant

(B) condescension. . disinclined

(C) histrionics. . unlikely

(D) cleverness. . eager

(E) mediocrity. . desperate
  普通的，平庸的

7. Any language is a conspiracy against experience in the sense that it is a collective at-

tempt to ____ experience by reducing it into discrete parcels.

(A) extrapolate 推断

(B) transcribe 誊写，抄录

(C) complicate 变复杂

(D) amplify

(E) manage 处理

SECTION 18 解答

1. 【正确答案】C

   【中文释义】这个委员会批评立法机构,因为其使得大学的入学依赖于能否支付的能力,指责道：这必然导致成百的有资格入学的年轻人将被剥夺掉继续深造的教育机会。

   【解题分析】空格既然是 charge 的内容,故应为不好的内容,答案为 C。

   【重点词条】entitle v. ①定名,命名(to give a title to, designate)

   ②使有权利,使具资格(to furnish with proper grounds for seeking or claiming something) 例 this ticket～s the bearer to free admission

2. 【正确答案】E

   【中文释义】在大多数土著美洲文化中,一个在宗教祈祷和宗教仪式上所使用的物品在制作时充分注意并且充满了大量的花纹:它比一件类似的意欲用于日常生活的物品装饰得更多。

   【解题分析】冒号之后的显然是一个一套比较结构的比较句,故比较双方应相反,比较双方为(it) an article used in prayer or ritual 和 an article intended for ____ use。故空格里显然应填上宗教用途截然相反的用途,与宗教生活相反的是世俗的生活,故正确答案为 E。

   【重点词条】article n. ①(物品的)一件,物件

   ②条款,规定

   ③文章,论文,报道

3. 【正确答案】C

   【中文释义】由于没有道德约束感,席普勒在做一件事情之后很少受到道德良心的谴责,同样地,他在做一件事情之前也不是由于道德良心的驱使而产生动机的。

   【解题分析】本句的句型结构颇为复杂。我们先看一种简单的解法,第二个空格出现在 by 之后,显然与 by 之前构成一个目的和手段的关系,句子填空中的 by 之后如果是动词的抽象名词,或者动名词结构的话,此时 by 之前的结果往往就是这个抽象名词或动名词再变成动词即可,常见的格式为 be criticized by his criticism

或 be encouraged by his encouragement 等等。同样地,如果空格之前的动词已经存在,而需要填空格之后的动名词或抽象名词,我们也同样将 by 之前的动词改变一下词性即可。如此句中的 by 之后的空格,在考场上的第一反应就应该是 motivating（motivated 变化而来）。五个选项中构成此含义是 C 的 prompting。答案 D 的 allure 可用于指邪恶的念头引诱人去做某事,而不能用于道德指导人去行善这种场合,故正确答案为 C。本句的结构中的 as...as... 并不是通常所见的小连接结构,小连接结构中 as...as... 连接两个形容词,且这两个形容词为同义词。而此句中第一个 as 之后为表语,第二个 as 之后为一整句,故显然不是小连接结构,先举一简单的例子如下:

He is as smart as he is healthy.   译文:他既聪明又健康。

首先请注意 smart 和 healthy 无任何同义含义。事实上我们可以将 healthy 换成其他的褒义词,如 strong, honest, warmhearted 等等,句子结构仍然正确,所以请不要误以为这种 as...as... 结构连接的双方会有同义关系。

其次请注意如果我们要将这句话改造成"他既不聪明也不健康"此时只需在 smart 之前加上 never, little 等否定副词即可,而不需要在 healthy 之前加上任何否定词,故请不要将下句的 he was motivated by its prompting 译作"被良心的驱使而产生动机",应该在 was 之后加上省略掉的"never"。

最后,此句的逻辑关系上,as 所联接的两个成分无同义关系不宜做推理,而真正的推理关系在何处呢？ 正确的理解是:句首的原因状语对全句做出原因说明,因而分别和后文的两个结果构成因果关系,其一是"由于没有道德责任感,所以做事情之后不会受到道德良心的谴责",其二是"由于没有道德良心感,所以做事情之前不会受道德良心的驱使而产生动机",请注意这种特殊的推理线路,并加以运用。（请用此思路解 SECTION 27 的第 4 题。）

【重点词条】qualm *n*.①晕眩,恶心(a sudden attack of illness, faintness, or nausea)

②疑惧,忧虑(a sudden access of disturbing emotion such as doubt or fear)

③内疚,良心责备(a feeling of uneasiness about a point esp. of conscience or propriety)

atonement *n*.①补偿(reconciliation)

②赎罪(the reconciliation of God and man through the sacrificial death of Jesus Christ)

balm *n*.①香膏(a balsamic resin, one from small tropical evergreen trees)

②芳香(a spicy aromatic odor)

③安慰物(a soothing restorative agency)

4.【正确答案】A

【中文释义】弗洛伊德非直接地获知孩提时代的心理分析学情况:他们成年后的回忆中复现出童年。

【解题分析】冒号之后重复前文,如何间接地获知病人童年的情况？ 如果了解弗洛伊德的做法,不难知其用询问、催眠等等方式目的无非是让病人回忆起来童年时代所受过的精神创伤,并以此作为成年之后精神病病因的解释。故 A 为正确答案。此题具有文化背景十分容易解题,否则难以判断,这是一道针对北美学生的练习题,故不足为奇,在中国考区的考题中从未出现此种背景知识题。

【重点词条】**reconstruct** v. ①重建,修复(to establish or assemble again)
②使再现(to build up again mentally) 例 ~ing a lost civilization

incorporate v. ①包含,吸收,把…合并(to unite or work into something already existent so as to form an indistinguishable whole, to blend or combine thoroughly)
②体现(to give material form to)

release v. ①释放,解放(to set free from restraint, confinement, or servitude)
例 ~hostages/~pent-up emotions/~the brakes
②放开(to give permission for publication, performance, exhibition, or sale of, to make available to the public) 例 ~a new movie

5.【正确答案】E
【中文释义】尽管她当初遭到了很多先驱人物的命运——不被她的同僚所理解,但这位八十多岁的诺贝尔奖获得者芭芭拉·麦克林多克一直活到了来享受她的曾经是异端的理论的胜利。

【解题分析】句首的 initially 与句末的 once 是全句中惟一的表示时间的词,并且都表示过去,故第二个空格只需重复上文过去的状态即可。过去她的理论不被她的同僚接受,也即被同僚们看成 heterodox。故正确答案为 E。

【重点词条】**descry** v. 看见,望见,辨认出(to catch sight of, to find out, discover)
perpetuate v. 使永久,使长存(to make perpetual or cause to last indefinitely)
例 ~the species

6.【正确答案】E
【中文释义】百老汇的听众已经对平庸的作品失去判断能力,并且如此极度渴望被取悦以至于使得他们欣欣然的热烈掌声失去了他们为面前演出作品的质量评价的意义。

【解题分析】该句选取百老汇的听众做为研究样本,用群体心理学的观点做出了分析,因而句意比较难懂,解题时我们只需牢牢地抓住其逻辑关系即可,本句的 so...as to...显然构成了一组因果关系。So 之后的 to be pleased 为被取悦之意,演员在舞台上演出的目的就是使观众获得美的享受,也即取悦他们,观众是被取悦的对象。观众如果被取悦,典型的反应就是鼓掌。As to 之后为结果,此结果可分解为两个方面:其一是观众们欣欣然地愿意(ready)热烈鼓掌(ovation),其二是这种掌声是毫无意义的。那么原因 so 之后的那个单词就应该针对这两点给出解释。首先是针对"愿意热烈鼓掌"这一点可知,观众的确是被取悦了,故可选 D 和 E,其次由针对"这掌声毫无意义"可知,原因也应为一贬义的原因,

因果句的原因和结果始终是同褒贬的,而 D 和 E 的区别正在于褒贬性上,贬义
的原因为 E 的 desperate,故 E 为正确答案。

【重点词条】 **inure** *v.* 习惯于,适应于(to accustom to accept something undesirable)

　　　　　　please *v.* 取悦,使高兴,使满意(to afford or give pleasure or satisfaction)

　　　　　　desperate *adj.* ①绝望的(having lost hope) 例 a～spirit crying for relief

　　　　　　　　　　　②孤注一掷的,不顾一切的(involving or employing extreme measures in an attempt to escape defeat or frustration) 例 made a～leap for the rope

　　　　　　　　　　　③极度渴望的,极需要的(suffering extreme need or anxiety) 例 ～for money

　　　　　　　　　　　④危急的,极严重的(involving extreme danger or possible disaster) 例 a～situation

　　　　　　　　　　　⑤极度的,极强烈的(of extreme intensity)

7.【正确答案】E

　【中文释义】语言是反对经验的一种阴谋,因为从某种意义上说它是一个集体的企图来通过将经验变化为不连续的部分的方式来控制经验。

　【解题分析】尽管此句的含义更为晦涩,但仍可由一些简单的规律来判断答案。首先 in the sense that 为一种因果关系,也可以翻译成"部分上原因是…",所以空格里应填一贬义词来照应上文的 conspiracy,可以候选 C、D 和 E。需要指出的是 B 的 transcribe 为"抄写,誊写,改写,改编"等意,无"篡改"之意。再由 by 的手段和结果的关系进一步区分 C、D 和 E。C 和 D 的"复杂化"与"放大"显然与" reduce to"这个动作背道而驰,故正确答案为 E。关于此句子进一步理解请参阅 SECTION 32 的第 3 题句意,此句的观点是简化后即为"语言并不能表达经验,因为它表达的同时就控制分割肢解了经验",这个观点又为一固定观点,并且诸如"language of art"等也都是不能完美地表达其对应的经验世界。

　【重点词条】 **reduce to** ①数量变少

　　　　　　　　　　　②状态变化

　　　　　　　　　　　③身分地位下降

　　　　　　　　　　　④归纳总结为某一类型

　　　　　　transcribe *v.* ①抄写,誊写(to make a written copy of)

　　　　　　　　　　　②把…改成另一种形式(to transfer data from one recording form to another)

　　　　　　manage *v.* 控制(to keep or make submissive)

SECTION 19

1. There is perhaps some truth in that waggish   old definition of a scholar—a siren that calls

滑稽,玩笑的.

attention to a fog without doing anything to
____ it.

(A) describe

(B) cause

(C) analyze

(D) dispel

(E) thicken

2. Cryogenic energy storage has the advantage
of being suitable in any ____ , regardless of
geography or geology, factors that may ____
both underground gas storage and pumped
hydroelectric storage.

(A) location. . limit

(B) climate. . deter

(C) site. . forebode

(D) proportion. . typify

(E) surface. . hamper

3. The newborn human infant is not a passive
figure, nor an active one, but what might
be called an actively ____ one, eagerly attentive as it is to sights and sounds.

(A) adaptive

(B) selective

(C) inquisitive

(D) receptive

(E) intuitive

4. Opponents of the expansion of the market e-
conomy, although in ____ , continued to
constitute ____ political force throughout the
century.

(A) error. . an inconsequential

(B) retreat. . a powerful

(C) disarray. . a disciplined

(D) jeopardy. . an ineffective

(E) command. . a viable

5. Nature's energy efficiency often ____ human technology: despite the intensity of the
light fireflies produce, the amount of heat is
negligible; only recently have humans developed chemical light-producing systems
whose efficiency ____ the firefly's system.

(A) engenders. . manipulates

(B) reflects. . simulates

(C) outstrips. . rivals

(D) inhibits. . matches

(E) determines. . reproduces

6. Scholars' sense of the uniqueness of the central concept of "the state" at the time when
political science became an academic field
quite naturally led to striving for a correspondingly ____ mode of study.

(A) thorough

(B) distinctive

(C) dependable

(D) scientific

(E) dynamic

7. Just as astrology was for centuries ____
faith, countering the strength of established
churches, so today believing in astrology is
an act of ____ the professional sciences.

(A) an individual. . rebellion by

(B) an accepted. . antagonism toward

(C) an underground. . defiance against

(D) a heretical. . support for

(E) an unknown. . concern about

SECTION 19 解答

1.【正确答案】D

【中文释义】在学者的滑稽的老的定义中可能存在一些真理。学者就如一报警器可以唤起对一团浓雾的注意但却不能做任何事情来驱散浓雾。

【解题分析】一个典型的比喻句,破折号之后均为喻体层面,故 it 之前的空格仍为 siren 所做的动作,正确答案为 D。"驱散迷雾"对应的本体意为"解决问题",也即选项 C 的动词。做比喻句能分清本体和喻体一般都能做对,请参阅 SECTION 13 的第 3 题。

【重点词条】siren *n*. 海上女妖,汽笛,警报声

2.【正确答案】A

【中文释义】物理的低温能量储存方式有在任何地理位置,不管地理还有地质情况如何,都适用的优点,这两个因素却会限制地下气体储存方式和泵压水力发电的储存方式。

【解题分析】第一个空格之后出现了分隔,可据此推知空格中所填的词应同时包含地理和地质两方面情况,故可选 A 和 C。A 和 C 的第二个词应选 A 的 limit,判断方法如下:上文的 cryogenic energy storage 不受这两个因素的影响,而下文为另外两种方式 underground gas storage,显然文句的这种书写方式强调了这两种 storage 和第一种 storage 的不同,故第一种方式不受影响,第二、三种方式应受影响,也即 A 的 limit。

【重点词条】**proportion** *n*. ①均衡(harmonious relation of parts to each other or to the whole, balance, symmetry)

②部分(proper or equal share) 例 each did her~of the work

③比例(the relation of one part to another or to the whole with respect to magnitude, quantity, or degree, ratio)

cryogenic *adj*. 低温的(of or relating to the production of very low temperatures, being or relating to very low temperatures)

typify *v*. ①代表,象征(to represent in typical fashion, to constitute a typical mark or instance of)

②作为…的典型(to embody the essential or salient characteristics of, be the type of)

3.【正确答案】D

【中文释义】新出生的人类婴儿既不是一个消极的人物,也不是一个积极的人物,而是可被称之为一个积极地接收的人物,正如他对光和声音一样主动积极地注意接收。

【解题分析】由文中 not...but 结构可知 but 之后应与 no 之后反义,故 but 之后的 actively 显然与 not 之后的 passive 反义,而空格就应该与 nor 之后的 active 反义,故空格应填一个表示"消极被动"的词,A、B、C 均为主动动作的词义,D 的 receptive 为"接收",与"给予"正好构成一组反义,故"接收"为一被动动作,E 的 intuitive 也不表示被动。正确答案为 D。

　　另外我们也可以由分隔的角度来解题,eagerly attentive 即是对前文的重复,eagerly 重复 actively,故空格应该填上 attentive,D 的 receptive 正是 attentive 的同义词。此句对婴儿的行为做出了描述,婴儿很少主动向外界发表信息,但也从不拒绝外界的各种刺激,而是非常饶有兴趣地躺在摇篮里对外界一切声响光线做出敏感的反应。

【重点词条】**adaptive** *adj*. 适应的,适合的(showing or having a capacity for or tendency toward adaptation)

　　　　　　attentive *adj*. ①注意的,关心的(mindful, observant) 例 ~ to what he is doing

　　　　　　　　　　　　②殷勤的,恳切的(heedful of the comfort of others, solicitous)

　　　　　　　　　　　　③当心的,倾听的(offering attentions in or as if in the role of a suitor)

　　　　　　receptive *adj*. ①能接受的,善于理解的(able or inclined to receive, open and responsive to ideas, impressions, or suggestions)

　　　　　　　　　　　　②感受敏锐的(fit to receive and transmit stimuli)

4. 【正确答案】B

【中文释义】市场经济扩张的反对者们,尽管处于后退中,但却继续在整个世纪中构成了一支强大的政治势力。

【解题分析】本文又是 continue 和 remain 的考法之一,请参阅 SECTION 16 的第 3 题。

【重点词条】**inconsequential** *adj*. ①不连贯的,不合逻辑的(illogical)

　　　　　　　　　　　　②不相干的(irrelevant)

　　　　　　　　　　　　③不重要的,微不足道的(of no significance, unimportant)

　　　　　　disarray *n*. ①混乱,紊乱(a lack of order or sequence, confusion, disorder)

　　　　　　　　　　②衣服不整齐(disorderly dress)

　　　　　　viable *adj*. ①(婴儿脱离母体之后无须特殊护理)能养活的(capable of living, capable of surviving outside the mother's womb without artificial support) 例 the normal human fetus is usually ~ by the end of the seventh month

　　　　　　　　　　②(种子)能发芽生长的,(卵等)能生长发育的(capable of growing or developing) 例 ~ seeds/~ eggs

　　　　　　　　　　③能独立生存发展的(capable of existence and development as an independent unit) 例 the colony is now a ~ state

　　　　　　　　　　④可望成功的(having a reasonable chance of succeeding) 例 a ~ candidate

　　　　　　　　　　⑤切实可行的(financially sustainable) 例 a ~ enterprise

5. 【正确答案】C

【中文释义】大自然的能量效率通常胜过人的技术:不管萤火虫发出的光的强度是多大,但(产生的)热量却是微乎其微的;只在最近人才发展出化学发光系统,这种系统的能量效率可与萤火虫系统相抗衡。

【解题分析】上半句的冒号后实际上已经提供了答案,具有理工背景知识的同学都能知道一个发光系统所有的能量都用于发光,而没有一丁点儿浪费在发热上,这说明这个系统的能量效率已达登峰造极的无与伦比的境界,而萤火虫当然是大自然能量效率的化身,故第一个空格当然填"超过,胜过"等词义。如果没有理工知识背景,我们可以从分号句的角度分析,分号句下半句的时间状语 only recently 告诉我们上下句为反义重复,故应在两空格填同义词(A>B;B>A)。五个选项中构成同义词的选项为 C。

【重点词条】**negligible** *adj*. 可略而不计的,微不足道的(so small or unimportant or of so little consequence as to warrant little or no attention, trifling)

　　　　　outstripe *v*. ①(在竞速中)比…来得快(to go faster or farther than)

　　　　　　　　②把…抛在后面,超过,胜出(to get ahead of, leave behind) 例 Has civilization outstripped the ability of its users to use it?

　　　　　rival ①*n*. 对手,敌手,竞争者(one of two or more striving to reach or obtain something that only one can possess, one striving for competitive advantage)

　　　　　　　　②*v*. 与…匹敌,比得上(to possess qualities or aptitudes that approach or equal those of another)

6. 【正确答案】B

【中文释义】在政治学变成一个学术领域的时候,学者们关于国家这个中心概念独特性的认识就导致他们努力追求一个相应的独特的研究方法。

【解题分析】句子结构加以简化后即为"scholar' sense of uniqueness led to striving for a correspondingly ____ mode of study",由 corresponding 可知空格应该填上与 uniqueness 相应的词。

【重点词条】**dependable** *adj*. 可靠的,可信赖的(capable of being depended on, reliable)

　　　　　dynamic *adj*. ①有活力的,活动的(marked by usu. continuous and productive activity or change) 例 a～city

　　　　　　　　②精力充沛的 (energetic, forceful) 例 a～personality

7. 【正确答案】C

【中文释义】正如占星术几个世纪以来是一种反对正统力量的信仰,它反对国立教堂的力量,所以今天相信占星术是一种反抗专业科学的行为。

【解题分析】第一个空格后即出现分隔,由分隔可知空格应填"反对正统力量的",故 C 和 D 候选,而下文的 so 告诉我们今天其仍然是一种反对正统力量的行为,文中的"professional sciences"即为今天的正统力量,故 C 和 D 当中选 C。

【重点词条】**underground** *adj*. 地下的,秘密的,不公开的(clandestine conspiratorial organization set up for revolutionary or other disruptive purposes esp. against a civil order)

　　　　　established church 国立教堂,由国家认为的最权威的并提供资金的教堂。

SECTION 20

1. Despite the fact that the two council members belonged to different political parties, they ____ the issue of how to finance the town debt.
   (A) complicated
   (B) avoided
   (C) attested to
   (D) reported on
   (E) agreed on

2. The breathing spell provided by the ____ arms shipments should give all the combatants a chance to reevaluate their positions.
   (A) plethora of
   (B) moratorium on
   (C) reciprocation of
   (D) concentration on
   (E) development of

3. The notion that cultural and biological influences ____ determine cross-cultural diversity is discredited by the fact that, in countless aspects of human existence, it is cultural programming that overwhelmingly accounts for cross-population variance.
   (A) jointly
   (B) completely
   (C) directly
   (D) equally
   (E) eventually

4. Because medieval women's public participation in spiritual life was not welcomed by the male establishment, a compensating ____ religious writings, inoffensive to the members of the establishment because of its

____, became important for many women.
   (A) involvement with. . privacy
   (B) attention to. . popularity
   (C) familiarity with. . scarcity
   (D) dissatisfaction with. . profundity
   (E) resistance to. . domesticity

5. This final essay, its prevailing kindliness ____ by occasional flashes of savage irony, bespeaks the ____ character of the author.
   (A) illuminated. . imperturbable
   (B) marred. . dichotomous
   (C) untainted. . vindictive
   (D) exemplified. . chivalrous
   (E) diluted. . ruthless

6. Although his attempts to appear psychotic were so ____ as to be almost ____, there is evidence that Ezra Pound was able to avoid standing trial for treason merely by faking symptoms of mental illness.
   (A) spontaneous. . amusing
   (B) contrived. . believable
   (C) clumsy. . ludicrous
   (D) stylized. . distressing
   (E) sporadic. . premeditated

7. The ____ questions that consistently structure the study of history must be distinguished from merely ____ questions, which have their day and then pass into oblivion.
   (A) recurrent. . practical
   (B) instinctive. . factual
   (C) ingrained. . discriminating
   (D) philosophical. . random
   (E) perennial. . ephemeral

SECTION 20 解答

1.【正确答案】E

【中文释义】尽管事实是两个议员属于不同的政党,但他们却就如何为这个城镇的债务而募集资金这一问题达成了一致见解。

【解题分析】空格显然应与上文的 different 构成反义词,答案为 E。

【重点词条】finance v.①供资金给(to raise or provide funds or capital for) 例 ~ a new house

②为…筹措资金(to furnish with necessary funds) 例 ~ a son through college

2.【正确答案】B

【中文释义】由停止武器运输所导致的休息的一段时间应给所有的作战人员一个机会来重新评价他们的战略地位。

【解题分析】主语 breathing spell 后的分隔成分为解题点,思路为"何种武器运输的情况会导致战场上的暂时休息?"五个选项中只有 B 的 moratorium on 构成了正确的解释。

【重点词条】breathing spell 喘息的机会,短暂的休息,考虑的机会(some time in which to recover, get organized, or get going)

moratorium n.①延期偿付,延期履行债务(a legally authorized period of delay in the performance of a legal obligation or the payment of a debt)

②暂停,中止(a suspension of activity)

reciprocation n.①互换(a mutual exchange)

②酬报,回报(a return in kind or of like value)

3.【正确答案】D

【中文释义】这个概念,即文化和生物的影响因素平等地决定了跨文化的差异,被下文的事实驳斥了,这个事实是,在无数的人类存在的方方面面中,是文化的因素绝对地构成了跨人口的差异。

【解题分析】文句的主框架提供了逻辑结构,The notion is discredited by the fact。故 notion 后的从句应和 fact 后的从句反义,fact 之后的从句用了强调句型来强调文化的因素更重要。故上句相反的说法应为生物的因素更重要,或者两者平等重要。上句 notion 之后的从句为并列主句,故只能表达出一个概念,即两者同等重要,故正确答案为 D 的 equally。

【重点词条】programming n.①编制程序(the planning, scheduling, or performing of a program)

②编制教学计划(the process of preparing an instructional program)

overwhelmingly *adv.* 势不可挡的,压倒一切的(tending or serving to overwhelm) 例 an~majority

4. 【正确答案】A

   【中文释义】由于中世纪妇女公开加入宗教生活是不被男性宗教建立者们所欢迎的,一个补偿的加入到宗教写作中去对于许多妇女就变得非常重要,而这种做法由于其隐蔽性而对建立者们无冒犯之处。

   【解题分析】文句中的 male establishment 与下文的 members of the establishment 构成了一组重复,所以上文对这些人冒犯的,让他们生气,不欢迎的方式为 public participation,下句对他们不冒犯的方式当然就应为 public participation 的反义词,故选 A 的 privacy。至于参加到宗教写作中为何就具有了隐蔽性的理解,有背景知识的同学就会知道,所有宗教经文,以及宣传教义的书一般都不会签署作者的姓名,因为一切都是神的指喻,而不是平凡庸俗的人所能创作的,故而参加宗教写作就具有了这层特殊的隐蔽关系。

   【重点词条】**spiritual** *adj.* ①精神上的,灵魂的(of, relating to, consisting of, or affecting the spirit, incorporeal) 例 man's~needs

   ②神圣的,崇高的(of or relating to sacred matters) 例 ~songs

   ③脱俗的(ecclesiastical rather than lay or temporal) 例 ~authority/~lords

   profundity *n.* ①(思想等的)深度(intellectual depth)

   ②深奥,深刻(something profound or abstruse)

   ③深邃(the quality or state of being profound or deep)

   domesticity *n.* ①爱家(the quality or state of being domestic or domesticated)

   ②家庭生活 (domestic activities or life)

   ③家务(domestic affairs)

5. 【正确答案】B

   prevailing

   【中文释义】最后这一篇散文,它的占主导地位的友善被偶尔出现的一句句野蛮的讽刺的话语所破坏了,这就表明了作者的自相矛盾的性格。

   【解题分析】作者和作者的书,一个人和其所说过的话等等类似的关系都是同义词关系,故文中用 kindliness 和 savage irong 修饰作者的话,从而作者本人也应如此,故选答案 B 的 dichotomous。

   【重点词条】**illuminate** *v.* ①照明,照亮(brightened with light)

   ②阐明,启迪(intellectually or spiritually enlightened)

   ③使容光焕发,使辉煌(to make illustrious or resplendent)

   ④以金字装饰,显赫(to decorate as a manuscript with gold or silver or brilliant colors or with often elaborate designs or miniature pictures)

   exemplify *v.* ①例示(to show or illustrate by example)

   ②是…的例证,典型(to be an instance of or serve as an example,

to be typical of)

  dilute *v*. ①稀释,使变淡(attenuate)

    ②使变细(to make thinner or more liquid by admixture)

    ③减轻,削弱(to diminish the strength, flavor, or brilliance of by admixture)

6. 【正确答案】C

 【中文释义】尽管他企图显得精神失常的尝试是如此地笨拙以至于几乎显得可笑,但有证据表明,埃诺·庞德能够仅仅通过伪装精神病的症状来避免忍受叛国罪的审判。

 【解题分析】上下文的 appear psychotic 与 faking symptoms of mental illness 为同义词复述,下文称这种做法使得庞德成功,故上句应称这种做法本身并不优秀。第二个空格应填贬义词,C 为最佳候选,D 的 distreessing 为"使别人痛苦"之义,并且D的前后两词无 so...as to... 所要求的因果关系,而 C 的 so clumsy as to be almost ludicrous 为正常逻辑关系,故 C 为正确答案。

 【重点词条】**spontaneous** *adj*. ①自然的,天真率直的(proceeding from natural feeling or native tendency without external constraint)

    ②自发的,不由自主的(arising from a momentary impulse, controlled and directed internally, self-acting) 例 ~ movement characteristic of living things

  contrived *adj*. 人工制成的,不自然的,非即兴而发的(to form or create in an artistic or ingenious manner) 例 contrived household utensils from stone

  distress *n*. ①悲痛,忧虑(pain or suffering affecting the body, a bodily part, or the mind, trouble) 例 gastric~

    ②危险(a state of danger or desperate need) 例 a ship in~

  premeditate *v*. ①预先考虑(to think about and revolve in the mind beforehand)

    ②预谋(to think, consider, or deliberate beforehand)

7. 【正确答案】E

 【中文释义】那种永远构成历史学研究的永恒的问题必须与另外一种问题区分开来,这种问题昙花一现然后就被人们所遗忘。

 【解题分析】句子结构非常规范,两个问题各有一个定语从句,故两个从句之间互为对比关系,对比点显然是 consistently 与 have their day then pass into oblivion,也即强调时间延续长短的对比,从这个角度去选词,E 为正确答案。

 【重点词条】**recurrent** *adj*. 反复出现的,周期性的(returning or happening time after time) 例 ~complaints

  ingrained *adj*. 根深蒂固的(forming a part of the essence or inmost being, deep-seated) 例 ～ prejudice

discriminating *adj*. ①区别性的(making a distinction, distinguishing)

②具备识别能力的,敏锐的(marked by discrimination,

discerning, judicious)

SECTION 21

1. Despite the apparently bewildering complexity of this procedure, the underlying ____ is quite ____.

(A) simplicity. . calculated

(B) principle. . elementary

(C) confusion. . imaginary

(D) purpose. . effective

(E) theory. . modern

2. In television programming, a later viewing time often ____ a more ____ audience and, therefore, more challenging subjects and themes.

(A) requires. . critical

(B) evinces. . affluent

(C) implies. . mature

(D) eliminates. . realistic

(E) invites. . general

3. The cultivation of the emotion of natsukashii, interpretable as "pleasant sorrow," brings Japanese to Kyoto in the spring, not to ____ the cherry blossoms in full bloom but to ____ the fading, falling flowers.

(A) mourn. . exclaim over

(B) honor. . protect

(C) describe. . rejoice over

(D) arrange. . preserve

(E) savor. . grieve over

有欣赏之意

4. Adam Smith's Wealth of Nations (1776) is still worth reading, more to appreciate the current ____ of Smith's valid contributions to economics than to see those contributions as the ____ of present-day economics.

(A) disregard. . outgrowths

(B) reaffirmation. . concerns

(C) relevance. . precursors 先驱区

(D) acceptance. . byproducts

(E) importance. . vestiges

5. At several points in his discussion, Graves, in effect, ____ evidence when it does not support his argument, tailoring it to his needs.

(A) addresses

(B) creates

(C) alters

(D) suppresses

(E) substitutes

6. Regardless of what ____ theories of politics may propound, there is nothing that requires daily politics to be clear, thorough, and consistent-nothing, that is, that requires reality to conform to theory.

(A) vague

(B) assertive

(C) casual

(D) vicious

(E) tidy

相当好的,清晰

7. Exposure to sustained noise has been claimed

to ____ blood pressure regulation in human beings and, particularly, to increase hypertension, even though some researchers have obtained inconclusive results that ____ the relationship.

(A) sharpen. . conflate
(B) increase. . diminish
(C) aggravate. . buttress
(D) disrupt. . neutralize
(E) impair. . obscure

SECTION 21 解答

1.【正确答案】B
　【中文释义】尽管这个程序具有表面上的令人头昏眼花的复杂性,但是其内部的原则却是相当简单的。
　【解题分析】上句 apparently 与下句的 underlying 构成反义,故上句为表面上复杂,下句应为内部简单。第二个空格为修饰内部事物的形容词,故填简单,B 的 elementary。
　【重点词条】confusion *n*. 混乱,混淆(the quality or state of being confused)
　　　　　　 calculated *adj*. 精心策划的,蓄意的

2.【正确答案】C
　【中文释义】在电视节目的安排中,一个较晚的收视时间通常意味着更加成熟的观众,因此意味着更加发人深思的素材和主题。
　【解题分析】文中提示点甚多,later 既是时间又是比较,move 告诉我们存在一个对比。思路应为 later 当然与稍早一点的时间对比,这两段时间的收视观众又有何种对比呢? 当然结论很简单,稍早的时间往往为儿童节目,稍后的收视时间当然意味着成熟的观众,因而选 C。此题不少考生误选为 A。这些考生往往未注意到上文明显的对比提示,而是从 therefore 入手,应该说,这也是一种正确的思路,但是什么样的观众需要 challenging subjects and themes 呢? 这时有很多考生犯了错误,认为 critical audience 需要更 challenging subjects,仔细思考不难发现,两者其实并无瓜葛,再次 A 的 require 也不正确,收视时间和收视观众之间并不存在必然性的关系。
　【重点词条】challenging *adj*. ①挑战性的,考验人的(arousing competitive interest, thought, or action) 例 a～course of study
　　　　　　　　　　　　②激发好奇心的(invitingly provocative, fascinating) 例 a ～personality
　　　　　　 critical *adj*. ①重大的,关键的(of, relating to, or being a turning point or specially important juncture) 例 ～phase
　　　　　　　　　　②吹毛求疵的,爱挑剔的(inclined to criticize severely and unfavorably)
　　　　　　　　　　③审慎的,谨严的
　　　　　　　　　　④批评的,批判的,评论性的

evince *v*. ①显示出,表现出
②唤起,引起

3. 【正确答案】E

【中文释义】这种 natsukashii 的情绪气质,可以解释为"甜蜜的忧伤",带日本人到春天的京都去,并不是来欣赏盛开的樱花花朵,而是为那些凋零的、飘落的花而悲伤。

【解题分析】事实上该句的主干逻辑非常清晰:忧伤带日本人去干什么动作呢? 当然是忧伤的动作,因第二个空格为忧伤情绪所驱动的动作,所以第二空格的动词应具有伤感之意,E 的 grieve over 正确。

【重点词条】**mourn** *v*. ①感到痛心、遗憾(to feel or express grief or sorrow)
②表示哀悼服表(to show the customary signs of grief for a death, to wear mourning)

exclaim *v*. ①呼喊、惊叫(to cry out or speak in strong or sudden emotion)

例 ~ed in delight

②大声叫喊,激烈地表示意见(to speak loudly or vehemently)

例 ~ed against immorality

savor *v*. ①滋味,气味(the taste or smell of something)
②风味(a particular flavor or smell)
③声誉(a distinctive quality)
④品尝(to taste or smell with pleasure, relish)
⑤欣赏(to delight in, enjoy)

4. 【正确答案】C

【中文释义】亚当·斯密的《国富论》(1776 年)仍然值得一读,更多是为了斯密对经济学所做正确贡献在当今仍具有的相关性,而不仅仅是为了将这些贡献看成今天经济学的先驱。

【解题分析】文中的一套比较结构 more...than... 是解题的关键。根据一套比较结构中的比较双方应该构成一组比较的原则,上文的"the current ____"与下文的"the ____"应为一组反义词,事实上,上下文的"appreciate"与"see...as"也为重复,所以第二个空格里的词应与时间有关,并且与"现在"这个时间相反,可候选 A、C 和 E,A 和 E 都为之后的时间发生的情况,而亚当·斯密 1776 年的《国富论》显然应在今天经济学之前,故 A 和 E 都错,正确答案为 C。

【重点词条】**relevance** *n*. ①切题(relation to the matter at hand)
②关联(pertinence)

5. 【正确答案】C

【中文释义】在他谈论的几个观点中,格莱威事实上修改了那些不支持他观点的证据,根据自己的需要而剪裁证据。

【解题分析】Tailoring 引导的分隔直接重复前文,it 即为上文的 evidence,故空格填 tailor 即

可,答案为 C。

【重点词条】**tailor** *v*. 做修改,使适合特定需要,使适合(to make or fashion as the work of a tailor, to make or adapt to suit a special need or purpose)

　　　　　　suppress *v*. ①压制,镇压(to put down by authority or force, subdue)

　　　　　　　　　　②查禁(to keep from public knowledge, to keep secret, to stop or prohibit the publication or revelation of)

　　　　　　　　　　③抑制(to restrain from a usual course or action, arrest, to inhibit the growth or development of, stunt)

6.【正确答案】E

【中文释义】不管清晰的政治学理论会提出什么观点,没有什么能必然导致日常的政治行为清楚、彻底并且富有逻辑连贯性,没有什么事物能保证现实依从理论。

【解题分析】文中的 nothing 有两个 that 从句修饰,故出现了特殊并列句的句型:应在两个并列句之间进行推理重复,第一个并列句可得出结论:日常的政治行动是不清楚、不彻底、不具有逻辑连贯性的,而第二个并列句可得出结论:现实和理论不一样,由这两个并列句,再由日常政治行动即为现实可知:理论是清楚、彻底并且逻辑高度一致的。空格正是要求填一个修饰理论的形容词,故该形容词应表达出清楚、彻底、逻辑一致这几个概念,答案 E 的 tidy 正好表达了这个意思,tidy mind, tidy thought 是常见的短语,其中"清晰的思想"即指"清楚、彻底、逻辑一致的思想"。

【重点词条】**propound** *v*. 提出…供考虑或讨论(to offer for discussion or consideration)

　　　　　　consistent *adj*. ①一致的,稳定的(possessing firmness or coherence)

　　　　　　　　　　②调和的,相合的(marked by harmony, regularity, or steady continuity, free from variation or contradiction) 例 a～ style in painting

　　　　　　vicious *adj*. ①邪恶的,堕落的,道德败坏的(having the nature or quality of vice or immorality, depraved)

　　　　　　　　　　②恶意的,怀恨的(malicious, spiteful) 例 ～gossip

　　　　　　tidy *adj*. ①相当好的,令人满意的(adequately satisfactory, acceptable, fair) 例 a～solution to their problem

　　　　　　　　　　②整齐的,整洁的(neat and orderly in appearance or habits, well ordered and cared for)

　　　　　　　　　　③有条理的,精确的(methodical, precise) 例 a～mind

7.【正确答案】E

【中文释义】暴露在持续的噪音中被认为破坏了人体内的血压管制系统,并且尤其是增加了高血压,即使有些研究者已经获得了初步的结果,这些结果削弱了(上文所声称的)关联性。

【解题分析】第一个空格处于 and 所构成的小连接当中,所以第一个空格应表示血压管制失控的意思,这样才能与 and 之后的导致高血压构成小连接,C、D 和 E 可以候选。而下半句与上半句转折, the relationship 即指上文声称的噪音会导致高血压的关系, 所以第二个空格应反对这层关系, C、D 和 E 选项的第二单词恰好为支持, 中立, 反对削弱这三个义项, 正确答案为 E。

【重点词条】 **sustained** *adj*. 持续的, 经久不衰的

sharpen *v*. 使锐利(to make sharp or sharper)

conflate *v*. ①混合(to bring together, fuse)

②合并(to combine such as two readings of a text into a composite whole)

buttress *n*. ①扶墙, 拱壁(a projecting structure of masonry or wood for supporting or giving stability to a wall or building)

②支撑物(something that supports or strengthens) 例 a ~ of the cause of peace

obscure *adj*. ①阴暗的, 含糊的, 微弱的(dark, dim, shrouded in or hidden by darkness, not clearly seen or easily distinguished, faint)

②难解的, 神秘的(not readily understood or clearly expressed, mysterious)

③无名的(relatively unknown)

④偏僻的(remote, secluded)

SECTION 22

1. After a slow sales start early in the year, mobile homes have been gaining favor as _____ to increasingly expensive conventional housing.

(A) reaction

(B) an addition

(C) an introduction

(D) an alternative

(E) a challenge

2. Just as such apparently basic things as rocks, clouds, and clams are, in fact, intricately structured entities, so the self, too, is not an "elementary particle," but is _____ construction.

(A) a complicated

(B) a convoluted

(C) a distorted

(D) an amorphous

(E) an illusory

3. Considering how long she had yearned to see Italy, her first reaction was curiously _____.

(A) meditative

(B) tepid 微温的, 平静

(C) categorical

(D) unoriginal

(E) insightful

4. The successful _____ of an archaeological site requires scientific knowledge as well as cultural _____.

(A) evolution . . awareness

(B) revelation . . depth

(C) reconstruction . . sensitivity

(D) analysis . . aesthetics

(E) synthesis. . understanding

5. As painted by Constable, the scene is not one of bucolic ___; rather it shows a striking emotional and intellectual ___.

(A) intensity. . boredom

(B) complacence. . detachment

(C) serenity. . tension 张力

(D) vitality. . excitement

(E) nostalgia. . placidity

6. Our times seem especially ___ to bad ideas, probably because in throwing off the shackles of tradition, we have ended up being quite ___ untested theories and untried remedies.

(A) impervious. . tolerant of

(B) hostile. . dependent on

(C) hospitable. . vulnerable to

(D) prone. . wary of

(E) indifferent. . devoid of

7. Although he attempted repeatedly to ___ her of her conviction of his insincerity, he was not successful; she remained ___ in her judgment.

(A) remind. . forceful

(B) convince. . unfeigned

(C) exorcise. . indulgent

(D) disabuse. . adamant

(E) free. . unsure

SECTION 22 解答

1.【正确答案】D

【中文释义】在年初缓慢的销售之后,流动房屋作为对越来越贵的传统房屋的代替物而获得了欢迎。

【解题分析】此句做错的考生甚多,as 所引导的为主语同位语,所以将 as 之后的名词放到主语位置上也应正确才对。正确答案 C 的 an alternative 为候选物、代替物之意,我们可以说“一个代替物受到市场消费者的欢迎”,但我们绝对不会说“一个挑战受到了市场消费者的欢迎”。消费者所欢迎的绝不是一个抽象名词“challenge”或“reaction”。

【重点词条】**alternative** *n*. ①取舍,抉择(an opportunity for deciding between two or more courses or propositions)

②供抉择的解决方法,可供选择的替代途径(something which can be chosen instead) 例 the only~ to intervention

2.【正确答案】A

【中文释义】正如那些表面上简单的事物,如石头、云彩和河蚌事实上是构造复杂的物品,所以人自身也不是一个“基本粒子”而是一个复杂的构件。

【解题分析】文中的 not...but... 结构,以及 just as...so... 结构均为提示,空格应填上 intricately 的同义词,或者 elemthtary 的反义词,答案为 A,B 的 convoluted 本意为“旋绕的”,比喻义为“令人费解的”,该词并不从物理构成的角度强调“复杂”。

【重点词条】**entity** *n*. ①实际存在物,实体存在(being, existence, independent, separate, or self-contained existence)

②本质(the existence of a thing as contrasted with its attributes)

③独立自主体(something that has separate and distinct existence and objective or conceptual reality)

convoluted *adj.* ①盘绕的,卷曲的(having convolutions)

②繁复晦涩的(involved, intricate)

amorphous *adj.* ①无固定形状的(having no definite form, shapeless) 例 an~ cloud mass

②难以归类的,不规则的(being without definite character or nature, unclassifiable) 例 an~segment of society

③无组织的(lacking organization or unity) 例 an~style

④模糊的(having no real or apparent crystalline form, uncrystallized) 例 an~mineral

3.【正确答案】B

【中文释义】考虑到她如此长久地渴望见到意大利,她的第一反应是如此让人惊奇地平静。

【解题分析】文中的 curiously 提示我们她的反应与正常状态不一样,正常状态下人们见到久已渴望的东西终于出现时,一定会激动不已。所以空格应填"激动不已"的反义词,为 B。

【重点词条】**meditative** *adj.* 沉思冥想的(disposed or given to meditation, marked by or conducive to meditation)

tepid *adj.* ①微温的(moderately warm, lukewarm) 例 a~bath

②不热烈的(lacking in passion, force, or zest) 例 a~joke

③不热情的(marked by an absence of enthusiasm or conviction) 例 a~interest

categorical *adj.* ①绝对的,无条件的(absolute, unqualified) 例 a~denial

②类的(of, relating to, or constituting a category)

③范畴的(involving, according with, or considered with respect to specific categories)

4.【正确答案】C

【中文释义】成功地复建考古学遗址需要科学知识和文化敏感性。

【解题分析】美国是一个强调历史和考古的国家,而中国学生往往缺乏考古方面的背景知识,该题是针对美国学生的练习题,故对考古要求比较深入的了解,答案 A 的 evolution 显然不是人力所能为的事件,A 错,B 是一个具有高度迷惑的选项,而实际上发现遗址或者需要高科技,或者需要文化知识,两者具备一个往往就可导致遗址的发现,原文中用了 as well as 短语,就是强调了两者必须同时具有,这与许多实践中都是不相符合的。D 答案错在第二个词,a culture aesthetics 为文化审美之意,而事实上分析遗址的确需要文化知识,但却未必是文化审美,E 的第一个词就错了。C 为正确答案,比如复建金字塔,科学技术自然需要,而金字塔方方面面的细节,比如空间方位的摆向应与天体的运行相关,恐怕需要极高的文化敏感才行。

【重点词条】**aware** *adj*. ①机警的(watchful, wary)

②知觉的,有认识的(having or showing realization, perception, or knowledge)

5.【正确答案】C

【中文释义】正如康斯德柏所画的一样,这场景不是一幅田园牧歌式的宁静,相反它表现了震撼心灵的情感和精神的张力。

【解题分析】文中的逻辑关系明确告诉我们前后应为一组反义词,并且第一空格为田园牧歌式的风格。不难选出答案为 C。

【重点词条】**intensity** *n*. ①强烈,紧张(the quality or state of being intense, extreme degree of strength, force, energy, or feeling)

②强度,明亮度(the magnitude of a quantity such as force or energy per unit such as of area, charge, mass, or time)

③饱和度(saturation)

complacence *n*. 自满,沾沾自喜,满足(calm or secure satisfaction with oneself or one's lot, self-satisfaction)

vitality *n*. ①生命力(the peculiarity distinguishing the living from the nonliving)

②生机,活力(capacity to live and develop, physical or mental vigor when highly developed)

③生存力,持久力(power of enduring)

④生动性,有力性(lively and animated character)

nostalgia *n*. ①思乡病(the state of being homesick, homesickness)

②恋旧,怀旧(a wistful or excessively sentimental yearning for return to or of some past period or irrecoverable condition)

6.【正确答案】C

【中文释义】我们的时代看上去尤其愿意接受坏的思想,可能是因为在摆脱了传统思想桎梏的同时,我们已经变得对那些未测试过的思想和未证明过的方法变得毫无抵制能力。

【解题分析】上下句中的 our times 和 we 构成了一组同义词,而 bad ideas 与下文的 untested theories and untried remedies 构成上下义,那些未测试过的理论中包含了坏的思想,正如我国 80 年代初期的一句流行的话"窗户打开了,苍蝇也飞了进来",所以上下句的同义重复关系非常明显,并且 end up being sth 这个短语的含义为"以…结局收场""以…为结果",being 之后的状态是结果状态,也即变化后的现在的状态,千万不要理解成结束了 being 这个状态,所以上下句的两个空格为一组同义词。故选答案为 C

【重点词条】**hospitable** *adj*. ①好客的,殷勤款待的(given to generous and cordial reception

of guests, promising or suggesting generous and cordial welcome, offering a pleasant or sustaining environment)

②(对思想)愿意接受的,开通的(readily receptive, open)

例 ~ to new ideas

vulnerable *adj*. ①易受伤的(capable of being physically wounded)

②易受武力攻击的,难防御的(open to attack or damage, assailable)

7.【正确答案】D

【中文释义】尽管他一再尝试打消她的认为自己是不诚实的这个想法,但他没有成功;她继
续顽固地坚持她的判断。

【解题分析】女孩子继续自己的判断是他未成功的结果,说明他企图改变女孩子对他的判
断,从而第一空格应为"改变"、"消除"等含义。A、B 均错误,C 和 D 的第一个
选项候选。E 的 free 可作免除这个动词的同义来解释,但仍然不正确。C 和 D
的第二个选择是很容易判断的,正确答案为 D。

【重点词条】**exorcise** *v*. ①(用符咒、祈祷或仪式)驱除(to expel an evil spirit by adjuration)

②消除、除去恼人的、危险的事物(to get rid of something troublesome, menacing, or oppressive)

③驱除邪魔(to free of an evil spirit)

disabuse *v*. 去除…的谬误,使醒悟(to free from error, fallacy, or misconception)

indulgent *adj*. 纵容的,放纵的,溺爱的(indulging or characterized by indulgence, lenient)

free *v*. ①使自由,解放(to cause to be free)

②使解脱出来(to relieve or rid of what restrains, confines, restricts, or
embarrasses) 例 ~ a person from debt

③使摆脱,去除(disentangle, clear)

SECTION 23

1. Although adolescent maturational and devel-
opmental states occur in an orderly sequence, their timing ____ with regard to
onset and duration.

(A) lasts

(B) varies

(C) falters 摇摆,蹒跚

(D) accelerates

(E) dwindles

2. Many of the earliest colonial houses that are
still standing have been so modified and enlarged that the ____ design is no longer
____.

(A) pertinent. . relevant

(B) intended. . necessary

(C) embellished. . attractive

(D) appropriate. . applicable

(E) initial. . discernible

3. While the delegate clearly sought to _____ the optimism that has emerged recently, she stopped short of suggesting that the conference was near collapse and might produce nothing of significance.

(A) substantiate

(B) dampen

(C) encourage

(D) elucidate

(E) rekindle

4. The old man could not have been accused of _____ his affection; his conduct toward the child betrayed his _____ her.

(A) lavishing. . fondness for

(B) sparing. . tolerance of

(C) rationing. . antipathy for

(D) stinting. . adoration of

(E) promising. . dislike of

5. A leading chemist believes that many scientists have difficulty with stereochemistry because much of the relevant nomenclature is _____, in that it combines concepts that should be kept _____.

(A) obscure. . interrelated

(B) specialized. . intact

(C) subtle. . inviolate

(D) descriptive. . separate

(E) imprecise. . discrete

6. Among the many _____ of the project, expense cannot be numbered; the goals of the project's promoters can be achieved with impressive _____.

(A) highlights. . efficiency

(B) features. . savings

(C) disadvantages. . innovation

(D) claims. . speed

(E) defects. . economy

7. Though science is often imagined as a _____ exploration of external reality, scientists are no different from anyone else: they are _____ human beings enmeshed in a web of personal and social circumstances.

(A) fervent. . vulnerable

(B) neutral. . rational

(C) painstaking. . careless

(D) disinterested. . passionate

(E) cautious. . dynamic

SECTION 23 解答

1. 【正确答案】B

【中文释义】尽管青春期的成熟和发展阶段以有序的顺序发生,但它们的时间安排比如开始的时间和持续的时间却在变化。

【解题分析】13 岁到 16 岁为青春期可分为一前一后两个阶段,虽然每个人都是先入成熟期,后进入发展期,但下句与上句转折,所以他们的时间安排就应是无序的方式,也即没有方向,没有明确规律的变化,B 选项的 vary 恰好表达了这种观点,故正确答案为 B。

【重点词条】**timing** *n*. ①时间选择,时间安排(selection or the ability to select for maximum effect of the precise moment for beginning or doing something)

例 haven't got my~down

②时机掌握(observation and recording such as by a stopwatch of the elapsed time of an act, action, or process)

onset *n*. ①攻击,袭击(attack, assault) 例 withstand the～of the army

　　　　②开始(beginning, commencement) 例 the～of winter

dwindle *v*. 缩小,减少(to become steadily less, shrink)

2.【正确答案】E

【中文释义】很多仍然站立的早期殖民地时期的房屋已经被如此地修改和扩大了,以至于最初的设计不再能分辨出来。

【解题分析】文中的 so...that 结构为一很明显的因果结构,而 that 从句中的 no longer 更具提示作用,no longer 只对过去的动作状态等提出否定,故每见 no longer 应先考虑过去的那个状态或动作,此句中 no longer 当然是否定"过去"的设计,故第一个空格,选 E 的 initial。

【重点词条】**embellish** *v*. ①美化,装饰,修饰(to make beautiful with ornamentation, decorate)

　　　　　　　②润饰(to heighten the attractiveness of by adding ornamental details, enhance) 例 ～ed our account of the trip

3.【正确答案】B

【中文释义】尽管这位代表意图明确地力图打击近期出现的乐观主义情绪,但她及时停住了,差一点就说出这个会议几乎崩溃并且不会产生任何有重要性的结果。

【解题分析】Short of 短语出现在 stopped 这个动词之后,故其为副词短语,含义是"差一点就…"。所以在原句中这个短语一方面表示这位代表没有说出这句措辞过于严厉的话,但另外一方面也表明她一直是在批评这个会议,所以第一个空格应表示她一直力图批评这个会议,也即打击乐观主义情绪,故答案为 B。

【重点词条】**dampen** *v*. ①使扫兴,使沮丧,抑制,降低(to check or diminish the activity or vigor of, deaden) 例 the heat～ed our spirits

　　　　　　②弄湿(to make damp) 例 the shower barely～ed the ground

kindle *v*. ①点燃(to start a fire burning, light)

　　　　②激起(to stir up, arouse) 例 ～interest

4.【正确答案】D

【中文释义】这位老人不应被指责为吝啬他的爱;他对这个小孩的行为就表现了他对她的溺爱。

【解题分析】显然第一个空格应该填贬义词,因为它是 accuse 的内容,只有 A、B、D 选项为贬义,下句的 betray 为"表现","显示"之意。因而第二个空格为他的真实的动作,第一个空格为他被误解的,因而是不应该指责的,与真实动作相反的动作。所以两个空格应为一组反义词,只有 D 正确。

【重点词条】**lavish** *v*. 滥施,浪费(expending or bestowing profusely, prodigal)

spare *v*. ①宽恕,赦免(to forbear to destroy, punish, or harm)

　　　　②节约,吝惜(to use or dispense frugally) 例 don't～the syrup

ration *v*. ①定量供给(to supply with or put on rations)

②节约地使用(to use sparingly)

5. 【正确答案】E

【中文释义】一个领先化学家认为许多科学家对立体化学有困难是因为大量相关的命名是不精确的,因为它结合了一些本应该保持分离的概念。

【解题分析】文句的结构为特殊并列句结构,because 引导的原因从句与 in that 引导的原因从句为一组重复,in that 引导的从句中的空格可以由句子内部推断出来,即空格应填"combine"的反义词这一步尚好判断,可选 D 和 E。重要的是要认识到两个原因从句是并列关系,所以第一空格的信息应来源于第二个原因从句,从而得出结论第一空格应为"不该结合的概念却结合起来的导致的一种状态",这种状态当然就是 E 的 imprecise,而不会是 specialized 和 descriptive。

【重点词条】nomenclature *n*. ①名称(name, designation)

②术语,专门名词(a system or set of terms or symbols esp. in a particular science, discipline, or art)

specialized *adj*. ①专科的(characterized by or exhibiting biological specialization, highly differentiated esp. in a particular direction or for a particular end)

②专门的(designed or fitted for one particular purpose or occupation) 例 ~personnel

interrelated *adj*. 相互关系的,相互关联的(having a mutual or reciprocal relation)

inviolate *adj*. 未受侵犯的,未受亵渎的,纯洁的(not violated or profaned, pure)

6. 【正确答案】E

【中文释义】费用不能被归类为这个工程项目和诸多缺点之中,这个工程开发商的目标能够以给人强烈印象的节约的方式来实现。

【解题分析】尽管上半句的短语 be number among(被归类为,被归结为),被倒装了,从而造成很多同学对上半句理解的失误,但此句的解题并不依赖于此。事实上该句是一个分号句,所以上下句必然重复,上句只谈了一个简单的事物:费用。所以下半句当然只能重复"费用",下半句中出现过的单词都没有这个含义,所以空格必然为"费用"这个含义,五个选项中的 E 表示"费用很少",是费用的直接重复,故可选 E。

【重点词条】be numbered among 被归类,归结为…

7. 【正确答案】D

【中文释义】尽管科学通常被想象成对外部现实的公正无私的探索,但科学家却和其他人没有任何区别:他们是具有情感的人,被包裹在一张由人际社会关系和社会环境所构成的网当中。

【解题分析】本句实际上又是填空中的固定观点句"科学通常被认为是客观公正的,但现在

认为它是主观偏见的"的重复,第一个空格可直接填"客观公正",答案为 B 和
D。B 和 D 的第二个词中 B 的 rational 仍然是客观公正理性之意,故选 D 的
passionate。

【重点词条】**painstaking** *adj*. 勤恳的,煞费苦心的,精心的(taking pains, expending,
　　　　　　　　　showing, or involving diligent care and effort)

　　　　　　passionate *adj*. ①易怒的(easily aroused to anger)

　　　　　　　　　②感情热烈的,情绪激昂的(capable of, affected by, or ex-
　　　　　　　　　pressing intense feeling)

　　　　　　　　　③ 热情的(enthusiastic, ardent)

　　　　　　　　　④多情的,易动情的(swayed by or affected with sexual de-
　　　　　　　　　sire)

　　　　　　fervent *adj*. ①炽热的(very hot, glowing)

　　　　　　　　　②热情的,热诚的,强烈的(exhibiting or marked by great inten-
　　　　　　　　　sity of feeling, zealous) 例 ~prayers

SECTION 24

1. Social scientists have established fairly clear-cut _____ that describe the appropriate behavior of children and adults, but there seems to be _____ about what constitutes appropriate behavior for adolescents.

   (A) functions. . rigidity

   (B) estimates. . indirectness

   (C) norms. . confusion

   (D) regulations. . certainty

   (E) studies. . misapprehension

2. As long as nations cannot themselves accumulate enough physical power to dominate all others, they must depend on _____.

   (A) allies

   (B) resources

   (C) freedom

   (D) education

   (E) self-determination

3. We realized that John was still young and impressionable, but were nevertheless surprised at his _____.

   (A) naivete

   (B) obstinateness

   (C) decisiveness

   (D) ingeniousness

   (E) resolve

4. Although Mount Saint Helens has been more _____ during the last 4,500 years than any other volcano in the coterminous United States, its long dormancy before its recent eruption _____ its violent nature.

   (A) awe-inspiring. . restrained

   (B) gaseous. . confirmed

   (C) explosive. . belied

   (D) familiar. . moderated

   (E) volatile. . suggested

5. Changes of fashion and public taste are often _____ and resistant to analysis, and yet they are among the most _____ gauges of the state of the public's collective consciousness.

(A) transparent. . useful

(B) ephemeral. . sensitive

(C) faddish. . underutilized

(D) arbitrary. . problematic

(E) permanent. . reliable

6. The poet W. H. Auden believed that the greatest poets of his age were <u>almost necessarily irresponsible,</u> that the possession of great gifts ____ the ____ to abuse them.

(A) negates. . temptation

(B) controls. . resolution

(C) engenders. . propensity

(D) tempers. . proclivity

(E) obviates. . inclination

7. The self-important cant of musicologists on record jackets often suggests that true appreciation of the music is an ____ process closed to the uninitiated listener, however enthusiastic.

(A) unreliable

(B) arcane

(C) arrogant

(D) elementary

(E) intuitive

SECTION 24 解答

1.【正确答案】C

【中文释义】社会科学家已经建立了概念相当清晰的描绘儿童和成年人正确行为的行为准则,但是看上去何种行为构成青少年的正确行为却存在混乱。

【解题分析】第一个空格后的分隔结构直接提示了空格中应填一个描述正确行为的事物,当然 C 正确,D 的 regulation 为法律法规之意,这不是由 social scientist 制定的,而应由立法机构制定。E 的 studies 与分隔无关。故正确答案可直接选 C,当然也可以利用上下文的转折关系解题。第二个空格应与上文的 clear-cut 构成反义,同样是 C 的 confusion 最为恰当。

【重点词条】**clear-cut** *adj*. 概念和概念之间界定得很清楚的

misapprehension *n*. 误会,误解(to apprehend wrongly, misunderstand)

2.【正确答案】A

【中文释义】只要国家不能自己积累足够多的军事力量来控制其他国家,他们就必须依赖联盟的方式。

【解题分析】上句的 not 否定的是其后的 themselves,"非自己"的方式就是合作的方式,故选 A。

【重点词条】**ally** *n*. ①同盟国,同盟者

②助手,支持,辅助物

③同类物

3.【正确答案】A

【中文释义】我们认识到琼仍然年轻,易受别人的影响,但是仍然惊讶于他的幼稚。

【解题分析】请注意文句的转折方式,but nevertheless 同时出现时意味着递进转折,所以空格中应填一个比 young and impressionable 程度加深的词,答案为 A 的 naivete。

答案 B 的 obstinateness 与上文构成了对立面转折而不是递进转折。

通常递进转折为：even though, but nevertheless, though…even。

【重点词条】**impressionable** *n*. 易受影响的，敏感的（capable of being easily impressed）

decisiveness *n*. ①决定性（having the power or quality of deciding）

②坚定，果断（resolute, determined）

③确定，明确（unmistakable, unquestionable） 例 a～superiority

resolve *n*. ①决心，决定（fixity of purpose, resoluteness）

②（会议的）正式决定，决议（a legal or official determination, esp. a formal resolution）

4. 【正确答案】C

【中文释义】尽管圣海伦火山在过去的 4500 年中一直比其他美国国境内的火山更加猛烈，但是最近一次爆发之前的长期的休眠却削弱了它的猛烈性质。

【解题分析】下句的空格前后分别为 dormancy 和 violent nature，正好为一组相反事物，故空格动词应该表示"反对""削弱""破坏"等词义，可以候选 A、C 和 D。故下句的含义即为削弱或压抑了猛烈的性质。所以上句的转折应该反过来强调圣海伦火山的 violent nature。第一空格可选 C 的 explosive，表示"猛烈的，爆炸的"。

【重点词条】**coterminous** *adj*. ①有共同边界的，邻接的（having the same or coincident boundaries）例 ～states

②（在时空、范围方面）同样广大的，同始终的（coextensive in scope or duration）例 an experience of life～with the years of his father

belie *v*. ①掩饰，使人对…误解

②证明…为虚假，与…抵触，违背

volatile *adj*. ①易挥发的（readily vaporizable at a relatively low temperature）

②变化无常的，暴躁的（unable to hold the attention fixed because of an inherent lightness or fickleness of disposition, characterized by or subject to rapid or unexpected change）

③短暂的（difficult to capture or hold permanently, evanescent, transitory）

5. 【正确答案】B

【中文释义】时尚和公众口味的改变通常是稍纵即逝的并且难于分析，然而，它们属于最灵敏的衡量公众集体意识状态的标准。

【解题分析】文中的 and yet 表转折，故前文称时尚和公众口味的改变是难于分析的，一种贬义的说法，后文应转而赞美时尚和公众口味，所以第二空格应选褒义词。A、B 和 E 候选。A、B 和 E 的第一个词必须能够与其后的 and resistant to analysis 构成一个小连接，A 为"一目了然"的，故不正确，B 和 E 相比较，当然是 ephemeral 较 permanent 更难于分析，因而选 B。

【重点词条】**collective consciousness** *n*. 集体意识

faddish *adj*. 喜欢赶时髦的，一时流行的（a practice or interest followed for a time with exaggerated zeal, craze)

underutilize *adj*. 未充分加以利用的,浪费使用的(to utilize less than fully or below the potential use)

6.【正确答案】C

【中文释义】诗人 W·H·奥汀认为他那个时代的伟大的诗人几乎必然地不负责任,也就是说拥有伟大的天赋导致滥用天赋的倾向。

【解题分析】文中 believe 的宾语从句有两个,因而这两个宾语从句构成了特殊并列句。这两句应相互重复。the greatest poets 重复下文的 the possession of great gifts, irresponsible 与下文的 to abuse them 重复,所以下句的两个空格应与上句的 were almost necessary 重复,表示一种必然性,五个选项中 C 为正确答案,A、B、D 和 E 正好相反。

【重点词条】**temptation** *n*. ①引诱,诱惑(the act of tempting or the state of being tempted esp. to evil, enticement)

②诱惑物(something tempting, a cause or occasion of enticement)

resolution *n*. ①分解,解析(the act or process of reducing to simpler form, the act of analyzing a complex notion into simpler ones)

②决定(something that is resolved) 例 made a ～ to mend my ways

③决心(firmness of resolve)

④决议,裁决(a formal expression of opinion, will, or intent voted by an official body or assembled group)

temper *v*. ①调和,使缓和(to dilute, qualify, or soften by the addition or influence of something else, moderate) 例 ～justice with mercy

②锻炼(to make stronger and more resilient through hardship, toughen) 例 troops～ed in battle

proclivity *n*. 坏的癖性,倾向(an inclination or predisposition toward something, esp. a strong inherent inclination toward something objectionable)

inclination *n*. ①倾向,爱好,癖好(natural disposition, character, a particular disposition of mind or character, propensity, esp. liking)

例 had little～for housekeeping

②趋向,趋势(an act or the action of bending or inclining)

7.【正确答案】B

【中文释义】磁带封皮上的音乐学家的自负的术语总是暗示着对音乐的真正理解是一个秘不外传的过程,对所有未被传授专业知识的人,不管他有多么热情,都是关闭着的。

【解题分析】空格修饰 process,而 process 之后又直接出现一个分隔,因而可将分隔的内容直接填写到空格中即可, uninitiated 的含义是"未被传授知识的", 对于这些人音乐的大门永远关闭着, 也就是说音乐是只对专业学生敞开了大门, 对外则秘不外传, 答案 B 的 arcane 正好是"秘不外传"之意。它的名词 arcanum 为秘不外传的知识。

【重点词条】**self-important** *adj*. 自负的, 自高自大的

        cant *n*. ①言不由衷之词, 伪善言辞(affected singsong or whining speech)

            ②(下层社会的)黑话(the private language of the underworld)

            ③专业术语, 行话(the phraseology peculiar to a religious class or sect, jargon, a set or stock phrase)

            ④惯用套语(the expression or repetition of conventional or trite opinions or sentiments; esp. the insincere use of pious words)

        uninitiated *adj*. ①未被接纳入会的, 未入门的

            ②外行的, 缺乏某种特定知识和经验的, 不熟悉某种特定情况的(not initiated, inexperienced)

        jacket *n*. (书的)护封, 封面, 唱片套

SECTION 25

1. Many artists believe that successful imitation, far from being symptomatic of a lack of ____, is the first step in learning to be creative.

  (A) elegance

  (B) resolution

  (C) goodness

  (D) originality

  (E) sympathy

2. As serious as she is about the bullfight, she does not allow respect to ____ her sense of whimsy when painting it.

  (A) inspire

  (B) provoke

  (C) suppress

  (D) attack

  (E) satisfy

3. No one is ____ about Stephens; he inspires either uncritical adulation or profound ____

不加鉴别的赞颂

in those who work for him.

  (A) neutral. . antipathy

  (B) infuriated. . aversion

  (C) worried. . anxiety

  (D) enthusiastic. . veneration

  (E) apprehensive. . consternation

4. Before about 1960, virtually all accounts of evolution assumed most adaptation to be a product of selection at the level of populations; recent studies of evolution, however, have found no ____ this ____ view of selection.

  (A) departures from. . . controversial

  (B) basis for. . pervasive

  (C) bias toward. . unchallenged

  (D) precursors of. . innovative

  (E) criticisms of. . renowned

5. The new biological psychiatry does not deny the contributing role of psychological factors

in mental illnesses, but posits that these factors may act as a <u>catalyst</u> on existing physiological conditions and _____ such illnesses.

(A) disguise

(B) impede

(C) constrain

(D) precipitate

(E) consummate

6. During periods of social and cultural stability, many art academies are so firmly controlled by _____ that all real creative work
must be done by the _____.

(A) dogmatists. . disenfranchised

(B) managers. . reactionaries

(C) reformers. . dissatisfied

(D) imposters. . academicians

(E) specialists. . elite

7. The First World War began in a context of
<u>jargon and verbal delicacy</u> and continued in a
cloud of _____ as _____ as language and literature, skillfully used, could make it.

(A) circumlocution. . literal

(B) cliche. . lucid

(C) euphemism. . impenetrable

(D) particularity. . deliberate

(E) subjectivity. . enthralling

SECTION 25 解答

1.【正确答案】D

【中文释义】很多艺术家认为成功的模仿,并不是缺乏创造性的症状,而是学得具有创造性
的第一步。

【解题分析】文中的 far from 与下句构成转折,故空格里应填上 creative 的同义词。答案为
D 的 originality。

【重点词条】**resolution** *n*. ①分解,解析,解决(the act or process of reducing to simpler
form, the act of analyzing a complex notion into simpler
ones)

②决定(something that is resolved) 例 made a~to mend my
ways

③决心(firmness of resolve)

④决议,裁决(a formal expression of opinion, will, or intent
voted by an official body or assembled group)

elegance ①文雅,高尚(refined grace or dignified propriety, urbanity)

②优美(dignified gracefulness or restrained beauty of style, polish)

例 The essay is marked by lucidity, wit, and~.

③简洁(scientific precision, neatness, and simplicity) 例 the~of a
mathematical proof

2.【正确答案】C

【中文释义】尽管她对斗牛很严肃认真,但当她绘制斗牛作品时却不允许尊敬崇拜压制她
的古怪的,异想天开的灵感。

【解题分析】句首的 as serious as 表示了一种让步转折关系,是全句解题的关键。类似的句

子如:As poor as he is, he is honest。或者如:As smart as he is, he made such a silly mistake。转折后下句应表示她绘画时并非 serious 的态度,下句中的 respect 为 serious 态度的一种。而 whimsy 为 serious 的反义词,故应让 whimsy 占主体地位,这样整体上才能表现出 whimsy,而非 serious 的态度,故选答案 C。

【重点词条】**whimsy** *n.* ①怪念头,离奇的想法(whim, caprice)

②心血来潮,随心所欲(the quality or state of being whimsical or fanciful) 例 The designer's new line showed a touch of ～.

suppress *v.* ①压制(to put down by authority or force, subdue)

②禁止,查禁(to keep from public knowledge, to keep secret, to stop or prohibit the publication or revelation of)

3.【正确答案】A

【中文释义】没有人对史蒂汶的态度是客观的;他在那些为他工作的人之间激发起了或者是不加鉴别的赞美,或者是深深的厌恶。

【解题分析】分号下半句中的 either…or… 连接一组反义词,所以第二个空格应填 adulation 的反义词,可以候选 A 和 B。再由分号句上下文重复的观点可知,既然大家对他或是极端的赞美或是深深的厌恶,都是极端的态度,因而上句表达为没有人对他持中性客观的态度,选 A。

【重点词条】**uncritical** *adj.* ①不加批评的,不做批判的(not critical, lacking in discrimination)

②不加鉴别的(showing lack or improper use of critical standards or procedures)

infuriate *v.* 激怒(to make furious)

furious *adj.* ①狂暴的,狂怒的(exhibiting or goaded by anger, indicative of or proceeding from anger)

②猛烈的(giving a stormy or turbulent appearance) 例 ～ bursts of flame

apprehensive *adj.* ①善于领会的,能理解的(capable of apprehending or quick to do so, discerning)

②忧虑的,担心的,疑惧的(viewing the future with anxiety or alarm)

consternation *n.* 惊恐,惊愕(amazement or dismay that hinders or throws into confusion) 例 The two boys stared at each other in ～, and neither knew what to do.

4.【正确答案】B

【中文释义】在 1960 年之前,几乎所有关于演变的文章都假设大多数的适应是在种群水平上选择的结果;最近的关于演变的研究却没有发现这个普遍的进化观的事实基础。

【解题分析】句首的时间状语就已明确提示该句应用时间提示型来解题,果然分号下半句的时间为 recent。下半句的 this ____ view of selection 显然只能指上半句的观点,故现在的研究应反对、驳斥之,所以第一个空格先选,应表示对其后的观点的驳斥,只有 B 正确。并且 B 答案的第二个词 pervasive 重复了上文的 virtually all。

【重点词条】**virtually** *adv.* ①差不多(almost entirely, nearly)

②事实上,实际上(for all practical purposes) 例 ~unknown

account *n.* ①记述,描述,报道

②解释

③理由,根据

renowned *adj.* 有名的(having renown, celebrated)

5. 【正确答案】D

【中文释义】新的生物的精神病疗法并不否认精神病当中心理因素确实起作用,但指出这些因素可能起一种催化剂的作用,作用在现存的生理条件上,并且加速这些疾病。

【解题分析】空格处于 and 构成的小连接中,简化之后实际上为:act as a catalyst and such illness。故空格中显然应填"加速",答案为 D。

【重点词条】**contribute** *v.* ①资助(to give a part to a common fund or store)

②有助于,促成(to play a significant part in bringing about an end or result)

③投稿(to submit articles to a publication)

posit *v.* ①安置,安排(to dispose or set firmly, fix)

②假定,设想(to assume or affirm the existence of, postulate)

③建议(to propose as an explanation, suggest)

precipitate *v.* ①使突如其来地发生,促使…加快

②使陡然下降或跌落

consummate *v.* ①完成,实现

②使完美无缺,使完美

6. 【正确答案】A

【中文释义】在社会和文化的稳定期间,许多艺术学院如此被教条主义者牢牢地控制着以致于所有真正具有创造性的工作都必须被非主流艺术家来完成。

【解题分析】由句首状语可知 C 不对,D 选项又十分荒谬。如果稍加分析又可知 B 也不对,因为任何时候都是被管理人员控制一个机构,这种无明确含义的词一般都不会成为答案。比如存在 vary, increase 和 decrease 三个选项时,可立刻排除 vary 或者存在 character, defect, highlight 时先排除 character。此时只剩下 A 和 E,再由 so…that…因果关系来判断。A 为正确答案,因为教条主义者控制艺术学院,所以他们是主流人物,而教条主义者的定义即为不能干创造性的工作,所以如果主流人物不能干创造性工作的话,那么就只能由非主流艺术家来完成了,A 的 disenfranchised 本义是"被剥夺了选举权的",引申即为"非主流

的"。而 E 答案的前后却无任何因果关系,故选答案 A。

【重点词条】disenfranchise *v.* 剥夺…的公民权(选举权),剥夺…的权利,终止…的特许
　　　　　　　　　　 权(disfranchise, to deprive of a franchise, of a legal right,
　　　　　　　　　　 or of some privilege or immunity; esp. to deprive of the
　　　　　　　　　　 right to vote)

　　　　　academician *n.* ①院士(a member of an academy for promoting science, art,
　　　　　　　　　　　 or literatur)

　　　　　　　　　　　②墨守成规的学究(a follower of an artistic or philosophical
　　　　　　　　　　　 tradition or a promoter of its ideas)

　　　　　　　　　　　③学者(academic)

　　　　　elite *n.* ①出类拔萃的人物,精英
　　　　　　　　　　②(总称)上层掌权人物,实力集团

7.【正确答案】C

【中文释义】第一次世界大战开始于一个充满专业术语和精微的语言的环境中,并且继续
　　　　　 发展在一个委婉精致的话语环境中,这些委婉语难于理解到了语言文字在熟
　　　　　 练运用的情况下所可能制造出来的极限。

【解题分析】文中的 continue 又是一典型考法,请参阅 SECTION 17 第 3 题的解答。第一空
　　　　　 格中应填上文的 jargon and verbal delicacy,故正确答案为 C 的 euphemism。
　　　　　 需要进一步指出文中的 as…as… 结构又是一特殊的 as…as… 结构,第一个
　　　　　 as 之后为形容词 impenetrable,而第二个 as 之后却为一个整句:language and
　　　　　 literature could make it。所以此时 as…as… 并非小连接结构,连接的双方并
　　　　　 无同义词关系,此句中第二个 as 短语实际上起到了对第一个 as 之后的形容词
　　　　　 的修饰作用,强调它是语言文字中最难懂的那一种。
　　　　　 请大家参阅 SECTION 18 第 3 题中的对 as…as… 的解释,比较这两种特殊的
　　　　　 as…as… 结构的用法。两者都是不对称结构,都不是小连接,因为第二个 as
　　　　　 之后为一个句子。两者不同之处在于本句的第二个 as 结构为第一个 as 引导
　　　　　 的形容词的修饰结构。而 SECTION 18 中的那个 as…as… 结构却为一种并
　　　　　 列结构,翻译为"既…又…"。区分这两种 as…as… 结构的方法是看第二个 as
　　　　　 引导的句子中有没有出现:can may could might permit 等几个表可能性的词,
　　　　　 如果有则与本文的用法相同,如果没有则与 SECTION 18 中的那道题用法相
　　　　　 同。请参阅 SECTION 18 的第 3 题的解答。事实上,我们可以一言以蔽之,除
　　　　　 非 as…as… 为小连接,否则解题时根本不需要理解它,这样做就避开了对
　　　　　 as…as… 的复杂用法的分析。

【重点词条】jargon *n.* ①胡言乱语(confused unintelligible language)

　　　　　　　　　　②莫名其妙的话(a strange, outlandish, or barbarous language or di-
　　　　　　　　　　 alect)

　　　　　　　　　　③行话(the technical terminology or characteristic idiom of a special
　　　　　　　　　　 activity or group)

　　　　　particularity *n.* ①特殊性,特征(a minute detail, particular, an individual characteristic, peculiarity; singularity)

②个性,癖性(the quality or state of being particular as distinguished from universal)

③详尽,详细,精细(attentiveness to detail, exactness)

deliberate *adj*. ①慎重的,深思熟虑的(characterized by or resulting from careful and thorough consideration) 例 a~decision

②故意的,蓄意的(characterized by awareness of the consequences) 例 ~falsehood

③从容的,悠闲的(slow, unhurried, and steady as though allowing time for decision on each individual action involved) 例 a~pace

enthralling *adj*. 迷人的,吸引人的(to hold spellbound, charm)

SECTION 26

1. Because no comprehensive ____ exist regarding personal reading practices, we do not know, for example, the greatest number of books read in an individual lifetime.
   - (A) records
   - (B) instincts
   - (C) remedies
   - (D) proposals
   - (E) commercials

2. In our corporation there is a ____ between male and female ____ because 73 percent of the men and 34 percent of the women polled believe that our company provides equal compensation to men and women.
   - (A) contrast. . stereotypes
   - (B) difference. . perceptions
   - (C) variation. . salaries
   - (D) resemblance. . employees
   - (E) similarity. . aspirations

3. The wonder of De Quincey is that although opium dominated his life, it never ____ him; indeed, he turned its use to ____ when

he published the story of its influence in the London Magazine.
   - (A) overcame. . altruism 无私主义
   - (B) intimidated. . triumph
   - (C) distressed. . pleasure
   - (D) conquered. . gain
   - (E) released. . necessity

4. The reduction of noise has been ____ in terms of ____ its sources, but the alternative of canceling noise out by adding sound with the opposite wave pattern may be more useful in practice.
   - (A) justified. . diffusing
   - (B) accomplished. . tracking
   - (C) conceived. . concealing
   - (D) explained. . isolating
   - (E) approached. . eliminating

5. While Parker is very outspoken on issues she cares about, she is not ____; she concedes the ____ of opposing arguments when they expose weaknesses inherent in her own.
   - (A) fickle. . validity
   易变的

(B) arrogant. . restraint

(C) fanatical. . strength

(D) congenial. . incompatibility

(E) unyielding. . speciousness

6. Hampshire's assertions, far from showing that we can ＿＿ the ancient puzzles about objectivity, reveal the issue to be even more ＿＿ than we had thought.

(A) adapt. . pressing

(B) dismiss. . relevant

(C) rediscover. . unconventional

(D) admire. . elusive

(E) appreciate. . interesting

7. Usually the first to spot data that were inconsistent with other findings, in this particular experiment she let a number of ＿＿ results slip by.

(A) inaccurate

(B) verifiable

(C) redundant

(D) salient

(E) anomalous

SECTION 26 解答

1. 【正确答案】A

【中文释义】因为没有关于人们阅读活动的全面的记录,所以我们不知道,比如,在一个人一生中所读的书的最大数目。

【解题分析】本题甚为简单,我们不知道这个最大数,当然是因为没有这个最大数。五个选项中能提供人一生读书最大数目的只有 A 的 records,它是记录所读书数目的文件,由于它不存在,我们当然无从知晓最大的数字究竟是多少,答案为 A。

【重点词条】**instinct** *n*. ①天资(a natural or inherent aptitude, impulse, or capacity)

例 had an～for the right word

②直觉,天性,本能(a largely inheritable and unalterable tendency of an organism to make a complex and specific response to environmental stimuli without involving reason)

commercial *n*. ①商业广告

②宣传,吹嘘

2. 【正确答案】B

【中文释义】在我们公司里,男性和女性的理解存在着差异,因为投票的 73% 的男性和投票的 34% 的女性认为我们的公司给男性和女性提供了平等的工资报酬。

【解题分析】由原因从句可知男性中有大多数人认为工资是平等的,但女性中只有少部分人持有这一观点,故男性和女性之间的分歧是很明显的。A、B、C、的第一个词可以候选。D 和 E 认为男性和女性之间是类似的关系,显然错。A 的第二个词 stereotype 不符句意。关键问题是 B 和 C 第二词的区分。在西方社会女士很容易获得工作机会,在生活中也享受极大的便宜,因为"lady first"是西方社会的基本行为准则。但在另外一方面,女性也很难获得重大的升迁机会,很难掌握权力。在这种局面下女性的工资水准普遍低于男性。但有些人认为,女性干的工作比较轻松,承担的责任也相对较少,故工资略低也是正常的,公平的。但另外一些人认为工资的低就反应出了男女的不平等。所以此句应选 B。
主要是理解的不平等。细读原句会发现 C 选项是非常荒谬的。因为男女工资
方面是否有差异只需简单地比较一下薪金数字即可,而不必劳师动众地全公
司选举表决,更不可能出现薪金数字比较时大多数男性和大多数女性不一致
的场面,试想,如果男性平均工资 10000 元,女性平均工资 6000 元,有可能出
现出现全公司表决,并且对 10000 和 6000 孰大孰小众说纷芸的奇特场面吗?

【重点词条】**stereotype** *n*. ①铅版印刷(a plate cast from a printing surface)

②陈规,老套,刻板模式(something conforming to a fixed or general pattern; esp. a standardized mental picture that is held in common by members of a group and that represents an oversimplified opinion, prejudiced attitude, or uncritical judgment)

aspiration *n*. ①呼吸(audible breath that accompanies or comprises a speech sound)

②强烈的愿望,抱负(a strong desire to achieve something high or great)

③志向(an object of such desire)

3.【正确答案】D

【中文释义】德·昆西的奇迹是尽管鸦片充满了他的生活,但却从来没有征服他;事实上,他在"London Magazine"发表关于鸦片的药效的文章的时候,就已经将它的用途转到益处上去了。

【解题分析】分号后的 turn to 是一常见的表对立面转折的短语,用法与 shift from...to, oscillate between...and... 相同。鸦片的用途无非是好坏两方面,由其后的 when 引导从句可知,此句中当然要将它的用途转到好的方面,故空格中应填"益处"、"好处"、"好的用途",只有 D 的 gain 为这一词义,故选 D。

【重点词条】**influence** *n*. 药效

release *v*. ①释放,解除(to set free from restraint, confinement, or servitude) 例 ~ hostages／~ pent-up emotions／~ the brakes

②解放(to relieve from something that confines, burdens, or oppresses) 例 She was released from her promise.

③让渡(to give up in favor of another, relinquish) 例 ~ a claim to property

④准予发表(to give permission for publication, performance, exhibition, or sale of; to make available to the public) 例 The commission released its findings. ／~ a new movie

intimidate *v*. 恫吓,恐吓,威胁(to make timid or fearful, frighten; esp. to compel or deter by or as if by threats)

4.【正确答案】E

【中文释义】消除噪音可以用消除声源的方法实现,但另外一种消除噪音的方法,也即加上一个具有相对波形的声音的方法,可能在实践中更加有效。

【解题分析】请注意 in terms of 这个短语,它等同于 by,连接一组手段和目的的关系,在此句中,in terms of 重复了下文的 by,因而第二个空格应填上"adding sound"的反义词,从而选 E 的 eliminating。

【重点词条】diffuse *v.* ①扩散,弥漫(being at once verbose and ill-organized)

②传播,普及(not concentrated or localized) 例 ~sclerosis

track *v.* ①跟踪(to follow the tracks or traces of, trail)

②追踪(to search for by following evidence until found) 例 ~down the source

conceive *v.* ①怀胎(to become pregnant with young)

②创立(to cause to begin, originate)

③构想出,设想(to form a conception of, imagine)

④懂得,理解(to apprehend by reason or imagination, understand)

⑤认为(to be of the opinion)

⑥怀有,体验到

⑦表达

5.【正确答案】C

【中文释义】尽管帕克对于自己喜欢的观点总是非常直言不讳,但她并不固执;当对立面观点暴露出她自己观点内在的缺陷时,她承认对立面观点的正确性。

【解题分析】第二个空格应填 weakness 的反义词,因为自己的观点错了,当然就可推知对立面观点正确。所以第二个空格可以候选 A、C。再由分号句上下重复可知上文第一个空格应与下文的"知错就改,承认错误"的做法相反,应该为"不承认错误,死不悔改",这就是顽固的意思,也即 C 答案的 fanatical,它的含义是"狂热的,固执的"。

【重点词条】outspoken *adj.* ①直言的,坦率的(direct and open in speech or expression, frank) 例 ~in his criticism

②毫无保留地表示的(spoken or expressed without reserve) 例 his~advocacy of gun control

fickle *adj.* 易变的,无常的(marked by lack of steadfastness, constancy, or stability, given to erratic changeableness)

fanatical *adj.* 狂热的,盲信的,入迷的,盲目热衷的(marked by excessive enthusiasm and often intense uncritical devotion) 例 They're~about politics.

unyielding *adj.* ①不易弯曲的,坚挺的(characterized by lack of softness or flexibility)

②坚定的,顽强的(characterized by firmness or obduracy)

incompatibility *n.* ①不相容性(the quality or state of being incompatible)

②无法共存(mutually antagonistic things or qualities)

6. 【正确答案】B

   【中文释义】罕布什尔的断论,并不是说明我们可以不重视这个自古以来的关于客观公正性的疑惑,反而说明这个问题比我们曾经认为的更加重要。

   【解题分析】原句的逻辑关系非常简单,far from showing 与主干的 reveal 显然是一组反义动词,因而两个空格就应表示对 the issue 的完全相反的态度。第一个空格是动词,第二个空格却是形容词,这两者如何构成反义词呢? 这种词性不同却需构成同反义词的情况非常多,在本书中同反义词的概念与通常的概念是有区别的,它忽略了词性的差别。当词性不同却需要判断是否两个词为同反义词时,我们应该将所有非形容词性的词转化为形容词去考虑,比如本题的选项 A 的 adapt 可转换成形容词 adaptable 去考虑,adaptable 与第二选项 pressing 并不构成反义词,故 A 不正确。B 的第一选项动词 dismiss 可转化为 unimportant 去考虑,因为"忽略"这个动作所体现出的态度正好就是认为某物"不重要",unimportant 与第二选项 relevant 构成了反义词,故 B 正确,对于选项 C、D 和 E,请同学们用同样的思路去分析。

   这种不同词性的词构成同义词或反义词的现象在填空中比比皆是,大家一定要掌握好这个思路。

   【重点词条】**pressing** *adj*. ①紧迫的,迫切的

   ②热切的,坚持的

   unconventional *adj*. ①不依惯例的,非常规的(not conventional)

   ②不符习俗的(not bound by or in accordance with convention)

   ③异常的(being out of the ordinary)

7. 【正确答案】E

   【中文释义】通常她总是第一个来发现与其他发现结果不一致的数据,在这个独特的实验中她却让一些反常的数据从眼皮底下溜走了。

   【解题分析】上下两句明显是时间对比:usually 和 in this particular experiment。所以上下两句的情况也应相反,上句发现了"不一致"的数据,下句应没有发现"不一致"的数据,所以空格应填"不一致的",答案为 E 的 anomalous,即"与其他事物不一致的"。

   【重点词条】**spot** *v*. ①玷污,玷辱(to stain the character or reputation of, disgrace)

   ②准确地定位(to locate or identify by a spot)

   ③认出,发现(to single out, identify; esp. to note as a known criminal or a suspicious person detect, notice) 例 ~a mistake

   let something slip by   让…从眼皮下滑走

   salient *adj*. ①跳跃的(moving by leaps or springs, jumping)

   ②向上喷的(jetting upward) 例 a~fountain

   ③突出的,显著的(standing out conspicuously, prominent; esp. of

notable significance) 例 similar to...prohibition, but there are a couple of~differences

redundant *adj* . ①多余的,过剩的(exceeding what is necessary or normal, superfluous)

②累赘的,冗长的(characterized by or containing an excess; using more words than necessary)

SECTION 27

1. Psychology has slowly evolved into an ____ scientific discipline that now functions autonomously with the same privileges and responsibilities as other sciences.

(A) independent

(B) unusual

(C) outmoded

(D) uncontrolled

(E) inactive

2. A major goal of law, to deter potential criminals by punishing wrongdoers, is not served when the penalty is so seldom invoked that it ____ to be a ____ threat.

(A) tends. . serious

(B) appears. . real

(C) ceases. . credible

(D) fails. . deceptive

(E) seems. . coercive

3. When people are happy, they tend to give ____ interpretations of events they witness: the eye of the beholder is ____ by the emotions of the beholder.

(A) charitable. . colored

(B) elaborate. . disquieted

(C) conscientious. . deceived

(D) vague. . sharpened

(E) coherent. . confused

4. Even those who disagreed with Carmen's views rarely faulted her for expressing them, for the positions she took were as ____ as they were controversial.

(A) complicated

(B) political

(C) subjective

(D) commonplace

(E) thoughtful

5. New research on technology and public policy focuses on how seemingly ____ design features, generally overlooked in most analyses of public works projects or industrial machinery, actually ____ social choices of profound significance.

(A) insignificant. . mask

(B) inexpensive. . produce

(C) innovative. . represent

(D) ingenious. . permit

(E) inopportune. . hasten

6. Paradoxically, Robinson's excessive denials of the worth of early works of science fiction suggest that she has become quite ____ them.

(A) reflective about

(B) enamored of

(C) skeptical of

(D) encouraged by

(E) offended by

7. Cezanne's delicate watercolor sketches often served as ____ of a subject, a way of gathering fuller knowledge before the artist's final engagement of the subject in an oil painting.

(A) an abstraction
(B) an enhancement
(C) a synthesis
(D) a reconnaissance
(E) a transcription

SECTION 27 解答

1.【正确答案】A
   【中文释义】心理学已经缓慢地发展成为一门独立的科学学科,这门学科现在以与其他学科一样的权利和责任在独立自主地运作。
   【解题分析】空格应填形容词修饰名词,而名词 scientific discipline 之后又出现了定语从句分隔,故空格中填上定语从句表达的内容即可,应填上 autonomously 的同义词,答案为 A。
   【重点词条】**autonomous** *adj*. ①自治的(having the right or power of self-government)
   ②独立自主的(undertaken or carried on without outside control, self-contained) 例 an~school system
   ③独立存在的(existing or capable of existing independently)
   ④自发的(responding, reacting, or developing independently of the whole) 例 an~growth
   outmoded *adj*. 过时了的,废弃了的(not being in style, no longer acceptable, current, or usable) 例 ~customs

2.【正确答案】C
   【中文释义】法律的主要目标,即通过惩罚犯人来威慑潜在犯罪分子的目的,并没有起作用,因为这些惩罚很少实施以至于法律不能成为一个可信任的威胁力量。
   【解题分析】法律主要目标 deter(威慑)未起作用,也即未成为一个威慑,这就应该是 when 从句所描写的内容,尤其是每一个空格前的 it 指代法律,第二空格后的 threat 与 deter 直接相关,可见此处是重复上句,五个选项中,只有 C 表示法律没有成为一个威慑的力量,故选 C。
   【重点词条】**deter** *v*. ①威慑,阻拦,使不敢(to turn aside, discourage, or prevent from acting)
   ②禁止(inhibit)
   invoke *v*. ①乞灵于(to appeal to or cite as authority)
   ②乞求神灵保佑(to call forth by incantation, conjure)
   ③恳(乞)求(to make an earnest request for, solicit)
   ④行使,实行(to put into effect or operation, implement)
   ⑤导致,引起(bring about, cause)

cease *v*. 停止,结束(to cause to come to an end esp. gradually, no longer continue)

3. 【正确答案】A

【中文释义】当人们高兴的时候,他们倾向于给他们目击到的事件以欢快的解释:眼睛总是被它的拥有者的情绪所干扰。

【解题分析】由句首状语修饰主句这个简单的判断即可知,第一个空格应为 happy 的同义词,只有 A 的 charitable 正确。

【重点词条】**charitable** *adj*. ①慈悲的,慈悲为怀的(full of love for and goodwill toward others, benevolent)
②宽厚的(merciful or kind in judging others, lenient)

elaborate *adj*. ①煞费苦心的(planned or carried out with great care) 例 took ~precautions
②复杂的,精心制作的,详尽阐述的(marked by complexity, fullness of detail, or ornateness) 例 ~prose

conscientious *adj*. ①按良心办事的(governed by or conforming to the dictates of conscience, scrupulous) 例 a~public servant
②认真的,全神贯注的(meticulous, careful) 例 a~listener

disquiet *v*. 打搅,使忧虑,使烦恼(to take away the peace or tranquillity of, disturb, alarm)

4. 【正确答案】E

【中文释义】即使是那些不同意卡门观点的人也很少因为她表达了这些观点而指责她,因为她的观点是既具有思辨性又没有定论的。

【解题分析】此句中的 as...as...结构的用法与 SECTION 18 的第 3 题是同样的,请参阅相应讲解。本题的推理方向并不是由 controversial 推空格,而应是分两条线路,由 they were controversial 可解释上句的结果,对于"没有定论的"理论学说,即使对方不赞同一个观点,也只能各自保留意见,不会相互指责对方是错的;另外一条线路是由空格这个性质也应能推出上文的结果——即使对方不同意,也不会指责你的观点为错。五个选项中 E 的 thoughtful 可以构成这个结果的解释,所谓 thoughtful 即为"富有思辨色彩的",如"先有鸡还是先有鸡蛋"这样的课题,任何结论都似是而非,但永远都不会有最终正确答案。有相当一部分同学误选 A 的 complicated,但我们的生活中,即使是一个复杂的问题,只要有标准答案存在,那么解答错了也照样会遭到指责。所以 A 并不正确。

【重点词条】**positions** *n*. 立场,观点

controversial *adj*. ①争论的,成问题的(of, relating to, or arousing controversy)
②被议论的(given to controversy, disputatious)

thoughtful *adj*. ①沉思的,思考的(absorbed in thought, meditative, characterized by careful reasoned thinking

②经过缜密思考的(given to or chosen or made with heedful anticipation of the needs and wants of others)

5. 【正确答案】A

【中文释义】对技术和公共政策的新的研究着重强调那些看上去不重要的设计特征,通常会在大多数对公共工程项目或工业机械的分析中被忽略掉的设计特征,是如何实际上背后代表着具有深刻意义的社会选择的。

【解题分析】第一个空格修饰名词,而其后的分析结构直接提供了答案,第一空格应填"generally overlooked"的同义词,五个选项中 A 的 insignificant 为正确答案,因为"被忽略的"就是"不受重视的"也即 insignificant。当然全句的含义比较晦涩,在工业产品设计中,外形,功能等设计都是重要的设计,但另外有一些很小的设计却更能抓住市场人心,也即"背后代表了深刻的社会选择",如有一种小闹钟将声音变成了公鸡打鸣的声音,虽然这一设计工艺非常简单,但却由于其迎合了城市人的回归自然的社会选择而大受欢迎,所以现在的设计研究不再是简单地研究物理功能和外形。更强调那些表面不重要,但却渗透了文化,心理和价值取向的,能带来极大市场的设计,这就是本句的含义。

【重点词条】**mask** v. ①遮盖(to take part in a masquerade)

②掩饰,伪装(to disguise one's true character or intentions)

6. 【正确答案】B

【中文释义】自相矛盾的是,鲁宾逊对早期科幻作品的过度的否定就说明了她对这些作品非常的喜爱。

【解题分析】由句首的 paradoxically 即可知下句会出现一组反义词,空格填鲁宾逊对科幻作品的态度,上文表达过的一种态度为 excessive denials 所以此处应填它的反义词,答案为 B。

【重点词条】**reflective** adj. ①反射的,反映的(capable of reflecting light, images, or sound waves)

②思考的,沉思的(marked by reflection, thoughtful, deliberative)

enamor v. ①使倾心,使喜爱(to inflame with love)

②使迷恋(fascinate)

offend v. ①冒犯,得罪(to transgress the moral or divine law, sin) 例 If it be a sin to covet honor, I am the most～ing soul alive.

②触犯法律,犯错(to violate a law or rule, do wrong) 例 ～against the law

③使厌恶作呕(to cause difficulty, discomfort, or injury) 例 took off his shoe and removed the～ing pebble

7. 【正确答案】D

【中文释义】塞尚精致的水彩画练习作品常起到了对一个主题调查勘探的作用,也就是一个方法,在该艺术家最终将这个主题表现在油画中之前来收集更全面的信息。

【解题分析】空格后的分隔成分"a way of..."一段是给空格提供答案的,空格中直接填上
　　　　　　"gathering further knowledge"这样的信息即可。答案为 D 的 reconnaissance。

【重点词条】**sketch** *n*. ①草图(a rough drawing representing the chief features of an object
　　　　　　　　　　or scene and often made as a preliminary study)

②初稿(a tentative draft as for a literary work)

③素描,速写(a brief description such as of a person or outline)

④概述,纲要(a short literary composition somewhat resembling the
short story and the essay but intentionally slight in treatment, discursive in style, and familiar in tone)

reconnaissance *n*. 侦察,预先调查,勘察,草测(a preliminary survey to gain
information; esp. an exploratory military survey of enemy
territory)

SECTION 28

1. Though it would be ＿＿＿ to expect Barnard
to have worked out all of the limitations of
his experiment, he must be ＿＿＿ for his ne-
glect of quantitative analysis.
   (A) unjust..pardoned
   (B) impudent..dismissed
   (C) unrealistic..criticized
   (D) pointless..examined
   (E) inexcusable..recognized

2. The hierarchy of medical occupations is in
many ways a ＿＿＿ system; its strata remain
＿＿＿ and the practitioners in them have very
little vertical mobility.
   (A) health..skilled
   (B) delivery..basic
   (C) regimental..flexible
   (D) training..inferior
   (E) caste..intact

3. Noting the murder victim's flaccid muscula-
ture and pearlike figure, she deduced that
the unfortunate fellow had earned his living

in some ＿＿＿ occupation.
   (A) treacherous
   (B) prestigious
   (C) ill-paying
   (D) illegitimate
   (E) sedentary

4. In Germany her startling powers as a novel-
ist are widely ＿＿＿, but she is almost un-
known in the English-speaking world be-
cause of the difficulties of ＿＿＿ her eccentric
prose.
   (A) ignored..editing
   (B) admired..translating
   (C) espoused..revealing
   (D) obscured..comprehending
   (E) dispersed..transcribing

5. Liberty is not easy, but far better to be an
＿＿＿ fox, hungry and threatened on its hill,
than a ＿＿＿ canary, safe and secure in its
cage.
   (A) unfriendly..fragile

(B) aging. . young

(C) angry. . content

(D) imperious. . lethargic

(E) unfettered. . well-fed

6. Remelting old metal cans rather than making primary aluminum from bauxite ore shipped from overseas saves producers millions of dollars in ＿＿ and production costs.

(A) distribution

(B) salvage

(C) storage

(D) procurement

(E) research

7. Johnson never ＿＿ to ignore the standards of decent conduct mandated by company policy if ＿＿ compliance with instructions from his superiors enabled him to do so, whatever the effects on his subordinates.

(A) deigned. . tacit

(B) attempted. . halfhearted

(C) intended. . direct

(D) scrupled. . literal

(E) wished. . feigned

SECTION 28 解答

1.【正确答案】C

【中文释义】尽管期待勃纳德解决他实验的所有缺陷是不现实的,但他必须因为他忽略了数量分析而受到批评。

【解题分析】第二个空格处于一个直接的因果句中,可选 B 和 C,再由上下句的转折关系可知 C 正确。

【重点词条】work out ①制定(计划)

②解决(问题)

③理解、弄懂

impudent adj. ①放肆无礼的(lacking modesty)

②厚颜无耻的(marked by contemptuous or cocky boldness or disregard of others, insolent)

pointless adj. ①无意义的(devoid of meaning, senseless) 例 a～remark

②不得要领的,没有目的的(devoid of effectiveness, flat)

例 ～attempts to be funny

inexcusable adj. 无法辩解的,不可原谅的,不可宽恕的(being without excuse or justification)

2.【正确答案】E

【中文释义】医疗职业的等级制度在许多方面是一个等级制度;它的各个阶层保持不动并且各阶层的从业人员只有很少的升降流动性。

【解题分析】上半句主干简化后即为"The hierarchy is a ＿＿ system"。当然选 E 的 caste,一个无聊的直接重复而已。

【重点词条】caste n. ①种姓制度(one of the hereditary social classes in Hinduism that restrict the occupation of their members and their association with the members of other castes)

②等级地位(a division of society based on differences of wealth, inherited rank or privilege, profession, or occupation)

③社会阶级制度(a system of rigid social stratification characterized by hereditary status, endogamy, and social barriers sanctioned by custom, law, or religion)

regimental *adj.* ①军团的(of or relating to a regiment)

②独裁的,专断的(authoritative, dictatorial)

inferior *adj.* ①(地位、等级等)低等的,下级的(situated lower down, lower)

②(质量等)差的,次的,较差的(of low or lower degree or rank, of poor quality, mediocre)

③不重要的(of little or less importance, value, or merit) 例 always felt ~ to his older brother

3.【正确答案】E

【中文释义】注意到了这个谋杀案牺牲者的松软的肌肉组织和梨一样的体型,她推断这个不幸的小伙子在某种久坐不动的职业中谋生。

【解题分析】此句甚为简单,并且文中的 pearlike figure 令人忍俊不住,这是一个腹部脂肪堆积臀部肥大的人,造成这体型的职业往往是 E 的 sedentary。

【重点词条】**ill-paying** *adj.* 收入低微的

sedentary *adj.* ①定栖的,静止的(not migratory, settled) 例 ~ birds

②坐着的,不活动的(doing or requiring much sitting)

4.【正确答案】B

【中文释义】在德国她的令人叹为观止的小说家的才能受到广泛地崇拜,但是她在英语世界国家中几乎是不为人所知的,因为翻译她古怪的文句非常困难。

【解题分析】由转折关系可知第一空格应与下文的 unknown 构成反义词,可选 B 和 C。由两个状语的对比,in Germany 和 in the English-speaking world 的对比,可知造成差别的原因是语言的差异,所以第二个空格中填 B 的 translating。有些同学误选 C 的 revealing。如果是由于揭示她的古怪的文句的含义比较困难,那么在英语国家和在德语国家就应该都难于揭示其文句的含义就不会造成原句中的差异了。也有同学选 E 的 disperse,如果主语是 reputation 的话,选 disperse 表声誉传播了。但此句的主语为 power,选 disperse 的含义为"才能很分散",正确答案为 B。

【重点词条】**startling** *adj.* 令人惊吓的,使人惊跳的,惊人的(causing momentary fright, surprise, or astonishment)

disperse *v.* ①驱散(to cause to break up) 例 police dispersed the crowd

②使分散(to cause to become spread widely)

③散发,传播(to spread or distribute from a fixed or constant source, disseminate)

5.【正确答案】E

　【中文释义】自由并不容易,但更应该做一个不受束缚的狐狸,在山头上又饥饿又受到威胁,也强胜于做一人喂得饱饱的金丝雀,在笼子里很安全并且有物质保障。

　【解题分析】全句为一转折结构,上半句否定 liberty。所以下半句应肯定 liberty。下句肯定,推崇的显然是第一个空格,所以第一个空格应为 liberty 的同义词,答案为 E。

　【重点词条】**secure** *adj*. ①安心的,无虑的(unwisely free from fear or distrust, overconfident, easy in mind, confident, assured in opinion or expectation, having no doubt)

　　　　　　　　②安全的(free from danger, free from risk of loss)

　　　　　　　　③可靠的,稳固的(trustworthy, dependable) 例 ～foundation

　　　　imperious *adj*. ①专横的,老爷式的,傲慢的(befitting or characteristic of one of eminent rank or attainments, commanding, dominant) 例 an～manner

　　　　　　　　②迫切的,紧急的(intensely compelling, urgent) 例 the～problems of the new age

　　　　lethargic *adj*. ①昏睡的,没精打采的,呆滞的,懒散的(of, relating to, or characterized by lethargy, sluggish)

　　　　　　　　②冷漠无情的,漠不关心的(indifferent, apathetic)

6.【正确答案】D

　【中文释义】熔化旧的金属罐头而不是利用海外运回的铝土矿石来提炼原铝,这种做法节约了生产厂商成千上万的采购和生产费用。

　【解题分析】该句的谓语动词是 save,之前均为主语,由于句子结构不均衡造成了众多考生分不清句子结构,事实上,只要分清结构后,由答案必须重复这个观点即可知:production cost 重复上文的 making primary aluminum,空格就只能对应于上文的 shipped from overseas,故空格里可直接选 D,意为采购费用。A 为零售费用,B 为打捞费用,C 为仓储费用,E 为研究费用。

　【重点词条】**procure** *v*. ①取得,获得(to get possession of, obtain by particular care and effort)

　　　　　　　　②拉皮条,作淫媒(to get and make available for promiscuous sexual intercourse)

　　　　　　　　③实现,引起(bring about, achieve)

7.【正确答案】D

　【中文释义】琼森肆无忌惮地违反由公司政策颁布的行为准则,条件是遵守上级的指令可以使他这样做,而不管对他的下级的影响。

　【解题分析】第二个空格填一词修饰下级对上级的服从这个名词。在填空中,下级永远服从上级,故 B、D 都不对。另外,琼森本应该以正确的行动为下级作表率,而原句中出现"whatever the effects on his subordinates",可以推知琼森做了不光彩的事情,在本句中只能指违反公司的行为规则,而 A 和 C 却使得琼森未作这种违反公司准则的事,所以 A 和 C 都错,正确答案为 D 的 scrupled。通常该词与 never 连用,never scrupled to do sth 意为"肆无忌惮地做某事"。

【重点词条】**deign** v. 降低身分,屈尊,俯就,垂顾(to condescend reluctantly and with a strong sense of the affront to one's superiority that is involved)

　　　　　<u>scruple</u> adj. ①(由于道德原因而感到)迟疑不安的,踌躇的,顾忌的(an ethical consideration or principle that inhibits action)

　　　　　　　　②一丝不苟的,小心的,谨慎的(the quality or state of being scrupulous)

　　　halfhearted adj. 半心半意的,兴趣不大的,不热心的(lacking heart, spirit, or interest)

 literal adj. ①照字面的,刻板的(according with the letter of the scriptures)
　　　　　②如实不夸张的(free from exaggeration or embellishment) 例 the ～truth
　　　　　③只讲究实际的(characterized by a concern mainly with facts) 例 a very～man

SECTION 29

1. Although the feeding activities of whales and walruses give the seafloor of the Bering Shelf a <u>devastated</u> appearance, these activities seem to be actually ____ to the area, ____ its productivity.

(A) destructive. . counterbalancing

(B) rehabilitative. . diminishing

(C) beneficial. . enhancing

(D) detrimental. . redirecting

(E) superfluous. . encumbering

2. In an age without radio or recordings, an age ____ by print, fiction gained its greatest ascendancy.

(A) decimated

(B) denigrated

(C) dominated

(D) emphasized

(E) resurrected

3. Scientists' pristine reputation as devotees of the disinterested pursuit of truth has been ____ by recent evidence that some scientists have deliberately ____ experimental results to further their own careers.

(A) reinforced. . published

(B) validated. . suppressed

(C) exterminated. . replicated

(D) compromised. . fabricated

(E) resuscitated. . challenged

4. Although Johnson's and Smith's initial fascination with the fortunes of those jockeying for power in the law firm ____ after a few months, the two paid sufficient attention to determine who their lunch partners should be.

(A) revived

(B) emerged

(C) intensified

(D) flagged

(E) persisted

5. A war, even if fought for individual liberty and democratic rights, usually requires that these principles be ____, for they are ____ the <u>regimentation and discipline</u> necessary for military efficiency.

(A) espoused. . contrary to

(B) suppressed. . fulfilled through

(C) suspended. . incompatible with

(D) followed. . disruptive of

(E) rejected. . inherent in

6. To test the ____ of borrowing from one field of study to enrich another, simply investi-

gate the extent to which terms from the one may, without forcing, be ____ the other.

(A) risk. . confused with

(B) universality. . applied to

(C) decorum. . illuminated by

(D) rate. . superseded by

(E) efficacy. . utilized by

7. The English novelist William Thackeray considered the <u>cult</u> of the criminal so dangerous that he criticized Dickens' Oliver Twist for making the characters in the thieves' kitchen so ____.

(A) threatening

(B) riveting

(C) conniving

(D) fearsome

(E) irritating

SECTION 29 解答

1. 【正确答案】C

【中文释义】尽管鲸鱼和海象的觅食活动给白令海峡的海底一个被毁灭的外观,但这些活动看上去事实上对该地区有益,增进了它的生产率。

【解题分析】由转折句可知第一个空格为褒义词,第二个空格为分隔重复前文,所以仍然为褒义,正确答案为C。

【重点词条】**devastate** *v*. ①使荒芜,破坏,蹂躏(to bring to ruin or desolation by violent action)

②压倒,使垮掉,使混乱(to reduce to chaos, disorder, or helplessness, overwhelm) 例 devastated by grief/Her wisecrack devastated the class.

counterbalance *v*. 使平衡,抵消,补偿(to oppose or balance with an equal weight or force)

rehabilitative *adj*. ①恢复名誉的(to restore to good repute, reestablish the good name of)

②修复的,复兴的(to restore to a former state such as of efficiency, good management, or solvency) 例 ~ slum areas

③康复的,改造的(to restore or bring to a condition of health or useful and constructive activity)

> **redirect** *v.* 改变方向(to change the course or direction of)
>
> **encumber** *v.* ①使负担沉重,拖累(weigh down, burden)
> ②妨碍,阻碍,堵塞(to impede or hamper the function or activity of, hinder)

2. 【正确答案】C

　　【中文释义】在一个没有收音机和录音机的年代,一个被印刷占据的时代,小说获得了它的统治地位。

　　【解题分析】事实上文中的 fiction 和 print 是密不可分的,所以主句称小说获得了统治地位,就是说印刷占有统治地位,故选 B 的 dominated。

　　【重点词条】**ascendancy** *n.* 优势,统治或支配地位(governing or controlling influence, domination)

> **resurrect** *v.* ①使死而复生,复活(to raise from the dead)
> ②重新启用,使再度流行(to bring to view, attention, or use again)

3. 【正确答案】D

　　【中文释义】科学家最初的对真理无私追求的献身者的声誉被最近的证据所削弱了,这些证据表明有些科学家故意地捏造实验结果来推进他们的学术生涯。

　　【解题分析】由 pristine 和 recent 的一组对比即可知第一个空格应填"反对""削弱"等词意,C 和 D 候选。而第二个空格又必须表明科学家非客观公正的动作,D 的 fabricate 为正确答案。C 的 replicate 用于科学方面复制实验时,表示检验和核实,一旦其他的独立实验室不能复制出某一科学家公布的结果,就可以证明该科学家的宣称为假,文中的 replicate experimental result 即为"核实实验结果之意",无任何非公正,非客观的含义。

　　【重点词条】**pristine** *adj.* ①本来的,初期的(belonging to the earliest period or state, original) 例 the hypothetical~lunar atmosphere

> ②原始的(not spoiled, corrupted, or polluted such as by civilization, pure) 例 a~forest
>
> ③新鲜的(fresh and clean as or as if new) 例 ~ hard-backs in uniform editions to fill our built-in bookcases

> **exterminate** *v.* 根除,灭绝,消除(to get rid of completely usu. by killing off) 例 ~crabgrass from a lawn

> **compromise** *v.* ①通过互让解决(to adjust or settle by mutual concessions)
> ②泄露(to reveal or expose to an unauthorized person and esp. to an enemy) 例 confidential information was compromised
> ③连累,危及,损害(to cause the impairment of) 例 a compromised immune system/a seriously compromised patient

resuscitate *v.* 使复活,复生,使复兴,使恢复(to revive from apparent death or from unconsciousness; revitalize)

4. 【正确答案】D

【中文释义】尽管琼森和史密斯当初的强烈兴趣——对律师事务所中那些运用手段追求权力的人的前途命运的兴趣——几个月之后消退了,但是这两个人仍然给予足够多的注意力来决定谁应该成为他们的午餐伙伴。

【解题分析】将上半句简化之后即为"initial fascination _____ after a few month",由时间对比型的规律可直接选出答案 D。全句的含义相当晦涩。事实上,上句这两人关心那些政途上正在上升的人的前途的行为是为了自己,因为只有判断清楚谁会接管权力,他们才能知道究竟该跟从追随谁,以便等他登上权力巅峰后也能"鸡犬升天"。而下句他们关心和谁一起吃午饭仍是一种权术的表现。午餐是社交的一个重要部分,他们希望通过午餐的方式来接触某人,或是巩固与某人的关系,全句的转折关系实际上为"尽管对权术斗争的兴趣减轻了,但却继续存在"。

【重点词条】jockey *v.* ①欺骗(to deal shrewdly or fraudulently with)

②骑马,驾驭(to ride or drive a horse as a jockey, drive, operate)

③耍手段谋取(to maneuver or manipulate by adroit or devious means) 例 was ~ed out of the job

flag *v.* ①无力地下垂,(植物)萎垂(to hang loose without stiffness)

②变弱,疲乏(to become unsteady, feeble, or spiritless)

③失去吸引力(to decline in interest or attraction flag)

revive *v.* ①苏醒,复苏(to return to consciousness or life)

②复原,重振,复兴(become active or flourishing again)

5. 【正确答案】C

【中文释义】一场战争,即使是为了个人自由和民主权力而战,却通常要求这些原则被暂时终止搁置,因为他们与军事效率所必须的组织化纪律化相冲突。

【解题分析】由 even 所导致的转折关系可知第一个空格为贬义词,可选 B、C 和 E;由 for 所引导的因果句可知,第二个空格也应为贬义,从而可直接选 C。

【重点词条】suppress *v.* ①压制,镇压(to put down by authority or force, subdue)

②查禁,禁止(to keep from public knowledge, to keep secret, to stop or prohibit the publication or revelation of)

③抑制(to exclude from consciousness)

fulfill *v.* ①实践,履行(to put into effect, execute)

②结束(to bring to an end)

③满足(to measure up to, satisfy)

④实现(to convert into reality)

disruptive *adj.* 分裂的,破坏性的,搅乱的

6. 【正确答案】E

【中文释义】为了证明从一个学术领域借专业术语来丰富另外一个学术领域的这种做法的效力，只需简单地调查一下从一个学科中来的术语可以毫不勉强地被别的学科用上的程度。

【解题分析】句子与常见的题目相比略显古怪，实际上只是一个 to 引导的目的状语加上一个祈使句而已。做题的基本思路仍然是"答案必须重复"，下半句中的"terms from the one"重复上句的"borrowing from one field of study"，下句中的"the other"重复上句的"another"，所以空格里应直接重复上文的"enrich"即可。也即专业术语可以被别的学科使用，可候选 B 和 E。第一个词的判断比较简单，下句强调借来的术语可以毫不勉强地被用上的程度，也就是强调这种借术语的行为非常有效。故应选 E 的 efficacy。如果要证明 B 的 universality，那就只能在下半句证明各个学科之间都在相互借用专业术语。B 错。

【重点词条】**decorum** *adj*. ①正派得体，端庄稳重(literary and dramatic propriety, fitness)
②合宜，相称，高雅(propriety and good taste in conduct or appearance)
③恪守礼仪(orderliness)
④合乎经典，规范性(the conventions of polite behavior)

illuminate *v*. ①启迪(to enlighten spiritually or intellectually)
②照亮(to supply or brighten with light)

efficacy *n*. 功效，效力，效验(the power to produce an effect)

rate *v*. 评价，估计，给…定级，把…列为，将…认定为

7. 【正确答案】B

【中文释义】英文作家威廉·莎克莱认为对罪犯的喜爱是如此危险以致于他批评狄更斯的"Oliver Twist"，因为这本书将小偷厨房里的角色塑造得如此惹人喜爱。

【解题分析】由 so…that… 结构可知威廉·莎克莱批评狄更斯小说的原因是因为"the cult of criminal"，而 making 所引导的正是狄更斯小说的内容，其中 thieves 又与上文的 the criminal 重复，所以空格里填上"cult"的同义词即可，答案为 B。

【重点词条】**cult** *n*. 膜拜，狂热，崇拜，迷信

riveting *adj*. 饶有兴味的，非常动听的，强力吸引人的(having the power to fix the attention, engrossing, fascinating)

conniving *v*. ①默许，纵容(to pretend ignorance of or fail to take action against something one ought to oppose)
②共谋，密谋，取得默契(to be indulgent or in secret sympathy, wink, to cooperate secretly or have a secret understanding, conspire, intrigue)

fearsome *adj*. 可怕的，畏怯的(causing fear, timid, timorous)

irritate *v*. 激怒，使人不快(to provoke impatience, anger, or displeasure in, annoy)

SECTION 30

1. The discovery that, friction excluded, all bodies fall at the same rate is so simple to state and to grasp that there is a tendency to ____ its significance.
   (A) underrate
   (B) control
   (C) reassess
   (D) praise
   (E) eliminate

2. Their mutual teasing seemed ____, but in fact it ____ a long-standing hostility.
   (A) aimless. . produced
   (B) friendly. . masked
   (C) playful. . contravened
   (D) bitter. . revealed
   (E) clever. . averted

3. Noting that few employees showed any ____ for complying with the corporation's new safety regulations, Peterson was forced to conclude that acceptance of the regulations would be ____, at best.
   (A) aptitude. . unavoidable
   (B) regard. . indeterminate
   (C) respect. . negotiable
   (D) patience. . imminent
   (E) enthusiasm. . grudging

4. It has been argued that politics as ____, whatever its transcendental claims, has always been the systematic organization of common hatreds.
   (A) a theory
   (B) an ideal
   (C) a practice
   (D) a contest
   (E) an enigma

5. In many science fiction films, the opposition of good and evil is portrayed as a ____ between technology, which is ____, and the errant will of a depraved intellectual.
   (A) fusion. . useful
   (B) struggle. . dehumanizing
   (C) parallel. . unfettered
   (D) conflict. . beneficent
   (E) similarity. . malevolent

6. Although scientists claim that the seemingly ____ language of their reports is more precise than the figurative language of fiction, the language of science, like all language, is inherently ____.
   (A) ornamental. . subtle
   (B) unidimensional. . unintelligible
   (C) symbolic. . complex
   (D) literal. . allusive
   (E) subjective. . metaphorical

7. In recent decades the idea that Cezanne influenced Cubism has been caught in the ____ between art historians who credit Braque with its invention and those who ____ Picasso.
   (A) crossfire. . tout
   (B) interplay. . advocate
   (C) paradox. . prefer
   (D) deliberation. . attribute
   (E) tussle. . substitute

SECTION 30 解答

1. 【正确答案】A

   【中文释义】这个发现——摩擦排除在外,所有的物品以相同的速度下降——表达起来和理解起来都如此简单以至于有一种低估它的重要性的心理倾向。

   【解题分析】此句甚简单,只有一个简单的 so…that…结构,不难得知,我们对于简单的东西通常会是一种什么心理倾向。答案为 A。有极少的同学选 E 的 eliminate。这个词指主动的动作,即使我们心理上有轻视简单事物的倾向,也极少有人主动去著书立说,去巡回演讲来告诉世人应轻视这个简单的事物。所以 E 并不正确。

   【重点词条】**tendency** *n*. ①趋势(direction or approach toward a place, object, effect, or limit)

   　　　　　　　　②倾向(a proneness to a particular kind of thought or action)

2. 【正确答案】B

   【中文释义】他们的相互逗弄看上去友好,但实际上它背后代表着长期的敌意态度。

   【解题分析】前后对立面转折,而后文讲述的是与 hostility 相关的态度,所以前文也应是 hostility 的同义或反义,可候选 B 和 C,构成转折的是 B。

   【重点词条】**bitter** *adj*. ①有苦味的,苦的

   　　　　　　　　②令人不愉快的,难以接受的

   　　　　　　　　③流露心头痛苦的

   　　　　　　　　④充满仇恨的

   　　　　contravene *v*. ①违反,触犯法律(to go or act contrary to, violate) 例 ~a law

   　　　　　　　　②否认,反驳,与…冲突(to oppose in argument, contradict) 例 ~a proposition

3. 【正确答案】E

   【中文释义】注意到了很少有雇员显示出任何热情来遵守公司的新的安全管制,彼德森被迫得出结论:对新规则的接受最多只是勉强的。

   【解题分析】文末的 at best 修饰一个轻微的贬义词。所以第二个空格应为修饰"acceptance"的轻微贬义词,只有 E 的 grudging 构成了"勉强地接受"这样的轻微的贬义。正确答案为 E。

   【重点词条】**indeterminate** *adj*. ①模糊的(not definitely or precisely determined or fixed, vague)

   　　　　　　　　②不确定的(not known in advance)

   　　　　　　　　③无结果的(not leading to a definite end or result)

   　　　　negotiable *adj*. ①可磋商的(capable of being negotiated)

   　　　　　　　　②可转让流通的(transferable from one person to another by being delivered with or without endorsement so that the title passes to the transferee) 例 ~securities

③可通行的,可进行的(capable of being traversed, dealt with, or accomplished) 例 a difficult but~road/~demands

grudging *adj.* 勉强的,不情愿的(unwilling, reluctant, done, given, or allowed unwillingly, reluctantly, or sparingly) 例 ~compliance

4. 【正确答案】C

【中文释义】有人指出政治作为一种实践活动,不管它的理论上宣称是什么,总是有系统地组织共同仇恨的行为。

【解题分析】空格后的分隔结构非常清楚地提示空格应与"transcendental claims"构成反义词,与理论相反的当然是实践,所以正确答案为C。

【重点词条】**transcendental** *adj.* ①超越的,卓越的(transcendent)

②超自然的(supernatural)

③抽象的,玄奥的(abstruse, abstract)

④先验的,超验的(of or relating to transcendentalism)

5. 【正确答案】D

【中文释义】在许多科幻电影中,善和恶的对立被描绘成向善的技术和堕落的知识分子的邪恶意愿之间的冲突。

【解题分析】全句实际上即为"the opposition is portrayed as a ____",可由此知答案在B和D中。并且不难判断出"the opposition"之后的介词短语与第一个空格之后的介词短语为重复关系,由于errant will已经与上文的"evil"重复,所以第二个空格应与上文的"good"重复。答案为D。

【重点词条】**fusion** *n.* ①熔解(the act or process of liquefying or rendering plastic by heat)

②融合,溶合(a union by or as if by melting, a merging of diverse, distinct, or separate elements into a unified whole)

dehumanizing *adj.* 失去人性的,非人化的

parallel *n.* ①平行线(或面)

②可相比拟的事物,相似处

③比拟,显示相似处的比较

malevolent *adj.* ①含有恶意的(having, showing, or arising from intense often vicious ill will, spite, or hatred)

②恶毒的,有害的(productive of harm or evil)

6. 【正确答案】D

【中文释义】尽管科学家认为他们科学汇报中看上去非比喻性的语言比小说的比喻性语言更精确,但科学的语言和其他所有语言一样是内在上比喻性的。

【解题分析】文中的一套比较结构非常明显,"...language of their reports"与"figurative language of fiction"构成对比,所以空格中应填上figurative的反义词,答案为D。

【重点词条】**ornamental** *adj.* 装饰的,装饰性的,华丽的(of, relating to, or serving as ornament; grown as an ornamental)

unidimensional *adj* . 一纬度的,只涉及一个方面的(one-dimensional)

unintelligible *adj* . 不可理解的,晦涩难懂的

literal(见 SECTION 28 第 7 题的注释)

allusion *n* . ①隐喻(an implied or indirect reference esp. in literature; the use of such references)

　　　　　　　　②暗示(the act of alluding or hinting at)

metaphorical *adj* . 使用隐喻的,比喻的(a figure of speech in which a word or phrase literally denoting one kind of object or idea is used in place of another to suggest a likeness or analogy between them such as in drowning in money, figurative language)

7.【正确答案】A

　【中文释义】最近这十年以来,塞尚影响了立体主义的思想被置于了两种人的交叉火力反对之中,其一是那些因布拉克的发明而推崇布拉克的艺术史学家,其二是那些极力推崇毕加索的艺术史学家。

　【解题分析】该句中出现了三个画家,Cezanne 、Braque、Picasso,对于美国学生而言都应该了如指掌,所以出现在这道针对北美考生的考题中,中国考区的考题从不考这类考题。在绘画史上 Braque 和 Picasso 总是被相提并论,所以第二个空格也应填上文的"credit",可选 A、B、C。D 为 attribute,缺少"to"构不成正确短语,这是一个罕见的语法错误的选项,国内题中也从来不设计有语法错误的选项。由于支持塞尚影响立体主义的艺术史学家与下文的两种人观点都不同,所以他会遭到两者的反对,也即选项 A 的 be caught in the crossfire。

　【重点词条】**interplay** *n* . 相互影响,相互作用(interaction) 例 the～of opposing forces

　　　　　　tout *v* . ①侦查,查看(to spy on, watch)

　　　　　　　　②下赌注(to give a tip or solicit bets on a racehorse)

　　　　　　　　③盛赞,吹捧,吹嘘(to praise or publicize loudly or extravagantly)

　　　　　　　　　例 ～ed as the...most elaborate suburban shopping development

　　　　　　tussle *v* . ①扭打,争斗(a physical contest or struggle, scuffle)

　　　　　　　　②争执,争辩(an intense argument, controversy, or struggle)

SECTION 31

1. Agronomists are increasingly worried about "desertification", the phenomenon that is turning many of the world's ____ fields and pastures into ____ wastelands, unable to support the people living on them.

　(A) fertile. . barren

　(B) productive. . blooming

　(C) arid. . thriving

　(D) poorest. . marginal

　(E) largest. . saturated

2. Old beliefs die hard: even when jobs became ____, the long-standing fear that unemployment could return at a moment's notice ____.

 (A) vacant. . perished
 (B) easier. . changed
 (C) plentiful. . persisted
 (D) protected. . subsided
 (E) available. . receded

3. Intellectual ____ and flight from boredom have caused him to rush pell-mell into situations that less ____ spirits might hesitate to approach.

 (A) restlessness. . adventurous
 (B) agitation. . passive
 (C) resilience. . quiescent
 (D) tranquility. . versatile
 (E) curiosity. . lethargic

4. Science advances in ____ spiral in that each new conceptual scheme ____ that phenomena explained by its predecessors and adds to those explanations.

 (A) a discontinuous. . decries
 (B) a repetitive. . vitiates
 (C) a widening. . embraces
 (D) an anomalous. . captures
 (E) an explosive. . questions

5. Politeness is not a ____ attribute of human behavior, but rather a central virtue, one whose very existence is increasingly being ____ by the faddish requirement to "speak one's mind".

 (A) superficial. . threatened
 (B) pervasive. . undercut
 (C) worthless. . forestalled
 (D) precious. . repudiated
 (E) trivial. . affected

6. The painting was larger than it appeared to be, for, hanging in a darkened recess of the chapel, it was ____ by the perspective.

 (A) improved
 (B) aggrandized
 (C) embellished
 (D) jeopardized
 (E) diminished

7. Because folk art is neither completely rejected nor accepted as an art form by art historians, their final evaluations of it necessarily remain ____.

 (A) arbitrary
 (B) estimable
 (C) orthodox
 (D) unspoken
 (E) equivocal

SECTION 31 解答

1.【正确答案】A
【中文释义】农业经济学家越来越担心沙漠化,这种现象正将世界上肥沃的土地和牧场转变为贫瘠的荒地,根本无法养活在这块土地上生活的人们。
【解题分析】动词短语 turn...to... 表示一种对立面转变,故第一空格和第二空格应构成一组反义词。
【重点词条】 thriving adj. 繁荣的,兴旺的,旺盛的(to grow vigorously, flourish, to gain in wealth or possessions, prosper, to progress toward or realize a goal)

saturated *adj.* ①浸透的,渗透的(full of moisture, made thoroughly wet)

②饱和的(being a solution that is unable to absorb or dissolve any more of a solute at a given temperature and pressure)

2.【正确答案】C

【中文释义】老的信念消失得很慢:即使当工作机会很多的时候,长期的害怕情绪——失业很快就会回来——仍然存在。

【解题分析】冒号前后为重复结构。冒号前的 old belief 与冒号后的 the long-standing fear 为重复短语,故第二空格应与上文的 die hard 重复,可选 C。

【重点词条】**at a moment's notice**　一经通知立即…

give a worker a month's notice　给一个工人一个月的最后期限

(do sth) at a short notice　突然做某事

perish *v.* ①卒,凋谢

②被摧毁,消亡

③颓丧,堕落

④腐烂,硬化

3.【正确答案】A

【中文释义】精神上的不安分守己以及永不知疲倦使得他匆匆忙忙地冲进了很多局面当中,而一个不是有如此冒险精神的人就不会去这样做。

【解题分析】Less 后的空格里要求填一个形容词,表示某种精神状态,这种隐含的比较结构是考试的一大热点。一定要找到这种隐含的比较结构的比较双方究竟是什么,此句中显然是在和前文的 rush pell-mell 这种精神状态做比较,除此之外别无选择,五个选择答案中能够描绘出 rush pell-mell 精神状态的只有 A。

【重点词条】**pell-mell** *adj.* ①乱糟糟的(in mingled confusion or disorder)

②忙乱的,匆忙的(in confused haste)

③不加区分选择的

restlessness *adj.* ①得不到休息的(lacking or denying rest, uneasy)例 a~ night

②不安宁的(continuously moving, unquiet)例 the~ sea

③焦虑的,不满足的(characterized by or manifesting unrest esp. of mind)例 ~pacing

resilience *n.* ①弹性,灵活性(the capability of a strained body to recover its size and shape after deformation caused esp. by compressive stress)

②恢复力,适应力(an ability to recover from or adjust easily to misfortune or change)

4.【正确答案】C

【中文释义】科学以变宽的螺旋的方式取得进展,因为每一个新的概念体系都包括被之前的体系解释过的现象,同时又对这些解释做补充。

【重点词条】**vitiate** *v.* ①损坏(to make faulty or defective, impair) 例 The comic impact is vitiated by obvious haste.

②使变质,污染(to debase in moral or aesthetic status) 例 a mind vitiated by prejudice

③造成…无效(to make ineffective) 例 Fraud～s a contract.

④败坏,使堕落

5.【正确答案】A

【中文释义】礼貌并不是人们行为的一个无关紧要的品德,而是一个核心品德,这种品德的存在正被一个时尚的要求所威胁,这个时尚的要求是"有话直说"。

【解题分析】由 not...but 结构可判断出第一个空格应与下文的 central 构成反义词,可选 A、C、E。后文的 by 短语是第二解题点,"speak one's mind"是美国俚语短语,需要考生临时揣摩含义,而它的含义必然是和礼貌相关的。因为与这个短语发生关系的是 one, politeness 的重复。从这个角度去考虑,"speak one's mind"当然就是属于不礼貌的行为,所以礼貌越来越受到这种时尚的破坏作用。E 答案未明确说明是哪一种,好还是坏的影响,当然错。C 答案的 forestall 是一个终结性的动作,根本不可能由原文中的 increasingless 修饰。正确答案选 A。

【重点词条】**forestall** *v.* ①抢在…之前行动,垄断市场(to prevent the normal trading in by buying or diverting goods or by persuading persons to raise prices)

②(用先发制人的手段)排斥,阻碍,防止(to exclude, hinder, or prevent by prior occupation or measures)

③抢先,预先(to get ahead of, anticipate)

6.【正确答案】E

【中文释义】这幅画比它看上去的要大,因为挂在教堂黑暗的凹处时,它被透视法缩小了。

【解题分析】上半句玩了一个概念游戏,画比看上去的要大,也就是看上去的要比画本身要小,下句当然选择被透视法缩小了。

【重点词条】**perspective** *n.* ①透视画法(the technique or process of representing on a plane or curved surface the spatial relation of objects as they might appear to the eye; representation in a drawing or painting of parallel lines as converging in order to give the illusion of depth and distance)

②视角,观点(the interrelation in which a subject or its parts are mentally viewed) 例 places the issues in proper～

③远景,展望(the appearance to the eye of objects in respect to their relative distance and positions)

7.【正确答案】E

【中文释义】因为民间艺术作为一种艺术形式既不被艺术史学家们完全接受,也不被完全反对,他们对民间艺术的最终评价一直是模棱两可的。

【解题分析】五个答案中能够表达出既不肯定又不否定概念的只有 E,答案 A 的 arbitrary 也有"反复无常"的意思,但仍然不通顺,句子并不是强调他们的主见天天改变反复无常,而是讲他们没有主见,从来都没有明确的定论。

【重点词条】arbitrary *adj.* ①随心所欲的,个人武断的
　　　　　　　　　　　　　②反复无常的
　　　　　　　　　　　　　③专制的,任意的
　　　　　　　equivocal *adj.* ①模棱两可的(subject to two or more interpretations and usu. used to mislead or confuse)
　　　　　　　　　　　　　②有歧义的(uncertain as an indication or sign)
　　　　　　　　　　　　　③可疑的,靠不住的(of doubtful advantage, genuineness, or moral rectitude) 例 ~behavior

SECTION 32

1. Because it is ____ to ____ all the business costs related to employee discontent, an accurate estimate of the magnitude of these costs is not easily calculated.

   (A) difficult. . measure
   (B) impossible. . justify
   (C) improper. . overlook
   (D) useless. . discover
   (E) necessary. . pinpoint

2. Consider the universal cannibalism of the sea, all of whose creatures ____ one another.

   (A) hide from
   (B) ferret out
   (C) prey on
   (D) glide among
   (E) compete against

3. How could words, confined as they individually are to certain ____ meanings specified in a dictionary, eventually come, when combined in groups, to create obscurity and actually to prevent thought from being ____?

   (A) indefinite. . articulated
   (B) conventional. . conceivable
   (C) unlikely. . classified
   (D) archaic. . expressed
   (E) precise. . communicable

4. Even though they tended to be ____ strangers, fifteenth-century Europeans did not automatically associate ____ and danger.

   (A) trusting of. . diversity
   (B) haughty with. . nonconformity
   (C) interested in. . enmity
   (D) antagonistic to. . rudeness
   (E) hostile to. . foreignness

5. The Modern age is a permissive one in which things can be said explicitly, but the old tradition of ____ dies hard.

(A) garrulousness

(B) exaggeration

(C) excoriation

(D) bombast

(E) euphemism

6. Although many findings of the Soviet and United States probes of Venus were complementary, the two sets of atmospheric results clearly could not be ____ without a major change of data or ____.

(A) obtained. . experimentation

(B) completed. . position

(C) matched. . implementation

(D) reconciled. . interpretation

(E) produced. . falsification

7. While it is assumed that the mechanization of work has a ____ effect on the lives of workers, there is evidence available to suggest that, on the contrary, mechanization has served to ____ some of the traditional roles of women.

(A) salutary. . improve

(B) dramatic. . undermine

(C) benign. . revise

(D) debilitating. . weaken

(E) revolutionary. . reinforce

SECTION 32 解答

1.【正确答案】A

【中文释义】因为难于衡量出由雇员不满所导致的费用,所以对这些费用多少的精确测量是不容易计算出来的。

【解题分析】一个典型的 GRE 式的因果句,原因和结果只是重复了一下而已,如果将上半句的形式主语 it 换成它真正的主语,上下句之间几乎没有任何差别。GRE 句子填空中的因果句几乎都是同义重复或上下义重复,不需要大家真正地根据原因去推测结果。

【重点词条】**pinpoint** *v.* ①准确地定出…的位置(to locate or aim with great precision or accuracy)

②确认,确定(to fix, determine, or identify with precision)

③强调(to cause to stand out conspicuously, highlight)

④刺破,刺穿

2.【正确答案】C

【中文释义】考虑到海洋中普遍存在的同类相食现象,所有生物都在捕食别的生物。

【解题分析】该题只是考察 cannibalism 的含义,词汇不过硬的考生当然一筹莫展。

【重点词条】**ferret** *v.* ①用雪貂猎取,追逐(to hunt with ferrets)

②搜出,查获(to search about)

3.【正确答案】E

【中文释义】每个单词都被规定到词典里详细说明过的精确含义上,当他们结合成一个集合时,这些词汇是如何最终逐渐地创造出了不可理解性并且使得思维不能交流呢?

【解题分析】第一个空格的形容词修饰 meanings,而 meanings 后又有一个分隔结构,故空格里就应填上分隔所表示的含义,可得答案 E,第一个短语的结构需要澄清一下,confined to 是一个固定搭配,confined 后的 as 短语是副词短语修饰 confined 这个动词。

【重点词条】**obscurity** *n*. ①模糊的东西,费解的文字(one that is obscure)

②晦涩,费解(the quality or state of being obscure)

③无名,默默无闻

conceivable *adj*. 可想象的,想得到的(imaginable)

4. 【正确答案】E

【中文释义】即使他们倾向于对陌生人采取敌意的态度,15 世纪的欧洲人并不自动地将外来思想和危险联系起来。

【解题分析】在这个上下句中,下句的名词当然由上句提供,根本不可能由下句推理产生,上句提供的名词只有一个 stranger,故下句填 foreignness。

【重点词条】**nonconformity** *n*. ①不墨守成规(refusal to conform to an established or conventional creed, rule, or practice)

②不一致,不符合(absence of agreement or correspondence)

faulty *adj*. 有缺点的,不完善的(marked by fault or defect, imperfect)

5. 【正确答案】E

【中文释义】现代这个时代是一个宽容的时代,事件可以直接表达出来,但老的婉转语的风俗消失得很慢。

【解题分析】Modern age 与下文 old tradition 构成反义词,故空格中应填上"不能直接说"的意思。

【重点词条】**permissive** *adj*. ① 宽容的(granted on sufferance, tolerated)

②放任的(granting or tending to grant permission, tolerant)

③放纵的(deficient in firmness or control, indulgent, lax)

④予以选择的,自由的(allowing discretion, optional) 例 reduced the~ retirement age from 65 to 62

excoriation *n*. ①擦伤皮肤,剥皮(to wear off the skin of, abrade)

②严厉指责,痛骂(to censure scathingly)

6. 【正确答案】D

【中文释义】尽管苏联和美国的金星探测器的许多发现结果是互为补充的,但这两套太空观测结果,如果缺少一个对数据式描述的大的转化的话,显然是不能相互调和的。

【解题分析】转折句的上半句为一个判断句,所以下半句转折应针对 complementary 这个判断词来进行。第一个空格里应填上 complementary 的同义词,可候选的是 C 和 D,只有这两个词表达出了两个方面的相互概念。C 和 D 的第二个词能和 data 构成并列的是 D,事实上这儿所讲的转变就是坐标系的转变,因为苏联和美国的金星探测器不会在同一个空间轨道上,因而需要一个数据的坐标变换才能使双方的数据调和起来。

【重点词条】 complementary *adj.* ①互补色的(relating to or constituting one of a pair of contrasting colors that produce a neutral color when combined in suitable proportions)

②补充的,补足的(serving to fill out or complete)

③互补的(mutually supplying each other's lack)

④互为余角的,互余的(being complements of each other) 例 ~acute angles

falsification *n.* ①证明(某事物)为假(to prove or declare false)

②窜改,伪造(to make false, to make false by mutilation or addition)

③歪曲(to represent falsely, misrepresent)

7.【正确答案】E

【中文释义】尽管有人认为工作的机械化对工人的生活起到了一个革命性的效果,相反,有证据表明机械化起到了增强妇女传统角色的作用。

【解题分析】前后句的两个空格分别表示工作的机械化的两种相反的效果,应填反义词,尤其是第二个空格后出现妇女传统地位这个词组,所以工作机械化的作用显然和传统地位相关,那么第一个空格中所填的作用和第二个空格的作用相反,也应和传统相关,而有此含义的词只有答案 E。

【重点词条】 benign *adj.* ①善良的,宽厚的(of a gentle disposition, gracious) 例 a~teacher

②慈祥的,和善的(showing kindness and gentleness) 例 ~faces

③温和的,宜人的(favorable, wholesome) 例 a~climate

④良性的,无危险的(of a mild type or character that does not threaten health or life) 例 a~tumor

⑤无害的(having no significant effect, harmless) 例 environmentally~

dramatic *adj.* ①戏剧的(of or relating to the drama)

②戏剧性的(suitable to or characteristic of the drama)

③给人深刻印象的,突然的(striking in appearance or effect)

④雄壮的,生动的(of an opera singer, having a powerful voice and a declamatory style)

debilitate *v.* 削弱…的力量,使衰弱(to impair the strength of, enfeeble)

SECTION 33

1. Although economists have traditionally considered the district to be solely an agricultural one, the _____ of the inhabitants' occupations makes such a classification obsolete.

(A) productivity

(B) diversity

(C) predictability

(D) profitability

(E) stability

2. The author of this book ____ overlooks or minimizes some of the problems and short-comings in otherwise highly successful for-eign industries in order to ____ the points on which they excel and on which we might try to emulate them.

(A) accidentally. . exaggerate

(B) purposely. . emphasize

(C) occasionally. . counterbalance

(D) intentionally. . confuse

(E) cleverly. . compound

3. Crosby's colleagues have never learned, at least not in time to avoid embarrassing themselves, that her occasional ____ air of befuddlement ____ a display of her formidable intelligence.

(A) genuine. . dominates

(B) alert. . contradicts

(C) acute. . precludes

(D) bogus. . presages

(E) painstaking. . succeeds

4. To ensure the development and exploitation of a new technology, there must be a con-stant ____ of several nevertheless distinct ac-tivities.

(A) interplay

(B) implementation

(C) comprehending

(D) improvement

(E) exploration

5. Some customs travel well; often, however, behavior that is considered the epitome of ____ at home is perceived as impossibly rude or, at the least, harmlessly bizarre abroad.

(A) novelty

(B) eccentricity

(C) urbanity

(D) coarseness

(E) tolerance

6. The ____ of the early Greek philosophers' attempts to explain the operations of the cosmos led certain later thinkers to inquire into the ____ of human reason.

(A) difficulty. . origin

(B) meaning. . supremacy

(C) complexity. . reality

(D) equivocations. . subtlety

(E) failures. . efficacy

7. Ever prey to vagrant impulses that impelled him to ____ his talents on a host of unwor-thy projects, his very ____ nonetheless en-hanced his reputation, for the sheer energy of his extravagance dazzled observers.

(A) undermine. . enthusiasm

(B) isolate. . selectiveness

(C) display. . affability

(D) squander. . dissipation

(E) implicate. . genius

SECTION 33 解答

1.【正确答案】B

【中文释义】尽管经济学家们传统上认为这个地区完全是一个农业区,当地居民职业的多样性就使得这个分类过时不适用了。

【解题分析】Solely an agriculture one 中的 solely 就是 only 的意思,这两个单词一旦出现都应给予高度重视,因为它们表示出了惟一性、排他性。空格填的词使得上文的分类不适用,所以空格里应填与上文相反的词,diversity 正好与 solely 相反。

【重点词条】**solely** *adv*. ①独自地,单独地(without another, singly) 例 went~on her way

②仅仅,完全(to the exclusion of all else) 例 done~for money

diversity *n*. 不同,变化多端,多样性(the condition of being diverse, variety)

2.【正确答案】B

【中文释义】这本书的作者故意忽略或是尽管减少外国工业的缺点和问题,这些外国工业在其他方面都是高度成功的,目的是为了强调他们想赞美的观点,对于这些优点我们可以赶超。

【重点词条】**otherwise** *adv*. ①否则,要不然(if not)

②以另外方式(differently)

③在其他方面地(under other conditions)

counterbalance *n*. ①平衡(a weight that balances another)

②抵消(a force or influence that offsets or checks an opposing force)

3.【正确答案】D

【中文释义】克罗庇的同伴们从来不知道,至少也不是及时地知道以避免使自己尴尬,她偶尔假装出来的糊里糊涂的表情预示了她即将表现出她的极为强大的智慧。

【解题分析】最后一行的 her formidable intelligence 用了物主代词加特殊性格的方式,所以我们的思路是,一个具有强大智慧的人永远都不会糊涂,那么上文的 air of befuddlement 前的形容词应该否定这种糊涂的表情是真的,因而选 D。

【重点词条】**bogus** *adj*. 假冒的,伪造的(not genuine, counterfeit, sham)

painstaking *adj*. 辛劳的,刻苦的,勤恳的,仔细的(taking pains, expending, showing, or involving diligent care and effort)

4.【正确答案】A

【中文释义】为了保障新技术的开发和利用,就必须不断地综合那些在其他情况下就绝无关系的活动。

【解题分析】该题中的 nevertheless 是解题点,它被用作副词,含义为"under other conditions",所以推理思路为:在其他情况下绝无关系,那么在本句中应产生相互关系,能表达相互关系的词即为 A。

【重点词条】**nevertheless** *adv*. 仍然,尽管如此,然而(in spite of that, however) 例 her childish but~real delight

interplay *n*. 相互作用,相互影响(interaction) 例 the~of opposing forces

5.【正确答案】C

　　【中文释义】有些风俗传播得很好：但是通常在国内被看成优雅行为典范的行为却会在国
　　　　　　　　外被视为无法忍受的粗鲁，或者至少也是没有伤害性的滑稽可笑的行为。

　　【解题分析】冒号后出现转折连词，所以这一个冒号句是反义重复，冒号后应表示出某些风
　　　　　　　　俗未得到传播，尤其是冒号后的两个地点状语：at hoem 和 abroad 更是点明了
　　　　　　　　逻辑关系为反义关系，空格里应该填上 rude 或 bizarre 的反义词。

　　【重点词条】epitome *n*. ①梗概(a summary of a written work)

　　　　　　　　　　　　　　　②节录(a brief presentation or statement of something)

　　　　　　　　　　　　　　　③典型，象征(a typical or ideal example, embodiment) 例 The
　　　　　　　　　　　　　　　British monarchy itself is the~of tradition.

　　　　　　　　　　　　　　　④缩影(brief or miniature form)

　　　　　　　　novelty *n*. ①新鲜的事物，新奇的东西(something new or unusual)

　　　　　　　　　　　　　　　②新颖，新奇(the quality or state of being novel, newness)

　　　　　　　　　　　　　　　③新颖小巧的物品(a small manufactured article intended mainly
　　　　　　　　　　　　　　　for personal or household adornment)

　　　　　　　　urbanity *n*. 彬彬有礼，温文尔雅(the quality or state of being urbane)

6.【正确答案】E

　　【中文释义】早期的希腊哲学家解释宇宙运作的企图的失败就导致后来的思想家们对人类
　　　　　　　　的推理认知能力产生了怀疑。

　　【解题分析】句子结构简化后即为空格导致了对人的推理的怀疑，所以空格中当然表现了
　　　　　　　　人的推理认知能力的缺陷，所以答案选 E，表示古希腊哲学家一次推理认知的
　　　　　　　　企图的失败。A 和 D 并不正确，因为企图 attempt 本身并不具有 difficulty 或者
　　　　　　　　equivocation 的性质。

　　【重点词条】inquire *v*. ①询问(to put a question, seek for information by questioning)

　　　　　　　　　　　　　例 inquired about the horses

　　　　　　　　　　　　　②调查(to make investigation or inquiry)

　　　　　　　　supremacy *n*. ①至高无上(the quality or state of being supreme)

　　　　　　　　　　　　　　　②霸权地位，优势(supreme authority or power)

7.【正确答案】D

　　【中文释义】总是成为毫无目标的冲动的捕获品，这些冲动驱使他将自己的才能浪费在了
　　　　　　　　一大堆毫无价值的项目上，但他的这种浪费无论如何说都是提高了他的声誉，
　　　　　　　　因为他的挥霍中的巨大的才能使得围观者叹为观止。

　　【解题分析】这一句的结构较复杂，但第二个空格在 his 这个物主代词之后，所以应该填特
　　　　　　　　殊动作或特征性格，而在其后不远就重复了他的特征动作为 his extravagance，
　　　　　　　　所以第二个空格直接填上 extravagance 的同义词即可。

　　【重点词条】dissipation *n*. ①浪费，消耗(the action or process of dissipating, the state of
　　　　　　　　　　　　　　　being dissipated)

　　　　　　　　　　　　　　　②放荡，乱闹(an act of self-indulgence; one that is not harmful，amusement)

　　　　　③驱散

implicate *v.* ①含有…的意思(to involve as a consequence, corollary, or natu-

　　　　　ral inference, imply)

　　　　　②纠缠在一起(to fold or twist together, entwine)

　　　　　③使某人牵连于罪行(to bring into intimate or incriminating con-

　　　　　nection)

SECTION 34

1. Given the existence of so many factions in the field, it was unrealistic of Anna Freud to expect any ＿＿＿ of opinion.

　(A) freedom

　(B) reassessment

　(C) uniformity

　(D) expression

　(E) formation

2. Although specific concerns may determine the intent of a research project, its results are often ＿＿＿.

　(A) unanticipated

　(B) beneficial

　(C) expensive

　(D) spectacular

　(E) specialized

3. To list Reilly's achievements in a fragmentary way is ＿＿＿, for it distracts our attention from the ＿＿＿ themes of her work.

　(A) unproductive. . disparate

　(B) misleading. . integrating

　(C) pragmatic. . comprehensive

　(D) logical. . important

　(E) inevitable. . unsettling

4. People frequently denigrate books about recent catastrophes as morally ＿＿＿ attempts to profit, from misfortune, but in my view our desire for such books, together with the venerable tradition to which they belong, ＿＿＿ them.

　(A) inopportune. . encourages

　(B) fortuitous. . fosters

　(C) treacherous. . safeguards

　(D) despicable. . legitimizes

　(E) corrupt. . generates

5. That many of the important laws of science were discovered during experiments designed to ＿＿＿ other phenomena suggests that experimental results are the ＿＿＿ of inevitable natural forces rather than of planning.

　(A) analyze. . foundations

　(B) disprove. . predecessors

　(C) alter. . adjuncts

　(D) illuminate. . consequence

　(E) verify. . essence

6. Although in eighteenth-century England an active cultural life accompanied the beginnings of middle-class consumerism, the ＿＿＿ of literacy was ＿＿＿ with the rise of such consumerism in the different areas of the country.

　(A) repudiation. . reconciled

(B) renewal. . inconsistent

(C) promotion. . combined

(D) spread. . compatible

(E) degree. . uncorrelated

7. The trainees were given copies of a finished manual to see whether they could themselves begin to ____ the inflexible, though tacit, rules for composing more of such instructional materials.

(A) design

(B) revise

(C) disrupt

(D) standardize

(E) derive

SECTION 34 解答

1. 【正确答案】C

   【中文释义】考虑到在这个领域存在如此多的党派,安娜·佛洛伊德期待会有一个统一的观点是不现实的。

   【解题分析】下句为上句的双重否定形式。

   【重点词条】**assessment** *n*. ①估价,估定(the action or an instance of assessing, appraisal)
   ②估定额(the amount assessed)

2. 【正确答案】A

   【中文释义】尽管特定的关心内容会决定一个研究项目的目标,但它的结果却往往是出乎人们意料的。

   【解题分析】上下句的目标 intent 和 result 构成反义词,相应的修饰语也应构成反义词,specific 的反义词为 unanticipated。

   【重点词条】**spectacular** *adj*. 蔚为壮观的,惊人的,突出的(of, relating to, or being a spectacle, striking, sensational) 例 a~display of fireworks

3. 【正确答案】B

   【中文释义】将蕾莉的成就用分散的方式列举出来是具有误导性的,因为这种做法将我们的注意力从她作品的统一的主题上分散开来。

   【解题分析】For 引导的原因句用了 distract 这个词,所以上句的结果同样应是贬义词,可选 A 和 B。A 的第二个词 disparate 的含义是"根本不同的",这已经不可能进一步分散了,正确答案为 B,将注意力从统一的主题上分散开来,才构成一个正常的合乎逻辑的搭配。

   【重点词条】**fragmentary** *adj*. 片段的,破碎的,不完整的(consisting of fragments, incomplete)

             productive *adj*. ①生产性的,多产的(having the quality or power of producing esp. in abundance) 例 ~fishing waters

             ②能产的(effective in bringing about) 例 Investigating committees have been~of much good.

             ③有用的(yielding results, benefits, or profits)

disparate *adj.* 全异的,异种类的,不相干的(markedly distinct in quality or character)

4. 【正确答案】D

【中文释义】人们总是贬低内容为近期灾难的书,认为它们是一种道德上可鄙的企图,想从灾难中赢利,但是我认为,我们对这种书的的渴求,以及这些书所具有的久远的传统就使得这些书得到了大众的认可。

【解题分析】全句的结构简化后即为 people denigrate books, but our desire ＿＿ them (books),所以第二个空格填上 denigrate 的反义词,并且第一个空格很容易判断出应为描绘一种恶劣的道德的形容词,符合第一空格的选项为 C、D、E。A 为 inopportune,该词并不表达恶劣的道德;符合第二空格的选项为 D,答案 C 的 safeguard 并不是指心理上的支持,而偏重于行动上的支持,D 的 legitimize 除了有合法化的意思外,还有本句所用的意思"合情合理化,使获得大家的认可",即指心理上的支持,与心理上的反对 denigrate 构成反义。

【重点词条】**venerable** *adj.* ①值得敬重的(deserving to be venerated)

②神圣庄严的(made sacred esp. by religious or historical association)

③德高望重的,肃然起敬的(calling forth respect through age, character, and attainments)

legitimize *v.* ①使合法(理),批准

②证明…为有理(正当)

safeguard *v.* ①保护,保卫(to provide a safeguard for)

②使安全(to make safe, protect)

5. 【正确答案】D

【中文释义】许多重大的科学法则是在本来设计来阐明其他现象的科学实验中发现的,这就说明实验结果是不可避免的自然因素而不是人为计划的后果。

【解题分析】宾语从句的主干为 results are the ＿＿ of inevitable natural forces rather than planning,能构成正确搭配的只有答案 D。

【重点词条】**adjunct** *n.* ①附属物,辅助物(something joined or added to another thing but not essentially a part of it)

②附加语,修饰语(an adverb or adverbial attached to the verb of a clause esp. to express a relation of time, place, frequency, degree, or manner)

③助手,副手(an associate or assistant of another)

6. 【正确答案】E

【中文释义】尽管在 18 世纪的英格兰,一种积极的文化生活伴随中产阶级的消费主义的出现而同时发生,但是,在这个国家的不同地区,这种文化普及的程度却与这种消费主义的上升不相关联。

【解题分析】下句的 such consumerism 与上文的 middle-class consumerism 重复,而 literacy 显然又和上文的 active cultural life 重复,所以第二空格应与上文的 accompanied 重复,可以选择 B 或者 E。而答案 B 的第一个词 renewal 表达了一种荒谬的意思,即识字的程度、文化普及的程度会再兴起。众所周知,民众的文化普及程度是不可逆转的,除非是以极长的历史空间的角度去看,否则不可能出现识字程度的倒退过程,从而也就不可能出现再兴起这个过程。正确答案 E 的 degree 事实上是照应其后的 rise,文化程度越高对应着消费主义上升得越快。下句就是强调两者之间没有发展一致性的关联,尽管两者同时发生。

【重点词条】renewal *n*. ①重兴(the act or process of renewing, repetition)

②恢复(the quality or state of being renewed)

③延期(something such as a subscription to a magazine renewed)

④更新(something used for renewing; an expenditure that betters existing fixed assets)

⑤复兴,重建(the rebuilding of a large area such as of a city by a public authority)

literacy *n*. ①识字,有文化,读写能力

②熟谙文学,善于写作

7. 【正确答案】E

【中文释义】给受训者一份已完成了的手册的副本,来看一看他们能否自己开始提炼出僵化的、又不言而喻的规则来指导他们自己创作更多这样的指导材料。

【解题分析】Such instructional materials 是重复了上文的 manual,为了创作出类似的指导材料,中间过程是经由 rules 来实现的,rules 指导新的写作,那么为了保证新文件和范本的手册一致,那么这个写作的 rules 必须和范本中的 rule 一致。而五个选项中,A 是指设计新的 rule;B 是指修改旧的 rule;C 是指破坏旧的 rule;D 是指使 rule 标准化,也就是变化改变这些 rule 使之标准化,仍然是改变了范本的 rule。答案 E 才正确地表达出了范本的 rule 和指导新写作的 rule 相同的概念。

【重点词条】derive *v*. ①获得(to take, receive, or obtain esp. from a specified source)

②推论(infer, deduce)

③起源,得来(to trace the derivation of)

standardize *v*. ①按标准检验,校准(to compare with a standard)

②使标准化,使合乎标准(to bring into conformity with a standard)

finished *adj*. ①完结(成)了的

②精致完美的,绝顶的,有高度才艺的

SECTION 35

1. The availability of oxygen is an essential
   ____ for animal life, while carbon dioxide is
   equally ____ for plant life.
   (A) choice. . optional
   (B) duplication. . selective
   (C) conversion. . exchangeable
   (D) condition. . necessary
   (E) luxury. . harmful

2. Prudery actually draws attention to the vice
   it is supposed to ____; the very act that for-
   bids speech or prohibits sight ____ what is
   hidden.
   (A) condemn. . distorts
   (B) monitor. . signals
   (C) repress. . dramatizes
   (D) obviate. . fosters
   (E) divulge. . conceals

3. After thirty years of television, people have
   become "speed watchers"; consequently, if
   the camera lingers, the interest of the audi-
   ence ____.
   (A) broadens
   (B) begins
   (C) varies
   (D) flags
   (E) clears

4. Compared mathematically to smoking and
   driving, almost everything else seems relatively risk-free, ____ almost nothing seems
   worth regulating.
   (A) yet
   (B) since
   (C) so

(D) even though
(E) as long as

5. Ironically, Carver's precision in sketching
   lives on the edge of despair ensures that his
   stories will sometimes be read too narrowly,
   much as Dickens' social-reformer role once
   caused his broader concerns to be ____.
   (A) ignored
   (B) reinforced
   (C) contradicted
   (D) diminished
   (E) diversified

6. The demise of the rigorous academic curricu-
   lum in high school resulted, in part, from
   the progressive rhetoric that ____ the study
   of subjects previously thought ____ as part
   of school learning.
   (A) advocated. . necessary
   (B) enhanced. . indispensable
   (C) restricted. . impractical
   (D) undermined. . popular
   (E) sanctioned. . inappropriate

7. While some see in practical jokes a wish for
   mastery in miniature over a world that
   seems very ____, others believe that the
   jokes' purpose is to disrupt, by reducing all
   transactions to ____.
   (A) dubious. . confusion
   (B) disorderly. . symmetry
   (C) harmonious. . dissonance
   (D) unruly. . chaos
   (E) turbulent. . uniformity

SECTION 35 解答

1.【正确答案】D
  【中文释义】可获得氧气是动物生命的必要条件,然而对于植物,二氧化碳同样地必要。
  【解题分析】下句的 equally 这个词就提示我们应将上文的 essential 填到空格里去,类似作
          用的词有 such, similar, corresponding。
  【重点词条】luxury *n*. ①奢华,奢侈(a condition of abundance or great ease and comfort,
          sumptuous environment)例 lived in~
          ②奢侈品(something adding to pleasure or comfort but not absolutely
          necessary)

2.【正确答案】D
  【中文释义】拘谨的行为事实上吸引注意力到它设法隐藏的邪恶的念头上;恰恰是这种压
          抑语言表达和禁止东张西望的行为使得它隐藏的事物变得引人注目。
  【重点词条】prudery *n*. ①过分拘谨,故作正经,假道学(the characteristic quality or state of
          a prude)
          vice *n*. ①恶习,堕落(moral depravity or corruption, wickedness, a moral fault
          or failing, a habitual and trivial defect or shortcoming, foible)
          例 suffered from the~of curiosity
          ②缺点,瑕疵(blemish, defect, a physical imperfection, deformity, or
          taint)
          ③丑角(a character representing one of the vices in an English morality
          play)
          ④卖淫(sexual immorality; prostitution)
          dramatize *v*. ①改编成戏剧,用戏剧形式表现(to be suitable for dramatization)
          ②戏剧性地描述,生动地表述(to behave dramatically)
          divulge *v*. ①公开(to make public, proclaim)
          ②泄露秘密(to make known such as a confidence or secret)

3.【正确答案】D
  【中文释义】30 年的电视观看经验之后,人们已经变成了"速看人";相应地,如果电视画面
          停滞不动的话,观众的兴趣会下降。
  【解题分析】下句的动词 linger 实际上和上文的 speed watcher 构成对立,观众的兴趣当然
          会由此而下降。
  【重点词条】flag *v*. ①变弱(慢),疲乏,衰退
          ②变得枯燥无味
          ③(植物)萎垂

4.【正确答案】C

【中文释义】从数学角度看来,与抽烟或驾车相比较,几乎所有其他事物都显得相对零风险,因此几乎没有什么事情值得管制了。

【解题分析】惟一的一道填连词的填空题。据统计死于战争的人远远没有死于车祸的人多。

【重点词条】relatively *adv*. 相当地,比较地(to a relative degree or extent, somewhat)

5. 【正确答案】A

【中文释义】具有讽刺意味的是,卡佛对绝望边缘的人的精确描写导致了他的小说有时被读得太狭隘;正如狄更斯的社会改革家的人物角色曾经导致他的更广泛深远的关心主题被忽略掉了。

【解题分析】分号句的上下句重复,尤其是下句的 much as 这个短语更明确表明了这一关系,故空格里而应同样填上 be read too narrowly,吻合的答案为 A。答案 D 是众多考生误选的答案,事实上 D 的语态是被动语态,如果改成主动语态那就是读者消除了狄更斯作品的更广泛的主题。这显然是荒谬的,狄更斯的作品一旦完成后,就再也没有可能被读者来消除重要的主题,只有可能是读者自身没有品味到这些更广泛深刻的主题。

【重点词条】precision *n*. ①精确(the quality or state of being precise, exactness)

②精密度(the degree of refinement with which an operation is performed or a measurement stated)

6. 【正确答案】E

【中文释义】高中的严谨的学术课程的消失部分是由激进的言论导致的,这种激进的言论批准了过去被认为是不恰当的学术课题。

【解题分析】下句中的 previously thought 指的就是过去的严谨的设置课程的观点,而第一个空格表示新的、激进的观点,两者应该相反,因为激进的言论导致了严谨的课程的消失,五个选项中构成反义词的为 D 和 E,进一步分析可发现,D 的 undermine 并不正确。因为即使是激进的言论也不会去主动破坏一个课题,并且破坏课题和流行的课题(popular)实际上并无反义关系。

【重点词条】indispensable *adj*. ①责无旁贷的(not subject to being set aside or neglected)

例 an~obligation

②必不可少的(absolutely necessary, essential) 例 an~member of the staff

7. 【正确答案】D

【中文释义】尽管有些人在恶作剧中看出一个愿望,以微观的方式来控制这个看上去混乱不堪的世界,其他人则认为恶作剧的目的是通过将所有过程转变为混乱的方式来搞乱这个世界。

【解题分析】上下句的对比关系非常明显:some 与 others, wish 与 propose,那么上句的 mastery over 就应与下句的 disrupt 构成对比。Disrupt 的含义是"搞得混乱不堪",所以 mastery over 的含义就成为"管制得井井有条",那么第一个空格就应该填上"混乱"的意思。第二个空格较好判断,by 引导的方式状语重复前面的 disrupt,所以第二个空格也应为"混乱"的意思,符合这两个条件的选项为 D。

【重点词条】 disorderly *adj*. ①妨碍治安的(engaged in conduct offensive to public order) 例 charged with being drunk and~

       ②混乱的,杂乱的(characterized by disorder) 例 a~pile of clothes

  unruly *adj*. 难驾驭控制的,不守秩序的,不守法的(not readily ruled, disciplined, or managed) 例 an~crowd/a mane of~hair

  uniformity *n*. 无差异,无变化,相同,一致(the quality or state of being uniform)

SECTION 36

1. Aspartame, a new artificial sugar substitute, is only ____ replacement for saccharin because, unlike saccharin, it breaks down and loses its sweetening characteristics at high temperatures, making it ____ for baking.

    (A) an interim. . ideal
    (B) an apparent. . excellent
    (C) a potential. . versatile
    (D) a significant. . problematic
    (E) a partial. . unsuitable

2. Trapped thousands of years ago in Antarctic ice, recently discovered air bubbles are ____ time capsules filled with information for scientists who chart the history of the atmosphere.

    (A) inconsequential
    (B) broken
    (C) veritable
    (D) resplendent
    (E) impenetrable

3. In the days before the mass marketing of books, censorship was ____ source of ____, which helped the sale of the book and inspired Ralph Waldo Emerson to remark: "Every burned book enlightens the world".

    (A) a respected. . opinion
    (B) a constant. . guidance
    (C) a prime. . publicity
    (D) an unnoticed. . opposition
    (E) an unpromising. . criticism

4. It was not only the ____ of geologists that ____ earlier development of the revolutionary idea that the Earth's continents were moving plates; classical physicists, who could not then explain the mechanism, had declared continental movement impossible.

    (A) indecisiveness. . challenged
    (B) radicalism. . deterred
    (C) conservatism. . hindered
    (D) assumptions. . hastened
    (E) resistance. . mandated

5. Although often extremely critical of the medical profession as a whole, people are rarely willing to treat their personal doctors with equal ____.

    (A) impetuosity
    (B) sarcasm

(C) mockery

(D) contempt

(E) condescension

6. Aalto, like other modernists, believed that form follows function; consequently, his furniture designs asserted the ____ of human needs, and the furniture's form was ____ human use.

(A) universality. . refined by

(B) importance. . relegated to

(C) rationale. . emphasized by

(D) primacy. . determined by

(E) variability. . reflected in

7. A ____ acceptance of contemporary forms of social behavior has misled a few into believing that values in conflict with the present age are for all practical purposes ____ .

(A) casual. . reliable

(B) superficial. . trenchant

(C) complacent. . superseded

(D) cautious. . redemptive

(E) plaintive. . redundant

SECTION 36 解答

1.【正确答案】E

【中文释义】Aspartame,一种新的糖的人工代替品,仅仅是糖精的部分代替物,因为它和糖精不一样,在高温的时候会分解并且失去其使别的东西变甜的特性,从而使得它不适合烘烤。

【解题分析】尽管 Aspartame 这个单词谁也不认识,事实上是一种复杂的化学物质(天冬氨酰苯丙氨酸甲酯),但这一题的逻辑结构却非常简单,一个简单的因果句而已。

【重点词条】interim *adj*. ①间歇的(done, made, appointed, or occurring for an interim)

②暂时的,临时的

2.【正确答案】C

【中文释义】被封存在几千年前的南极之冰中,最近又被发现的空气泡泡是名副其实的时间胶囊,充满了绘制大气层变化历史的科学家所需要的信息。

【解题分析】Time capsule 后的分隔结构说明了 time capsule 是一个受欢迎的事物,因而空格应填褒义词,可以候选的为 C 和 D。D 的 resplendent 在修饰物质名词时表示辉煌的、发光的,故不正确。

【重点词条】veritable *adj*. 名副其实的,十足的,真实的(being in fact the thing named and not false, unreal, or imaginary, often used to stress the aptness of a metaphor) 例 a～mountain of references

inconsequential *adj*. ①不合逻辑的(illogical)

②离题的,不相关的(irrelevant)

③微不足道的(of no significance, unimportant)

3.【正确答案】C

【中文释义】在书籍的大规模市场营销之前,审查制度是一个主要的广告源泉,它帮助了书的销售并激发爱默生评论道:"每本被烧毁的书都照亮了我们的世界。"

【解题分析】第二个空格后的从句结构为一分隔,直接提供第二个空格的答案,在五个选项中能够帮助书籍销售的为 B 和 C。B 的第一个词与上句的时间状语冲突。

4.【正确答案】C

【中文释义】不仅仅是地质学家的保守主义阻碍了早期的关于地球陆地是漂移的板块的这个革命性思想的发展,而且还有古典物理学家们,他们不能够解释这个机制,因而宣称大陆移动是不可能的。

【解题分析】该句中 not only…but also 短语省略了 but also 下句中的物理学家反对大陆漂移,所以上句的地质学家也应反对这一学说,可以候选的第二个空格选项为 B 和 C,而 B 和 C 的第一个单词正好是一组反义词,使得思路很好发展,究竟是保守主义的还是激进主义会阻碍一个新思想呢? 当然选 C。

【重点词条】indecisiveness *n*. ①优柔寡断,犹豫不决(marked by or prone to indecision, irresolute)

②模糊,不确定(not clearly marked out, indefinite)

5.【正确答案】D

【中文释义】尽管人们通常会对医疗职业整体持极端的挑剔态度,但人们很少用同样的轻蔑态度对待他们的私人医生。

【解题分析】下文的 equal 提示我们应该填 extremely critical,但五个选项中没有它的同义词,这时应选它的近义词,请仔细阅读难词注解,正确答案为 D。

【重点词条】sarcasm *n*. 讽刺,挖苦,嘲笑(a sharp and often satirical or ironic utterance designed to cut or give pain) 例 tired of continual~s

mockery *n*. ①嘲笑,嘲弄(insulting or contemptuous action or speech, derision)

②笑柄(a subject of laughter, derision, or sport)

③学样(a counterfeit appearance, imitation)

④恶劣的事例(something ridiculously or impudently unsuitable)

condescension *n*. ①俯就,屈尊(voluntary descent from one's rank or dignity in relations with an inferior)

②傲慢态度,恩赐态度(patronizing attitude or behavior)

6.【正确答案】D

【中文释义】艾尔塔和其他现代派一样,以为形式应遵从功能;相应地,他的家具设计肯定了人的需求的首要地位。并且让家具的形式由人的用途来决定。

【解题分析】分号上下句重复,所以第二个空格是最好判断的,直接可得 D。

【重点词条】rational *adj*. ①理智的,有理性的(having reason or understanding)

②合理的(relating to, based on, or agreeable to reason, reasonable) 例 a~explanation/~behavior

③有理数的(involving only multiplication, division, addition, and subtraction and only a finite number of times)

rationale *n*. ①原理的阐述,解释

②全部理由,根本原因,逻辑依据

primary *n.* ①首位,卓越(something that stands first in rank, importance, or value, fundamental)

②教皇的职责(地位,身分)

7.【正确答案】C

【中文释义】对当代社会行为模式的夜郎自大式的接受已经误导了一些人,使得他们认为与当今年代冲突的价值观实际上都是过时陈旧的。

【解题分析】由 misled 可判断出第一个空格填贬义,可选 B 和 C。第二个空格显然应填贬义,因为接受当代价值观的人会认为与当代价值观冲突的都是不可接受的。正确答案因而可知为 C。

【重点词条】**complacent** *adj.* ①自满的(self-satisfied) 例 a～smile

②殷勤恭敬的(complaisant)

③漠不关心的(unconcerned)

redemptive *adj.* ①赎回的(of, relating to, or bringing about redemption)

②(宗教)救赎的,赎世的

SECTION 37

1. With its maverick approach to the subject, Shere Hite's book has been more widely debated than most; the media throughout the country have brought the author's ＿＿＿ opinions to the public's attention.

   (A) controversial

   (B) authoritative

   (C) popular

   (D) conclusive

   (E) articulate

2. Though many medieval women possessed devotional books that had belonged to their mothers, formal written evidence of women bequeathing books to their daughters is scarce, which suggests that such bequests were ＿＿＿ and required no ＿＿＿.

   (A) unselfish. . rationalization

   (B) tangential. . approval

   (C) customary. . documentation

   (D) covert. . discretion

   (E) spurious. . record

3. Although their initial anger had ＿＿＿ somewhat, they continued to ＿＿＿ the careless worker who had broken the machine.

   (A) blazed. . assail

   (B) diminished. . appease

   (C) abated. . berate

   (D) subsided. . condone

   (E) intensified. . torment

4. Borrowing a copyrighted book from a library amounts to a form of theft ＿＿＿ by entrenched custom: the copyright owner's property, the book, is used repeatedly without ＿＿＿ for such use.

   (A) engendered. . application

   (B) anticipated. . acknowledgement

   (C) sanctioned. . compensation

(D) provoked. . adjustment

(E) perpetrated. . permission

5. The notion that a parasite can alter the behavior of a host organism is not mere fiction; indeed, the phenomenon is not even ____.

(A) observable

(B) real

(C) comprehended

(D) rare

(E) imaginable

6. Although Shakespeare received little formal education, scholarship has in recent years ____ the view that he was ____ the work of classical authors.

(A) substantiated. . unimpressed by

(B) eroded. . obsessed by

(C) supported. . oblivious to

(D) questioned. . influenced by

(E) undermined. . unfamiliar with

7. Darwin's method did not really ____ the idea of race as an important conceptual category; even the much more central idea of species was little more than a theoretical ____.

(A) require. . convenience

(B) apply. . measurement

(C) exclude. . practice

(D) subsume. . validation

(E) reject. . fact

SECTION 37 解答

1. 【正确答案】A

【中文释义】由于他对这个课题的与众不同的研究方法,希尔·黑尔特的书受到了最广泛的讨论;整个国家的媒体使作者的富有争议的观点引起了公众的注意。

【解题分析】With 引导了一个原因状语。下句重复上句,最适合的做法是将 maverick 直接填到空格里去,答案 A 的 controversial 与 maverick 在"与众不同,易引起争议"这一意项上是同义词。

【重点词条】controversial *adj*. ①争论的,成问题的(of, relating to, or arousing controversy)

②可疑的,被议论的(given to controversy, disputatious)

maverick *n*. ①未打过烙印的牲口,尤指迷失的小牛(an unbranded range animal; esp. a motherless calf)

②(党派中)闹独立的人,背离团体自行其是的人(an independent individual who does not go along with a group or party)

2. 【正确答案】C

【中文释义】尽管很多中世纪的妇女拥有曾经属于她们的母亲的用于祈祷的书,关于妇女遗留书给她们女儿的正式书面证据却很稀少,这就说明这种遗赠行为是风俗性的,并不需要证明文件。

【解题分析】第二空格中显然应填上文出现过的 formal written evidence。这样就构成了一个很简单流畅的重复语句"遗赠的书面证据很少,这就说明遗赠不需要书面证据"。可以候选的答案为 C 和 E,再以第一个词的角度来看,C 构成了一个正确的顺承并列关系。

【重点词条】**bequeath** *v.* ①(按遗嘱)把…遗留给(to give or leave by will)

②传给(to hand down, transmit)

tangential *adj.* ①正切的(of, relating to, or of the nature of a tangent)

②离题的(divergent, digressive)

③略为触及的(touching lightly, incidental, peripheral) 例 ~ involvement

covert *adj.* ①隐蔽的,掩饰的,秘密的(not openly shown, engaged in, or avowed, veiled) 例 a~ alliance

②在保护下的(covered over, sheltered)

3. 【正确答案】C

【中文释义】尽管他们起初的愤怒某种程度上减轻了,但是他们继续训斥那个粗心的毁坏了机器的工人。

【解题分析】Continue to 后应该继续跟一个表"愤怒"的动词,可候选的为 A、C、E,第一个词能和下文构成转折的只有 C。

【重点词条】**appease** *v.* ①平息,抚慰(to bring to a state of peace or quiet, calm)

②缓解,使…得以满足(pacify, conciliate; esp. to buy off an aggressor by concessions usu. at the sacrifice of principles)

torment *v.* ①使痛苦,使苦恼(to cause severe usu. persistent or recurrent distress of body or mind to) 例 cattle~ed by flies

②歪曲,扭曲(distort, twist)

4. 【正确答案】C

【中文释义】从图书馆里借一本注了版权的书等同于一种由根深蒂固的风俗所批准的偷窃:版权拥有者的财产,这本书,被反复使用而没有任何经济补偿。

【解题分析】第一个空格后出现 by 短语,by 后如果接动词或其变化的形式则可以直接用于解题,事实上填空当中几乎都是这样的句式:被某人的鼓励所鼓励了,被某人的批评所批评了。该句 by 后的 entrench 的含义是"确立,批准"的意思,所以第一个空格与之同义的只有 C。

【重点词条】**entrench** *v.* ①以壕沟防护(to place within or surround with a trench esp. for defense)

②建立(to establish solidly) 例 ~ed themselves in the business

③挖壕沟(to cut into, furrow; to erode downward so as to form a trench)

5. 【正确答案】D

【中文释义】寄生虫会改变寄主生物的行为的概念并不是虚构;事实上,这个现象甚至都不罕见。

【解题分析】分号后出现的 indeed 在填空中都表示肯定和递进。

【重点词条】**fiction** *n.* ①小说(a work of fiction; esp. novel)

②假设(an assumption of a possibility as a fact irrespective of the question of its truth) 例 a legal~

③虚构,捏造(the action of feigning or of creating with the imagination)

6.【正确答案】E

【中文释义】尽管莎士比亚只受到过很少的正规教育,学者们这几年反对这种观点,即莎士比亚对古典作家的作品很不熟悉。

【解题分析】上下句转折所针对的角度即为 formal education,下句的 work of classical authors 即是指 formal education,所以第二个空格可以填 receive 或者 not receive 而不可能是其他情况,这样才可以与上句构成转折关系,此时可候选的为 D 和 E,而 D 的第一个单词使得上下句不能成为转折关系,故选 E。

【重点词条】**obsess** *v.* ①困扰(to haunt or excessively preoccupy the mind of) 例 was~ed with the idea

②使着迷,使心神不宁

oblivious *adj.* ①忘却的,健忘的(lacking remembrance, memory, or mindful attention)

②不注意的,不知觉的(lacking active conscious knowledge or awareness)

7.【正确答案】A

【中文释义】达尔文的方法并不真正地需要属的思想作为一个重要的概念范畴;即使是更中心的种的思想也只不过是理论上的图方便而已。

【解题分析】下句的 little more than 就提示我们后面的空格应该填上一个贬义的词,A 的 convenience 作"方便"解释时,并不是贬义词,但作"图方便的、权宜的"解释时,便是贬义。B、C、D、E 都是客观事物或褒义词,故可直接选 A。此句的含义比较晦涩,达尔文用门纲目科属种的概念体系来作分类描述,如果这种描述是真理,那么它的描述就应该是惟一的,因为客观存在是惟一的存在,相应的描述这种惟一存在的理论体系,也只应是一系列惟一对应的概念体系,而此句说达尔文的概念是并非必然需要的,或者只是理论上的图方便,实指达尔文的理论并非真实描绘存在,而只是描绘的存在影子而已。

【重点词条】**subsume** *v.* 把…归入,纳入(to include or place within something larger or more comprehensive, encompass as a subordinate or component element)

例 red, green, and yellow are subsumed under the term "color"

SECTION 38

1. The functions of the hands, eyes, and brain are so ____ that using the hands during early childhood helps to promote the child's entire ____ development.
   (A) intertwined. . perceptual
   (B) unalterable. . intellectual
   (C) enigmatic. . psychological
   (D) regulated. . adolescent
   (E) individualized. . social

2. Before 1500 North America was inhabited by more than 300 cultural groups, each with different customs, social structures, world views, and languages; such diversity ____ the existence of a single Native American culture.
   (A) complements
   (B) implies
   (C) reiterates
   (D) argues against
   (E) explains away

3. That dealers ____ enough to nurture a young modern painter's career rather than plunder it exist is not impossible, but the public's ____ appetite for modern art makes such dealers less and less likely.
   (A) chivalrous. . discriminating
   (B) magnanimous. . quirky
   (C) patient. . insatiable
   (D) cynical. . finicky
   (E) reckless. . zealous

4. In the absence of any ____ caused by danger, hardship, or even cultural difference, most utopian communities deteriorate into ____ but enervating backwaters.
   (A) turmoil. . frantic
   (B) mistrust. . naive
   (C) amelioration. . ignorant
   (D) decimation. . intrusive
   (E) stimulation. . placid

5. As Juanita argued, this new code of conduct is laughable; its principles are either ____, offering no wisdom but the obvious, or are so devoid of specific advice as to make almost any action ____.
   (A) irresolute. . unlikely
   (B) corroborative. . redundant
   (C) platitudinous. . justifiable
   (D) homogeneous. . impartial
   (E) labyrinthine. . unacceptable

6. Histocompatibility antigens that attack foreign tissue in the body cannot have been ____ through evolution expressly to ____ organ transplantation; on the contrary, they have been found to facilitate many essential biological functions.
   (A) designed. . retain
   (B) produced. . aid
   (C) developed. . enhance
   (D) selected. . promote
   (E) conserved. . foil

7. Their air of cheerful self-sacrifice and endless complaisance won them undeserved praise, for their seeming gallantry was wholly motivated by a ____ wish to avoid conflict of any sort.
   (A) poignant

(B) sincere   (D) laudable

(C) plaintive   (E) craven

SECTION 38 解答

1. 【正确答案】A

   【中文释义】手,眼睛和大脑的功能是如此交织在一起,以至于在孩童早期使用手有助于促进小孩全部感观和思维的发展。

   【解题分析】句中表达的变化非常明显,首先是手,眼睛和大脑,接着只谈了手,而其后的第二个空格前又谈了整个的发展,不难推知,第一个空格应填手,眼睛和大脑是相互有关联的,或类似的词,正确答案 A。

   【重点词条】perceptual *adj.* 感知的,感觉的(of, relating to, or involving perception esp. in relation to immediate sensory experience)

2. 【正确答案】D

   【中文释义】在 1500 年之前北美居住着超过 300 个文化部落,每一个文化部落都有不同的风俗,社会结构,世界观和语言;这种多样性推翻了只存在一个土著美洲印第安文化的说法。

   【重点词条】reiterate *v.* 反复做,反复讲,反复重申(to state or do over again or repeatedly sometimes with wearying effect)

   argue against   驳斥,推翻

   argue for   支持,提倡

   explain away   通过解释来消除 例 She explains away the child's fear.

3. 【正确答案】C

   【中文释义】有足够耐心来培养一个年轻的现代画家的职业生涯而不是掠夺他的画商存在,这一点并不是不可能的,但是公众对现代艺术的毫不知足的需求使得这样的交易商越来越不可能。

   【解题分析】上半句为大主语,that 构成主语从句,主语从句的谓语动词为 is not impossible。主语从句内部的主语为 dealers,谓语为 exist,分析清楚全句的结构后,答案就很好分析了,下句称这样的画商越来越少,也就是说培养画家而不是掠夺画家的画商越来越少,换种说法就是掠夺画商的交易商越来越多,也就说明画商需要大量的画来满足公众的需求,从而可知公众的需求是非常大量的,可选答案 C。

4. 【正确答案】E

   【中文释义】缺少任何由危险,困境或者文化差异所造成的刺激,大多数乌托邦国家恶化成为平静但是死气沉沉的与世隔绝的环境。

   【解题分析】第一个空格后的 by 并不能用于解题,我们通常将 by 后出现的动词或动词的变化形态,甚至是动词的抽象名词作为解题点加以注意,但此处的 by 后未出现任何动词及其变化形式,所以不宜由此入手解题,第二个空格与 enervating 共同修饰 backwaters,这儿出现了两个形容词用 but 连接同时修饰一个名词的

情况,这时 but 左右并不是对立面反义词,而应该是一个褒贬转折。正确答案可据此判断为 E,大家应该记住两个形容词用 but 连接同时修饰一个名词的特殊考法。这种情况的变化形态 ①adj1, albeit adj2 N ②N of 形容词的抽象名词,这种考法近几年频频出现。

【重点词条】**amelioration** *n*. 改善,改良,减轻(to make better or more tolerable)

intrusive *adj*. 侵入的,闯入的,打扰的(intruding where one is not welcome or invited)

5. 【正确答案】C

【中文释义】正如詹安尼所指出的一样,这个新的行为规则是可笑的;它的条款或者是陈腐的,没有任何智慧都是显而易见的,或者是如此地缺乏明确的指导以至于使得任何行为都正当合理。

【解题分析】第一个空格后显然是一个分隔成分,直接给前文提供答案,能表达出分隔含义的选项为 C。

【重点词条】**platitudinous** *adj*. 老生常谈的,陈腐的(having the characteristics of a platitude, full of platitudes) 例 ～remarks

corroborative *adj*. 使更加确凿的,确证的(to support with evidence or authority, make more certain)

labyrinthine *adj*. 迷宫的,错综复杂的(of, relating to, or resembling a labyrinth, intricate, involved)

6. 【正确答案】E

【中文释义】攻击异体组织的适应性抗原不可能通过演变保留下来专门去破坏器官移植;相反,它们被发现有助于很多必须的生理功能。

【解题分析】分号下半句重复上半句,而分号后的 on the contrary 就告诉读者应为反义重复,所以上句中适应性抗原的作用应和下句的 facilitate 正好相反,上句中表示适应性组织抗原作用的空格为第二空格,第一空格表示的是适应性组织抗原所被动遭受的动作而不表示其主动的作用,所以 facilitate 的反义词应填入第二空格,可得答案 E,值得强调的是上半句否定的并不是 conserve,否定的是 expressly to do sth。也就是说适应性组织抗原确实保存了下来,但保存的目的不仅仅是为了破坏器官的移植,下句接着强调,它们有很多重要的生理功能。

【重点词条】**essential** *adj*. ①基本的,本质的(of, relating to, or constituting essence, inherent)

②必要的,必不可少的(of the utmost importance, basic, indispensable, necessary) 例 ～foods/an～requirement for admission to college

foil *v*. ①挫败(to prevent from attaining an end, defeat)
②阻挠(to bring to naught, thwart)

7. 【正确答案】E

【中文释义】他们愉快的自我牺牲以及无休止的殷勤为他们赢得了不配享有的赞扬,因为他们看起来的骑士风度完全是由一种来避免一切冲突的胆怯愿望所激发的。

【解题分析】全句为一个因果关系句,既然上文认为他们的种种自我牺牲以及殷勤都不值得表扬,那么下句就应该提出原因表示出一个不值得表扬的愿望,五个选项中,贬义词只有 E。

SECTION 39

1. Though some of the information the author reveals about Russian life might surprise Americans, her major themes are ____ enough.

   (A) familiar
   (B) thorough
   (C) vital
   (D) original
   (E) interesting

2. In the early twentieth century, the discovery of radium ____ the popular imagination; not only was its discoverer, Marie Curie, idolized, but its market value ____ that of the rarest gemstone.

   (A) stormed. . sank to
   (B) horrified. . approached
   (C) taxed. . was equal to
   (D) enflamed. . exceeded
   (E) escaped. . was comparable to

3. The president's secretary and his chief aide adored him, and both wrote obsessively ____ personal memoirs about him; unfortunately, however, ____ does not make for true intimacy.

   (A) fatuous. . frankness
   (B) devoted. . idolatry
   (C) garrulous. . confidentiality
   (D) candid. . discretion
   (E) rancorous. . criticism

4. Despite claims that his philosophy can be traced to ____ source, the philosophy in fact draws liberally on several traditions and methodologies and so could justifiably be termed ____.

   (A) a particular. . consistent
   (B) a schematic. . multifaceted
   (C) a dominant. . cogent
   (D) an authoritative. . derivative
   (E) a single. . eclectic

5. Du Bois' foreign trips were the highlight, not the ____, of his travels; he was habitually on the go across and around the United States.

   (A) idiosyncrasy
   (B) result
   (C) precursor
   (D) culmination
   (E) totality

6. Business forecasts usually prove reasonably accurate when the assumption that the future will be much like the past is ____; in times of major ____ in the business environment, however, forecasts can be dangerously wrong.

   (A) specified. . discontinuities
   (B) questioned. . surges
   (C) contradicted. . improvements
   (D) entertained. . risks
   (E) satisfied. . shifts

7. It is almost always desirable to increase the

yield of a crop if ____ increases are not also necessary in energy, labor, and other inputs of crop production.

(A) predetermined

(B) commensurate

(C) compatible

(D) measured

(E) equivocal

SECTION 39 解答

1. 【正确答案】A

   【中文释义】尽管这位作者所揭示出的一些关于俄国人生活的消息会让美国人惊奇,但她的重要主题却是非常为人们所熟悉的。

   【解题分析】空格里填上文 surprise 的反义词。

   【重点词条】**thorough** *adj*. ①彻底的(carried through to completion, exhaustive) 例 a~ search
   ②对(细节)不厌其烦的,全然的(marked by full detail) 例 a~ description
   ③严谨的(careful about detail, painstaking) 例 a~scholar
   ④通过的(passing through)

2. 【正确答案】D

   【中文释义】在二十世纪早期,镭的发现激发点燃了公众的想象力;不仅仅是它的发现者,玛丽·居里被偶像般崇拜,而且镭的市场价格超过了最稀缺的宝石。

   【解题分析】下句的居里受到偶像化崇拜,以及其递进关系所表达的镭的市价很高都是对上文的解释,下句的现象表明公众极为热情,所以上句只能填 D。

   【重点词条】**storm** *v*. 强烈感染,使着迷,使神魂颠倒

   tax *v*. ①抽税(to levy a tax on)
   ②指责,责备(charge, accuse) 例 ~ed him with neglect of duty
   ③使负担,受压力(to make onerous and rigorous demands on) 例 The job~ed her strength.

3. 【正确答案】B

   【中文释义】总统的秘书和他的第一助理崇拜总统,两人都写了令人难忘的虔诚的关于总统的个人回忆录;不幸的是,然而,崇拜并不能导致真正的了解。

   【解题分析】分号下半句重复上半句,第二个空格能和上文重复的词只有一个 adore,答案为 B。

   【重点词条】**make for** 有助于,导致,产生

   intimacy *v*. ①深知,了解(a relationship marked by depth of knowledge)
   ②亲昵的言语(行为)
   ③私下,秘密

4. 【正确答案】E

【中文释义】尽管有这样的观点，即他的哲学可以被回溯到一个单一的源头，但是这位哲学家事实上自由地利用了好几个传统和方法论，因而可以被非常公允地定义为折中的。

【解题分析】第一个空格应和 several traditions and methodologies 构成反义，第二个空格应表达出这个哲学有好几个源头这一概念，吻合的只有 E。

【重点词条】**eclectic** *adj*. ①选择的(selecting what appears to be best in various doctrines, methods, or styles)

②折中的，兼收并蓄的(composed of elements drawn from various sources; heterogeneous)

cogent *adj*. ①强有力的(having power to compel or constrain) 例 ~ forces

②有说服力的(appealing forcibly to the mind or reason, convincing) 例 ~ evidence

③相关的(pertinent, relevant) 例 a ~ analysis of a problem

5.【正确答案】E

【中文释义】杜·波伊斯的外国旅行是精彩的部分，但不是他旅行的全部；他总是习惯性地在旅途生活中，这种旅途既在美国国内四处旅游也会穿越到美国之外去旅游。

【解题分析】分号句的上半句在谈论外国旅行部分，而下半句则讲他的旅行既有国内又有国外，故可知空格的概念。

【重点词条】**go** *n*. 旅途，旅行

6.【正确答案】E

【中文释义】当这样的假设满足时，也即未来会和过去高度相似的假设成立时，商业预测总是证实为相当精确；在商业环境大变动的时代里，然而，预测却是非常危险的错误。

【解题分析】上下句预测的结果迥然不同是由两个不同的条件所导致的，上句为过去和未来会十分相像这个条件，所以下句的条件应为过去和未来不一样，这时可得出 A 和 E 的第二选择正确，接着分析第一个空格，A 表示这种假设被详细说明过，和这个假设是真的是两个完全不同的概念，也即上句并没有认为过去和未来是一样的，当然和下半句就没有构成任何对比，而 E 却满足了这个不同的条件不同结果的逻辑结构。

【重点词条】**surge** *v*. ①起伏，颠簸(to rise and fall actively, toss) 例 a ship surging in heavy seas

②汹涌，奔腾(to rise and move in waves or billows, swell)

③猛冲，急剧上升(to rise suddenly to an excessive or abnormal value) 例 The stock market ~ ed to a record high.

④浪涛般汹涌奔腾(to move with a surge or in surges) 例 felt the blood surging into his face

entertain *v*. ①怀有，抱有，心存(to keep, hold, or maintain in the mind) 例

I~grave doubts about her sincerity.

②接受,考虑(to receive and take into consideration) 例 refused

to~our plea

③给…娱乐,款待(to provide entertainment for)

7.【正确答案】B

【中文释义】这总是受欢迎的,如果可以增加稻谷的产量而不需要同样地增加能量和人力和其他的稻谷生产的投入。

【解题分析】此句中的 yield 和最后一行的 input 构成一组反义词明确说明了此句为投入和产业的关系。

【重点词条】measured *adj*. ①整齐的

②从容不迫的

③(诗歌)有节奏的

④(言辞等)慎重的,经仔细考虑的,有分寸的

SECTION 40

1. Job failure means being fired from a job, being asked to resign, or leaving _____ to protect yourself because you had very strong evidence that one of the first two was _____.

   (A) voluntarily. . impending

   (B) abruptly. . significant

   (C) knowingly. . operative

   (D) understandably. . pertinent

   (E) eventually. . intentional

2. The tone of Jane Carlyle's letter is guarded, and her feelings are always _____ by the wit and pride that made _____ plea for sympathy impossible for her.

   (A) masked. . a direct

   (B) bolstered. . a needless

   (C) controlled. . a circumspect

   (D) enhanced. . an intentional

   (E) colored. . an untimely

3. French folktales almost always take place within the basic _____ that correspond to the _____ setting of peasant life: on the one hand, the household and village on the other, the open road.

   (A) contexts. . hierarchical

   (B) structures. . personal

   (C) frameworks. . dual

   (D) chronologies. . generic

   (E) narratives. . ambivalent

4. Nurturing the Royal Ballet's artistic growth while preserving its institutional stability has been difficult, because the claims of the latter seem inescapably to _____ development; apparently, attaining artistic success is simpler than _____ it.

   (A) ensure. . promoting

   (B) inhibit. . perpetuating

   (C) undermine. . resurrecting

   (D) modify. . appreciating

   (E) supplement. . confining

5. Inspired interim responses to hitherto un-

known problems, New Deal economic stratagems became _____ as a result of bureaucratization, their flexibility and adaptability destroyed by their transformation into rigid policies.

(A) politicized

(B) consolidated

(C) ossified

(D) ungovernable

(E) streamlined

6. Biologists _____ isolated oceanic islands like the Galapagos, because, in such small, laboratory-like settings, the rich hurly-burly of continental plant and animal communities is reduced to a scientifically _____ complexity.

(A) explore. . diverse

(B) desert. . manageable

(C) exploit. . intimidating

(D) reject. . intricate

(E) prize. . tractable

7. The startling finding that variations in the rate of the Earth's rotation depend to an _____ degree on the weather has necessitated a complete _____ of the world's time-keeping methods.

(A) unexpected. . overhaul

(B) anticipated. . recalibration

(C) indeterminate. . rejection

(D) unobservable. . review

(E) estimated. . acceptance

SECTION 40 解答

1. 【正确答案】A

   【中文释义】工作的失败就意味着被解雇,或者被要求主动辞职,或者自动离开来保护自己,因为你自己有足够的证据表明前两者之一正在临近。

   【解题分析】显然第一个空格填出后仍然表示被辞职,因为它与前面两种方式并列,所以第二个空格解释第一个空格的行为,实际上就是解释为何要辞职,五个选项中 A 构成了解释,即辞职的原因是迫不得已。

   【重点词条】**operative** *adj*. ①有效的(producing an appropriate effect, efficacious)

   ②起作用的(exerting force or influence, operating)

   ③操作着的(having to do with physical operations such as of machines)

   ④工作着的(working) 例 an~craftsman

2. 【正确答案】A

   【中文释义】卡莉丽的信的语调是谨慎提防的,并且她的感情总是被巧妙的言语和骄傲所掩饰,这就使得直接请求别人的同情对她而言是根本不可能的事。

   【解题分析】Pride 后作分隔的定语从句显然应由 pride 推断答案,所以,思路简化为"骄傲的情绪就使什么样的请求同情不可能发生",可以候选的答案为 A,骄傲的人都不会直接请求别人的同情,当然,会有些同学认为 D 或者 C 似乎也没有太大的错误。那么,再分析一下第一选项,第一选项中问及她的感觉,她的心情被怎么样了,而 and 之前明确表达出,她的感情是提防谨慎,不轻易外露的;故可选的答案当然是 A。

【重点词条】wit *n.* ①风趣(clever or apt humor)

②智者(a person of superior intellect，thinker)

③领悟

④机智

3.【正确答案】C

【中文释义】法国的民间故事总是发生在一个基本的框架之中,这个框架与农民生活的双重环境相对应,这双重环境一方面是指家庭和村庄,另一方面是指畅通的道路。

【解题分析】冒号前后表示解释,冒号后谈到两个方面,故第二个空格必须包括这两个方面。明确表达这一点的为答案 C。尽管我们对这两方面具体所指并不熟悉,但在考场上请记住重复才是正确的选择。事实上这里所指的两方面是指法国农民的特殊的双重性格,既有保守的渴望宁静安详的生活的态度,又有一种超越的积极进取的心态。

【重点词条】ambivalent *adj.* ①矛盾的(simultaneous and contradictory attitudes or feelings such as attraction and repulsion toward an object，person，or action)

②摇摆不定的(continual fluctuation between one thing and its opposite)

③模棱两可的(uncertainty as to which approach to follow)

4.【正确答案】B

【中文释义】培养皇家芭蕾舞剧团艺术上的成长,同时又保持它的机制的稳定是困难的,因为后者的目标看上去不可避免地抑制发展;很明显,获得艺术的成功比使之永恒要简单得多。

【解题分析】上半句中称两者同时干是有困难的,提出的原因中当然是应该认为两者有不可调和、不可共存的性质,此时可以选 C 和 B。分号句下句要重复上句,获得艺术的成功显然是对应上半句中的艺术的成长,所以第二个空格应该对应于机制的稳定不变,B 和 C 的第二个词表示稳定不变的词是 B 的 perpetuate。此句的意思较为隐晦,它谈了一个发展与稳定的问题。事实上一个成熟的艺术家都会有自己的固定风格(institutional stability),而如果他要继续发展,他就必须打破这个风格,所以艺术家总是称自己在痛苦地脱胎新生,但是发展中的艺术形态没有固定的风格又很难获得认可。有人称"风格就是艺术",但如果形成风格后就不再发展那就是固步自封。

【重点词条】perpetuate *v.* 使永久,使长存,使不朽(to make perpetual or cause to last indefinitely) 例 ~ the species

5.【正确答案】C

【中文释义】作为一种富有灵感的,临时的对迄今为止尚不知晓的问题的反应策略,罗斯福新政的经济政策被官僚化的结果是变得僵化,它们的灵活性和适应性被转变为僵化的政策所彻底摧毁。

【解题分析】空格后的分隔明确指出了,灵活性和适应性被摧毁当然就会表现为僵化不灵活,故空格选 C。

【重点词条】**ossify** *v*. ①使骨化(to change into bone)

②使僵化,使硬化(to become hardened or conventional and opposed to change)

ungovernable *adj*. 无法控制的,难治理的,难约束的(not capable of being governed, guided, or restrained)

6.【正确答案】E

【中文释义】生物学家认为像戈拉帕哥这样的与外界隔离的大洋中的小岛很有价值,因为在这样小的、实验室一般的环境里,大陆动植物群的大量的混乱复杂被削减为一个科学上可控制的复杂性。

【解题分析】生物学家与大洋小岛要有一个动词发生关系,这是很奇怪的。GRE 的句子从来都是在讨论特征人物的特征动作,生物学家只应该研应生物,而不是大洋中的小岛,带着这个疑问下文很快就作出了解释,such 这个词明确告诉我们这个小岛是生物学家的实验室,所以第一个空格就成为科学家与他的实验室之间的关系,可以候选的是 C 和 E。下句的因果句来表达为何科学家利用实验室(C),或者认为实验室有价值(E),当然都会是正面色彩的原因,故只能选 E。

【重点词条】**hurly-burly** *n*. 骚动,喧哗,吵闹,混乱(uproar, tumult)

tractable *adj*. ①驯服(顺)的(capable of being easily led, taught, or controlled, docile) 例 a～horse

②易处理的(easily handled, managed, or wrought, malleable)

manageable *adj*. 易处理的,易驾驭的(capable of being managed)

desert *v*. ①抛弃,遗弃(to withdraw from or leave usu. without intent to return)

②擅离职守(to quit one's post, allegiance, or service without leave or justification; esp. to abandon military duty without leave and without intent to return)

7.【正确答案】A

【中文释义】这个令人吃惊的发现,地球自转速度的变化依赖气候到了一个令人吃惊的程度,使得我们必须完全地重新调整地球的时间记录方法。

【解题分析】主语之后的分隔中有一个空格,所以分隔当中的空格应直接由前文获得,故选 unexpected 填到空格中。

【重点词条】**startling** *adj*. 令人惊吓的,使人惊跳的,惊人的(causing momentary fright, surprise, or astonishment)

overhaul *v*. ①彻底检查(to examine thoroughly)

②彻底革新(to renovate, revise, or renew thoroughly)

calibration *n*. 量口径,校准刻度(the act or process of calibrating)

SECTION 41

1. In the British theater young people under thirty-five have not had much ____ getting recognition onstage, but offstage—in the ranks of playwrights, directors, designers, administrators—they have mostly been relegated to relative obscurity.
   - (A) trouble
   - (B) satisfaction
   - (C) curiosity about
   - (D) success at
   - (E) fear of

2. An institution concerned about its reputation is at the mercy of the actions of its members; because the misdeeds of individuals are often used to ____ the institutions of which they are a part.
   - (A) reform
   - (B) coerce
   - (C) honor
   - (D) discredit
   - (E) intimidate

3. Since many casual smokers develop lung cancer and many ____ smokers do not, scientists believe that individuals differ in their ____ the cancer-causing agents known to be present in cigarette smoke.
   - (A) heavy. . susceptibility to
   - (B) chronic. . concern about
   - (C) habitual. . proximity to
   - (D) devoted. . reliance upon
   - (E) regular. . exposure to

4. We accepted the theory that as people become more independent of one another, they begin to feel so isolated and lonely that freedom becomes ____ condition that most will seek to ____.
   - (A) a permanent. . postpone
   - (B) a common. . enter
   - (C) a negative. . escape
   - (D) a political. . impose
   - (E) an irreparable. . avoid

5. If animal parents were judged by human standards, the cuckoo would be one of nature's more ____ creatures, blithely laying its eggs in the nests of other birds, and leaving the incubating and nurturing to them.
   - (A) mettlesome
   - (B) industrious
   - (C) domestic
   - (D) lackluster
   - (E) feckless

6. The current penchant for ____ a product by denigrating a rival, named in the advertisement by brand name, seems somewhat ____: suppose the consumer remembers only the rival's name?
   - (A) criticizing. . inefficient
   - (B) touting. . foolhardy
   - (C) enhancing. . insipid
   - (D) evaluating. . cumbersome
   - (E) flaunting. . gullible

7. His imperturbability in the face of evidence indicating his deliberate fraud failed to reassure supporters of his essential ____; instead, it suggested a talent for ____ that

they had never suspected.

(A) culpability．．intrigue

(B) wisdom．．reproof

(C) remorse．．loquacity

(D) probity．．guile

(E) combativeness．．compromise

SECTION 41 解答

1.【正确答案】A

【中文释义】在英国的剧院里 35 岁以下的年轻人在舞台上获得声誉并没有遇到多大麻烦，但是在舞台下，在剧作、导演、布景和剧务这些阶层中，他们总是被贬低到相对不重要的地位。

【解题分析】上下句用 onstage 和 offstage 来表示了一种对比关系，故下句称他们总是被贬低到不重要的地位，上句则应称他们容易获得声誉。双重否定的说法就是没有困难，也即容易的意思。

【重点词条】relegate *v.* ①驱逐(to send into exile, banish)

②贬低，贬谪(assign to a place of insignificance or of oblivion, put out of sight or mind)

③指派，指定(to assign to an appropriate place or situation on the basis of classification or appraisal)

obscurity *n.* ①无关紧要的人(one that is obscure)

②无足轻重的地位(the quality or state of being obscure)

2.【正确答案】D

【中文释义】一个关心它自己声誉的机构受制于其成员的行为；因为个人的错误行为总是被用于否定一个他们所工作的那个机构的声誉。

【解题分析】Be at the mercy of 的含义是受到控制，所以上句的含义即为个人的行为和整个单位的声誉总是相一致，所以下句的个人的错误行为与机构的声誉相一致，当然也是使这个机构获得不好的声誉，故选 D。

【重点词条】**be at the mercy of**　处于…的支配控制之中

3.【正确答案】A

【中文释义】既然许多偶尔才吸烟的人得了肺癌，而许多抽烟很重的人却没有，所以科学家认为人和人之间在他们对香烟中存在的致癌物的吸收上是有差别的。

【解题分析】上半句是非常对称的结构，偶尔抽烟的人得肺癌，那么不得肺癌的就是那些总抽烟的人，可选 A、B、C、E，由因果句可推断出答案 A 正确。

【重点词条】susceptibility *n.* 易感染，易屈服，高度脆弱(the quality or state of being susceptible; esp. lack of ability to resist some extraneous agent, such as a pathogen or drug, sensitivity)

4.【正确答案】C

【中文释义】我们认可了这样的理论学说；当人们之间变得越来越独立，他们就开始觉得如

此地与世隔绝和孤独以至于自由变成了一个负面的条件,大多数人都寻求
摆脱。

【解题分析】此句的 so...that 因果结构指向的结果应该是贬义的,因为其原因是贬义的,
故可选 C。

【重点词条】**irreparable** *adj*. 无可救药的,无法弥补的(irremediable) 例 ～damage

5.【正确答案】E

【中文释义】如果动物的父母用人的标准去衡量的话,杜鹃是大自然中最不负责任的动物,
他们非常愉快地将他们的蛋产在别的鸟的巢里,并且将孵化和培养下一代的
工作留给别的鸟去干。

【解题分析】很有趣的题目。由空格后的一长串分隔,不难得知杜鹃作为父母是多么的不
负责任。不过也正如句中所强调的一样,这是"judged by human standards"后
的结论,焉知杜鹃作如何感想。正如人总是偷窃并享用完蜂蜜后给蜜蜂加上
一个无私的奉献的美名一样,人类社会里错误地运用判断标准,强盗般地运用
错误判断标准,以及有选择性地强盗般地错误地运用标准几乎已经成为司空
见惯的、必不可少的现象。

【重点词条】**mettlesome** *adj*. 精神抖擞的(full of mettle, spirited)

　　　　lackluster *adj*. 目光迟滞的,缺乏活力的,平庸的(lacking in sheen, brilliance,
　　　　　　　　or vitality, dull, mediocre)

　　　　feckless *adj*. ①虚弱的,无效的(weak, ineffective)
　　　　　　　　②无价值的,不负责任的(worthless, irresponsible)

　　　　blithely *adj*. ①愉快的,轻松的(of a happy lighthearted character or disposi-
　　　　　　　　tion)
　　　　　　　　②随意的,散漫的(lacking due thought or consideration, casual,
　　　　　　　　heedless)

6.【正确答案】B

【中文释义】目前通过贬低对手来宣传一个产品的倾向,并且对手产品在宣传广告中居然
是以其品牌名称出现的,(这种倾向)看上去有点愚蠢:假设消费者只记住了竞
争对手的品牌名称呢?

【解题分析】第一个空格后的 by 提供了解题线索,贬低对手这种手段当然就是为了宣传吹
捧自己的产品,可以候选的答案为 B 和 E。C 答案是指促进一个产品的质量或
功能而非广告中的提高知名度,B 和 E 选项的第二个词很好判断,如果消费者
只记住竞争对手的品牌,那这种广告当然就是愚蠢失败的。

【重点词条】**foolhardy** *adv*. 卤莽冲动地(foolishly adventurous and bold, rash)

　　　　insipid *adj*. ①无味的(lacking taste or savor, tasteless)
　　　　　　　　②索然无味的,令人乏味的(lacking in qualities that interest,
　　　　　　　　stimulate, or challenge, dull, flat)

　　　　cumbersome *adj*. ①沉重的, 不方便的(burdensome, troublesome)

②费力的(unwieldy because of heaviness and bulk)

③沉重的,移动缓慢的(slow-moving, ponderous)

7.【正确答案】D

　【中文释义】他在揭示他故意欺骗行为的证据面前表现出来的镇定自若没有能够使他的支持者们确信他的本质的正直;相反,这却表明了一种他们从来没有猜想过的欺骗的天赋。

　【解题分析】分号句下句要求填上这个骗子的天赋才能,当然就应该填上骗术。这可以从分号句上半句的 his deliberate fraud 这个特征动作中得来。而第一行的他面对证据仍然镇定自若,并不是表示他的特征性格是镇定,而是表明他极善于欺骗。

　【重点词条】**reassure** *v*. ①再次肯定,证实(to assure anew) 例 reassured him that the work was on schedule

②安慰,恢复信心(to restore to confidence) 例 felt reassured by their earnest promise to do better

　　　　culpability *n*. ①罪恶,罪恶感(guilty, criminal)

②应受诅咒的(meriting condemnation or blame) 例 ~ negligence

SECTION 42

1. Although providing wild chimpanzees with food makes them less ____ and easier to study, it is also known to ____ their normal social patterns.

(A) interesting. . reinforce

(B) manageable. . upset

(C) shy. . disrupt

(D) poised. . inhibit

(E) accessible. . retard

2. There is something ____ about the way the building of monasteries proliferated in eighteenth-century Bavaria, while in the rest of the Western world religious ardor was ____ and church building was consequently declining.

(A) enigmatic. . coalescing

(B) destructive. . changing

(C) immutable. . dissipating

(D) incongruous. . diminishing

(E) momentous. . diversifying

3. Because they had various meanings in nineteenth-century biological thought, "mechanism" and "vitalism" ought not to be considered ____ terms; thus, I find the recent insistence that the terms had single definitions to be entirely ____.

(A) univocal. . erroneous

(B) problematic. . anachronistic

(C) intractable. . obtuse

(D) congruent. . suspect

(E) multifaceted. . vapid

4. Many Americans believe that individual initiative epitomized the 1890's and see the entrepreneur as the ____ of that age.

(A) caricature

(B) salvation

(C) throwback

(D) aberration

(E) personification

5. Neither the ideas of philosophers nor the practices of ordinary people can, by themselves, ____ reality; what in fact changes reality and kindles revolution is the ____ of the two.

 (A) constitute. . divergence

 (B) affect. . aim

 (C) transform. . interplay

 (D) preserve. . conjunction

 (E) alter. . intervention

6. There has been a tendency among art historians not so much to revise as to eliminate

the concept of the Renaissance to ____ not only its uniqueness, but its very existence.

 (A) explain

 (B) extol

 (C) transmute

 (D) regret

 (E) contest

7. Employees had become so inured to the caprices of top management's personnel policies that they greeted the announcement of a company-wide dress code with ____.

 (A) astonishment

 (B) impassivity

 (C) resentment

 (D) apprehension

 (E) confusion

SECTION 42 解答

1.【正确答案】C

【中文释义】尽管给黑猩猩提供食物使得他们不会太害羞,因而易于研究,但这种做法同样也会破坏他们的正常的社会模式。

【解题分析】第一个空格应和其后的更容易研究构成小连接,只能选 C。

【重点词条】upset v. ①推翻(to force out of the usual upright, level, or proper position, overturn)

②干扰(to trouble mentally or emotionally, disturb the poise of)

③颠覆(to defeat unexpectedly)

④使…不适(to cause a physical disorder in; to make somewhat ill)

disrupt v. ①打碎,分裂(to break apart, rupture)

②搅乱(to throw into disorder) 例 agitators trying to~the meeting

③破坏(to interrupt the normal course or unity of)

retard v. ①阻碍(to slow up esp. by preventing or hindering advance or accomplishment, impede)

②保守(to delay academic progress by failure to promote)

2.【正确答案】D

【中文释义】这种现象中有一些不协调的因素,一方面是在 18 世纪的巴伐利亚修道院建筑非常兴旺,而另一方面在其他的西方世界地区宗教热忱还在减少,教堂建筑也随之衰败。

【解题分析】原句中的 building of monasteries proliferated 与 church building was declining 显然是在对比,两种截然相反的情况,故第一个空格可填 A 和 D。而 A 的第二个词并不能与其后的句子构成并列,故选 D。

【重点词条】**coalesce** *n*. 结合,合并,兼并

incongruous *adj*. ①不统一的,不和谐的(lacking congruity, not harmonious or incompatible) 例 ~colors

②违反规定的(not conforming, disagreeing) 例 conduct ~ with principle

③自相矛盾的(inconsistent within itself) 例 an ~ story

④不正确的,不相宜的(lacking propriety, unsuitable) 例 ~ manners

3.【正确答案】A

【中文释义】因为"机械论"和"生机论"在 19 世纪的生物学思维中各自有着许多不同的定义,所以他们不应该被认为是单义的术语,因此,我发现现在的这种坚持,认为这两个术语有单一定义是完全错误的。

【解题分析】此句考得非常细腻,请注意文中的 single definitions,这个短语用 single 来修饰复数的 definitions,这种表达很少见,它只能表示一种含义即"生机论"和"机械论"各有一个定义,如果文中表达的是 single definition,那么就成为这两个学说有一个共同的定义,这正是许多同学误解的含义,所以上文第一个空格应填 A 的 univocal,即单义的,而不是 D 的 congruent,即两者同意的。

【重点词条】**univocal** *adj*. 含义单一的(having one meaning only)

obtuse *adj*. ①不尖锐的,不精明的(not pointed or acute, blunt)

②钝角的(of an angle, exceeding 90 degrees but less than 180 degrees) 例 an ~ triangle

③不敏感的,不聪明的(lacking sharpness or quickness of sensibility or intellect, insensitive, stupid)

④难以理解的(difficult to comprehend, not clear or precise in thought or expression)

4.【正确答案】E

【中文释义】很多美国人认为个人的进取心象征了美国的 18 世纪 90 年代,并且将企业家看成那个年代的人格化身。

【解题分析】此句关键是要理解企业家就是个人进取心的代表,从而企业家就代表了那个时代的精神,成为个人进取心的代表。

【重点词条】**caricature** *n*. ①滑稽可笑(exaggeration by means of often ludicrous distortion of parts or characteristics)

②讽刺作品(a representation esp. in literature or art that has the qualities of caricature)

③滑稽的性格(a distortion so gross as to seem like caricature)

throwback *n*. ①返祖(reversion to an earlier type or phase, atavism)

②返祖现象或人物(one that is suggestive of or suited to an earlier time or style) 例 His manners were a~ to a more polite era.

personification *n*. 人格化身,人格化(representation of a thing or abstraction as a person or by the human form)

5.【正确答案】C

【中文释义】既不是哲学家的思想,也不是普通人的实践活动就可以凭自身的力量来改造现实;真正改变现象并且点燃革命的是两者力量的结合。

【解题分析】分号句下句的 reality 前的动词为 change,所以上半句的空格填上 change 的同义词,可选 C 和 E,第二个空格显然是针对上文的 by themselves 提出一种不同的方式,故选 C 答案。

【重点词条】**interplay** *v*. 交互作用(interaction) 例 the~of opposing forces

intervention *n*. ①插入(to occur, fall, or come between points of time or events)

②突兀之物(to enter or appear as an irrelevant or extraneous feature or circumstance)

③干预,干涉(to come in or between by way of hindrance or modification) 例 ~to stop a fight

6.【正确答案】E

【中文释义】在艺术史学家之间存在一个倾向,这种倾向与其说是修订不如说是消除文艺复兴这个概念,也就是说不但是否认它的独特性,更是否定它的真实存在。

【解题分析】破折号之前的连词短语 not so much…as…是"与其说…不如说…"的意思,所以上句肯定的是动词 eliminate,破折号后重复时应重复 eliminate,答案为 E。

7.【正确答案】B

【中文释义】雇员们已经对顶层管理的劳工政策的多变性感到麻木不仁了,以至于他们用一种冷漠的态度对待全公司范围内的着装规定的宣布。

【解题分析】由 so…that…结构可知,雇员对新的政策应该是 inured 的态度,故选 B 答案。

【重点词条】**impassivity** *n*. ①毫无痛觉(unsusceptible to pain)

②无知觉(unsusceptible to physical feeling, insensible)

③冷淡(unsusceptible to or destitute of emotion, apathetic)

④面无表情(giving no sign of feeling or emotion, expressionless)

confusion *n*. ①混淆(an act or instance of confusing)

②混乱不堪(the quality or state of being confused)

③混合物(a confused mass or mixture) 例 a~of voices

SECTION 43

1. Even though formidable winters are the norm in the Dakotas, many people were unprepared for the ____ of the blizzard of 1888.
   - (A) inevitability
   - (B) ferocity
   - (C) importance
   - (D) probability
   - (E) mildness

2. As the first streamlined car, the Airflow represented a ____ in automotive development, and although its sales were ____, it had an immense influence on automobile design.
   - (A) milestone. . disappointing
   - (B) breakthrough. . significant
   - (C) regression. . unimportant
   - (D) misjudgment. . calculable
   - (E) revolution. . tolerable

3. While nurturing parents can compensate for adversity, cold or inconsistent parents may ____ it.
   - (A) exacerbate
   - (B) neutralize
   - (C) eradicate
   - (D) ameliorate
   - (E) relieve

4. The architects of New York's early skyscrapers, hinting here at a twelfth-century cathedral, there at a fifteenth-century palace, sought to legitimize the city's social strivings by ____ a history the city did not truly ____.
   - (A) revealing. . deserve

   - (B) displaying. . desire
   - (C) evoking. . possess
   - (D) preserving. . experience
   - (E) flouting. . believe

5. Actual events in the history of life on Earth are accidental in that any outcome embodies just one ____ among millions; yet each outcome can be ____ interpreted.
   - (A) coincidence. . randomly
   - (B) relationship. . predictably
   - (C) fact. . readily
   - (D) happening. . uniquely
   - (E) possibility. . rationally

6. Although some of her fellow scientists ____ the unorthodox laboratory methodology that others found innovative, unanimous praise greeted her experimental results: at once pioneering and ____.
   - (A) ignored. . untrustworthy
   - (B) complimented. . foreseeable
   - (C) welcomed. . mundane
   - (D) decried. . unexceptionable
   - (E) attacked. . inconclusive

7. Early critics of Emily Dickinson's poetry mistook for simplemindedness the surface of artlessness that in fact she constructed with such ____.
   - (A) astonishment
   - (B) vexation
   - (C) allusion
   - (D) innocence
   - (E) cunning

SECTION 43 解答

1. 【正确答案】B

　【中文释义】即使可怕的冬天在达科他州是司空见惯的事情,人们仍然没有预料到 1888 年
　　　　　　　暴风雪会如此猛烈。

　【解题分析】上下句由 even though 指出了递进转折的关系,所以下句应填上一个比
　　　　　　　formidable 递进的词,答案为 ferocity。通常能够构成递进转折的连词有 even
　　　　　　　though, but nevertheless 或者从句用 though 引导,主句用 even 引导。

2. 【正确答案】A

　【中文释义】作为第一辆流线型的汽车,"气流"代表了汽车发展中的一块里程碑,尽管它的
　　　　　　　销售让人失望,但它却对汽车的设计有巨大的影响。

　【解题分析】此句有两个空格,我们通常从有明确解题点的或者有明确逻辑关系的空格开
　　　　　　　始着手解题。第一个空格并不处于一个明确的逻辑关系中,所以我们从第二
　　　　　　　个空格着手,构成明确转折关系的是 A 和 C,再由第一个空格判断为 A。

　【重点词条】**streamline** *v.* ①设计为流线形(to design or construct with a streamline)
　　　　　　　　　　　　　　②现代化(to bring up to date, modernize)
　　　　　　　　　　　　　　③组织,条理化(to put in order, organize)
　　　　　　　　　　　　　　④使更有效率(to make simpler or more efficient)

3. 【正确答案】A

　【中文释义】充满爱心的父母会对儿童成长中的困境苦难作出补偿,而冷酷的或者言行不
　　　　　　　一的父母往往会加重这些痛苦。

　【解题分析】While 只能表示对照而不表示转折,此句中标识逻辑关系的是一组形容词 nur-
　　　　　　　turing 和 cold and inconsistent。所以空格里填上前文 compensate 的反义词。

　【重点词条】**relieve** *v.* ①减轻负担(to free from a burden, give aid or help to)
　　　　　　　　　　　　　②免除责任(to set free from an obligation, condition, or restriction)
　　　　　　　　　　　　　③使轻松愉快

4. 【正确答案】C

　【中文释义】纽约市的早期摩天大楼的建筑家们,在这儿用一个 12 世纪的大教堂暗示一
　　　　　　　下,在那儿又用一个 15 世纪的大宫殿暗示一下,希望凭借这种激发出一种这
　　　　　　　个城市并未真正拥有过的历史感的方式来力图使这个城市的努力成果获得大
　　　　　　　家的认可。

　【解题分析】此句的主干为 The architects sought to legitimize the city's social strivings by
　　　　　　　____ a history。事实上 by 之后动名词的逻辑主语仍然是建筑家们,所以我们
　　　　　　　需要在原文中寻找一个建筑家们做过的动作来填进这个空格。建筑家们曾对
　　　　　　　历史做过什么动作当然不可能由我们各自的专业知识提供,答案必须由原文
　　　　　　　提供。原文中建筑家做了的动作只有一个 hinting。所以空格里直接填暗示出

历史就可以了。A 和 B 都是明确地展示,D 和 E 显然都没有关系,答案 C 的 e-voke 就是 hint 的意思。

　　第二种解法是直接做第二个空格,空格里要求填一个词来表达历史和这个城市的关系,这也必须在原文中表达出来,因为考生们也不可能通过自己的专业知识来填写这个空格。原文中提到历史的只有 12 世纪、15 世纪等字样。"五月花"号,May Flower 是 17 世纪到的美洲大陆,所以 12 世纪和 15 世纪的宏伟建筑对于这块土地纯属无稽之谈。所以第二个空格可直接选 A,C 和 D,而 A 和 D 的第一个动词显然又错了,因为 reveal 不可能指揭示或展示出一个不存在的东西,同样 preserve 也不可能保存一个不存在的东西。

　　第三种解法基于对全句结构的深刻把握上,hinting 所引导的一段文字事实上是谓语动词的方式状语,而 by 所引导的一段文字也是谓语动语的方式状语,故两者应相同,可以得知将 hinting 填到第一空格即可。

【正确答案】legitimize *v*. ①使合法化
　　　　　　　　　　　②使合情理

evoke *v*. ①祈求,请求(to call forth or up, as a conjure)
　　　　　②提示,暗示(to bring to mind or recollection) 例 This place ∼ s memories.

5.【正确答案】E
　【中文释义】地球生命史中的真实事件是随机的,因为任何出现的生物仅包含了成千上万个可能性中的一种;但是每一个出现的生物可以被理性地解释。
　【解题分析】上句的主句为判断句,所以 accidental 为主体词。因果句即解释 accidental,而下句的转折仍然是针对 accidental。从第二个空格看与 accidental 能构成转折关系的是 B 和 E,有些考生误选 D,事实上 D 的第二选项 uniquely 和 accidental 无任何反义关系,我们甚至可以说随机事件是很独特的,两者无反义关系。B 和 E 当中第一个词填回原文后能解释 accidental 的为 E。
　【重点词条】readily *adv*. ①愿意地(in a ready manner, without hesitating, willingly)
　　　　　　　　　　例 ∼ accepted advice
　　　　　　　　②简单地(without much difficulty, easily) 例 for reasons that anyone could ∼ understand

6.【正确答案】D
　【中文释义】尽管她的同行科学家中有一些人贬低她的非正统的实验室方法,而其他人认为其有新意,但是她的实验结果却受到了全体一致的表扬:在那时候具有先锋性质并且无懈可击。
　【解题分析】由从句中的 some 和 others 的对比可知第一个空格应填一个贬义词,可选 A,D 和 E,由下句的 and 小连接可知第二空格要填褒义词,可选 D。
　【重点词条】foreseeable *adj*. ①可预料到的(being such as may be reasonably anticipated)
　　　　　　　　　　例 ∼ problems

②在可预见的范围内的(lying within the range for which forecasts are possible) 例 in the~future

unexceptionable *adj.* 无可指责的,无可驳斥的(not open to objection or criticism, beyond reproach, unimpeachable)

exceptional *adj.* ①特别的(forming an exception, rare) 例 an~number of rainy days

②优秀的(better than average, superior) 例 ~skill

exceptionable *adj.* 会引起反感或厌恶的(being likely to cause objection, objectionable) 例 visitors even drink the~beer

7.【正确答案】E

【中文释义】早期的艾默莉·狄金森诗歌的评论家们将诗歌表面的质朴无华误解为诗人的思维简单,而事实上诗人煞费苦心才营建出这种质朴无华。

【解题分析】上文的结构首先要分清楚,mistake A for B 是一个正常的表达,而此句中为了平衡句子结构,变成了 mistake for B A 的结构,所以评论家们因误解而认为诗人思维简单,所以下句转折后应该表达出诗人事实上思维精细复杂,答案为 E。有很多同学将上句理解成,"评论家们误以为诗歌没有艺术性",所以下半句就转折为事实上诗歌很有艺术性。从而错选 C。

【重点词条】**allusion** *n.* ①暗喻(an implied or indirect reference esp. in literature; also: the use of such references)

②暗示(the act of alluding or hinting at)

simplemindedness *n.* 思维简单

artlessness *n.* ①缺乏艺术(lacking art, knowledge, or skill, uncultured)

②毫无技巧(made without skill, crude)

③自然(free from artificiality, natural) 例 ~grace

④质朴(free from guile or craft, sincerely simple)

SECTION 44

1. This project is the first step in a long-range plan of research whose ____ goal, still many years off, is the creation of a new prototype.

(A) cooperative

(B) reasoned

(C) original

(D) ultimate

(E) intentional

2. Eric was frustrated because, although he was adept at making lies sound ____ when telling the truth, he ____ the power to make himself believed.

(A) plausible..lacked

(B) convincing..held

(C) honest..found

(D) true..acquired

(E) logical..claimed

3. In certain forms of discourse such as the parable, the central point of a message can be effectively communicated even though this point is not ____.
   - (A) preferred
   - (B) explicit
   - (C) inferable
   - (D) discerned
   - (E) illustrated

4. Always circumspect, she was reluctant to make judgments, but once arriving at a conclusion, she was ____ in its defense.
   - (A) nonplussed
   - (B) obsequious
   - (C) intransigent
   - (D) deferential
   - (E) negligent

5. The techniques now available to livestock breeders will continue to be ____ but will probably be ____ by new ones under development.
   - (A) fruitful. . reversed
   - (B) refined. . upgraded
   - (C) inconvenient. . reassessed
   - (D) used. . supplemented
   - (E) harmless. . improved

6. Any population increase beyond a certain level necessitates greater ____ vegetable foods; thus, the ability of a society to choose meat over cereals always arises, in part, from ____ the number of people.
   - (A) reliance on. . replenishing
   - (B) production of. . estimating
   - (C) spending on. . concealing
   - (D) recourse to. . limiting
   - (E) attention to. . varying

7. Ethologists are convinced that many animals survive through learning—but learning that is ____ their genetic programming, learning as thoroughly ____ as the most instinctive of behavioral responses.
   - (A) superseded by. . primitive
   - (B) compatible with. . transient
   - (C) complementary to. . familiar
   - (D) derived from. . inventive
   - (E) dictated by. . stereotyped

SECTION 44 解答

1. 【正确答案】D

   【中文释义】这个项目是一个长期研究计划的第一步,这个研究计划多年之后的最终目标是创造出新的原型。

   【解题分析】空格里需要填形容词修辞名词 goal,而紧随其后的就是一个分隔,所以空格里应填写上"很多年之后的目标",能吻合的是 D。

   【重点词条】intentional *adj*. 故意的,有意的(done by intention or design, intended) 例 ~ damage

   　　　　　　prototype *n*. ①原型,样本
   　　　　　　　　　　　　②模范,典型

   　　　　　　reasoned *adj*. 经缜密推断分析的,详尽论述的

2. 【正确答案】A

【中文释义】埃利克很沮丧,因为尽管他能很熟练地将谎言编造得合情合理,但当他讲真话时,他缺乏能力使别人相信自己。

【解题分析】真正的原因从句就是最后一小段文字而已,能构成使埃利克沮丧的原因只有 A。

【重点词条】frustrate *v*. ①使灰心(to induce feelings of discouragement in)

②阻止,阻碍(impede, obstruct, to make invalid or of no effect)

plausible *adj*. 貌似有理(或真实)的(superficially fair, reasonable, or valuable but often specious) 例 a~pretext

3.【正确答案】B

【中文释义】在某些文章体裁,比如说是寓言中,中心信息可以被有效地表达出来,即使这个信息并不明显。

【解题分析】Even though 是表递进转折的连词,所以空格里应填上比上文"effectively communicated"更加有效的交流方式,据此可判断 B 正确。C,D 和 E 都是一种间接没有效率的方式。A 不相关。尤其是答案 E 的 illustrate 的含义是"用图画式形象的方式来表达",这正是寓言的表达方式。

【重点词条】explicit *adj*. ①详述的,明确的(fully revealed or expressed without vagueness, implication or ambiguity, leaving no question as to meaning or intent) 例 ~instructions

②直露的(open in the depiction of nudity or sexuality) 例 ~ books and films

③成熟的(fully developed or formulated) 例 an~plan/an~notion of our objective

④坦率的(unambiguous in expression) 例 was very~on how we are to behave

4.【正确答案】C

【中文释义】总是顾忌重重,她总是勉强犹豫地做出决定,但是一旦得到一个结论,她却会坚定不移地支持这个结论。

【解题分析】应该针对上句的主体词 reluctant 转折。

【重点词条】obsequious *adj*. 卑躬屈膝的,拍马奉承的(marked by or exhibiting a fawning attentiveness)

intransigent *adj*. 不妥协的,不让步的,不调和的(refusing to compromise or to abandon an extreme position or attitude, uncompromising)

circumspect *adj*. 谨慎小心的,慎重的(careful to consider all circumstances and possible consequences, prudent)

5.【正确答案】D

【中文释义】家畜饲养者们现在可利用的技术会继续被使用,但是可能会被处于发展中的新技术所加强。

【解题分析】原文中的 continue 提示应将 available 直接填回第一空格即可。这是 continue 的最直接的考法。另外一种考法是 continue 之前并没有提供过去的状态,但是却出现一个 although 加空格的结构,此时应在空格里直接选一个表程度下降的词(速度变慢,体积减小等等)。并且此句中的 A 选项 fruitful,选项 D 的 used 与选项 E 的 harmless 实为一组词,一组表程度减弱的词。既然是 continue,所以应与前文一模一样重复,A 和 E 在程度上就犯了错误。

【重点词条】**supplement** *n*. ①补给,补充(something that completes or makes an addition)

例 dietary～s

②补遗,附录,增刊(a part added to or issued as a continuation of a book or periodical to correct errors or make additions)

③补角(an angle or arc that when added to a given angle or arc equals 180 degrees)

6.【正确答案】D

【中文释义】任何超过一定水平限度后的人口增长都必然导致对蔬菜类食物的更大的依赖;因此,一个社会选择肉食而不选择谷类食品能力的上升部分来源于削减人口数目。

【解题分析】此句为一个典型的分号句,上句为人口增长导致蔬食的增长。分号句的下半句空格后显然是上文 population 的重复。所以在阅读第二空格之前的文字的时就应充分注意将之转化为蔬菜类食物的角度去理解,从而理解为蔬食的下降,这样上下句之间的关系就凸现出来,上句为人口增长导致蔬食的增长,所以下句当然是一个逆否命题——蔬食的下降导致人口下降,故第二个空格先填出一个下降的单词,答案为 D。该句的重复关系望大家充分领会。一般来讲,如果上下句出现了 A→B; B→A 的结构,则重复关系可能是主动被动句重复,或逆否命题重复。如果出现了 by, is the result of, is the product of, is the outgrowth of 这几个短语则必然为则重复关系可能是主动被动句重复,否则为逆否命题重复。相关例题请参阅 SECTION 10 的第 7 题。

7.【正确答案】E

【中文释义】动物行为学家确信许多动物是通过学习获得生存的,这种学习是被它们的遗传图谱所完全规定的,这种学习与它们的最本能的行为反射一样的固定僵化。

【解题分析】此句中的 but 引导 learning 的同位语,起到对前一个 learning 的词义的限定说明作用,其后的两个 learning 又处于并列关系,并且各有一个定语从句。所以这两个定语从句就成为特殊并列句,应该含义相同,所以可以得知第一个空格应该强调这种学习是本能的行为,也即由遗传图谱所描述规定好的行为,可以选 E,D 和 B,而 B 的第二个词 transient 是形容后天行为反射的,并非先天反射(后天反射会随时向推移而淡忘,因此称为短暂的;先天条件反射会终生伴随)。D 的第二个词 inventive 显然也不能用于描述先天的行为反射。答案 E 的第二个选项非常恰当,既然是由遗传决定的学习行为,那么所有该物种的学习过程和方法都会一样(stereotype),如所有的小猫的学习过程和方式都惊人地相似。

【重点词条】**stereotype** *n*. ①铅版(a plate cast from a printing surface)

②老套,旧习(something conforming to a fixed or general pattern; a standardized mental picture that is held in common by members of a group and that represents an oversimplified opinion, prejudiced attitude, or uncritical judgment)

stereotyped *adj*. ①已成陈规的,刻板的

②固定不变的,定型的

SECTION 45

1. Nonviolent demonstrations often create such tensions that a community that has constantly refused to ____ its injustices is forced to correct them: the injustices can no longer be ____.

   (A)acknowledge. . ignored

   (B)decrease. . verified

   (C)tolerate. . accepted

   (D)address. . eliminated

   (E)explain. . discussed

2. Since 1813 reaction to Jane Austen's novels has oscillated between ____ and condescension; but in general later writers have esteemed her works more highly than did most of her literary ____.

   (A)dismissal. . admirers

   (B)adoration. . contemporaries

   (C)disapproval. . readers

   (D)indifference. . followers

   (E)approbation. . precursors

3. There are, as yet, no vegetation types or ecosystems whose study has been ____ to the extent that they no longer ____ ecologists.

   (A)perfected. . hinder

   (B)exhausted. . interest

   (C)prolonged. . require

   (D)prevented. . challenge

   (E)delayed. . benefit

4. Under ethical guidelines recently adopted by the National Institutes of Health, human genes are to be manipulated only to correct diseases for which ____ treatments are unsatisfactory.

   (A)similar

   (B)most

   (C)dangerous

   (D)uncommon

   (E)alternative

5. It was her view that the country's problems had been ____ by foreign technocrats, so that to invite them to come back would be counterproductive.

   (A)foreseen

   (B)attacked

   (C)ascertained

   (D)exacerbated

   (E)analyzed

6. Winsor McCay, the cartoonist, could draw with incredible ____: his comic strip about Little Nemo was characterized by marvelous draftmanship and sequencing.

(A)sincerity
(B)efficiency
(C)virtuosity
(D)rapidity
(E)energy

7. The actual ＿＿ of Wilson's position was always ＿＿ by his refusal to compromise after having initially agreed to negotiate a settlement.

(A)outcome..foreshadowed
(B)logic..enhanced
(C)rigidity..betrayed
(D)uncertainty..alleviated
(E)cowardice..highlighted

SECTION 45 解答

1. 【正确答案】A

【中文释义】非暴力的游行示威总是产生这样的紧张局面,也即一个过去一直拒绝承认其有不公正现象的国家现在被迫来改正这些不公正做法,不公正现象再也不能被故意忽略了。

【解题分析】上下文有一组时间提示 constantly refused 与 no longer,分别表示两个截然相反的时间中不做某些事,故第一个空格与第二个空格应为反义词,可选择的只有 A。

【重点词条】**acknowledge** v. ①承认,承认⋯的权威
②告知,确认
③就⋯表示谢忱,报偿
④对⋯作出反应

demonstration n. ①证明(conclusive evidence, proof)
②(产品等)展示(a showing of the merits of a product or service to a prospective consumer)
③感情的流露(an outward expression or display)
④炫耀武力(a show of armed force)
⑤示威游行(a public display of group feelings toward a person or cause)

2. 【正确答案】B

【中文释义】自从 1813 年以来对简·奥斯汀小说的反响一直在赞美和轻蔑中摇摆;但整体上说来,后来的作家比她的大多数同时代作家更看重她的作品。

【解题分析】此句中的 oscillate between⋯and⋯ 中应连接一组反义词,故可选 B 和 E,而 E 的第二个词 precursor 又不可能对简·奥斯汀的作品作出任何评价,故不可能成为比较句的一方,故正确答案为 B。或者此句可由比较句的规律:"一套比较结构,比较双方应构成对比"出发,得 B 和 E,再由常识排除 E。

【重点词条】**esteem** v. ①评估(appraise)
②把⋯视作(to view as, consider) 例 ~ it a privilege

③尊敬,尊重(to set a high value on, regard highly and prize accordingly)

approbation *n*. ①认可,证明(proof)

②批准,许可(an act of approving formally or officially)

③称赞,嘉许(commendation, praise)

3. 【正确答案】B

【中文释义】到目前为止,没有植物类型或者生态系统的研究已经彻底到这种程度以至于它们不再吸引生态学家。

【解题分析】此句中出现了 no longer 来表否定,no longer 在英文中表示对过去的状态或动作的否定,因此第二个空格应填上一个过去的情况或通常的情况,通常情况下课题和研究者之间的关系可以是 B,C 和 D 各自的第二词,而 C 和 D 各自的两个词均不能构成正常的因果推理结构,故 B 正确。有部分同学会受母语的影响而选择 A,但请一定记住英文中的 no longer 只否定过去的动作或一般性的动作,当课题尚未研究得完善的时候,课题与科学家之间的关系,我们通常不描写为 hinder,也即中文的拖后腿或妨碍的意思,如果想表达课题在过去很困难很难研究攻克,那么此时连接课题和科学家的动词通常用 challenge。关于 no longer 的这种解题思路请参阅 SECTION 11 的第 6 题,SECTION 23 的第 2 题。

【重点词条】**hinder** *v*. 阻碍,妨碍(to delay, impede, or prevent action)

exhaust *v*. 详尽无遗的论述(或研究)

benefit *n*. ①恩惠(an act of kindness, benefaction)

②好处(something that promotes well-being, advantage)

③帮助(useful aid, help)

④救济金(financial help in time of sickness, old age, or unemployment)

⑤义演(an entertainment or social event to raise funds for a person or cause)

4. 【正确答案】E

【中文释义】根据国家健康研究所最近通过的伦理学的指导方针,人类的基因只有在其他所有的治疗方案都不能令人满意的情况下才可以改变。

【解题分析】此句中的 only 极为重要,如果未仔细斟酌恐怕会选 B。正确答案为 E。Only 表示惟一性和排他性,故能与之相对应的是 alternative,而与 most(大多数)相对应的是"少部分"。

【重点词条】**manipulate** *v*. ①操作,利用(to treat or operate with the hands or by mechanical means esp. in a skillful manner)

②巧妙地处理,操纵,控制(to control or play upon by artful, unfair, or insidious means esp. to one's own advantage)

③窜改,改造(to change by artful or unfair means so as to serve one's purpose) adopt v. ①收养(to take by choice into a relationship, esp. to take voluntarily a child of other parents as one's own child)

②采用(to take up and practice or use) 例 ~ed a moderate tone

③正式通过(to accept formally and put into effect) 例 ~a constitutional amendment

④接受,采纳(to choose such as a textbook for required study in a course)

5. 【正确答案】D

【中文释义】按她的观点看来这个国家的问题已经被外国的技术论统治者们恶化了,因此邀请他们回来将会起相反的作用。

【解题分析】此句中的 come back 充分说明这些人当初曾经在这个国家呆过一段时间。既然推测他们回来后会有坏作用,可见当年也未起过好的作用。这就是第一个空格要填的词。有些同学会误选B,B 的 attack a problem 是"分析解决问题"的意思。

【重点词条】ascertain v. ①查明,弄清(to make certain, exact, or precise)

②探知,确定(to find out or learn with certainty)

6. 【正确答案】C

【中文释义】威瑟·梅凯这位卡通画家,可以以令人难以置信的精湛技巧作画:他的关于小兰姆连环漫画的特征是具有非同一般的技巧和高度的一致性。

【解题分析】冒号后表示重复,很显然 marvelous draftsmanship 应填到第一空格里去。至于 sequencing 的精确含义,解题时可不必拘泥于它,既然是和 marvelous drafts-manship 并列,所以理所当然地认为其就是指精湛的技术。这种思路近几年考试中屡屡出现,and 左右连接的一个是常见单词,一个是专业单词的特殊含义,这种情况下字读半边即可。sequencing 在此处的含义是指情节,环境,形象的高度一致性。如有些拙劣的漫画中主人公穿汗衫,背景却是雪山,或者一株只产于亚马逊河谷的植物长在了沙漠之上,或者一个人物在前面几集连续剧中有八只眼睛,到了后几集又忽然变成了九只眼睛,等等。都是由于漫画家缺乏整体谋篇技巧和笔法粗糙所导致的,而一个技巧精湛的画家就不会犯这样的错误。

【重点词条】incredible adj. 难以置信的,不可思议的(too extraordinary and improbable to be believed, hard to believe)

virtuosity n. ①对艺术品的爱好与鉴赏(a taste for or interest in virtu)

②精湛技艺(great technical skill such as in the practice of a fine art)

7. 【正确答案】C

【中文释义】在当初同意协商解决之后威尔逊又拒绝妥协,这就暴露了他立场的真实的僵化性。

【解题分析】文中的 by 表手段,直接反映出威尔逊的立场,可选 C 或 D,而 D 的第二个词为
         减轻的意思,所以 D 不正确。C 为正确答案。

【重点词条】**betray** *v*. ①使背叛(to lead astray, esp. seduce)

②泄露秘密(to deliver to an enemy by treachery)

③暴露(to reveal unintentionally)

alleviate *v*. 减轻,缓解(relieve, lessen, to make such as suffering more bear-

able) 例 Her sympathy alleviated his distress.

SECTION 46

1. The senator's reputation, though ____ by false allegations of misconduct, emerged from the ordeal ____.
   (A) shaken.. unscathed
   (B) destroyed.. intact
   (C) damaged.. impaired
   (D) impugned.. unclear
   (E) tarnished.. sullied

2. This poetry is not ____; it is more likely to appeal to an international audience than is poetry with strictly regional themes.
   (A) familiar
   (B) democratic
   (C) technical
   (D) complex
   (E) provincial

3. Experienced employers recognize that business students who can ____ different points of view are ultimately more effective as managers than are the brilliant and original students who ____ dogmatically to their own formulations.
   (A) discredit.. revert
   (B) assimilate.. adhere
   (C) impose.. refer
   (D) disregard.. incline
   (E) advocate.. relate

4. Poe's ____ reviews of contemporary fiction, which often find great merit in otherwise ____ literary gems, must make us respect his critical judgment in addition to his well-known literary talent.
   (A) thorough.. completed
   (B) petulant.. unpopular
   (C) insightful.. unappreciated
   (D) enthusiastic.. acclaimed
   (E) harsh.. undeserving

5. The significance of the Magna Carta lies not in its ____ provisions, but in its broader impact: it made the king subject to the law.
   (A) specific
   (B) revolutionary
   (C) implicit
   (D) controversial
   (E) finite

6. The theory of cosmic evolution states that the universe, having begun in a state of simplicity and ____, has ____ into great variety.
   (A) equilibrium.. modulated
   (B) homogeneity.. differentiated
   (C) contrast.. metamorphosed
   (D) proportion.. accelerated
   (E) intelligibility.. developed

7. Not wishing to appear ____ the junior members of the research group refrained from ____ any criticism of the senior members' plan for dividing up responsibility for the entire project.

(A) reluctant. . evaluating
(B) inquisitive. . offering
(C) presumptuous. . venturing
(D) censorious. . undercutting
(E) moralistic. . observing

SECTION 46 解答

1. 【正确答案】A
   【中文释义】这位议员的声誉,尽管被诬告他失职的虚假指控所动摇了,但又从这严峻的考验中恢复得完好如初。
   【解题分析】文中的 the ordeal 指代前文的 false allegations of misconduct。Emerge 是系动词,与 sound, look 或 continue 等用法相同。故第二空格里填的是表语,来描绘声誉恢复后的状态,既然是恢复后的状态当然应该选 A。
   【重点词条】impugn *v.* 指责,非难,抨击,质疑
   　　　　　　emerge *v.* ①出现(to become manifest)
   　　　　　　　　　　②露出(to rise from or as if from an enveloping fluid, come out into view)
   　　　　　　　　　　③出人头地(to rise from an obscure or inferior position or condition)
   　　　　　　　　　　④发生(to come into being through evolution)

2. 【正确答案】E
   【中文释义】这个诗歌并不是地方性的;它比那些严格意义上的地方性的诗歌更能吸引国际读者。
   【重点词条】provincial *adj.* ①乡气的(of, relating to, or coming from a province)
   　　　　　　　　　　②偏狭的(limited in outlook, narrow)
   　　　　　　　　　　③粗野的(lacking the polish of urban society, unsophisticated)
   　　　　　　　　　　④朴素平常的(of or relating to a decorative style such as in furniture marked by simplicity, informality, and relative plainness)

3. 【正确答案】B
   【中文释义】有经验的雇主认识到那些能吸取不同观点的商学院的学生作管理人员时比那些聪明而有独创性但却教条地坚持自己观点的学生更有效果。
   【解题分析】文中明显是一套比较结构,比较双方分别为两种学生,又各有一个定语从句,所以比较双方的对比就成为两个定语从句的对比。尤其是第二个定语从句的 dogmatically 更是提醒了我们,第二种学生是那种教条坚持自己的学生,第一种则可推理为能听取不同意见的学生,故选 B。
   【重点词条】assimilate *v.* ①吸收,消化(to take in and appropriate as nourishment, absorb into the system, to take into the mind and thoroughly compre-

hend)

②使同化(to make similar, to alter by assimilation)

③跟…相比(compare, liken)

4.【正确答案】C

【中文释义】爱伦·坡对当代小说的富有洞察力的评论,总是能够发现出在其他情况下都不被人欣赏的文学精品中的巨大优点,(这种富有洞察力的评论)一定会使我们尊崇他广为人知的文学天赋之外的判断能力。

【解题分析】主干为爱伦·坡的某种评论使得大家尊崇他的判断能力,故第一空格必为一个表现有很好判断能力的词,可以候选 C 和 A。第二个空格前的 otherwise 充分提示了第二个空格应与之前的一段文字相反义,故选 C。

【重点词条】acclaim v. ①报以掌声,称赞(applaud, praise)

②喝彩,欢呼(to declare by acclamation)

otherwise adv. ①否则,要不然(if not)

②以不同的方式(in a different way or manner) 例 He could not act~.

③在其他方面(in other respects) 例 weak but ~well

④在别的情况下(under other conditions) 例 ~he might won

5.【正确答案】A

【中文释义】英国大宪章的重要意义并不存在于它具体的条文上,而是在于它更深远的影响上:它第一次使国王受制于法律。

【解题分析】此句的逻辑关系非常明确,not…but…结构必然连接一组反义词,空格应和 broad impact 构成反义。问题出在第二步选词上(第一步分析句子结构,第二步根据结构进行推理)。究竟是哪个词和 broad impact 构在反义? 若干考生误选 E 的 infinite。Infinite 的含义是时间,空间或数量的有限,那么它的反义词应该是时间,空间和数量的无限,而后文的 broader impact 显然并非这几个义项。其冒号后的解释中并未涉及到这三方面的无限,而只是说法律第一次使国王受制于法律。此处的 broader impact 可理解为:更深远的影响,也即超越了本身行为的背后更深层次的影响。如攀登珠峰、漂流长江等行为一样,本身并不创造价值,但都有更深远的、超越了本身行为的更深层次的影响。此时 broader impact 的反义词应该为:具体的、事物本身所表现出的性质,应选 A。

此句非常典型。如果以后在考题当中,尤其是在后几道题目中,见到那些句子结构很简单,逻辑推理非常明确的句子,一定要仔细推敲第三步选词。这已成为国内考题的最新动向,对中级词汇的更高的要求是 GRE 这几次最新试卷的特点,正是因为如此,所以本书才加强了对词汇的注释,希望大家认真对待这些英文词汇注释,在反复的学习揣摩中增强词汇修养,毕竟这不是一朝一夕之功。

【重点词条】infinite adj. ①无限的(extending indefinitely, endless) 例 ~space

②没有穷尽的(immeasurably or inconceivably great or extensive, inexhaustible) 例 ~patience

implicit *adj.* ①不言明的,含蓄的(capable of being understood from something else though unexpressed, implied) 例 an~assumption

②内含的,固有的(involved in the nature or essence of something though not revealed, expressed, or developed, potential) 例 A sculptor may see different figures~in a block of stone.

③无保留的,绝对的(being without doubt or reserve, unquestioning)

6.【正确答案】B

【中文释义】宇宙演变的理论陈述道:宇宙已经分化进入巨大的变化之中,尽管其开始在一个简单同质的状态当中。

【解题分析】本句中的 begin 就在提示着时间对比型,大家要记住几个有时间提示的动词:begin, start, initial, launch, end, finish, conclude。既然后文的 has 加动词构成了现在完成时态,那么它与 began 的时间状态应该截然相反,故第一空格里填上与 great variety 相反的词,答案 B。

【重点词条】**modulate** *v.* ①控制嗓音(to tune to a key or pitch)

②调节(to adjust to or keep in proper measure or proportion, temper)

③调整(to vary the amplitude, frequency, or phase of a carrier wave or a light wave for the transmission of intelligence such as by radio)

intelligibility *n.* 易于理解,清晰易懂(capable of being understood or comprehended)

7.【正确答案】C

【中文释义】由于不希望显得好高自大,所以研究小组中的低级成员克制自己,不大胆提出任何针对高级成员关于在整个项目中实行分权责任制度计划的批评。

【解题分析】此句中出现一组特征人物,低级成员和高级成员,由 GRE 句子填空人物之间的单向性可知,低级成员应永远服从高级成员,绝对不会提出任何批评意见。(这一点可以脱离原文得出结论)。故第二空格可以选 B 和 C,答案 A 的 evaluating 填回原文后的意思是:不评价其他人提出的批评意见是否正确。并不是自己不提出批评意见,所以并不是低级成员的特征动作。B 和 C 的第一个单词显然选 C,因为句子反过来理解就是:一旦低级成员对高级成员的计划提出批评意见,他们就会显得好高自大,而不会是显得有好奇心。

【重点词条】**presumptuous** *adj.* 专横的,傲慢的,放肆的(overstepping due bounds such as of propriety or courtesy, taking liberties)

venture *v.* ①敢于做(to expose to hazard, risk, gamble) 例 ventured a buck or two on the race

②冒险(to undertake the risks and dangers of, brave) 例 ventured the stormy sea

③大胆表示(to offer at the risk of rebuff, rejection, or censure)

例 ～an opinion

undercut *v*. ①潜挖,切除…的下部(to cut away the underpart of) 例 ～a vein of ore

②浮雕(to cut away material from the underside of an object so as to leave an overhanging portion in relief)

③由下往上击球(to strike a ball with a downward glancing blow so as to give a backspin or elevation to the shot)

④削弱,暗中破坏(to undermine or destroy the force, value, or effectiveness of) 例 Inflation～s consumer buying power.

moralistic *adj*. 道德说教的(characterized by or expressive of a concern with morality)

SECTION 47

1. The Chinese, who began systematic astronomical and weather observations shortly after the ancient Egyptians, were assiduous record-keepers, and because of this, can claim humanity's longest continuous _____ of natural events.

   (A)defiance
   (B)documentation
   (C)maintenance
   (D)theory
   (E)domination

2. Because many of the minerals found on the ocean floor are still _____ on land, where mining is relatively inexpensive, mining the ocean floor has yet to become a _____ enterprise.

   (A)scarce. . common
   (B)accessible. . marginal
   (C)unidentified. . subsidized
   (D)conserved. . public
   (E)plentiful. . profitable

3. The valedictory address, as it has developed in American colleges and universities over the years, has become a very strict form, a literary _____ that permits very little _____.

   (A)text. . clarity
   (B)work. . tradition
   (C)genre. . deviation
   (D)oration. . grandiloquence
   (E)achievement. . rigidity

4. A human being is quite _____ creature, for the gloss of rationality that covers his or her fears and _____ is thin and often easily breached.

   (A)a logical. . problems
   (B)a frail. . insecurity
   (C)a valiant. . phobias
   (D)an ambitious. . morality
   (E)a ludicrous. . laughter

5. Although the passage of years has softened the initially hostile reaction to his poetry, even now only a few independent observers _____ his works.

   (A)praise

(B)revile

(C)scrutinize

(D)criticize

(E)neglect

6. Unlike philosophers who constructed theoretically ideal states, she built a theory based on ____ ; thus, although her constructs may have been inelegant, they were ____ sound.

　(A)reality. . aesthetically

　(B)intuition. . intellectually

　(C)surmise. . scientifically

(D)experience. . empirically

(E)conjecture. . factually

7. Once a duckling has identified a parent, the instinctive bond becomes a powerful ____ for additional learning since, by ____ the parent, the duckling can acquire further information that is not genetically transmitted.

　(A)impulse. . surpassing

　(B)referent. . recognizing

　(C)force. . acknowledging

　(D)inspiration. . emulating

　(E)channel. . mimicking

SECTION 47 解答

1.【正确答案】B

　【中文释义】中国人,在古埃及人之后不久就开始了有系统的天文和大气的观测,是勤奋的簿记者,正是因为如此,才能宣称拥有人类最长最连续的关于自然现象的书面记载。

　【解题分析】此句主语之后出现了冗长的分隔,由于此分隔中以及分隔前的主干成分无空格,故此分隔属文字垃圾,可完全略而不看,节约考场上宝贵的时间。主干的推理是很简洁的,空格里由因果关系可直接填上文出现过的 record 即可。

　【重点词条】**claim** v. ①宣称拥有(权利)(to call for, require) 例 This matter～s our attention.

　　　　　　　②宣称具有所有权(to take as the rightful owner) 例 went to～their bags at the station

　　　　　　　③坚持某观点(to assert in the face of possible contradiction, maintain) 例 ～ed that he'd been cheated

　　　　　　　④ 对…提出索赔(claim against somebody)

　　　　　　n. ①索赔 (a demand for something due or believed to be due) 例 insurance～

　　　　　　　②(对债务,财产,特权等)权利(a right to something such as a title to a debt, privilege, or other thing in the possession of another)

　　　　　　　③宣言(an assertion open to challenge) 例 a～of authenticity

2.【正确答案】E

　【中文释义】因为很多在海底发现的矿物质在陆地上仍然很丰富,而开采陆地相对而言也不昂贵,所以开采海底到目前为止仍然不能成为一项有利可图的业务。

　【解题分析】请注意文中的 relatively,此词表示了和开采海底相比的意思,故文字的实际含义是:开采海底仍然是昂贵的,因而开采海底仍然没有变成一个有利可图的业务。这种隐含的比较是这几年的一大考点,另外有 compared with, in contrast to, beyond, in comparison with 或表示同级比较的如:as…as , to the same degree, matter neither more nor less than 等。

【重点词条】**marginal** *adj*. ①边缘的,边界的(of, relating to, or situated at a margin or border)

②不重要的(not of central importance) 例 regards violence as a ~ rather than a central problem

③边缘人的,边缘文化的(characterized by the incorporation of habits and values from two divergent cultures and by incomplete assimilation in either) 例 the ~ cultural habits of new immigrant groups

④被主流社会或主流思想所排斥的(excluded from or existing outside the mainstream of society, a group, or a school of thought)

subside *v*. ①下陷,降低

②入座(to let oneself settle down; sink) 例 subsided into a chair

③消退,平息(to become quiet or less) 例 as the fever ~ s/My anger subsided.

3.【正确答案】C

【中文释义】告别演说由于已经在美国的学院和大学里发展了很多年,现在已经成为一种非常严格的形式,一种不允许有任何差错的文学类型。

【解题分析】此句的主语后又出现一个冗余的分隔,其中没有空格,其前的主干也没有空格。主干结束后出现一段分隔,重复前文的一个结构:a very strict form。事实上这个重复与前文几乎是同样的结构:前文是形容词修饰名词,后文是定语从句修饰名词,所以两个名词同义,定语从句和形容词同义即可,定语从句在语法上的功能几乎等同于形容词,故第一空格填上 form 即可,答案为 C。

【重点词条】**genre** *n*. ①文学的体裁,文学的类型(a category of artistic, musical, or literary composition characterized by a particular style, form, or content)

②风俗画(painting that depicts scenes or events from everyday life usu. realistically)

grandiloquence *n*. 华丽,炫耀,张扬(的语言)(a lofty, extravagantly colorful, pompous, or bombastic style, manner, or quality esp. in language)

4.【正确答案】B

【中文释义】人类是一种非常脆弱的动物,因为掩盖他或她的害怕和不安全感的理性光辉是非常的薄弱并且很容易被击碎。

【解题分析】请注意,如果去掉 gloss of rationality 的定语从句(分隔)的话,我们的推理会简

洁得多,由贬义的原因我们可以轻松地得出贬义的结论 B 和 E,而 B 和 E 的第二个词能和 fear 构成并列的显然是 B。

【重点词条】 **phobia** *n.* 厌恶,憎恨(an exaggerated usu. inexplicable and illogical fear of a particular object, class of objects, or situation)

           morality *n.* 道德,道义,道德课,道德的行为

           ambitious *adj.* 雄心壮志的(having a desire to achieve a particular goal, aspiring)

5. 【正确答案】A

     【中文释义】尽管这许多年时间的消逝已经减轻了当初对他的诗歌的敌意态度,但是即使现在也只有一少部分的独立观察家表扬他的作品。

     【解题分析】文中的 initial 和 now 显然提示着一组时间对比,故相应的态度也应对比,空格里填上前文 initial hostile 的反义词即可。正确答案 A。事实上这种解法是纯经验的解法,切不可与精读的解法混为一谈,如果用精读的解法,初一看转折后的文意应为人们仍然采取敌意的态度,再细一看下文的主语并不是"人们",而是"人们"的对立面"只有一少部分的人们",故仍应选 A。这一番细读的两次周折完全可以在纯经验的解法中化解掉。我们需要的是非常功利地快速得到正确答案,而不是字斟句酌的浅吟低唱。精读的解法和纯经验的解法都不失为一种好办法,但在争分夺秒的考场上,孰优孰劣一眼便知。

     【重点词条】 **scrutinize** *v.* 详细地检查(to examine closely and minutely)

6. 【正确答案】D

     【中文释义】和那些营建理论上完善学说的哲学家们不一样,她将她的理论建立在经验的基础上;因而,尽管她的理论可能是不精致的,但它们却是在经验主义上合情合理的。

     【解题分析】由 unlike 可知逻辑关系为对立面的转折,与"理论上完善"构成转折的为 A 和 D;由分号后的 thus 可知因果关系,而构成因果句的实际上只是:she built a theory based on...; thus, they were...sound。A 和 D 当中当然可以一目了然地选出 D 正确。并且 A 的第二个词在分号后的转折关系中也不正确,一个理论学说在美学上合理就是指精致优雅 elegant 的意思。怎么可能同一个学说既 elegant 又 inelegant 呢? 一匹白色的黑马!

     【重点词条】 **construct** *n.* 人的创造物或创作作品(something that is constructed esp. by a process of mental synthesis)

7. 【正确答案】E

     【中文释义】一旦一只小鸭子认可了父亲或母亲,本能的纽带就成为后天学习的重要渠道,因为通过模仿它的父亲或母亲,这只小鸭子就可以学习到遗传上并没有传递给它的更多的信息。

     【解题分析】文中的 by 引导了一个手段方法以及该手段方法所欲实现的目标,文中的 for 又引导了一个目的以及实现该目的的手段方法,所以实际上是同一内容上换

了语言结构重复表达了一遍。我们可以清楚地看到上文的目的 additional learning 正是下文所表达的目的 further information。同样,两个空格均表示手段方法,第一空格中表示手段方法的只有 E。请注意 E 所表达的两个方法之间的关系是上下义的关系,也即包含关系。这一点与 SECTION 5 的第 3 题一模一样。

【重点词条】**identify** *v*. ①同化(to cause to be or become identical)

②认为相同(to conceive as united as in spirit, outlook, or principle) 例 groups that are identified with conservation

inspiration *n*. ①灵感,灵机一动(a divine influence or action on a person believed to qualify him or her to receive and communicate sacred revelation)

②吸取,吸气(the act of drawing in; specif: the drawing of air into the lungs)

③充满灵气的状态(the quality or state of being inspired) 例 a scheme that was pure~

SECTION 48

1. Nearly two-thirds of the country's mushroom crop is produced by 160 growers in a single county, the greatest ____ growers anywhere.

(A) cause of

(B) agreement among

(C) indication of

(D) interaction between

(E) concentration of

2. The disjunction between educational objectives that stress independence and individuality and those that emphasize obedience to rules and cooperation with others reflects a ____ that arises from the values on which these objectives are based.

(A) conflict

(B) redundancy

(C) gain

(D) predictability

(E) wisdom

3. It is ____ for a government to fail to do whatever it can to eliminate a totally ____ disease.

(A) folly. . innocuous

(B) irresponsible. . preventable

(C) crucial. . fatal

(D) instinctive. . devastating

(E) detrimental. . insignificant

4. Dramatic literature often ____ the history of a culture in that it takes as its subject matter the important events that have shaped and guided the culture.

(A) confounds

(B) repudiates

(C) recapitulates

(D) anticipates

(E) polarizes

5. The legislators of 1563 realized the ____ of trying to regulate the flow of labor without

securing its reasonable remuneration, and so the second part of the statute dealt with establishing wages.

(A)intricacy

(B)anxiety

(C)futility

(D)necessity

(E)decadence

6. Scientists who are on the cutting edge of research must often violate common sense and make seemingly ____ assumptions because existing theories simply do not ____ newly observed phenomena.

(A)radical..confirm

(B)vague..incorporate

(C)absurd..explain

(D)mistaken..reveal

(E)inexact..corroborate

7. The ____ with which the French aristocracy greeted the middle-class Rousseau was all the more ____ because he showed so little respect for them.

(A)deference..remarkable

(B)suspicion..uncanny

(C)reserve..unexpected

(D)anger..ironic

(E)appreciation..deserved

SECTION 48 解答

1.【正确答案】E

【中文释义】几乎这个国家蘑菇产量的三分之二是由一个小县城里的 160 个生产者种植出来的,这个小县城与任何其他地方比起来都是蘑菇生产者的最大集中地。

【解题分析】只要不将 county 混淆为 country 该题都能正确解答。

【重点词条】**anywhere** *adv*. ①任何地方(at, in or to any place or point) 例 loud sail～along the coast

②到…程度(used as a function word to indicate limits of variations) 例 ～from 10 to 30 minutes

2.【正确答案】A

【中文释义】两种教育目标之间存在冲突,一种教育目标强调独立性和个性自由,另一种强调遵守规则和与其他人的合作,这种冲突就反映了价值观之间的分歧,而这两个教育目标正是建立在这些价值观基础之上的。

【解题分析】本句的主干为 The disjunction reflects a ____. 可以直接得答案 A。类似的解题方法在填空中随处可见,与此题最类似的如 SECTION 30 的第 5 题。主语后冗长的分隔实际上一点解题上的意义都没有,因为只要是由价值观所产生的两个目标,如人生目标,世界观,历史观等等,都可以替换入原句而对解题无任何影响。

【重点词条】**gain** *v*. ①获得(to acquire or get possession of usu. by industry, merit, or craft) 例 ～an advantage/He stood to～a fortune.

②赢得(to win in competition or conflict) 例 the troops～ed enemy territory

③达到(to arrive at, reach, attain) 例 ～ed the river that night

④增进(to get by a natural development or process) 例 ～strength

⑤吸引(to cause to be obtained or given, attract) 例 ～attention

⑥走快(of a timepiece, to run fast by the amount of) 例 The clock～s a
minute a day.

3. 【正确答案】B

【中文释义】对于一个政府而言,不尽全力来消除可以预防的疾病是不负责任的。

【解题分析】Fail 后跟着两个动词不定式(其他语法书会有别解),所以两个动词不定式是并
列重复关系,相对应于"做它可以做的事",第二个动词不定式应为"消除它可
以消除的疾病"。由第二空格选词可得答案 B。

【重点词条】**folly** *n.* ①蠢笨(lack of good sense or normal prudence and foresight)
②愚蠢,愚行(criminally or tragically foolish actions or conduct)

4. 【正确答案】C

【中文释义】戏剧文学总是在简明扼要地复述文化史,因为它将那些曾经塑造和引导文化
的重大事件当作主题素材。

【解题分析】第一空格中的戏剧文学对文化史的动作显然应由原文提供,因为我们并不是
戏剧文学专家,而下文所提及的戏剧文学的动作只有 take important events as
its subject matter,也即描写那些文化史上的重大事件,故第一空格应为"挑选
重大事件加以描写",正确答案 C。

5. 【正确答案】C

【中文释义】1563 年的立法者们认识到了在不保障合情合理的工资报酬的情况下企图管制
劳动力流向的无效性,所以他们在法规的第二部分着手确立工资。

【解题分析】请注意文中的 without 表示条件。With 和 without 同样可以表示条件,原因或
者伴随状态,在填空题当中经常用于表示一种隐含的逻辑关系。此题中若认
识不到 without 引导的实为一条件的话,那么就会自然地探求该条件是否为必
要条件。紧随其后的文字就迎合了思路,告诉读者立法者在确立工资,由此可
知工资就是立法者们认为的必要条件,所以前文的推理就成为:必要条件未能
满足,所以企业必然失败。

【重点词条】**secure** *adj.* ①安心的,无虑的(unwisely free from fear or distrust, overconfident, easy in mind, confident, assured in opinion or expectation, having no doubt)
②安全的(free from danger)
③可靠的(trustworthy, dependable) 例 ～foundation
④确定的(assured, certain) 例 ～victory

6. 【正确答案】C

【中文释义】处于最前沿研究的科学家必定经常违反常识并且做出看上去荒谬的假设,因为现存的理论确实不能解释新观察到的现象。

【解题分析】文中的 and 为小连接,连接两个动宾短语。所以第一个定格可直接填上"违反常识的",可选 C,因为违反常识的就是看上去荒谬的或反常的。

【重点词条】radical *adj.* ①基本的(of, relating to, or proceeding from a root)

②根本的(of or relating to the origin, fundamental)

③极端的,激进的(marked by a considerable departure from the usual or traditional, extreme, tending or disposed to make extreme changes in existing views, habits, conditions, or institutions)

incorporate *v.* ①包含,吸收(to unite or work into something already existent so as to form an indistinguishable whole)

②使混合,使合并(to blend or combine thoroughly)

③具体化,体现(to give material form to, embody)

corroborate *v.* 证实,确证(to support with evidence or authority, make more certain)

simply *adv.* 坦白地,仅仅,简单地,单纯地,天真地,朴实地,彻底地

7. 【正确答案】A

【中文释义】法国贵族对待中产阶级卢梭的尊重态度是非常出乎人们意料的,因为卢梭对他们一点儿也不尊重。

【解题分析】由第一空格后的从句的动词短语 greet with 可知空格里应填贵族对卢梭的态度。而原因从句中表明卢梭对贵族不尊重。这两种人之间的相互态度在提示我们第一空格应填"尊重"或"不尊重"。符合的词意只有 A。通过这种解题思路,我们避开了原文中艰难的语法,all the 结构是一种现代英语中已经罕见的表达结构,起到强调表语的作用。后接形容词的比较级却并无比较的含义,只起强调作用,我们学习过强调主语的强调句型,强调谓语动词的 do 的用法,强调表语则应用此结构,答案 C 正是错在这个结构上,如果用 all the 强调 unexpected 则第一空应为 deference,这才是极端出乎人们意料的情况。如果不强调,将 all the 去掉,C 也是一个通畅的句子。当然 all the 后也可接名词,有若干复杂的含义,均极罕见,本书从略。但切不可以为 all the 后只能接 remarkable。五个选项从语法上看都应是正确的,这是 GRE 填空与 TOEFL 填空的重大区别之一。

【重点词条】remarkable *adj.* 异常的,卓越的,值得注意的(worthy of being or likely to be noticed esp. as being uncommon or extraordinary)

reserve *n.* ①拘谨,矜持

②严肃,节制

SECTION 49

1. Because they had expected the spacecraft Voyager 2 to be able to gather data only about the planets Jupiter and Saturn, scientists were ____ the wealth of information it sent back from Neptune twelve years after leaving Earth.
   (A) disappointed in
   (B) concerned about
   (C) confident in
   (D) elated by
   (E) anxious for

2. Wearing the latest fashions was exclusively the ____ of the wealthy until the 1850's, when mass production, aggressive entrepreneurs, and the availability of the sewing machine made them ____ the middle class.
   (A) aspiration. . disagreeable to
   (B) vexation. . superfluous for
   (C) bane. . profitable to
   (D) prerogative. . accessible to
   (E) obligation. . popular with

3. Linguists have now confirmed what experienced users of ASL—American Sign Language—have always implicitly known: ASL is a grammatically ____ language in that it is capable of expressing every possible syntactic relation.
   (A) limited
   (B) economical
   (C) complete
   (D) shifting
   (E) abstract

4. He was regarded by his followers, as something of ____, not only because of his insistence on strict discipline, but also because of his ____ adherence to formal details.
   (A) a martinet. . rigid
   (B) an authority. . sporadic
   (C) a tyrant. . reluctant
   (D) a fraud. . conscientious
   (E) an acolyte. . maniacal

5. The influence of the Timaeus among early philosophical thinkers was ____, if only because it was the sole dialogue ____ in Europe for almost 1,000 years.
   (A) pervasive. . available
   (B) inestimable. . suppressed
   (C) unnoteworthy. . abridged
   (D) underestimated. . studied
   (E) circumscribed. . translated

6. The Gibsons were little given to ____ in any form; not one of them was afraid of ____, of being and seeming unlike their neighbors.
   (A) humility. . absurdity
   (B) excellence. . mediocrity
   (C) anger. . confrontation
   (D) conformism. . singularity
   (E) ostentation. . eccentricity

7. Even after ____ against the ____ of popular sovereignty were included, major figures in the humanistic disciplines remained skeptical about the proposal to extend suffrage to the masses.
   (A) recommendations. . continuation
   (B) safeguards. . excesses

(C)arguments. . introduction   (E)laws. . creation

(D)provisions. . advantages

SECTION 49 解答

1. 【正确答案】D
   【中文释义】因为科学家们预期航海者二号飞行器只能收集关于木星和土星的数据,所以他们对于飞行器离开地球 12 年后又从海王星送回来的丰富的信息感到喜出望外。
   【解题分析】只要看到上句中的 only 后下句的 the wealth of (本身有褒义)就可以断定从第三颗星球送回的信息为额外的信息,科学家们对于意外收获当然会高兴,答案选 D。
   【重点词条】elate *v*. 使兴高采烈,使得意洋洋,使兴奋(to fill with joy or pride)

2. 【正确答案】D
   【中文释义】在 19 世纪 50 年代之前穿着最新的时髦服装一直是富人们的专有特权,从那以后,大规模的生产、有进取心的企业家以及缝纫机的利用就使得这些时髦服装对于中产阶级也是可获得的了。
   【解题分析】上下文的 the wealthy 和 the middle class 构成了一组对比,并且 until the 1850's 也提示了对比关系,所以上下文应当为反义关系,五个选项中能构成反义关系的只有 D。
   【重点词条】bane *n*. ①毒物(poison)

                   ②死亡,毁灭(death, destruction) 例 stop the way of those that seek my～

                   ③祸根(a source of harm or ruin, curse) 例 national frontiers have been more of a～than a boon for mankind

       obligation *n*. ①合约(something such as a formal contract, a promise, or the demands of conscience or custom that obligates one to a course of action)

                   ②债务(a debt security such as a mortgage or corporate bond)

                   ③恩惠(a condition or feeling of being obligated, a debt of gratitude)

                   ④义务,责任(something one is bound to do, duty, responsibility)

3. 【正确答案】C
   【中文释义】语言学家们现在才证实了那些美国手势语的有经验的使用者们早就暗暗知道的一个事实:美国手势语是一个语法上完备的语言,因为它能够表达出任何可能的句法结构。
   【解题分析】与空格相关联的是其后的因果结构,我们只关心那些和空格相关联的逻辑结构,因为只有这些逻辑才是对解题有帮助的逻辑,并且越直接的,越有利于推理,既然 ASL 能表达出任何句法结构,所以它在语法上当然就是全能的,也就是完备的,答案为 C。

【重点词条】complete *adj*. 完整的,完备的(persising, or nescessary parts, items, component, elements)

perfection *n*. ①完美,圆满(the quality or state of being perfect, freedom from fault or defect, flawlessness)

②成熟(maturity)

③尽善尽美(an exemplification of supreme excellence)

4.【正确答案】A

【中文释义】他被他的同伙们看成某种严格执行纪律的偏执狂,不单单因为他严格地坚持苛刻的纪律,而且因为他刻板地坚守日常细节。

【解题分析】在 not only...but also...构成的递进结构中,第二个空格只能继续表达他坚持纪律,所以 B 和 C 都不对,A、D、E 中 D 和 E 又显然不是坚持纪律的人,故选 A。A 的 martinet 是 1991 年的考卷后才添加到红宝书中的,所以我们有时并不排斥排除法,尤其是在有些生僻的单词不知晓的情况下,别无他法。

【重点词条】mania *n*. ①癫狂,狂乱(excitement manifested by mental and physical hyperactivity, disorganization of behavior, and elevation of mood)

②狂热,醉心(excessive or unreasonable enthusiasm) 例 a~for saving things

5.【正确答案】A

【中文释义】Timaeus 在早期哲学家之间的影响是很普遍的,只不过是因为它是整个欧洲一千年以来可获得的惟一的一本对话体哲学著作。

【解题分析】If only because 是一个连词短语,表作者所轻蔑的惟一的一个原因;only because 表示作者认为的惟一的一个原因。两者有明显的语言色彩的差别。首先五个选项中能构成一个原因解释的就只有 A。再细读发现 A 的语义充满了辛辣的讽刺。也就是说 Timaeus 这本哲学著作本身的内容并不优秀,欧洲人只不过没有同类的书看,迫不得已才看它而已。

【重点词条】inestimable *adj*. ①难以计算的,无法估计的(incapable of being estimated or computed) 例 Storms caused~damage.

②极宝贵的,无价的(too valuable or excellent to be measured or appreciated) 例 has performed an~service for his country

6.【正确答案】D

【中文释义】格伯森一家人很少屈从于任何形式的从众主义;他们当中没有人害怕显得独特,显得和周围的邻居们不一样。

【解题分析】分号句上下句重复,下句的空格显然应该填上其后分隔的内容。从而下句含义即为"格伯森一家人都很独特",相应地上句应为"格伯森一家人不屈从使他们与邻居一样的力量"也即"不屈服于从众主义",答案选 D。

【重点词条】**singularity** *n*. ①独一,罕有,非凡(something that is singular, a separate unit, unusual or distinctive manner or behavior, peculiarity)

②奇特,独特(the quality or state of being singular)

conformist *n*./*adj*. ①因循守旧的(人)(to be similar or identical; to be in a-greement or harmony)

②顺从(to be obedient or compliant)

③从俗,随大流 (to act in accordance with prevailing standards or customs)

7.【正确答案】B

【中文释义】即使在那些防止大众主权过滥的保护措施实施了之后,人文学科的主要人物仍然怀疑是否应该进一步扩展普选权给大众。

【解题分析】上下文中有一明显的重复:popular sovereignty 与 suffrage to mass。大众主权并不是指每个人都去当主席,而是指大众能行使普选权。故第二个空格应填相应的"extend"的名词形式,答案为 B。

【重点词条】**safeguard** *n*. ①保卫(convoy, escort)

②预防措施(a precautionary measure, stipulation, or device)

③保护设备(a technical contrivance to prevent accident)

excess *n*. ①过度,超过(the state or an instance of surpassing usual, proper, or specified limits, superfluity)

②过量,超额(the amount or degree by which one thing or quantity exceeds another) 例 an~of 10 bushels

③无节制 (undue or immoderate indulgence, intemperance; an act or instance of intemperance) 例 prevent~es and abuses by newly created local powers

SECTION 50

1. A recent survey shows that, while ninety-four percent of companies conducting man-agement-training programs open them to women, women are ____ only seventy-four percent of those programs.

(A)protesting against

(B)participating in

(C)displeased by

(D)allowed in

(E)refused by

2. Thomas Paine, whose political writing was often flamboyant, was in private life a sur-prisingly ____ man: he lived in rented rooms, ate little, and wore drab clothes.

(A)simple

(B)controversial

(C)sordid

(D)comfortable

(E)discourteous

3. Their ____ of loyalties is first to oneself, next to kin, then to fellow tribe members, and finally to compatriots.

(A) merging

(B) hierarchy

(C) definition

(D) judgment

(E) cognizance

4. The belief that science destroys the arts appears to be supported by historical evidence that the arts have ____ only when the sciences have been ____.

(A) declined. . attacked

(B) flourished. . neglected

(C) matured. . unconcerned

(D) succeeded. . developed

(E) floundered. . constrained

5. The action and characters in a melodrama can be so immediately ____ that all observers can hiss the villain with an air of smug but enjoyable ____.

(A) spurned. . boredom

(B) forgotten. . condescension

(C) classified. . self-righteousness

(D) plausible. . guilt

(E) gripping. . skepticism

6. In the design of medical experiments, the need for ____ assignment of treatments to patients must be ____ the difficulty of persuading patients to participate in an experiment in which their treatment is decided by chance.

(A) independent. . amended by

(B) competent. . emphasized by

(C) mechanical. . controlled by

(D) swift. . associated with

(E) random. . reconciled with

7. Though dealers insist that professional art dealers can make money in the art market, even an ____ knowledge is not enough: the art world is so fickle that stock-market prices are ____ by comparison.

(A) amateur's. . sensible

(B) expert's. . erratic

(C) investor's. . booming

(D) insider's. . predictable

(E) artist's. . irrational

SECTION 50 解答

1.【正确答案】B

【中文释义】最近的一项调查研究表明,尽管有94%开设管理训练课程的公司将该课程向妇女开放,妇女们只参加这些项目的74%。

【解题分析】此题的 only 甚为重要,它提醒这是一种程度对比,而非对立面转折,A、C、D 均犯了对立面转折的错误,而 D 的句意明显与上文不符合,故选 B。

【重点词条】displease v.①使不快,激怒(to incur the disapproval or dislike of esp. by annoying) 例 their gossip～s her

②冒犯,使厌恶(to be offensive to) 例 abstract art～s him

2.【正确答案】A

【中文释义】托马斯·潘恩,他的政治作品总是很华丽,但在个人生活中却让人吃惊地朴素:

他住在租来的房子里,吃得很少,穿着颜色不鲜艳的衣服。

【解题分析】此句中的 surprisingly 提示我们该选反义词,flamboyant 的反义词为 A simple。

【重点词条】**sordid** *adj.* ①卑鄙的(marked by baseness or grossness, vile) 例 ～motives

②肮脏污秽的(dirty, filthy)

③贪婪的,下贱的(meanly avaricious, covetous)

④暗色调的(of a dull or muddy color)

3.【正确答案】B

【中文释义】他们忠诚对象的等级首先是对自己,其次是对亲戚,然后是对本部落成员,最后才是对同胞。

【解题分析】句中的 first, next, then, finally 明显在提示选 B,并且请注意句中的短语为 loyalty to somebody。

【重点词条】**merge** *v.* ①合并(to cause to combine, unite, or coalesce)

②融合(to blend gradually by stages that blur distinctions)

cognizance *n.* ①认识,察知(knowledge, awareness) 例 had no～of the situation

②注意(notice, acknowledgment) 例 take～of their achievement

③审理,管辖权(jurisdiction, responsibility)

4.【正确答案】B

【中文释义】科学摧毁艺术的信念好像被下面的历史证据证实了;只有在科学被忽略的时候艺术才会兴旺。

【解题分析】上下句的结构很有特征:科学摧毁艺术;艺术与科技的关系。显然符合 A 增→B 减;B 减→A 增的逆否命题的结构。因此第一个空格直接填艺术被摧毁的反义词,则应为 B 或 C,相应的第二空格应表示科学的不良景象,则应为 B。答案 C 是颇具有迷惑性的选项,C 的第一个词 mature 与被摧毁无反义词关系。Mature 与幼稚构成反义词,并且艺术的成熟还是幼稚是个不可逆转的过程,根本不可能出现在一个逆否命题句中。

【重点词条】**flounder** *n.* 比目鱼类(a fish of either of two families such as Pleuronectidae and Bothidae that include important marine food fishes)

flounder *v.* ①挣扎(to struggle to move or obtain footing, thrash about wildly)

②笨拙的举动(to proceed or act clumsily)

ineffectually *adv.* ①没有效果地(not producing the proper or intended effect, futile)

②无效地,无益地(ineffective)

constrain *n.* ①强迫(to force by imposed stricture, restriction, or limitation)

②限制(to secure by or as if by bonds, confine, limit)

③做作(to force or produce in an unnatural or strained manner) 例 a～ed smile

④抑制（to hold back by or as if by force）例 ~ing my mind not to wander from the task

5. 【正确答案】C

【中文释义】善恶分明的轻松歌舞剧中的行为和角色可以被如此迅速地辨认出来以至于所有的观众都会带着一种沾沾自喜同时又是令人愉快的自我正直感的表情来嘘坏蛋。

【解题分析】本题最简单的解法是由第二个空格前的 enjoyable 得答案 C，因为其他几个选项都不能和 enjoyable 构成搭配关系。本题更深入的解法是判断出第二空格应和前面的 smug 构成褒贬转折，从而得出答案 C。Smug 与 self-rightousness 同时修饰 air，两者又用 but 连接，故只能构成褒贬转折。这已在 SECTION 6 的第 6 题中作了详细分析，请重视这种结构。

【重点词条】melodrama n. 善恶分明的轻松歌舞剧

spurn v. 狂傲地拒绝

6. 【正确答案】E

【中文释义】在医药实验的设计中，随机将治疗方案分配给病人的需求必须与下列困难协调起来，这个困难就是劝说病人参加到一个他们所接受的治疗方案由机率决定的实验中。

【解题分析】原文简化后即为 the need must be ____ the difficulty。在设计实验时有一个需要完成的任务 the need，同时又预料到会有一个障碍 the difficulty，因此主观上会产生强烈的愿望 must 去干什么呢？恐怕在制定计划时所有人想的都一样，都是想去克服困难。故可直接选 E。或者我们将全句视为三大块。第一块为主干，第二块为 the need 的修饰语 for 短语，第三块为 the difficulty 的修饰语 by 短语。那么 for 短语中的空格信息显然应由第三块文字提供，因为句子主干中根本未涉及到治疗，何谈治疗方案的分配方式？By 短语中关于治疗提及了 by chance，所以我们将之填到第一空格里去，这就是原文提示的信息，正确答案为 E。事实上医疗实验中都会设计阴性对照，阳性对照和零度参照组以核实用药过量，用药不足和不用药的各自效果，病人不愿意参加实验的主要恐惧来源于治疗方案的随机分配，担心自己会分配到一组恶劣的实验组中，千万不要误以为是病人担心治疗效果不确定。所以原句中的"their treatment is decided by chance"应理解为"他们所接受的治疗方案由机率决定"，而不是"他们所接受的治疗方案的成败由机率决定"。

【重点词条】reconcile v. ①和解（to restore to friendship or harmony）例 reconciled the factions

②调和（settle, resolve）例 ~differences

③使一致（to make consistent or congruous）例 ~ an ideal with reality

④使认命（to cause to submit to or accept something unpleasant）例 was reconciled to hardship

⑤使符合(to check a financial account against another for accuracy)

swift *adj*. ①快速进行的(moving or capable of moving with great speed)
②短暂的,突然的(occurring suddenly or within a very short time)
③机警的(quick to respond, ready)

7.【正确答案】D
　　【中文释义】尽管交易商们坚持认为职业的艺术交易商肯定会在艺术品市场上赚钱,但即
　　　　　　　　使一个内行的知识也是远远不够的:艺术品市场如此地变化多端以至于相比
　　　　　　　　之下股价都可以预料了。
　　【解题分析】由递进转折可知第一空格应填 professional 的递进词义,可选 B 或 D。而冒号
　　　　　　　　后的比较结构中强调艺术品市场变化多端,因而股价相比之下就缺乏变化,故
　　　　　　　　在 B 和 D 中选 D。
　　【重点词条】sensible *adj*. ①感觉到的(of a kind to be felt or perceived) 例 felt a~chill
　　　　　　　　　　　　　　②意识到的,认识到的(perceptible to the senses or to reason or
　　　　　　　　　　　　　　understanding) 例 Her distress was~from her manner.
　　　　　　　　　　　　　　③敏感的(receptive to external influences, sensitive) 例 the
　　　　　　　　　　　　　　most~reaches of the spirit
　　　　　　　　　　　　　　④明显的(convinced by perceived evidence, satisfied) 例 ~of
　　　　　　　　　　　　　　my error
　　　　　　　　　　　　　　⑤明智的(having, containing, or indicative of good sense or rea-
　　　　　　　　　　　　　　son, rational, reasonable) 例 ~people/made a~answer
　　　　　　　　　erratic *adj*. ①游移的(having no fixed course, wandering) 例 an~comet
　　　　　　　　　　　　　　②漂移的(transported from an original resting place esp. by a
　　　　　　　　　　　　　　glacier) 例 an~boulder
　　　　　　　　　　　　　　③不规则的(characterized by lack of consistency, regularity, or u-
　　　　　　　　　　　　　　niformity)
　　　　　　　　　　　　　　④古怪的(deviating from what is ordinary or standard, eccentric)
　　　　　　　　　　　　　　例 an~genius

SECTION 51

1. Contrary to the popular conception that it is
powered by conscious objectivity, science often operates through error, happy accidents,
_____ and persistence in spite of mistakes.
(A) facts
(B) controls

(C) hunches
(D) deductions
(E) calculations

2. The transition from the Paleolithic to the
Neolithic era is viewed by most art histori-

ans as a _____, because, instead of an increasingly _____ pictorial art, we find degeneration.

(A) milestone. . debased

(B) consolidation. . diverse

(C) calamity. . aberrant

(D) regression. . sophisticated

(E) continuation. . improved

3. Salazar's presence in the group was so _____ the others that they lost most of their earlier _____; failure, for them, became all but unthinkable.

(A) reassuring to. . trepidation

(B) unnoticed by. . curiosity

(C) unusual to. . harmony

(D) endearing to. . confidence

(E) unexpected by. . exhilaration

4. The eradication of pollution is not merely a matter of _____, though the majestic beauty of nature is indeed an important consideration.

(A) economics

(B) legislation

(C) cleanliness

(D) aesthetics

(E) restoration

5. Despite an agreement between labor and management to keep the print and electron-ic media _____ developments, the details of the negotiations were _____ all but a few journalists from the major metropolitan newspapers.

(A) abreast of. . disclosed to

(B) involved in. . leaded to

(C) apprised of. . withheld from

(D) speculating about. . denied to

(E) ignorant of. . suppressed by

6. Word order in a sentence was much freer in Old French than it is in French today, this _____ disappeared as the French language gradually lost its case distinctions.

(A) restriction

(B) license

(C) similarity

(D) rigidity

(E) imperative

7. Whereas biologists must maintain a _____ attitude toward the subjects of their research, social scientists must, paradoxically, combine personal involvement and scholarly _____.

(A) scrupulous. . sympathy

(B) careful. . abandon

(C) casual. . precision

(D) passive. . passion

(E) disinterested. . detachment

SECTION 51 解答

1. 【正确答案】C

【中文释义】和流行的观念——科学是被清醒的客观所推动的——相反,科学总是运作在错误、令人愉快的意外事件、直觉和顽固坚持错误中。

【解题分析】由 contrary to 可知主句中强调科学的非客观性。这就是四个并列成分的共同特征。五个选项中表示非客观的词为 C。

【重点词条】control n. 实验中的参照物

       hunch v. ①推开,挤开(jostle, shove)

                   ②弯成拱状(to thrust or bend over into a humped or crooked position)

                   ③向前挤进(to thrust oneself forward)

                   ④蹲伏(to assume a bent or crooked posture)

                   ⑤蜷曲(to draw oneself into a ball, curl up)

       hunch n. ①瘤,块(a thick piece, lump)

                   ②预感(a strong intuitive feeling concerning esp. a future event or result)

2.【正确答案】D

  【中文释义】从旧石器时代向新石器时代的转变被大多数艺术史学家看成一个倒退的过程,因为我们并没有发现一个越来越精致的视图艺术,反而是堕落倒退。

  【解题分析】此句中针对主干的原因从句为完整句:we find degeneration,由此原因推知主干的结论应为 D。

  【重点词条】**debase** v. ①贬低身分、人格、意义(to lower in status, esteem, quality, or character)

                       ②贬值(to reduce the intrinsic value of a coin by increasing the base-metal content)

         aberrant adj. ①偏离正路的(straying from the right or normal way)

                     ②反常的,异常的(deviating from the usual or natural type, atypical)

       sophisticated adj. 复杂的,精致的,经过仔细研究的

3.【正确答案】A

  【中文释义】萨拉特出现在小组中是如此地安慰镇定了其他人,以至于他们失去了大多数早期的恐慌之情;失败对他们而言变得几乎是不可想像的了。

  【解题分析】分号句的上半句出现了 earlier 这个既是时间又是隐含比较的词,所以我们希望在下句找到过去的情况或者现在的情况,结果下句中的 became 提示我们现在的情况是以为自己不可能失败,所以上句中 earlier 所修饰的情况则应为认为自己会失败,五个选项中与失败的情绪相地应的为 A。All but 后接名词时是大家熟悉的"除了…之外都…"的意思;all but 后接形容词时,等同于 almost。

  【重点词条】**reassure** v. ①向…再保证,安慰(to assure anew) 例 reassured him that the work was on schedule

                     ②使放心,使消除疑虑(to restore to confidence) 例 felt reassured by their earnest promise to do better

4.【正确答案】D

  【中文释义】消除污染不仅仅是一个美的问题,尽管大自然壮丽的美的确是一个重要的考虑因素。

  【解题分析】下半句肯定了美,所以上句程度否定的对象当然也是美,否则构不成转折,故

空格里填美的同义词,答案为 D。

【重点词条】restoration *n*. ①恢复

②复原,修整

③重新实施

④归还,返还

5. 【正确答案】C

【中文释义】尽管工会和管理层有一个协定,希望让新闻界报道谈判的发展过程,但是谈判的细节却对所有记者封锁了,而只透露给了一些大都市主要大报的记者。

【解题分析】Despite 使得上下文对立面转折,第一空格前的特征人物新闻界又提示我们空格只能填报道或不报道,所以相应的第二个空格只可能是报道或不报道二者的选择。又由于第二个空格后为 all but 的结构,不可能出现"对所有记者均开放消息,但对大报记者封锁"的场景,所以第二空格只能填"不报道",第一空格填"报道"。故选答案 C。

【重点词条】**abreast of** 同步报道

apprise *v*. (正式)通知,告知

withhold *v*. ①阻挡,使停止(to hold back from action, check)

②监督,保护(to keep in custody)

③拒给(to refrain from granting, giving, or allowing) 例 ~per-

mission

④扣除(to deduct from income)

6. 【正确答案】B

【中文释义】一个句子中词的顺序在古法语中比今天的法语更加自由;这个自由之所以消失是因为法语逐渐失去了它的格的区别。

【解题分析】分号句下半句中的 this 重复上文消失的自由,故空格填 B。

【重点词条】**license** *n*. ①行为的自由(permission to act, freedom of action)

②许可,特许(a permission granted by competent authority to en-

gage in a business or occupation or in an activity otherwise unlaw-

ful)

③执照(a document, plate, or tag evidencing a license granted)

④放纵(freedom that allows or is used with irresponsibility)

⑤(艺术创作的)破格,不拘一格(deviation from fact, form, or rule

by an artist or writer for the sake of the effect gained)

imperative *adj*. ①祈使式的(of, relating to, or constituting the grammatical

mood that expresses the will to influence the behavior of an-

other)

②命令的(expressive of a command, entreaty, or exhortation)

③强制的(having power to restrain, control, and direct)

④必须的(not to be avoided or evaded, necessary) 例 an~duty

7.【正确答案】E

【中文释义】尽管生物学家必须保持对研究课题的公正客观态度,社会科学家却必须非常矛盾地将个人情感与学者的公正结合起来。

【解题分析】文中的 paradoxically 提示我们该选一组反义词。Personal involvement 的反义词为 E 的 detachment。

【重点词条】**disinterested** *adj*. ①公正无私的,无偏的

②冷漠的,无兴趣的

scrupulous *adj*. ①有顾忌的,有道德原则的(having moral integrity, acting in strict regard for what is considered right or proper)

②细致认真的,一丝不苟的(punctiliously exact, painstaking)

例 working with～care

SECTION 52

1. Read's apology to Heflin was not exactly abject and did little to ____ their decades-long quarrel, which had been as ____ as the academic etiquette of scholarly journals permitted.

 (A) encourage..sporadic

 (B) dampen..courteous

 (C) obscure..ceremonious

 (D) resolve..acrimonious

 (E) blur..sarcastic

2. Certain weeds that flourish among rice crops resist detection until maturity by ____ the seedling stage in the rice plant's life cycle, thereby remaining indistinguishable from the rice crop until the flowering stage.

 (A) deterring

 (B) displacing

 (C) augmenting

 (D) imitating

 (E) nurturing

3. Although the architect's concept at first sounded too ____ to be ____, his careful analysis of every aspect of the project convinced the panel that the proposed building was indeed, structurally feasible.

 (A) mundane..attractive

 (B) eclectic..appealing

 (C) grandiose..affordable

 (D) innovative..ignored

 (E) visionary..practicable

4. Gould claimed no ____ knowledge of linguistics, but only a hobbyist's interest in language.

 (A) manifest

 (B) plausible

 (C) technical

 (D) rudimentary

 (E) insignificant

5. An obvious style, easily identified by some superficial quirk, is properly ____ as a mere mannerism, whereas a complex and subtle style ____ reduction to a formula.

(A) avoided. . risks

(B) decried. . resists

(C) prized. . withstands

(D) identified. . consists of

(E) cultivated. . demands

6. If efficacious new medicines have side effects that are commonly observed and ____, such medicines are too often considered ____, even when laboratory tests suggest caution.

(A) unremarkable. . safe

(B) unpredictable. . reliable

(C) frequent. . outdated

(D) salutary. . experimental

(E) complicated. . useful

7. Although a few delegates gave the opposition's suggestions a ____ response, most greeted the statement of a counterposition with ____.

(A) favorable. . approval

(B) dispirited. . reluctance

(C) surly. . resentment

(D) halfhearted. . composure

(E) vitriolic. . civility

SECTION 52 解答

1. 【正确答案】D

【中文释义】瑞德对赫夫琳的道歉并不是严格意义上的可怜而真诚的,因而没有解决他们长达几十年的争吵,这几十年的争吵一直都尖刻到学术杂志的学术礼节所允许的最大限度。

【解题分析】第一空格由 and 的顺承关系可知 B、C 和 D 候选,第二个空格修饰这长达几十年的争吵,B 和 C 当然都不行,故选 D,文中的 as. . .as 结构并非小连接结构,第二个 as 短语起到对第一个 as 所引导的形容词的修饰作用。

【重点词条】**abject** *adj*. ①绝望无援的,凄苦可怜的

②可鄙的

③奴性的,怯懦的

blur *v*. ①弄脏,玷污(to obscure or blemish by smearing)

②使模糊不清(to make cloudy or confused)

2. 【正确答案】D

【中文释义】某些在稻谷中繁荣生长的野草在成熟之前通过模仿稻谷生命周期的发芽阶段而难于被发现,因而它们直到开花期之前一直和稻谷真假难辨。

【解题分析】A 和 C 答案使得野草和稻谷有区别,而不是 indistinguishable,B 和 E 根本不可能发生,能使两者无法区分的只有 D。

【重点词条】**deter** *v*. 威慑住,阻止,使不敢

displace *v*. ①移动…的位置

②取代…的位置,置换

③撤换,免…的职

3. 【正确答案】E

【中文释义】尽管这位建筑家的设计观念起初听上去过于奇思妙想以至于显得不切实际，但他对工程各个方面的仔细分析使委员会确信提议中的建筑在结构上可行。

【解题分析】上下句转折句，且均为判断句，故直接让两个表语反义即可，所以第二空格应填上"structurally feasible"以便表达出"结构不可行"的概念，正确答案为 E。部分同学误选 C，C 的含义是财政支出的不可行，不能与下文的结构上可行构成反义。

【重点词条】mundane *adj*．①世俗的，尘世的(of, relating to, or characteristic of the world)

②单调平凡的(characterized by the practical, transitory, and ordinary, commonplace) 例 the～concerns of day-to-day life

visionary *adj*．①幻想的(of the nature of a vision, illusory)

②不切实际的(incapable of being realized or achieved, utopian)

例 a～scheme

③空想的(existing only in imagination, unreal)

4．【正确答案】C

【中文释义】邦德宣称没有语言学家的专业知识，但只有一个业余爱好者对语言的兴趣。

【解题分析】语言学家和 hobbyist 的对比充分说明了语言学家是个专业人士，故第一空格填"专业的"。答案 C。

【重点词条】manifest *adj*．①显然的(readily perceived by the senses and esp. by the sight)

②明了的(easily understood or recognized by the mind, obvious)

technical *adj*．技术的，专业的，专门性的

5．【正确答案】B

【中文释义】一个肤浅的风格，非常容易通过一些肤浅的奇怪言行辨认出来，是非常恰当地被指责为故作姿态；而一个复杂和精微的风格却难于归结为任何一种类型。

【解题分析】上下句的主语两种风格显然是在对比，故上文为 easily identified，则下文应为 hard to identify。下句的 reduction to 和 identify 同义，故空格里填上一个表困难的词即可，可选 B 或 C。上句的语言色彩决定了 B 和 C 中正确的为 B。

【重点词条】identify *v*．①使参与，使支持(to cause to be or become identical)

②认为…等同于(to conceive as united such as in spirit, outlook, or principle) 例 groups that are identified with conservation

③确定(to establish the identity of)

④认出，识别(to determine the taxonomic position of a biological specimen)

reduction to (reduce to)　①数量减少

②状态变差

③身份地位下降

④归结为一种不好的类型

6．【正确答案】A

【中文释义】如果一种有效的新药物有副作用,并且这种副作用司空见惯不显著的话,这样的药物总是被认为是安全的,即使当实验室的测试表明其危险性。

【解题分析】第一空格在小连接中,能和司空见惯(强调副作用的不严重)构成搭配的是 A。

【重点词条】side effect *n*. ①(药物)副作用

②(事态的)意外后果

7. 【正确答案】E

【中文释义】尽管一些代表给了反方的建议一个尖刻的回答,大多数代表用文明礼貌的方式对待反方的陈述。

【解题分析】前后转折,a few 和 most 构成强烈的对比,五个选项中构成反义词的是 A。

【重点词条】approval *n*. 赞同,赞成,包退包换(approbation, on approval, subject to a prospective buyer's acceptance or refusal) 例 stamps sent to collectors on approval

surly *adj*. ①傲慢的,倨傲的(arrogant, imperious)

②阴沉的,乖戾的(irritably sullen and churlish in mood or manner, crabbed)

③阴霾的(menacing or threatening in appearance) 例 ~ weather

resentment *n*. 愤恨,怨恨(a feeling of indignant displeasure or persistent ill will at something regarded as a wrong, insult, or injury)

SECTION 53

1. By idiosyncratically refusing to dismiss an insubordinate member of his staff, the manager not only _____ established policy, but he also _____ his heretofore good chances for promotion.

(A) instituted. . bettered

(B) recognized. . protected

(C) contravened. . jeopardized

(D) reiterated. . computed

(E) delimited. . restricted

2. Congress is having great difficulty developing a consensus on energy policy, primarily because the policy objectives of various members of Congress rest on such _____ assumptions.

(A) commonplace

(B) trivial

(C) explicit

(D) divergent

(E) fundamental

3. The widespread public shock at the news of the guilty verdict was caused partly by _____ news stories that had _____ acquittal.

(A) sensational. . condemned

(B) buried. . urged

(C) impartial. . mentioned

(D) biased. . predicted

(E) local. . denounced

4. The idealized paintings of nature produced in theeighteenth century are evidence that the medieval _____ natural settings had been

_____ and that the outdoors now could be enjoyed without trepidation.

(A)fear of. . exorcised

(B)concerns about. . regained

(C)affection for. . surmounted

(D)disinterest in. . alleviated

(E)enthusiasm for. . confronted

5. Some paleontologists debate whether the diversity of species has _____ since the Cambrian period, or whether imperfections in the fossil record only suggest greater diversity today, while in actuality there has been either _____ or decreased diversity.

(A)changed. . escalation

(B)increased. . stasis

(C)expanded. . discontinuity

(D)declined. . reduction

(E)improved. . deviation

6. Manipulating laboratory tissue cultures with hormones is one thing; using hormones to treat human beings, however, is contingent on whether hormones that _____ in the laboratory can affect _____ organisms, and in predictable ways.

(A) develop. . similar

(B) succeed. . simple

(C) fail. . cellular

(D) work. . whole

(E) reproduce. . unknown

7. The astronomer and feminist Maria Mitchell's own prodigious activity and the vigor of the Association for the Advancement of Women during the 1870's _____ any assertion that feminism was _____ in that period.

(A)exclude. . thriving

(B)contradict. . prospering

(C)pervade. . remote

(D)buttress. . dormant

(E)belie. . quiescent

SECTION 53 解答

1.【正确答案】C

【中文释义】通过固执地拒绝解雇一个不服从领导的下属,这个经理不但违反了已经建立的政策,而且危及到了他目前为止一直良好的提升机会。

【解题分析】文中的 heretofore 表到目前为止,所以他的行为使得他一直很好的提升机会从此丧失了,故两个空格里均应填不好的动作。

【重点词条】institute v. ①设立(to establish in a position or office)

②开创(to originate and get established, organize) 例 instituted reading clinics

③开始(to set going, inaugurate) 例 instituting an investigation of the charges

reiterate v. 反复做,反复重申(to state or do over again or repeatedly sometimes with wearying effect)

delimit v. 确定…界线,限定(to fix or define the limits of)

2.【正确答案】D

【中文释义】议会很难得到关于能量政策的一致意见,主要是因为议会的不同成员之间的政策目标建立在如此分歧的假设之上。

【解题分析】由很难得到一致结果可知其前提假设不一致,故空格里填 D 的 divergent。

【重点词条】divergent *adj*. ①有分歧的,不同的(differing from each other or from a standard, deviant) 例 the~interests of capital and labor

②发散的(relating to or being an infinite sequence that does not have a limit or an infinite series whose partial sums do not have a limit)

③分叉的,叉开的(causing divergence of rays) 例 a~lens

3.【正确答案】D

【中文释义】对于有罪判决消息的普遍的公众震惊部分上是由有偏见的新闻报导所导致,这些报导曾经预料为无罪释放。

【解题分析】对有罪的判决感到震惊,说明公众预期的是无罪释放,而第二空格果然出现 acquittal 无罪释放,且时态为过去完成时态,正好对应于公众过去的看法。所以第二空格可候选 B、C、或 D,第一空格填形容词修饰新闻报导,显然原文提供的信息表明新闻报导与实际判决相反,故可选 D。

【重点词条】buried *adj*. 被遗忘的

denounce *v*. ①谴责,指责(to pronounce esp. publicly to be blameworthy or evil)

②告发,控告(to inform against, accuse)

③通知废止(to announce formally the termination of such as a treaty)

4.【正确答案】A

【中文释义】这幅产生于 18 世纪的关于大自然完美主义的作品是证据,表明了中世纪对自然环境的害怕之情已经被驱逐掉并且室外风光现在可以被人们不带有恐惧之情地享受。

【解题分析】Evidence 之后有两个同位语从句,故此两同位语从句构成了特殊并列句,为互相重复的关系,第二个 that 从句中出现 now 又提示了一种时间对比型,故可立刻推知过去是 trepidation 而非 enjoy。第一个 that 从句中的 medieval 正好表示过去,故其后的空格填 trepidation 的同义词即可,答案为 A。

【重点词条】exorcise *v*. ①驱除(to expel an evil spirit by adjuration)

②消除,除去(to get rid of something troublesome, menacing, or oppressive)

surmount *v*. ①超越(to surpass in quality or attainment, excel)

②克服(to prevail over, overcome) 例 ~an obstacle

③登上(to get to the top of, climb)

5.【正确答案】B

【中文释义】有些古生物化石学家讨论道:或者物种的多样性自从寒武纪开始持续地增加,或者化石纪录的不完整性只能说明今天有更多的物种;而实际上是物种多样性并没有变化或下降。

【解题分析】本句的逻辑关系划分尤为重要,上句为一常见句式 debate whether... or whether...。下句用 while in actuality 引导,故第一层逻辑关系为转折关系。第二个空格里只可能填不变或上升。究竟是哪一种情况,由与上文对应的关系可获得,空格正上方的 greater diversity today 即说明上句认为是上升,故第二空格填不变,直接得答案 B。此句的理解关键在于第二个 whether 从句中的 only, 两个 whether 从句均认为物种是变多的,只不过第一个 whether 从句同时还认为变多的方式是持续增加(had increased)。第二个 whether 从句只认为是变多,对上升的方式采取不确定的态度,而本文的作者干脆将两个观点全部否定,认为是不变和下降。之所以造成如此多的不同理解,均是由于对化石纪录的理解造成的,由于化石记录中体现的物种数量并不能代表真实的当时物种数量,所以实际上三种可能都会发生。

【重点词条】imperfection *n*. 不完整(the quality or state of being imperfect; fault, blemish)

　　　　　escalation *n*. 逐步上升(增强,扩大),逐步升级(to increase in extent, volume, number, amount, intensity, or scope) 例 A little war threatens to~into a huge ugly one.

6. 【正确答案】D

【中文释义】用荷尔蒙激素处理实验室里的离体组织培养是一回事;用荷尔蒙激素来处理人体都取决于在实验室里起作用的荷尔蒙是否能以可预料的方式影响整体的有机体。

【解题分析】分号句上下句在对比,上句为荷尔蒙处理组织培养,下句为处理人体。第一个空格谈的是处理实验室的情况,故第二个空格只能指另外一个有机体,也即人体了,所以可直接选 D。

【重点词条】contingent *adj*. ①可能的(likely but not certain to happen, possible)

　　　　　　②偶发的(happening by chance or unforeseen causes)

　　　　　　③意外的(subject to chance or unseen effects, unpredictable)

　　　　　　④有条件的(dependent on or conditioned by something else)

7. 【正确答案】E

【中文释义】宇航员和女权主义者玛丽亚·密歇尔自身的大量活动和妇女促进提高会在19世纪70年代的活力证明了下列断言为假,即女权主义在那个时期处于安静期。

【解题分析】句中的 prodigious activity 和 vigor 均说明女权主义正在活动,能表达的选项为 E。

【重点词条】prodigious *adj*. ①异常的(resembling or befitting a prodigy, strange, unusual)

　　　　　　②惊人的(exciting amazement or wonder)

③庞大的,巨大的(extraordinary in bulk, quantity, or degree, enormous)

buttress *v.* 支持,支撑 (to furnish or shore up with a buttress; support, strengthen) 例 arguments~ed by solid facts

pervade *v.* 遍布,弥漫(to become diffused throughout every part of)

SECTION 54

1. Only by ignoring decades of mismanagement and inefficiency could investors conclude that a fresh infusion of cash would provide anything more than a ____ solution to the company's financial woes.

   (A) fair

   (B) temporary

   (C) genuine

   (D) realistic

   (E) complete

2. Although the discovery of antibiotics led to great advances in clinical practice, it did not represent a ____ bacterial illness, for there are some bacteria that cannot be ____ treated with antibiotics.

   (A) breakthrough in. . consistently

   (B) panacea for. . effectively

   (C) neglect of. . efficiently

   (D) reexamination of. . conventionally

   (E) resurgence of. . entirely

3. A misconception frequently held by novice writers is that sentence structure mirrors thought: the more convoluted the structure, the more ____ the ideas.

   (A) complicated

   (B) inconsequential

   (C) elementary

   (D) fanciful

   (E) blatant

4. Jones was unable to recognize the contradictions in his attitudes that were obvious to everyone else; even the hint of an untruth was ____ to him, but he ____ serious trouble by always cheating on his taxes.

   (A) acceptable. . risked

   (B) exciting. . averted

   (C) repugnant. . courted

   (D) anathema. . evaded

   (E) tempting. . hazarded

5. Even though the general's carefully qualified public statement could hardly be ____, some people took ____ it.

   (A) respected. . liberties with

   (B) inoffensive. . umbrage at

   (C) faulted. . exception to

   (D) credited. . potshots at

   (E) dismissed. . interest in

6. Though feminist in its implications, Yvonne Rainer's 1974 film ____ the filmmaker's active involvement in feminist politics.

   (A) preserved

   (B) portrayed

   (C) encouraged

   (D) renewed

   (E) antedated

7. The chances that a species will ____ are reduced if any vital function is restricted to a

single kind of organ;＿＿＿ by itself possesses
an enormous survival advantage.

(A)degenerate..complexity

(B)expire..size

(C)disappear..variety

(D)flourish..symmetry

(E)persist..redundancy

SECTION 54 解答

1. 【正确答案】B

   【中文释义】只有在忽略掉几十年的管理不善和低效率的情况下投资者们才能得出这样的结论:一批新的大量资金的注入会成为一个不仅仅是临时的针对公司财政危机的解决措施。

   【解题分析】此句是一种强调原因的句型,如果一种原因至关重要,我们可以这样强调它,即:如果没有这个原因的话,事情将会截然不同。常见的表达为 only by ignoring ,only by failing to see, only by failing to recognize。我们正确的做法是先按这个原因正常地推理,得出一个结论,然后在原句的结果中填上一个与正常推理相反的结果。如本题中,如果从正常的推理出发,这种给一个管理不良的公司贷款无疑是于事无补的,最多只是一个临时的解决方案。将此结论相反的意思带回原句,那就是不仅仅是一个临时的解决方案。文中的 anything more than 和正常推理中的"最多是临时的解决方案"构成反义。

   【重点词条】**at best**　最多…

   nothing more than/little more than　只不过是

   anything more than　不仅仅是

   nothing but　绝不是

2. 【正确答案】B

   【中文释义】尽管抗生素的发现导致了临床医学的极大的进步,但它并不是一个细菌疾病的万能药,因为有一些细菌不能被抗生素有效克服。

   【解题分析】第二空格填副词,我们通常将副词忽略不计,将第二句当成完整句去推理可知:有些能被治疗,有些不能治疗,因此抗生素并不是一个包治百病的万灵药。答案可选 B。

   【重点词条】**conventionally** *adv.*　①条约上地(formed by agreement or compact)

   ②常规地(according with, sanctioned by, or based on convention)

   ③陈旧地(lacking originality or individuality, trite)

   ④普通地(ordinary, commonplace)

   ⑤形式上地(according with a mode of artistic representation that simplifies or provides symbols or substitutes for natural forms)

   ⑥传统地(of traditional design)

   ⑦习惯地(of, resembling, or relating to a convention,

assembly, or public meeting)

    resurgence *n*. 复活,复苏,再现(a rising again into life, activity, or promi-
        nence, renascence)

3.【正确答案】A

   【中文释义】由初等作家普遍持有的错误观点是句子结构代表着思想,也就是说越复杂的
          结构,越复杂的思想。

   【解题分析】此句理解 mirror 即可。

   【重点词条】**fanciful** *adj*. ①富于幻想的(marked by fancy or unrestrained imagination
                 rather than by reason and experience) 例 a～person

                ②幻想的(existing in fancy only) 例 a～notion

                ③异想天开的(marked by or as if by fancy or whim) 例 gave
                their children～names

      blatant *adj*. ①喧闹吵嚷的(noisy esp. in a vulgar or offensive manner, clam-
                orous)

                ②炫耀的,俗丽的(completely obvious, conspicuous, or obtrusive
                esp. in a crass or offensive manner, brazen)

4.【正确答案】C

   【中文释义】琼斯不能够认识到他的态度行为中的矛盾,而这种矛盾对其他人是一目了然
          的;即使是一丝虚假也会令他不悦,但他却由于总是逃税漏税而招致了严重的
          麻烦。

   【解题分析】分号句下句重复上句谈及琼的态度行为相矛盾,所以我们在下半句重复的方
          式仍然是找出他的两个行为动作,并且使之矛盾即可。下句中他的两个动作
          一个是弄虚作假的逃税,另一个为听到虚假事实时他的反应,照常理这符合他
          的行为,他应该不会太反感,结果由上句中他的态度行为中有矛盾性可知,他
          会对虚假的东西表现出深恶痛绝,故选 C 和 D。只有 C 的第二个词才会将他
          的欺骗行为暴露出来,从而使大家发现一个平时连听到虚假都皱眉的人原来
          自己也是个偷税者,这样才能照应上文的另外一段文字,即其他人很了解他行
          为的矛盾性。

   【重点词条】**the hint of** 一些;痕迹

      hazard *v*. 冒险(venture, risk) 例 ～a guess as to the outcome

5.【正确答案】C

   【中文释义】即便将军谨慎、够水平的公众声明不太可能被指责为错误,有些人仍然反
          对它。

   【解题分析】第一个空格可直接由上半句内部推理知应填"认为是没有水平的",从而可以
          选 C 和 E,第二空格由全句的转折关系知应填"反对,认为不合格",故选 C。

   【重点词条】**take liberties with** 对…采取随意,自由的态度

      take umbrage at 对…很生气

　　　　　　take exception to　对…极端地反对
　　　　　　take potshots at　对…作随意的批评

6.【正确答案】E
　【中文释义】尽管伊沃娜·诺娜的 1974 年的电影在内涵上是女权主义的,但这部电影却比电影制作人积极参加到女权主义政治活动中提前了许多。
　【解题分析】上句为一省略句,省略了主语和系动词,feminist 为形容词,故转折后下句应该为电影制作人却不是女权主义者。这一步推理跨度较大,需详细解释。通常GRE 句子填空中会作一些特殊的同义词推理,这些同义词包括:作者和作者的书,一个人和其所说的话,科学家和其理论,甚至是苏格兰土地和土地上的道路,在上下句出现时我们将之当作同义词处理,用同样的形容词去修饰他们,用同样的动词作为他们的谓语等,在此句中出现了电影和电影制作人,如果不是转折句,下句的习惯推理应为“电影制作人也是一个女权主义者”。现在原文为转折句,故应推知其拍电影时还不是女权主义者,能表达该意思的为 E。
　【重点词条】**preserve** *v.* ①保护(to keep safe from injury, harm, or destruction, protect)
　　　　　　　　　　　　②维持(to keep alive, intact, or free from decay, maintain)
　　　　　　　　　　　　③腌制(to keep or save from decomposition, to can, pickle, or similarly prepare for future use)

7.【正确答案】E
　【中文释义】如果任何重要的功能都被限制在一个单种器官中的话,物种生存的机会就会减少;代偿物本身就拥有一个巨大的生存优势。
　【解题分析】分号句上下句重复。上句为某个条件导致某个结果,下句为某事物本身拥有巨大的生存机会,可见上文的机会减少对应于下文的巨大的生存机会,上文的机会减少只能和下文同义或反义,故只能为生存机会减少或死亡机会减少,也即生存机会增大,而上句的条件句中用了动词 restrict,故只能导致不好的结果,即生存机会减少,可选 D 和 E。那么第二个空格应对应于上文的条件句,且为相反的关系,而 D 的 symmetry 并不指多种,不能与上文的 single kind 构成反义,故选 E。Redundancy 指代偿物,如有些动物有一个备用的肾,虽然比正常工作的肾要小,功能简单一些,但当病毒攻击工作的肾时,这个备用的肾就可以起到延缓生命的作用,从而增大生存优势。
　【重点词条】**persist** *v.* ①坚持不懈,执意(to go on resolutely or stubbornly in spite of opposition, importunity, or warning)
　　　　　　　　　　　②持续(to remain unchanged or fixed in a specified character, condition, or position)
　　　　　　　　　　　③追问,坚持说(to be insistent in the repetition or pressing of an utterance such as a question or an opinion)
　　　　　　　　　　　④存留(to continue to exist esp. past a usual, expected, or normal time)
　　　　　　redundancy *n.* ①冗余(为补救错失、保证可靠性的一种方法)
　　　　　　　　　　　　②代偿物或代偿机制(生物体中的备用的器官或功能)

SECTION 55

1. It was a war the queen and her more prudent counselors wished to ____ if they could and were determined in any event to ____ as long as possible.
   - (A) provoke. . delay
   - (B) denounce. . deny
   - (C) instigate. . conceal
   - (D) curtail. . promote
   - (E) avoid. . postpone

2. Despite many decades of research on the gasification of coal, the data accumulated are not directly ____ to environmental questions; thus a new program of research specifically addressing such questions is ____.
   - (A) analogous. . promising
   - (B) transferable. . contradictory
   - (C) antithetical. . unremarkable
   - (D) applicable. . warranted
   - (E) pertinent. . unnecessary

3. Unlike other creatures, who are shaped largely by their ____ environment, human beings are products of a culture accumulated over centuries, yet one that is constantly being ____ by massive infusions of new information from everywhere.
   - (A) harsh. . unconfirmed
   - (B) surrounding. . upheld
   - (C) immediate. . transformed
   - (D) natural. . mechanized
   - (E) limited. . superseded

4. Edith Wharton sought in her memoir to present herself as having achieved a harmonious wholeness by having ____ the conflicting elements of her life.
   - (A) affirmed
   - (B) highlighted
   - (C) reconciled
   - (D) confined
   - (E) identified

5. In their preface, the collection's editors plead that certain of the important articles they ____ were published too recently for inclusion, but in the case of many such articles, this ____ is not valid.
   - (A) discussed. . replacement
   - (B) omitted. . excuse
   - (C) revised. . clarification
   - (D) disparaged. . justification
   - (E) ignored. . endorsement

6. The labor union and the company's management, despite their long history of unfailingly acerbic disagreement on nearly every issue, have nevertheless reached an unexpectedly ____, albeit still tentative, agreement on next year's contract.
   - (A) swift
   - (B) onerous
   - (C) hesitant
   - (D) reluctant
   - (E) conclusive

7. In response to the follies of today's commercial and political worlds, the author does not ____ inflamed indignation, but rather ____ the detachment and smooth aphoristic prose of an eighteenth-century wit.

(A)display..rails at   (D)express..affects

(B)rely on..avoids   (E)resort to..spurns

(C)suppress..clings to

SECTION 55 解答

1.【正确答案】E

【中文释义】对于这场战争女皇和她更加审慎的顾问都希望在力所能及的范围内避免掉，并且决定在任何情形下都尽可能拖延。

【解题分析】文中的 prudent 为人物的性格，由此可推知相应的动作，可直接选 E。答案 B 的 denounce 是控告、谴责的意思。这并不是一个谨慎的人的动作，应该是一个具有正义感的人的动作，而答案 D 的 curtail 的意思为缩短、减少，这也不是一个谨慎的人的动作，因为谨慎是指事情发生之前作决策时的状态，而不是指战争发生之后，再来缩短战争。当然，D 和 E 的第二个词能与其后的 as long as possible 构成搭配的也是 E。

【重点词条】**prudent** *adj*. ①精明的(shrewd in the management of practical affairs)

                     ②审慎的，小心的(marked by circumspection, discreet)

                     ③节俭的(provident, frugal)

2.【正确答案】D

【中文释义】尽管对煤的气化问题研究了几十年，但积累下来的数据却不能直接运用于环境问题；因此，一个新的专门解决这个问题的研究就必要合理。

【解题分析】尽管这道题只是第二道题，但错误率都较高，事实上解题方法不变；分号后注意重复语言现象即可。分号后的 such question 只能是指代上文的 environmental questions，而其前的 specifically 又对应了上文的 directly，故结论很快可以得出来：上文第一空格对应于 addressing，即解决、应用、处理的意思，五个选项中答案 D 的 applicable 表应用、解决的意思，而其他几个选项 A、B 和 E 都是一种间接的方式，而不是直接地应用，这就是选项之间的逻辑关系，实际上为反义关系。

【重点词条】**address** *v*. 对付，处理，着手解决，满足需要

           analogous *adj*. 相似的，可比拟的(showing an analogy or a likeness that permits one to draw an analogy)

           warrant *v*. ①确认(to declare or maintain with certainty, be sure that) 例 I'll ~he'll be here by noon.

                     ②确证(to assure a person of the truth of what is said)

                     ③向…保证(to guarantee to a person good title to and undisturbed possession of such as an estate)

                     ④允诺(to provide a guarantee of the security of such as title to property sold usu. by an express covenant in the deed of conveyance)

⑤授权给,批准(to give warrant or sanction to, authorize) 例 The law～s this procedure.；证明…是正当或有理(to serve as or give adequate ground or reason for) 例 promising enough to～further consideration

3.【正确答案】C

【中文释义】不像其他的动物,这些动物主要是由它们所处的当下环境所塑造的,人是一个积累了几个世纪的文化的产品,并且这个文化一直不停地被从各方面来的新信息的涌入所改造。

【解题分析】句首的 unlike 表明了一种对立面反义词的关系,而文中的两个动词短语 are shaped by 和 are products of 为同义动词短语,故相应地空格应与 a culture accumulated over centuries 相反义。与文化环境构成反义的为自然环境,可选 B、C、D,而另外一层信息即为文化是由几个世纪积累下来的,也就是说人所处的文化环境受到了过往的文化的影响,尽管我们生活在 21 世纪,但 19 世纪、18 世纪某个思想家的思想可能成为我们常识的一部分,仍然在影响我们,而动物生活的环境,现在是高山,所以它就会具有高山动物的特征,哪怕这座高山以前是片海洋,这座高山上的动物也不会受到这个过去因素的影响,所以上下文的对比中另外强调了时间因素的对比。B、C、D 三个选项中 B 和 D 均只涉及到了自然环境,闭口不谈时间因素,故都错。表达出时间对比的是 C。Immediate 表时间和空间的复接,并且需要指出的是,由 yet 引导的同位语 one,重复 culture,目的是作出进一步的修辞说明文化仍然会受将来的新信息的影响,所以人所处的文化环境是一个既受过去积累影响又受将来变化影响的环境,这就与动作所处的当下环境构成了一个完美严谨的对比。

【重点词条】**immediate** *adj*. ①直接的(acting or being without the intervention of another object, cause, or agency, direct) 例 the～cause of death

②直觉的(present to the mind independently of other states or factors) 例 ～awareness

③紧接的(being next in line or relation) 例 the～family

④贴近的(existing without intervening space or substance) 例 brought into～contact

⑤立刻的(occurring, acting, or accomplished without loss or interval of time, instant) 例 an～need

⑥目前的(of or relating to the here and now, current) 例 too busy with～concerns to worry about the future

4.【正确答案】C

【中文释义】爱迪丝·沃顿力图在她的回忆录中将自己表现为已经取得了和谐的统一人格,通过调和消除她的生活中种种相冲突的元素。

【解题分析】文中的 by 构成了一一对应的手段与结果的关系,前后的 harmonious 与 con-

flicting 显然是一组反义词,欲取得 harmonious wholeness 当然必须不存在 conflicting elements,故选 C。当然这儿的 harmonious wholeness 指的是人的道德修
养的最高境界,类似于中国孟子所说的"浩然正色",古代的另一句话说得更精
辟:"君子坦荡荡,小人常戚戚",这儿的坦荡荡并不只是做事说话很利落的意
思,它更倾于君子在取舍时的明确态度,而小人由于自身的价值取向和道德观
尚未完全确立,故选择时患得患失,即"常戚戚",可惜很多人一生都生活在痛
苦的患得患失当中。

【重点词条】**reconcile** *v*. ①和解(to restore to friendship or harmony) 例 reconciled the
factions

②调停(settle, resolve) 例 ~differences

③使一致(to make consistent or congruous) 例 ~an ideal with
reality

④使认命(to cause to submit to or accept something unpleasant)
例 was reconciled to hardship

⑤使符合(to check a financial account against another for accuracy)

5.【正确答案】B

【中文释义】在他们的前言当中,文集的编辑们辩解道有一些他们忽略掉的重要文章是发
表得太迟才没有被包含进文集中的,但是对于许多这样的文章而言,这个借口
是不正确的。

【解题分析】在全句的转折结构中,从句中出现一个 this,这当然是指代前文说明过的事物,
在主干这个转折层面上,能被 this 指代的只有 plead,至于 plead 的宾语从句已
经是全句的第二层逻辑层面了,故主干第一层逻辑层面上的 this 不会指代其
中的事物,this 后的空格应填 plead 的名词同义词,答案只有 B 正确。或者由第
一空格处于定语从句中,描述编辑对文章做的动作,原文告诉我们的动作只有
一个那就是"没有包含这些文章到文集中",故由此空格可知 B 和 E 候选,B 和
E 的第二个词经阅读判断,不难得知为 B。这是此题的第二解法。

【重点词条】**clarify** *v*. ①澄清(to make such as a liquid clear or pure usu. by freeing from
suspended matter)

②阐明(to make understandable)

justification *n*. ①辩解,辩明(the act or an instance of justifying, vindication)

②辩护的理由(something that justifies)

6.【正确答案】A

【中文释义】劳工工会和公司的管理阶层尽管长期以来总是对各个问题存有不同意见,但
却仍然就下一年度的合同达成了一个尽管仍然是暂时性的但却是出乎意料迅
速的一致意见。

【解题分析】请注意空格存在于一个独特的结构中:两个形容词用转折关系连接同时修饰

名词。此时空格的形容词应与其后的 tentative 构成特殊关系:首先必须转折,其次不能互为反义词,大多数情况下为褒贬转折。该题做错的同学往往错选 E,实际上 E 的 conclusive 与 tentative 恰好构成了一组对立面的反义词,为一典型错误,与 tentative 构成褒贬转折的是 A 的 swift 两词都是谈时间短暂,但是有褒贬转折,请牢记这种特殊的转折关系,这是一个考生常常失误的环节。

【重点词条】**unfailing** *adj*. ①经久不衰的(not failing or liable to fail, constant, unflagging)

②用不完的,无止息的(everlasting, inexhaustible) 例 a subject of～interest

③可靠的(infallible, sure) 例 an～test

onerous *adj*. ①繁重的,麻烦的(involving, imposing, or constituting a burden, troublesome) 例 an～task

②负有义务的,艰巨的(having legal obligations that outweigh the advantages) 例 ～contract

7.【正确答案】D

【中文释义】对今天政界和商界的愚蠢行为作出了反应,这位作者并没有表达出火冒三丈的愤怒,而是模仿了一位 18 世纪哲人的超然冷静的态度和流畅的格言式的文句。

【解题分析】文中的 but rather 明确提示前后应截然相反,而 inflamed indignation 与 detachment 已经构成了一组反义词,故两个空格的动词应该填同义词,答案为 D。

【重点词条】**rail at** 责备

suppress *v*. ①镇压(to put down by authority or force, subdue)

②查禁(to keep from public knowledge, to keep secret, to stop or prohibit the publication or revelation of)

③抑制(to exclude from consciousness)

affect *n*. 模仿

SECTION 56

1. Vaillant, who has been particularly interested in the means by which people attain mental health, seems to be looking for ____ answers: a way to close the book on at least a few questions about human nature.

    (A)definitive

    (B)confused

    (C)temporary

    (D)personal

    (E)derivative

2. The well-trained engineer must understand fields as diverse as physics, economics, geology, and sociology; thus, an overly ____ engineering curriculum should be avoided.

    (A)narrow

    (B)innovative

    (C)competitive

    (D)rigorous

    (E)academic

3. Although supernovas are among the most
____ of cosmic events, these stellar explo-
sions are often hard to ____, either because
they are enormously far away or because
they are dimmed by intervening dust and
gas clouds.
(A)remote. . observe
(B)luminous. . detect
(C)predictable. . foresee
(D)ancient. . determine
(E)violent. . disregard

4. During the widespread fuel shortage, the
price of gasoline was so ____ that suppliers
were generally thought to be ____ the con-
sumer.
(A)reactive. . shielding
(B)stable. . blackmailing
(C)depressed. . cheating
(D)prohibitive. . placating
(E)excessive. . gouging

5. Art ____ science, but that does not mean
that the artist must also be a scientist; an
artist uses the fruits of science but need not
____ the theories from which they derive.
(A)precedes. . anticipate
(B)incorporates. . understand
(C)transcends. . abandon
(D)imitates. . repudiate
(E)resembles. . contest

6. Imposing steep fines on employers for on-
the-job injuries to workers could be an effec-
tive ____ to creating a safer workplace, es-
pecially in the case of employers with poor-
safety records.
(A)antidote
(B)alternative
(C)addition
(D)deterrent
(E)incentive

7. Literature is inevitably a ____ rather than
____ medium for the simple reason that
writers interpose their own vision between
the reader and reality.
(A)distorting. . a neutral
(B)transparent. . an opaque
(C)colorful. . a drab
(D)flawless. . an inexact
(E)flexible. . a rigid

SECTION 56 解答

1.【正确答案】A
   【中文释义】维勒,他对人们获得精神健康的方法尤其地感兴趣,看上去正在寻找彻底的答
         案:一个能彻底解答至少一些关于人的本性的问题的答案。
   【解题分析】冒号后表示解释重点,理解 close the book on a few question 即可知,维勒是在寻
         求最彻底的解答,答案为 A。
   【重点词条】**close the book**　中止、停止;停止入账
         definitive *adj*. ①决定性的,最后的(serving to provide a final solution or to
            end a situation) 例 a~victory
               ②确定的,权威性的(authoritative and apparently exhaustive)
            例 a~edition

2.【正确答案】A

　【中文释义】受过良好训练的工程师必须理解诸如物理、经济学、地质学和社会学等非常多的课目;因此,一个过度狭隘的工程科课程应该设法避免。

　【解题分析】空格里填上 diverse 的反义词。

3.【正确答案】B

　【中文释义】尽管超新星属于宇宙中最明亮的天文现象,但是这些星星的爆炸却是难于预测的,或者是因为它们太遥远或者是因为它们被介入于其间的灰尘和气体云变得暗淡无光难于分辨。

　【解题分析】上半句的转折关系中前后都未提供信息,故无法推理。下半部分的因果关系却非常简单。由 dimmed 可知第二个空格应为 A 和 B。再由转折关系可得 B。

　【重点词条】**foresee** *v.* 预见(to see such as a development beforehand)

4.【正确答案】E

　【中文释义】在最近的能量短缺期间,汽油的价格是如此地高以至于供应商们普遍被认为是在敲榨消费者。

　【解题分析】由句首状语即可知,油价非常高,可选 D 和 E。再由 so...that 结构可得 E 答案,此题往往有一些学生钻进牛角尖选 C。事实上句首状语与主干并无转折关系,这是其一;其二,suppliers 用了复数形式来表达出所有供应商的概念,永远都不会存在一个国家所有供应商都欺骗顾客的情况。选 C 的同学思路上走了一段弯路。要切记,句子填空不存在反常识的含义,永远都是简单的思维占优势。

　【重点词条】**depressed** *adj.* ①抑郁的(low in spirits, sad, esp. affected by psychological depression)

②凹陷的(having the central part lower than the margin)

③萧条的,贫穷的(suffering from economic depression; esp. underprivileged)

④降低的,减少的(being below the standard)

shield *v.* ①保护(to protect with or as if with a shield, provide with a protective cover or shelter)

②隐藏(to cut off from observation, hide)

③防止(forbid)

placate *v.* 平息,安抚,抚慰(to soothe or mollify esp. by concessions, appease)

gouge *v.* ①挖取,掘取(to scoop out with or as if with a gouge)

②诈骗钱财,敲竹杠(to subject to extortion or undue exaction, overcharge)

5.【正确答案】B

【中文释义】艺术结合了科学,但这并不意味着艺术家必须同时成为一个科学家;一个艺术家使用科学的成果但不需要理解它们引用的理论。

【解题分析】分号处上下句重复。第一个空格应表达出艺术使用了科学的成果这个概念,第二个空格应填科学家必须做的动作,从第二个空格来看,可选 B。

【重点词条】precede *v*. ①高于(to surpass in rank, dignity, or importance)

②先于(to be, go, or come ahead or in front of)

③早于(to be earlier than)

④在…之前(to cause to be preceded, preface)

transcend *v*. ①超出,超越(to rise above or go beyond the limits of)

②克服(to triumph over the negative or restrictive aspects of, overcome)

③胜过(to outstrip or outdo in some attribute, quality, or power)

contest *n*. 竞争,辩驳,驳斥

6.【正确答案】E

【中文释义】针对工人的工伤事故而给雇主强行征收高额罚款会成为一个有效的刺激来产生更加安全的工作环境,尤其是针对那些有着非常恶劣的安全纪录的雇主。

【解题分析】此句并不难推理,但很多同学失误在选词上。首先,alternative 和 addition 都必须有一个本来的方法,否则谈不上其他的方法。Other 在考题中也有同样的用法,而 a deterrent to doing sth 的含义是阻止作某事,也即不做这件事。正确答案为 E。

【重点词条】steep *adj*. ①高的(lofty, high)

②险峻的(making a large angle with the plane of the horizon)

③陡峭的(mounting or falling precipitously) 例 The stairs were very～.

④过高的(extremely or excessively high) 例 ～prices

7.【正确答案】A

【中文释义】文学不可避免地是一种扭曲的而非客观的媒介,因为作者在读者和现实之间强行加入了自己的观点。

【解题分析】由 rather than 可知前后两个空格应为一组反义词,并且由 inevitablely 可知应为前贬后褒的一组反义词,满足的选项只有 A 的 distorting 和 neutral。其他几个选项均为前褒后贬。

【重点词条】opaque *adj*. ①不透明的(not transpar ent or clear)

②难懂的,晦涩的(difficult to uncler stand)

SECTION 57

1. A good doctor knows that knowledge about 　　　medicine will continue to ＿＿＿ and that,

therefore, formal professional training can never be an ____ guide to good practice.

(A) vary. . adaptable

(B) change. . absolute

(C) ossify. . inflexible

(D) pertain. . invaluable

(E) intensify. . obsolescent

2. Foucault's rejection of the concept of continuity in Western thought, though radical, was not unique; he had ____ in the United States who, without knowledge of his work, developed parallel ideas.

(A) critics

(B) counterparts

(C) disciples

(D) readers

(E) publishers

3. In retrospect, Gordon's students appreciated her ____ assignments, realizing that such assignments were specifically designed to ____ original thought rather than to review the content of her course.

(A) didactic. . ingrain

(B) intimidating. . thwart

(C) difficult. . discourage

(D) conventional. . explicate

(E) enigmatic. . stimulate

4. In sharp contrast to the intense ____ of the young republic, with its utopian faith in democracy and hopes for eternal human progress, recent developments suggest a mood of almost unrelieved ____.

(A) idealism. . cynicism

(B) individualism. . escapism

(C) sectarianism. . recklessness

(D) assertiveness. . ambition

(E) righteousness. . egalitarianism

5. Old age, even in cultures where it is ____, is often viewed with ____.

(A) venerated. . ambivalence

(B) rare. . surprise

(C) ignored. . condescension

(D) feared. . dismay

(E) honored. . respect

6. Unlike the easily studied neutral and ionized ____ that compose the primary disk of the Milky Way itself, the components of the ____ surrounding our galaxy have proved more resistant to study.

(A) figments. . envelope

(B) essences. . fluctuations

(C) elements. . problems

(D) calculations. . perimeter

(E) materials. . region

7. Although normally ____, Alison felt so strongly about the issue that she put aside her reserve and spoke up at the committee meeting.

(A) diffident

(B) contentious

(C) facetious

(D) presumptuous

(E) intrepid

SECTION 57 解答

1.【正确答案】B

【中文释义】一个好的医生知道医药的知识会继续改变,并且,由此可见,正规的职业训练永远都不可能成为优秀行医实践的绝对指导。

【解题分析】文中 knows 的宾语从句有两个,所以本句又构成了一个特殊并列句。这两个宾语从句之间应该互相推导,实际上 knowledge about medicine 就是下句主语 formal professional training 的一个对应物,因为正规的医疗训练正是传授医药知识的。所以上句认为 knowledge about medicine 会 continue,所以 formal professional training 也应 continue,从而知下句中的 never 之后应为"not continue"的方式,这样才能正确地重复上文,表示"not continue"方式的只有 B 的 absolute。

【重点词条】**ossify** *v*. ①骨化(to change into bone)

②硬化,墨守成规(to become hardened or conventional and opposed to change)

pertain *v*. ①从属,附属(to belong as a part, member, accessory, or product, to belong as an attribute, feature, or function) 例 the destruction and havoc～ing to war

②适应(to be appropriate to something) 例 the criteria will be different from those that～elsewhere

③有关,涉及(to have reference) 例 books～ing to birds

2. 【正确答案】B

【中文释义】福柯对西方思想中连续的概念的反对尽管很激进,却不是独有的:他在美国有一个思想相同的人,在不知道他的作品的情况下,发展出了相同的思想。

【解题分析】此句冒号前为一判断句,主体词为 not unique,所以冒号之后应予以重复,空格应填与"not unique"相同义的词,B 的 counterpart 即为"有相同的人或物"之义,故选 B;或者可以由另外一个途径分析得知答案,空格之后有一定语从句修饰该空格,这实际上就是一种分隔提供答案的方式而已,故空格中应填上"developed parallel ideas"这样的人,只有 B 的 counterparts 有此动作,故正确答案为 B。

【重点词条】**counterpart** *n*. ①副本(one of two corresponding copies of a legal instrument, duplicate)

②配对物(a thing that fits another perfectly)

③极相似的人或物(one remarkably similar to another)

④相当的人或物(one having the same function or characteristics as another) 例 college presidents and their～s in business

parallel *n*. ①平行线(a parallel line, curve, or surface)

②纬线(one of the imaginary circles on the surface of the earth paralleling the equator and marking the latitude; the corresponding line on a globe or map)

③相似处(something equal or similar in all essential particulars, counterpart)

3. 【正确答案】E

【中文释义】回想起来,戈登的学生非常欣赏她的神秘而让人费解的家庭作业,因为认识到这样的家庭作业是专门设计来刺激独创性思考的而不只是仅仅回顾一下她课程的内容而已。

【解题分析】由 rather than 可知前后的动词不定式短语应为反义重复,实际上又是一个小连接。所以由 rather than 之后的"仅仅回顾课程内容"与 rather than 之前给出的 original thought 结合即可知,作者在强调"仅仅回顾课程的内容"是"没有独创性思考的",所以 rather than 之前应表达出"有独创性思考"的含义,而五个选项中能够使学生自己产生独创性思考的只有 E 答案的 stimulate,故正确答案为 E。

【重点词条】**didactic** *adj*. ①教学的(designed or intended to teach)

②教诲的(intended to convey instruction and information as well as pleasure and entertainment)

③好说教的(making moral observations)

ingrain *v*. 使铭记,使根深蒂固(to work indelibly into the natural texture or mental or moral constitution)

thwart *v*. ①反对,阻挠(to run counter to so as to effectively oppose or baffle, contravene)

②挫败(to oppose successfully, defeat the hopes or aspirations of)

③横过(to pass through or across)

explicate *v*. ①解释(to give a detailed explanation of)

②引申(to develop the implications of, analyze logically)

4. 【正确答案】A

【中文释义】与年轻的共和国的强烈的理想主义——对民主有乌托邦式的理想并且希望人类永恒地进步——构成了尖锐的对比,最近的发展进程表明了一种几乎无法释怀的犬儒主义情绪。

【解题分析】文中的 with 引导的一段文字显然不是主干成分,故其为分隔,应该给空格提供答案,所以第一个空格中应表达出"对民主有乌托邦式的理想并且相信人类永恒地进步"只有 A 的 idealism 为此含义,故正确答案为 A。

【重点词条】**relieved** *adj*. 宽心的,宽慰的(experiencing or showing relief esp. from anxiety or pent-up emotions)

escapism *n*. 逃避现实(habitual diversion of the mind to purely imaginative activity or entertainment as an escape from reality or routine)

sectarianism *adj*. ①宗派主义的(of, relating to, or characteristic of a sect or sectarian)

②偏狭的(limited in character or scope, parochial)

egalitarianism *n*. 平等主义(a belief in human equality esp. with respect to social, political, and economic rights and privileges)

5. 【正确答案】A

【中文释义】古老的岁月,即使在某些文化中是受到尊重的,仍然被视之以怀疑的态度。

【解题分析】由 even 可知前后的转折关系,五个选项中表转折关系的只有 A,故为正确答案。

【重点词条】ambivalence *n*. ①矛盾情绪或态度(simultaneous and contradictory attitudes or feelings such as attraction and repulsion toward an object, person, or action)

②摇摆,举棋不定(continual fluctuation such as between one thing and its opposite)

6. 【正确答案】E

【中文释义】不像那些容易研究的中性的离子化的构成了银河系自身核心盘状物的那些物质,围绕着我们银河系的那个区域的组成元素被证实是难于研究的。

【解题分析】由第一个空格后的分隔可知 C 和 E 候选,因为能够构成银河系自身核心盘状物的只能是具体的物质,而不可能是 A,B 和 D 这三个抽象名词。由第二个空格之后的分隔可知 E 的正确答案,因为能够围绕着我们银河系的绝不可能是 C 的 problems,只可能是 E。

【重点词条】figment *n*. 臆造之事物(something made up or contrived)

ionized *adj*. 离子化的 (to convert wholly or partly into ions)

perimeter *n*. ①周长 (the length of a perimeter)

②周边,边缘 (a line or strip bounding or protecting an area)

7. 【正确答案】A

【中文释义】尽管通常很自卑,但艾丽森对于这个观点如此有信心以至于她抛弃了拘谨沉默的做法并且在委员会会议上发言。

【解题分析】前为一简单的转折句,能构成转折的显然为 A。

【重点词条】presumptuous *adj*. 专横傲慢的,冒昧放肆的(overstepping due bounds such as of propriety or courtesy, taking liberties)

fell strongly about sth 对…很有信心

reserve *n*. (言语行动)拘谨,矜持,寡言

SECTION 58

1. Contrary to the antiquated idea that the eighteenth century was a ____ island of elegant assurance, evidence reveals that life for most people was filled with uncertainty and insecurity.

(A) clannish

(B) declining

(C) tranquil

(D) recognized

(E) sprawling

2. The insecticide proved ____ by killing the

weak adults of a species, it assured that the strong ones would mate among themselves and produce offspring still more ____ to its effects.

(A) ineffective. . hostile

(B) cruel. . vulnerable

(C) feasible. . susceptible

(D) necessary. . immune

(E) counterproductive. . resistant

3. Many industries are so ____ by the impact of government sanctions, equipment failure, and foreign competition that they are beginning to rely on industrial psychologists to ____ what remains of employee morale.

(A) estranged. . guard

(B) beleaguered. . salvage

(C) overruled. . undermine

(D) encouraged. . determine

(E) restrained. . confirm

4. Fashion is partly a search for a new language to discredit the old, a way in which each generation can ____ its immediate predecessor and distinguish itself.

(A) honor

(B) repudiate

(C) condone

(D) placate

(E) emulate

5. Although ____ is usually thought to spring

from regret for having done something wrong, it may be that its origin is the realization that one's own nature is irremediably ____ .

(A) contrition. . resilient

(B) certitude. . confident

(C) skepticism. . innocent

(D) remorse. . flawed

(E) resignation. . frivolous

6. Numerous historical examples illustrate both the overriding influence that scientists' ____ have on their interpretation of data and the consequent ____ of their intellectual objectivity.

(A) prejudices. . impairment

(B) instruments. . abandonment

(C) theories. . independence

(D) conclusions. . coloration

(E) suppositions. . reinforcement

7. From the outset, the concept of freedom of the seas from the proprietary claims of nations was challenged by a contrary notion—that of the ____ of the oceans for reasons of national security and profit.

(A) promotion

(B) exploration

(C) surveying

(D) conservation

(E) enclosure

SECTION 58 解答

1.【正确答案】C

【中文释义】与这个古老过时的想法——18 世纪是一个充满优雅舒适的生活保障的宁静安祥小岛——相反,证据表明大多数人的生活充满了变幻无常和不安全感。

【解题分析】由空格之后的介词短语即可知这是一个令人向往的小岛。空格中应填褒义词,只有 C 正确。

【重点词条】clannish *adj*. ①氏族的,部落的(of or relating to a clan)

②排外的,抱成一团的(tending to associate only with a select group of similar background or status)

sprawl *v*. ①蔓生(to creep or clamber awkwardly)

②伸开手脚(to lie or sit with arms and legs spread out)

③不规则的散开(to spread or develop irregularly)

2.【正确答案】E

【中文释义】这个杀虫剂被证明具有反作用;通过杀死弱小的成虫,它保证了强壮的虫子会自行交配,并且产生对杀虫剂的效果更具有抵抗力的下一代。

【解题分析】由文中的 weak adults 与 strong ones 的对比可知作者的意图,所以第二个空格应该填更加强壮的虫子,也即更加对药的效果无所畏惧,可候选 D 和 E,而由句意可知第一空格应选 E 的 counterproductive。

【重点词条】immune *adj*. ①免除的(free, exempt) 例 ～from further taxation

②豁免的(marked by protection) 例 Some criminal leaders are～ from arrest.

③不受影响的(not susceptible or responsive) 例 ～to all pleas

④有免疫力的(having or producing antibodies or lymphocytes capable of reacting with a specific antigen) 例 an～serum

resistant *adj*. 有抵抗力的,耐…的(giving or capable of resistance, often used in combination) 例 wrinkle～ clothes

3.【正确答案】B

【中文释义】许多工业是如此地被政府处罚,设备失效及外国竞争所困挠,以至于他们开始依赖工业心理治疗医生来恢复所剩无几的雇员的士气。

【解题分析】由第二个空格前的 psychologist 即可知空格的动作只有能是"求援、治疗、恢复健康"等等特征动作,从而可选择的只有 B 的 salvage,根据特殊人物的职业来推断其动作是 GRE 填空中常规解题法之一。

【重点词条】sanction *v*. 批准,影响,处罚

beleaguer *v*. ①围困,围攻(besiege)

②困扰(trouble, harass) 例 ～ed parents

overrule *v*. ①压制(to rule over, govern)

②否决(to prevail over, overcome)

③推翻(to rule against)

④反对(to set aside, reverse)

4.【正确答案】B

【中文释义】时髦在一定程度上是寻找一种新的语言来否定老的事物,在这种方法中每一代人都能够否定它的前任并且使自己脱颖而出。

【解题分析】空格处于一分隔结构中,一定重复前文,而 its immediate predecessor 与前文的

the old 重复,所以空格应该重复 discredit,答案为 B 的 requdiate。

【重点词条】**distinguish** *v*. ①区别(to perceive a difference in, mentally separate) 例 so a-
like they could not be~ed

②使明显不同(to mark as separate or different)

③使扬名(to give prominence or distinction to) 例 ~ed themselves in music

④辨认(discern) 例 ~ed a light in the distance

5.【正确答案】D

【中文释义】尽管懊悔通常被认为来源于由于做错了事情所产生的后悔,但也有可能它的
根源是因为认识到一个人的本性是不可救药地有缺陷。

【解题分析】由第一个空格之后的 usually 可知第一个空格可按最通常想法去选择,可候选
A 和 D,这两种才有可能会由后悔所进一步导致,由第二个空格前的 irremediably 可知空格应填一贬义词,故选 D 的 flawed。

【重点词条】**contrition** *n*. 痛悔,悔罪(the state of being contrite, repentance)

remorse *n*. ①悔恨,自责(gnawing distress arising from a sense of guilt for past
wrongs, self-reproach)

②怜悯,同情(compassion)

resignation *n*. ①辞职,放弃(an act or instance of resigning so mething, surrender)

②听任,顺从(the quality or state of being resigned, submissive-
ness)

6.【正确答案】A

【中文释义】无数的历史证据表明了这两点:其一是科学家的偏见具有强大的影响,影响了
他们对数据的解释;其二是随之而来的对他们的智力活动客观性的损害。

【解题分析】由第一个空格处于物主代词之后这样的特征结构可知,第一空格应填特征动
作或特征性格,而科学家的特征性格式动作只有两个可能性:"客观"或"非客
观",五个选项中能表达这义项的只有 A 的 prejudice 故正确答案为 A。

【重点词条】**overridding** *adj*. ①压倒一切的,首要的

②盛气凌人的,傲慢的

supposition *n*. 假定,推测(the act of supposing)

coloration *n*. 改变颜色,歪曲,文饰,渲染

7.【正确答案】E

【中文释义】从一开始起,海洋应独立于国家宣布对其拥有私有权的声明之外的思想就受
到一个相反的观点的挑战,这个相反的观点是出于国家安全和利益的原因而
对海洋私有化。

【解题分析】文中的 freedom from 这个短语被许多考生误读了,理解成了海洋的自由,如果
是这种理解的话,from 就失去了任何搭配对象。由上文的海洋不应私有化的

宣称可知下句相反的观点应该是将海洋私有化,E 的 enclosure 为正确答案。此句的翻译为忠实于原文的结构而显得过于欧化,为便于同学们理解,下文给出一个意译的译句:从一开始起,关于海洋是否也应私有化这个问题就存在着截然相反的两个观点:其一是认为海洋应超然于任何国家对其所声称的私有权之外,根本不应私有化;其二是认为出于国家的安全和利益的角度考虑而将海洋私有化。

【重点词条】enclosure *n*. 围住,封闭,圈地(the act or action of enclosing, the quality or state of being enclosed)

         freedom from   摆脱…, 独立于(超然于)…之外

SECTION 59

1. The corporation expects only ＿＿ increases in sales next year despite a yearlong effort to revive its retailing business.
   - (A) unquestionable
   - (B) sequential
   - (C) modest
   - (D) exaggerated
   - (E) groundless

2. No computer system is immune to a virus, a particularly malicious program that is designed to ＿＿ and electronically ＿＿ the disks on which data are stored.
   - (A) prepare. . improve
   - (B) restore. . disable
   - (C) infect. . damage
   - (D) preserve. . secure
   - (E) invade. . repair

3. Recent research indicates that a system of particles which has apparently decayed to randomness from ＿＿ state can be returned to that state; thus the system exhibits a kind of memory of its ＿＿ condition.
   - (A) an equilibrium. . lesser
   - (B) an ordered. . earlier
   - (C) an unusual. . settled
   - (D) a chaotic. . last
   - (E) a higher. . present

4. A number of writers who once greatly ＿＿ the literary critic have recently recanted, substituting ＿＿ for their former criticism.
   - (A) lauded. . censure
   - (B) influenced. . analysis
   - (C) simulated. . ambivalence
   - (D) disparaged. . approbation
   - (E) honored. . adulation

5. She writes across generational lines, making the past so ＿＿ that our belief that the present is the true locus of experience is undermined.
   - (A) complex
   - (B) distant
   - (C) vivid
   - (D) mysterious
   - (E) mundane

6. Individual freedom of thought should be ＿＿ more absolutely than individual freedom of action, given that the latter, though also desirable, must be ＿＿ the limits imposed by the rights and freedom of

others.

(A) protected. . subject to

(B) assessed. . measured by

(C) valued. . superior to

(D) exercised. . indifferent to

(E) curtailed. . conscious of

7. Their ＿＿ was expressed in quotidian be-

havior: they worshipped regularly, ＿＿ all the regenerative processes of nature respect, and even awe.

(A) selflessness. . reserving to

(B) moderation. . extending to

(C) reverence. . exacting from

(D) piety. . according

(F) serenity. . refusing

SECTION 59 解答

1. 【正确答案】C

【中文释义】这个公司只期望销售额有适度的增长,尽管有长达一年之久的努力来复兴它的零售业务。

【解题分析】由 only 及 despite 可知此句为一程度转折句,通常情况下巨大的努力就应带来回报,所以 A 和 B 与下句构成了一个因果关系。C 为正确答案。D、E 显然不能构成程度转折。

【重点词条】exaggerate v. ①夸大,夸张(to enlarge beyond bounds or the truth, overstate)

例 a friend～s a man's virtues

②使过大 (to enlarge or increase esp. beyond the normal, overemphasize)

groundless adj. 无根据的,无理由的(having no ground or foundation) 例 ～ fears

2. 【正确答案】C

【中文释义】没有计算机系统对病毒是免疫的,病毒是一种尤为恶毒的程序,专门设计来侵染并且以电磁的方式上毁坏储存数据的磁盘。

【解题分析】由文中的 malicious 可知,两个空格的动词应为坏的动作,只有 C 正确。

【重点词条】malicious adj. 恶毒的,蓄意谋害的(given to, marked by, or arising from malice)

3. 【正确答案】B

【中文释义】最近的研究表明一个非常明显地从有序状态堕落到无序状态的粒子系统可以回到当初的状态;因此这个系统展示了一种对自身早期条件的记忆能力。

【解题分析】由文中的 from. . . to 即可知第一个空格应填"有序的"。答案为 B。

【重点词条】ordered adj. ①有条理的,整齐的

②有次序的

4. 【正确答案】D

【中文释义】一些曾经极度贬低这个文学评论家的作者最近公开认错,用表扬代替了过去

的批评。

【解题分析】由文中的 once 与 former criticism 即可知 once 之后也应为 criticism,从而选 D。

【重点词条】**recant** *v.* ①(正式并公开地)撤消,放弃(to withdraw or repudiate a statement or belief formally and publicly, renounce)

②取消(revoke)

③认错(to make an open confession of error)

5.【正确答案】C

【中文释义】她写作时跨越了时代界限,将过去塑造得如此栩栩如生以至于我们的信仰——目前是真正的经验中心——遭到了破坏。

【解题分析】文中显然有 the past 与 the present 这一组反义词对比,既然 the present 为 true 的信仰遭到了破坏,所以 the past 为 true,也即作者 making the past 为 true,所以空格中应填"true"的同义词,为 vivid,故正确答案为 C。

【重点词条】**vivid** *adj.* ①形象的,逼真的(having the appearance of vigorous life or freshness, lively)例 a～sketch

②光亮的(of a color, very strong, very high in chroma)

③鲜明的(producing a strong or clear impression on the senses, sharp, intense; producing distinct mental images)例 a～description

④活泼的(acting clearly and vigorously)例 a～imagination

locus *n.* ①地点(the place where something is situated or occurs, site, location)例 Was the culture of medicine in the beginning dispersed from a single focus or did it arise in several loci?

②中心(a center of activity, attention, or concentration)例 In democracy the～of power is in the people.

mundane *adj.* ①世俗的,尘世的(of, relating to, or characteristic of the world)

②单调平凡的(characterized by the practical, transitory, and ordinary, commonplace)例 the～concerns of day-to-day life

6.【正确答案】A

【中文释义】个人思想的自由应该比个人行动的自由更加绝对地受到保护,因为后者,尽管也是值得喜爱的,却必须受到限制,这种限制是由别人的自由和权利所导致的。

【解题分析】第二个空格处于一个简单的转折关系中,应填贬义词,可以候选的为 A,B 和 E,均表示行动的自由应该受到限制,而第一个空格处于比较结构中,既然行动的自由应该受到限制,那么思想的自由就不应该受到限制,所以应该选 A,表示思想的自由受绝对的保护,而 E 的 curtail 仍然表示限制,故不正确,而 B 的 assess 为评估之义,不正确。

【重点词条】**be measured by** 被限量,被限制

7.【正确答案】D

【中文释义】他们虔诚的性格在他们每日的行为中表现了出来:他们每日敬神,赋予大自然界所有再生的过程以尊敬甚至是敬畏。

【解题分析】第一个空格在物主代词 their 之后,故应为他们的特征动作、特征性格,冒号后表达出的动作只有一个,那就是 worship,所以空格应填上这个特征动作,答案 D 的 piety 即为此义。另外文末的分隔实际上是重复了 worship 这个动词。"Accord A to B"或者"accord B A"或者"accord to B A"都是 accord 的正常表达,表示"赋予 B 以 A"或"将 A 赋予给 B"。此处的"赋予大自然的所有再生过程以尊敬甚至敬畏"即为原始的宗教崇拜,即对 worship 的重复。

【重点词条】quotidian *adj*. ①每日发生的(occurring every day) 例 ~fever

②日常的(belonging to each day, everyday) 例 ~routine

③平凡的,普通的(commonplace, ordinary) 例 ~drabness

regenerative *adj*. 恢复的,新生的,复兴的(of, relating to, or marked by regeneration)

moderation *n*. ①温和,中庸

②缓和,减轻

③适度,节制

exact *v*. ①强求,索取(to call for forcibly or urgently and obtain, press for) 例 from them has been~ed the ultimate sacrifice

②严格要求(to call for as necessary or desirable)

SECTION 60

1. My family often found others laughable, but I learned quite early to be _____ while people were present, laughing only later at what was funny and mocking what to us seemed _____.

   (A)polite..bizarre

   (B)impatient..unfortunate

   (C)facetious..enviable

   (D)wistful..extraordinary

   (E)superficial..deplorable

2. The technical know-how, if not the political _____, appears already at hand to feed the world's exploding population and so to _____ at last the ancient scourges of malnutrition and famine.

   (A)will..weaken

   (B)expertise..articulate

   (C)doubt..banish

   (D)power..denounce

   (E)commitment..eradicate

3. In small farming communities, accident victims rarely sue or demand compensation: transforming a personal injury into a _____ someone else is viewed as an attempt to _____ responsibility for one's own actions.

   (A)conspiracy against..assume

   (B)claim against..elude

   (C)boon for..minimize

   (D)distinction for..shift

   (E)trauma for..proclaim

4. Dominant interests often benefit most from ____ of governmental interference in business, since they are able to take care of themselves if left alone.
(A) intensification
(B) authorization
(C) centralization
(D) improvisation
(E) elimination

5. The "impostor syndrome" often afflicts those who fear that true self-disclosure will lower them in others' esteem; rightly handled, however, ____ may actually ____ one's standing.
(A) willfulness.. consolidate
(B) imposture.. undermine
(C) affectation.. jeopardize
(D) candor.. enhance
(E) mimicry.. efface

6. The pungent verbal give-and-take among the characters makes the novel ____ reading, and this very ____ suggests to me that some of the opinions voiced may be the author's.
(A) disturbing.. flatness
(B) tedious.. inventiveness
(C) lively.. spiritedness
(D) necessary.. steadiness
(E) rewarding.. frivolousness

7. The fortresslike facade of the Museum of Cartoon Art seems calculated to remind visitors that the comic strip is an art form that has often been ____ by critics.
(A) charmed
(B) assailed
(C) unnoticed
(D) exhilarated
(E) overwhelmed

SECTION 60 解答

1. 【正确答案】A
【中文释义】我的家庭总是觉得别人可笑，但我很早就学会了当人们在场时保持礼貌，只在事后嘲笑那些滑稽可笑之物或者模仿那些我们看起来奇异可笑之事。
【解题分析】由文中 and 构成的小连接可知第二个空格应填 funny 的同义词，从而选 A。
【重点词条】enviable *adj.* 引起妒忌的，值得羡慕的（highly desirable）
　　　　wistful *adj.* ①渴望的，留恋的（full of yearning or desire tinged with melancholy; inspiring such yearning）例 a～memoir
　　　　　　②沉思的（musingly sad, pensive）
　　　　extraordinary *adj.* ①非常的（going beyond what is usual, regular, or customary）例 ～powers
　　　　　　②惊人的（exceptional to a very marked extent）例 ～beauty
　　　　　　③特别的，特派的（employed for or sent on a special function or service）例 an ambassador～
　　　　deplorable *adj.* 可叹的，悲惨的（deserving censure or contempt, wretched）

2.【正确答案】E

　　【中文释义】技术上的专业技能,如果不是政治的参与的话,看上去早就可以轻易地喂饱全
　　　　　　　　世界膨胀的人口,并且因此而最终消除自古以来的营养不良和大饥荒的灾祸。

　　【解题分析】由 and 构成的小连接可知空格应为"消除了"大饥荒,故选 E 的 eradicate,C 的
　　　　　　　　banish 为"从一个地方驱逐到另外一个地方"之义,在此句中不通,因为我们不
　　　　　　　　可能将饥荒驱逐到别的星球去。此句是小连接的一个典型题目,and 前后连接
　　　　　　　　动词不定式构成小连接的情况往往被许多同学忽略,从而导致解题的失败,切
　　　　　　　　记,见到连词先判断是否为小连接,如果是则可解题。

　　【重点词条】**know-how** *n*. 专业知识,专业技能

　　　　　　　　commitment *n*. 参加,参与;犯罪,做错事

　　　　　　　　be at hand to do sth　非常容易地做某事

　　　　　　　　ancient *adj*. 古代的,古老的,旧的(having the qualities of age or long exis-
　　　　　　　　tence)

3.【正确答案】B

　　【中文释义】在小的农业国中,意外事故的受伤人员很少起诉或者要求赔偿:将一个个人的
　　　　　　　　伤害转化对别人的索赔被看成逃避个人行为责任的企图。

　　【解题分析】冒号前后为重复关系,显然 personal injury 对应于上文的 victim,而 someone 只
　　　　　　　　能是冒号前隐含的起诉对象或索赔的对象,故空格里应填上文"sue or demand
　　　　　　　　compensation"的同义词,B 为正确答案。

　　【重点词条】**claim against**　索赔

　　　　　　　　boon *n*. ①恩惠(benefit, favor; one that is given in answer to a request)

　　　　　　　　　　　　②利益(a timely benefit, blessing)

　　　　　　　　trauma *n*. ①外伤(an injury such as a wound to living tissue caused by an ex-
　　　　　　　　　　　　trinsic agent) 例 surgical～

　　　　　　　　　　　　②(精神)创伤(a disordered psychic or behavioral state resulting from
　　　　　　　　　　　　mental or emotional stress or physical injury)

　　　　　　　　proclaim *v*. ①宣告,公布(to declare publicly, typically insistently, proudly, or
　　　　　　　　　　　　defiantly and in either speech or writing, announce)

　　　　　　　　　　　　②表明,显示(to give outward indication of, show)

　　　　　　　　　　　　③宣言,声明(to declare or declare to be solemnly, officially, or
　　　　　　　　　　　　formally) 例 ～an amnesty/～the country a republic

　　　　　　　　　　　　④赞扬(to praise or glorify openly or publicly, extol)

4.【正确答案】E

　　【中文释义】主要利益集团总是在消除政府对商业的干预中受益,因为如果允许自行其事
　　　　　　　　的话,他们能够很好地照料自己。

　　【解题分析】由下文的 if left alone 可知大利益集团倾向于自由决策,故上文政府的干预为
　　　　　　　　大利益集团所不希望发生的情形,应"消除",答案为 E。

　　【重点词条】**centralize** *v*. 集中,中央集权化(to form a center, cluster around a center)

　　　　　left alone　允许自行其事，自由自在

5.【正确答案】D

　【中文释义】"骗子综合症"总折磨那些担心真正的自我曝光会降低他们在别人心目中的地位的人；但如果恰当地处理的话，坦诚事实上会增强一个人的地位。

　【解题分析】分号句的上下句为重复关系，由分号后的 however 可知上下句为反义重复，故上句为"降低地位"，下文的 standing 之前的空格就应与上文的 lower 反义，可候选 A 和 D，而 D 的 candor 才是对上文 self-disclosure 的重复，故正确答案为 D。

　【重点词条】**esteem** *v*.①评价(appraise)

　　　　　　　　　　　②把⋯看作，认为(to view as, consider) 例 ~it a privilege

　　　　　　　　　　　③尊重，尊敬(to set a high value on, regard highly and prize accordingly)

　　　　　　standing *n*.级别，地位，身分，名声

6.【正确答案】C

　【中文释义】角色之间的辛辣的交谈使得小说读起来生动活泼，并且这种生动说明提出来的观点可能是作者自己的观点。

　【解题分析】由 this 可知第二个空格应重复上文的某个词，上文中只有 pungent 会在 this 之后重复，从而选 C 的 spiritedness。

　【重点词条】**pungent** *adj*.①痛的(sharply painful)

　　　　　　　　　　　②尖的(having a stiff and sharp point) 例 ~leaves

　　　　　　　　　　　③尖刻的，尖锐的(marked by a sharp incisive quality, caustic)

　　　　　　　　　　　例 a~critic／~language

　　　　　　　　　　　④有刺激性的，辛辣的(causing a sharp or irritating sensation; acrid)

　　　　　　give-and-take *n*.①公平交易，互让互谅(the practice of making mutual concessions, compromise)

　　　　　　　　　　　②交谈(a usu. good-natured exchange such as of ideas or comments)

　　　　　　spirited *adj*.精神饱满的，生气勃勃的，活泼的(full of energy, animation, or courage) 例 a~discussion

　　　　　　rewarding *adj*.①值得的，有价值的(yielding or likely to yield a reward, valuable, satisfying) 例 a~experience

　　　　　　　　　　　②报酬的(serving as a reward) 例 a~smile of thanks

7.【正确答案】B

　【中文释义】卡通艺术博物馆堡垒一般的正面看上去在故意提醒参观者，连环漫画这种艺术形式总是被评论家攻击。

【解题分析】由空格后的 by critics 可知空格中只能填"表扬、批评或评价"这三种词,又由 fortresslike 可知该城堡正面临攻击,故选 B。

【重点词条】**calculated** *adj*. ①可能的,适合的(apt, likely)

②计算过的(worked out by mathematical calculation)

③预估过的(engaged in, undertaken, or displayed after reckoning or estimating the statistical probability of success or failure) 例 a~risk

④故意的(planned or contrived to accomplish a purpose, deliberate, intended)

exhilarate *v*. ①使欢欣鼓舞(to make cheerful)

②使兴奋(enliven, excite)

③激励(refresh, stimulate)

overwhelm *v*. ①征服(upset, overthrow)

②淹没(to cover over completely, submerge)

③压倒(to overcome by superior force or numbers)

④使受不了,使不知所措(to overpower in thought or feeling)

SECTION 61

1. The fact that a theory is ____ does not necessarily ____ its scientific truth, which must be established by unbiased controlled studies.

(A) plausible. . ensure

(B) popular. . limit

(C) venerable. . override

(D) cohesive. undermine

(E) cumbersome. . alleviate

2. It is difficult to distinguish between the things that charismatic figures do ____ and those that are carefully contrived for effect.

(A) formally

(B) publicly

(C) prolifically

(D) spontaneously

(E) willfully

3. The development of containers, possibly made from bark or the skins of animals, although this is a matter of ____, allowed the extensive sharing of forage foods in prehistoric human societies.

(A) record

(B) fact

(C) degree

(D) importance

(E) conjecture

4. Although the young violinist's ____ performance, with the orchestra demonstrated his technical competence, his uninspired style and lack of interpretive maturity labeled him as a novice musician rather than as a truly ____ performer.

(A) spectacular. . conventional

(B) blundering. . artistic

(C) marginal. . inept

(D) steady. . accomplished

(E) dazzling. . unskilled

5. Even though political editorializing was not ____ under the new regime, journalists still experienced ____, though perceptible, gov-ernmental pressure to limit dissent.

(A) restricted. . clear

(B) encouraged. . strong

(C) forbidden. . discreet

(D) commended. . overt

(E) permitted. . regular

6. The trick for Michael was to ____ his son an illusory orderliness; only alone at night, when the boy was asleep, could Michael ____ the chaos he kept hidden from his son.

(A) explore with. . demonstrate

(B) conjure for. . acknowledge

(C) conceal from. . dispel

(D) demystify for. . escape

(E) endure with. . abandon

7. The ____ costumes of Renaissance Italy, with their gold and silver embroidery and figured brocades, were the antithesis of Spanish ____, with its dark muted colors, plain short capes, and high collars edged with small ruffs.

(A) striking. . obliqueness

(B) extravagant. . profligacy

(C) austere. . informality

(D) unpretentious. . asceticism

(E) sumptuous. . sobriety

SECTION 61 解答

1. 【正确答案】A

【中文释义】一个理论看上去似乎合理并不能必然确立其科学真理性,科学真理必须被没有偏见的对照研究所确立。

【解题分析】此句的结构几乎与我们曾详细解析过的 SECTION 3 第 5 题一模一样,请参阅并对比研究,本题中第一个空格应填 unbiased controlled studies 的反义词,第二个空格应填 establish 的同义词,答案为 A。

【重点词条】plausible adj. ①貌似有理的(superficially fair, reasonable, or valuable but of-ten specious) 例 a～pretext

②貌似可信的(superficially pleasing or persuasive) 例 a swindler. . ., then a quack, then a smooth, ～gentleman

cumbersome adj. ①麻烦的(burdensome, troublesome)

②难处理的(unwieldy because of heaviness and bulk)

③笨重的(slow-moving, ponderous)

2. 【正确答案】D

【中文释义】难以区分这两件事情,其一是具有领袖气质的人自然而然所做的事,其二是那些为了达到效果而事先设计好了的事情。

【解题分析】显然空格中应填一与 contrived 反义的词来构成一组对比,一组截然不同的两种事件。故正确答案为 D。

【重点词条】spontaneous adj. ①自发的,自然的(proceeding from natural feeling or native tendency without external constraint）

②无意识的，不由自主的（controlled and directed internally，self-acting）例 ～ movement characteristic of living things

contrive *v*. ①谋划，策划（devise，plan）例 ～ways of handling the situation

②发明，创造（to form or create in an artistic or ingenious manner）

例 contrived household utensils from stone

③设法（to bring about by stratagem or with difficulty，manage）

prolific *adj*. ①丰富的（producing young or fruit esp. freely，fruitful）

②富于创造力的（causing abundant growth，generation，or reproduction）

③多产的（marked by abundant inventiveness or productivity）

例 a～composer

3.【正确答案】E

【中文释义】容器的发展，有可能是用动物的皮肤或者树皮做的，尽管这只是一种猜测，却使得史前人类社会的大规模分享四处找到的食物成为可能。

【解题分析】文中的 this 显然重复前文的"possibly made from bark or the skins of animals"，故空格中只能填 E 的 conjecture，表示一种猜测的事实，A 和 B 正好相反，表示一个确凿的事实，C 和 D 强调的性质在原文中根本未出现过，正确答案为 E。

【重点词条】**conjecture** *n*. ①推测（inference from defective or presumptive evidence）

②猜测（a conclusion deduced by surmise or guesswork）

③假设（a proposition such as in mathematics before it has been proved or disproved）

forage *n*. ①草料，饲料（food for animals esp. when taken by browsing or grazing）

②搜寻粮草（the act of foraging，search for provisions）

4.【正确答案】D

【中文释义】尽管这位年轻的小提琴手在乐团中稳定的表演表明他技术上能胜任，但他缺乏灵感的风格以及对演绎的缺乏成熟就说明了他是一个初出茅庐的音乐家而不是一个真正老练的表演者。

【解题分析】由文末的 rather than 这个小连接可以轻松地得出答案为 D，即第二个空格应与 novice 反义。

【重点词条】**spectacular** *adj*. 壮观的，引人注目的（of，relating to，or being a spectacle，striking，sensational）例 a～display of fireworks

blunder *v*. ①笨拙地行动（to move unsteadily or confusedly）

②铸成大错（to make a mistake through stupidity，ignorance，or carelessness）

dazzling *adj*. ①炫目的（to lose clear vision esp. from looking at bright light）

②耀眼的(to shine brilliantly, to arouse admiration by an impressive display)

5.【正确答案】C

【中文释义】即使社论在新的政权下并不遭到禁止,但新闻记者仍然经历了谨慎的,仍可觉察出来的来自政府的限制不同政见的压力。

【解题分析】第二个空格与其后的 perceptible 构成转折,符合的只有 C 的 discreet,故 C 为正确答案。

【重点词条】editorialize v. ①发表社论(to express an opinion in the form of an editorial)

②编辑(to introduce opinion into the reporting of facts)

③发言,表态(to express an opinion such as on a controversial issue)

overt adj. 公开的,明显的(open to view, manifest)

6.【正确答案】B

【中文释义】迈克尔的鬼把戏是为他的儿子变幻出一个虚幻的有序性;只有在夜深人静之时,当这个小孩已沉睡过去,迈克尔才能独自面对从儿子身边隐藏掉的混乱心绪。

【解题分析】分号句和上下句为重复关系,orderliness 与下文的 the chaos 构成一组反义词,所以第一个空格应与 kept hidden from his son 构成反义。与"隐藏"相反的当然是"表现,表露出",只有 B 正确,B 的 conjure 通常为"恳求"的意思,另外一个意思为"变魔术,变幻出…"即为本句中所使用的含义。

此句含义甚为晦涩,事实上"*Sleepless in Seattle*"这部电影的观众恐怕都能理解,这儿的 the orderliness 与 the chaos 均指人的内心世界。在"*Sleepless in Seattle*"中,一位母亲过早地离开了小孩,小孩的成长空间就与别的小孩完全不一样,会遭受各种 chaos,而父亲为了安慰小孩不得不成天撒谎敷衍,这就是文中所说的 trick,等待夜深人静小孩熟睡之时,丈夫一人独自面对内心的痛苦和冲突,即本文的 acknowledge the chaos。

【重点词条】conjure v. ①恳求(to charge or entreat earnestly or solemnly)

②用魔法影响(to affect or effect by or as if by magic)

③想像(imagine, contrive) 例 We～up our own metaphors for our own needs.

④回忆(to bring to mind) 例 words that～pleasant images

⑤念咒召唤神灵等(to summon a devil or spirit by invocation or incantation)

⑥变魔术(to practice magical arts)

demystify v. 使非神秘化,使不再迷惑不解(to eliminate the mystifying features of)

acknowledge v. ①承认(to recognize the rights, authority, or status of)

②告知,确认(to disclose knowledge of or agreement with)

③就…表示谢忱,报偿(to express gratitude or obligation for)

④注意(to take notice of)

7.【正确答案】E

【中文释义】文艺复兴时期意大利的华美的服装,有着金银刺绣和提花锦缎,是西班牙俭朴服装的对立物,西班牙的服装有着灰色柔和的色彩,朴素的短斗篷,高高的衣领上只装饰着小的花边。

【解题分析】由两个分隔不难知第一空格就为"华美",第二个空格应为"俭朴",正确答案为 E。

【重点词条】**muted** *adj*. 柔和的

obliqueness *adj*. ①倾斜的(neither perpendicular nor parallel, inclined, having the axis not perpendicular to the base) 例 an~cone

②拐弯抹角的,不光明正大的(not straightforward, indirect; obscure)

unpretentious *adj*. 不矫饰的,不夸耀的,朴实无华的(free from ostentation, elegance, or affectation, modest) 例 ~homes

sumptuous *adj*. 奢侈的,豪华的,昂贵的,华丽的(extremely costly, rich, luxurious, or magnificent) 例 ~banquets/a~residence

SECTION 62

1. According to the newspaper critic, the performances at the talent contest last night ____ from acceptable to excellent.

   (A) varied

   (B) receded

   (C) swept

   (D) averaged

   (E) declined

2. For more than a century, geologists have felt comfortable with the idea that geological processes, although very ____, are also ____ and so are capable of shaping the Earth, given enough time.

   (A) minute. . sporadic

   (B) slow. . steady

   (C) complex. . discernible

   (D) unpredictable. . constant

   (E) ponderous. . intermittent

3. While not ____ with the colorfully obvious forms of life that are found in a tropical rain forest, the desert is ____ to a surprisingly large number of species.

   (A) brimming. . foreign

   (B) endowed. . detrimental

   (C) imbued. . hostile

   (D) teeming. . host

   (E) confronted. . home

4. Speakers and listeners arc often at odds: language that is easy for the receiver to understand is often difficult to ____, and that which is easily formulated can be hard to ____.

   (A) estimate. . confirm

(B) transmit. . defend

(C) produce. . comprehend

(D) suppress. . ignore

(E) remember. . forget

5. The current demand for quality in the schools seems to ask not for the development of informed and active citizens, but for disciplined and productive workers with abilities that contribute to civic life only ＿＿＿, if at all.

(A) indirectly

(B) politically

(C) intellectually

(D) sensibly

(E) sequentially

6. Because of its lack of theaters, the city came, ironically, to be viewed as an ＿＿＿

theater town, and that reputation led entrepreneurs to believe that it would be ＿＿＿ to build new theaters there.

(A) unprofitable. . risky

(B) untapped. . pointless

(C) unappreciated. . difficult

(D) unlikely. . appropriate

(E) unimpressed. . shrewd

7. He felt it would be ＿＿＿, in view of the intense ＿＿＿ that would likely follow, to make the sacrifice required in order to gain such little advantage.

(A) charitable. . growth

(B) welcomed. . prejudice

(C) futile. . encouragement

(D) academic. . acclaim

(E) unrealistic. . turmoil

SECTION 62 解答

1.【正确答案】A

【中文释义】依据报纸评论家看来,昨夜智力竞赛的表现在尚可接受到优秀之间变化。

【解题分析】能与其后的 from. . . to 构成搭配的只有 A。

【重点词条】**sweep** *v.* ①扫(to remove from a surface with or as if with a broom or brush) 例 swept the crumbs from the table

②扫荡,肃清(to destroy completely, wipe out, usu. used with away) 例 Everything she cherished might be swept away overnight.

③猛推(to remove or take with a single continuous forceful action) 例 swept the books off the desk

④清除(to remove from sight or consideration) 例 The problem can't be swept under the rug.

⑤环视(to cover the entire range of) 例 His eyes swept the horizon.

decline *v.* ①下降

②谢绝

2.【正确答案】B

【中文释义】长达一个多世纪以来,地质学家对这个观点非常满意,即地质的过程尽管非常慢,但却稳定,因而只要有足够多的时间就能够塑造地球。

【解题分析】请充分注意句末的 given enough time,这是一种隐含的条件句(另外也可用 with 或 without 表示隐含的条件),由该条件句即可知,给予足够的时间,地质过程就能改变地球,而如果时间不足则不能改变地球,所以第一个空格与第二个空格所描述的地质过程的属性应与时间高度相关,五个选项中表达出时间概念的只有 B,故 B 为正确答案。

【重点词条】**ponderous** *adj*. ①极重的(of very great weight)
②笨重的,难处理的(unwieldy or clumsy because of weight and size)
③冗长的,沉闷的(oppressively or unpleasantly dull, lifeless)
例 ~prose

intermittent *adj*. ①间歇的(coming and going at intervals, not continuous)
例 ~rain
②偶尔的(occasional) 例 ~trips abroad

3.【正确答案】D

【中文释义】尽管没有充满那些可以在热带雨林中找到的色彩鲜艳的各种生命形式,但是沙漠仍然是出乎人们意料的大量物种的寄居地。

【解题分析】文中的 tropical rain forest 与 desert 构成对比,故 desert 中不应有各种生命,而下文中又出现了一个关键的词 surprisingly,故沙漠中应有大量的生命,第二个空格可候选 D 和 E。D 和 E 的第一词符合句意的为 D 中的 teeming,故正确答案为 D。

【重点词条】**brim** *n*. ①边缘(an upper or outer margin, verge)
②水面(the upper surface of a body of water)
③容器的边(the edge or rim of a hollow vessel, a natural depression, or a cavity)
④帽缘(the projecting rim of a hat)

brim *v*. ①装满到边缘(to fill to the brim)
②充满,充溢(to be or become full often to overflowing)

imbue *v*. ①感染,弥漫(to permeate or influence as if by dyeing) 例 the spirit that~s the new constitution
②使浸透(to tinge or dye deeply)

teem *v*. ①充满(to become pregnant, conceive)
②涌现,丰富(to become filled to overflowing, abound) 例 lakes ~ with fish
③大量出现(to be present in large quantity)

4.【正确答案】C

【中文释义】演讲者和听众总是不一致：对于听众容易理解的语言通常难以形成，而容易形成的语言又总是难以理解。

【解题分析】冒号之后表示解释重复，所以第一个空格应填与 receiver 相反的人的动作，同理可知第二个空格内容，正确答案为 C。

【重点词条】**at odds** *prep.* 争执，不一致，冲突

5.【正确答案】A

【中文释义】目前学校对于质量的要求看上去并不是要求得到有教养的积极的市民，而是要求得到守纪律的并且富有效率的工人，这些工人的能力只能对文明生活做间接的贡献（如果真有的话）。

【解题分析】由文中的 not... but 结构可知 workers 在文中扮演的是"not informed and not active"的角色，这样的人对文明生活的贡献当然不会太大，空格应填贬义词，A 正确，或者由 if at all 来判断也可知空格应填贬义词。

【重点词条】**sensibly** *adv.* ①到能感觉到的地步，显著地，明显地（of a kind to be felt or perceived, perceptible to the senses or to reason or understanding）例 felt a～chill/her distress was～from her manner

②实在地（perceptible as real or material, substantial）例 the～world in which we live

③敏感地（receptive to external influences, sensitive）例 the most～reaches of the spirit

④明智地（having, containing, or indicative of good sense or reason, rational, reasonable）例 ～people/made a～answer

sequential *adj.* ①连续的，一系列的（of, relating to, or arranged in a sequence, serial）例 ～file systems

②按顺序的（following in sequence）

6.【正确答案】A

【中文释义】因为缺乏戏院，这个城市反而变得被人看成一个无利可图的戏剧城，而这个声誉导致企业家认为在那儿建一座新剧场将是很冒风险的。

【解题分析】下文的 that reputation 即指代上文第一个空格，而该声誉导致企业家做出了某种判断。企业家为一特征人物，永远只考虑是否赢利，所以这个声誉也应为是否赢利的声誉。通常如果一个地方缺乏戏院，会被看成有利可图，但文中又出现了一个 ironically，故反而是 unprofitable，正确答案为 A。

【重点词条】**untapped** *adj.* ①桶栓未拔开的（not subjected to tapping）例 an～keg

②未开发的，未利用的（not drawn upon or utilized）例 as yet ～markets

pointless *adj.* ①无意义的（devoid of meaning, senseless）例 a～remark

②没有效果的（devoid of effectiveness, flat）例 ～attempts to be funny

7.【正确答案】E

【中文释义】他觉得这种做法——做出所要求的牺牲只为了获得如此少的收益,并且考虑到随之而来的巨大的混乱——是不现实的。

【解题分析】只要清楚 it 为形式主语,真正的主语为 to 引导的动词不定式,即可知第一个空格应选 C 和 E,第二个空格仍应为贬义,故选 E。

【重点词条】**futile** *adj*. ①无益的,无效的(serving no useful purpose, completely ineffective) 例 Efforts to convince him were~.

②不重要的(occupied with trifles, frivolous)

③缺乏目的的

④愚蠢的

SECTION 62(2)

1. The academic education offered to university students is essential and must not be _____, but that does not mean universities should _____ the extracurricular, yet still important, aspects of university life.

   (A) impeded. . promote
   (B) debated. . victimize
   (C) protected. . broaden
   (D) maximized. . continue
   (E) compromised. . neglect

2. To understand fully the impact of global warming on the environment, one must recognize that the components of the problem are _____ and, therefore, a change in any one component will _____ the others.

   (A) distinct. . influence
   (B) unique. . clarify
   (C) linked. . affect
   (D) cyclical. . negate
   (E) growing. . exacerbate

3. Although the Impressionist painters appeared to earlier art historians to be _____ in their methods, recent analyses of their brushwork suggest the contrary—that, in fact, their technique was quite _____.

   (A) unstudied. . sophisticated
   (B) idiosyncratic. . effective
   (C) eclectic. . naive
   (D) lax. . fashionable
   (E) careless. . unpremeditated

4. Increased governmental alarm about global warming _____ the concern among scientists that such warming is occurring, though when to expect major effects is still _____.

   (A) echoes. . agreed on
   (B) precludes. . under consideration
   (C) reflects. . in dispute
   (D) obviates. . in doubt
   (E) encourages. . confirmed

5. For someone as _____ as she, who preferred to speak only when absolutely necessary, his relentless chatter was completely _____.

   (A) ingenuous. . ignorant
   (B) curt. . enchanting
   (C) cheerful. . idle
   (D) laconic. . maddening
   (E) forward. . pointless

6. Future generations will probably consider current speculations about humanity's place in the universe to be ＿＿ omissions and errors; even rigorous scientific views change, sometimes overnight.

   (A) immune from

   (B) marred by

   (C) uncorrupted by

   (D) correct despite

   (E) abridged by

7. Marshal Philippe Petain, unlike any other French citizen of this century, has been, paradoxically, the object of both great veneration and great ＿＿.

   (A) reverence

   (B) interest

   (C) empathy

   (D) contempt

   (E) praise

SECTION 62(2)解答

1. 【正确答案】E

  【中文释义】提供给大学生的学术教育是必不可缺的,因此不能被破坏,但这并不意味着大学就应该忽略课外的、但仍很重要的大学生活的那些方面。

  【解题分析】文中有一结构是考生常常忽略的——"the extracurricular, yet still important aspects",这一短语中强调的是"imporint"。因而第二个空格应填贬义词,而第一个空格非常容易判断,由 and 结构可知其也应为贬义词。正确答案为 E。

  【重点词条】**compromise** *v*. ①通过互让解决争端等

                         ②连累,危及,损害

                         ③放弃原则、理想等

          essential *adj*. ①本质的(of, relating to, or constituting essence, inherent)

                   ②必要的,必不可少的(of the utmost importance, basic, indispensable, necessary) 例 ～foods/an～requirement for admission to college

2. 【正确答案】C

  【中文释义】若想全面理解地球变暖对环境的影响,一个人就必须认识到这个问题的各组成部分是相关联的,因而,任何一个元素的改变将会影响其他元素。

  【解题分析】文中第二个空格尽管尚未明确,但至少可获知一个元素的改变会对其他元素产生某个动作,从而可判断第一个空可为这些元素之间至少应是有关联的,答案为 C。

  【重点词条】**cyclical** *adj*. 循环的,周期性的(of, relating to, or being a cycle, moving in cycles) 例 ～time

3. 【正确答案】A

  【中文释义】尽管印象派画家对于早期的艺术评论家而言,在作画方法上显得好像未曾钻研过,但是最近对他们的笔法的分析表明了相反的观点——事实上,他们的技术是非常精致的。

【解题分析】由转折及 the contrary 等明显的提示可知第一空格与第二空格应为一组反义词,表达出对印象派画家的两种截然不同的评价,五个选项中构成一组反义词的为 A。故正确答案为 A。

【重点词条】**sophisticated** *adj.* ①老于世故的,失去天真的,矫揉造作的

②老练的,富有经验的,精通的

③不落俗套的,深奥精妙的,精致的

④复杂的,精密的,尖端的

unstudied *adj.* ①未学过的,非由研究而获得的(not studied, not acquired by study)

②自然的,不勉强的(not forced, not done or planned for effect)

lax *adj.* ①松弛的(of the bowels, loose, open)

②软弱的,不严格的(deficient in firmness, not stringent) 例 ～control/a～foreman

4.【正确答案】C

【中文释义】政府增加的关于全球变暖的警报反映了科学家的忧虑——这种变暖正在发生,但何时能预期到其主要效果却仍然有分歧意见。

【解题分析】第二个空格处于一个简单的转折句中,可推知何时会有大的效果尚不知晓,也即尚未明确,故可候选 B、C 和 D,而 B 和 D 的第一词是荒谬的,意即政府越警报,科学家就越不关心,正确答案只能为 C,因为政府本身并不能做出任何科学的警报,它的警报只可能是来源于科学家不停地给政府所提出报告,故政府的警报从一个侧面反映出了科学家的态度。

【重点词条】**echo** *v.* ①附和,回响(to resound with echoes)

②发回声(to produce an echo)

5.【正确答案】D

【中文释义】对于像她这样简洁,只在绝对必要时才说话的人而言,他的无休无止的闲聊是完全疯狂的行为。

【解题分析】由第一个空格后的分隔可知空格可候选 B 和 D,由上下文的对比可知应选 D,这种性格的女孩应该不会太喜欢废话连篇的男孩。

【重点词条】**curt** *adj.* ①简明扼要的(sparing of words, terse)

②简短失礼的,唐突鲁莽的(marked by rude or peremptory shortness, brusque)

laconic *adj.* (言语、文章等)简洁的,精炼的(using or involving the use of a minimum of words, concise to the point of seeming rude or mysterious)

forward *adj.* ①热心的,乐意的(strongly inclined, ready)

②冒失的,卤莽的(lacking modesty or reserve, brash)

③早熟的(notably advanced or developed, precocious)

idle *adj*. ①无聊的(lacking worth or basis, vain) 例 ~chatter/~pleasure

②空闲的(not occupied or employed, having no employment, inactive) 例 ~workers

③闲置的(not turned to normal or appropriate use) 例 ~funds/~farmland

④懒惰的(shiftless, lazy)

⑤无根据的(having no evident lawful means of support)

6.【正确答案】B

【中文释义】未来的人们可能会认为今天的关于人类在宇宙中的地位的思考被各种错误和疏忽所损毁了;即使是严谨的科学观点也总是会改变的,有时候一夜之间就彻底变化了。

【解题分析】由文首的 future 及随后不远处的 current 即可知本题的答案,将来的人们会认为今天的思考错误,一个简单的时间对比型,B 为正确答案。下半句用的时态为一般现在时,表示一种永恒的规律,所以上半句也可由此推知将来的观点肯定与现在不一样,从而认为今天的是错的,正确答案为 B。

【重点词条】**abridge** *v*. ①减少(to reduce in scope, diminish) 例 attempts to~the right of free speech

②限制(to shorten in duration or extent) 例 modern transportation that~s distance

③节略,缩短(to shorten by omission of words without sacrifice of sense, condense)

mar *v*. 毁坏,玷污(to detract from the perfection or wholeness of, spoil)

7.【正确答案】D

【中文释义】菲利普·贝当元帅,和这个世纪的其他法国臣民不一样,非常矛盾的,受到了巨大的尊敬和巨大的轻蔑。

【解题分析】由 paradoxically 可知下文应出现一组反义词,因而空格中应填 veneration 的反义词,正确答案为 D。

【重点词条】**empathy** *n*. ①(审美)移情作用(the imaginative projection of a subjective state into an object so that the object appears to be infused with it)

②神入,神会(the action of understanding, being aware of, being sensitive to, and vicariously experiencing the feelings, thoughts, and experience of another of either the past or present without having the feelings, thoughts, and experience fully communicated in an objectively explicit manner)

SECTION 63

1. In some cultures the essence of magic is its traditional integrity; it can be efficient only if it has been ____ without loss from primeval times to the present practitioner.
   (A) conventionalized
   (B) realized
   (C) transmitted
   (D) manipulated
   (E) aggrandized

2. Although skeptics say financial problems will probably ____ our establishing a base on the Moon, supporters of the project remain ____, saying that human curiosity should overcome such pragmatic constraints.
   (A) beset. . disillusioned
   (B) hasten. . hopeful
   (C) postpone. . pessimistic
   (D) prevent. . enthusiastic
   (E) allow. . unconvinced

3. Before the Second World War, academics still questioned whether the body of literature produced in the United States truly ____ a ____ literature, or whether such literature was only a provincial branch of English literature.
   (A) symbolized. . local
   (B) constituted. . national
   (C) defined. . historical
   (D) outlined. . good
   (E) captured. . meaningful

4. Many more eighteenth-century novels were written by women than by men, but this dominance has, until very recently, been regarded merely as ____ fact, a bit of arcane knowledge noted only by bibliographers.
   (A) a controversial
   (B) a statistical
   (C) an analytical
   (D) an explicit
   (E) an unimpeachable

5. All ____ biological traits fall into one of two categories: those giving their possessors greater ____ the environment and those rendering them more independent of it.
   (A) widespread. . detachment from
   (B) beneficial. . control over
   (C) successful. . freedom from
   (D) neutral. . compatibility with
   (E) harmful. . advantage in

6. One of archaeology's central dilemmas is how to reconstruct the ____ of complex ancient societies from meager and often ____ physical evidence.
   (A) riddles. . obsolete
   (B) details. . irrefutable
   (C) intricacies. . equivocal
   (D) patterns. . flawless
   (E) configurations. . explicit

7. Just as the authors' book on eels is often a key text for courses in marine vertebrate zoology, their ideas on animal development and phylogeny ____ teaching in this area.
   (A) prevent
   (B) defy
   (C) replicate
   (D) inform
   (E) use

SECTION 63 解答

1. 【正确答案】C
   【中文释义】在有些文化中巫术的本质是它的传统的完整性:只有当巫术被毫无损失地从远古时代传递到今天的从业人员的手中时,它才会是有效的。
   【解题分析】由文中的 from 短语可知这是一个时间上传递的动作,故能修饰的动词只有 C。正确答案为 C。
   【重点词条】conventionalize *v*. ①使按习俗,使惯例化(according with, sanctioned by, or based on convention)
   　　　　　　　　　　　　　　　②使符合传统(lacking originality or individuality, trite)
   　　　　　　　　　　　　　　　③按传统手法表现(according with a mode of artistic representation that simplifies or provides symbols or substitutes for natural forms)

2. 【正确答案】D
   【中文释义】尽管怀疑主义者们认为财政问题将可能阻止我们在月球上建立一个基地,这个项目的支持者继续热情高涨,认为人类的好奇心应该克服这样功利的约束。
   【解题分析】由两个特征人物 skeptics 和 supports 可知第一个空格为反对的情绪,第二个空格为支持的情绪,故正确答案为 D。
   【重点词条】beset *v*. ①困扰,苦恼(trouble, harass) 例 inflation～s the economy
   　　　　　　　　　　②围攻(to set upon, assail) 例 the settlers were～by savages
   　　　　　　　　　　③包围(to hem in, surround)
   　　　　　　disillusion *n*. 理想幻灭(the condition of being disenchanted)

3. 【正确答案】B
   【中文释义】二战之前,学者们仍然怀疑在美国所产生的文学是否真正地构成了一种民族文学,或者这种文学只不过是一种英国文学的地方分支而已。
   【解题分析】文中出现了 question whether...or whether... 的句型结构,这是一种常见句型,两个 whether 从句中有一常规解题点"only",由此可推知上文的 whether 从句中不应为"provincial branch",而应相反。五个选项中,只有 B 的第二个词"national"与"provincial branch"相反,故正确答案为 B。
   【重点词条】outline *n*. ①外形,轮廓(a line that marks the outer limits of an object or figure, boundary, shape)
   　　　　　　　　　②略图,素描(a style of drawing in which contours are marked without shading)
   　　　　　　　　　③提纲(a sketch in outline)
   　　　　　　　　　④梗概(a summary of a written work, synopsis)

4. 【正确答案】B

【中文释义】更多的18世纪小说是由女性写的,而不是男性,但是这种优势直到最近都仅仅被看成是一个统计事实,一种只被文献目录学家所知道的秘不外传的知识。

【解题分析】由空格后的分隔可知,这是一种只能被文献目录学家所知道的知识,强调了某一种独特的知识。事实上任何一个对18世纪小说产生兴趣的人都会涉及某些作品,并有所了解,比如他们由此就获得了某些清晰"explicit"的知识,但只有文献目录学家知道的知识是什么呢? 只有文献目录学家才会对所有18世纪小说加以分类、整理、统计,一般人绝不会出于兴趣而去全面统计18世纪小说,因而只为文献目录学家所知晓的知识为 B 的 statistical。

【重点词条】**arcane** *adj*. ①秘密的,专门的(known or knowable only to the initiate, secret)

　　　　　　　例 the～rites of a mystery cult

　　　　　　　②神秘的,晦涩难懂的(mysterious, obscure) 例 the technical consultant's～explanations

　　　　unimpeachable *adj*. 无瑕疵的,无缺点的,完全可靠的(not impeachable, not to be called in question, not liable to accusation, irreproachable, blameless)

5.【正确答案】B

【中文释义】所有有益的生物特征可以归结为两大类:那些赋予这些特征拥有者更大的对环境的控制的特征和那些导致他们更加独立于环境之外的特征。

【解题分析】冒号前后为重复说明关系,冒号前称有益的生物特征可分为两大类,故冒号后为两类而不是一类,从而 A 和 C 错误,因为 independent of, detachment from, freedom from 为同义词。而 B、D、E 的第一个词显然构成了一组词:有益、有害、中立的。显然能导致生物更加独立于环境之外就导致生物有更多的生存机会,为有益的生物学特征,所以答案为 B。

【重点词条】**render** *v*. ①熬化(to melt down) 例 ～suet

　　　　　　②精炼(to treat so as to convert into industrial fats and oils or fertilizer)

　　　　　　③使成为(to transmit to another, deliver)

　　　　　　④投降,放弃(give up, yield)

　　　　　　⑤给予,提供

　　　　　　⑥提出,呈报

6.【正确答案】C

【中文释义】考古学的一个中心难题是如何由那些简单而模棱两可的物理证据中重现出复杂的古代社会的纷繁复杂的方方面面。

【解题分析】第二个空格与 meager 相并列,显然也是一种坏的情形,故可选 A 和 C,A 的第一个词 riddles 是不可能正确的,学者的目的永远都不会是为了创造或复现谜团,而 C 的第一个词 intricacies 事实上重复了其后的 complicate,故正确答案为 C。

【重点词条】**riddle** *v*. ①解谜(to find the solution of, explain)

　　　　　　②给…出谜(to set a riddle for, puzzle)

intricacy *n*. 错综复杂,难以了解(the quality or state of being intricate)

7.【正确答案】D

【中文释义】正如作者关于鳗鱼的书通常是海洋脊椎动物学课程的核心课程一样,他的关于动物发展和种系发生的理论指导了这个领域的教学。

【解题分析】文中出现了一组常见的同义词,the authors' book 与 their ideas 为同义词重复,因而空格应表现出他们的思想为核心思想这个概念,D 的 inform 为指导的意思。故正确答案为 D。

【重点词条】inform *v*. 渗透,贯穿于其中,使充满,充斥

SECTION 64

1. What is most important to the monkeys in the sanctuary is that they are a group; this is so because primates are inveterately ____ and build their lives around each other.
   (A) independent
   (B) stable
   (C) curious
   (D) social
   (E) proprietary

2. Often the difficulties of growing up in the public eye cause child prodigies to ____ the world of achievement before reaching adulthood: happily, they sometimes later return to competition and succeed brilliantly.
   (A) ridicule
   (B) conquer
   (C) retire from
   (D) antagonize
   (E) examine

3. In scientific studies, supporting evidence is much more satisfying to report than are discredited hypotheses, but, in fact, the ____ of errors is more likely to be ____ than is the establishment of probable truth.
   (A) formulation.. permitted

(B) correction.. ignored
(C) detection.. useful
(D) accumulation.. agreeable
(E) refinement.. conditional

4. Professional photographers generally regard inadvertent surrealism in a photograph as a curse rather than a blessing; magazine photographers, in particular, consider themselves ____ to the extent that they can ____ its presence in their photographs.
   (A) skillful.. enhance
   (B) inadequate.. eliminate
   (C) original.. demonstrate
   (D) fortunate.. minimize
   (E) conventional.. highlight

5. Marison was a scientist of unusual ____ and imagination who had startling success in ____ new and fundamental principles well in advance of their general recognition.
   (A) restiveness.. acknowledging
   (B) precision.. coordinating
   (C) aggression.. resisting
   (D) candor.. dispelling
   (E) insight.. discerning

6. Unenlightened authoritarian managers rarely recognize a crucial reason for the low levels of serious conflict among members of democratically run work groups: a modicum of tolerance for dissent often prevents ____.

   (A) demur
   (B) schism
   (C) cooperation
   (D) compliance
   (E) shortsightedness

7. Carruthers' latest literary criticism ____ her reputation for trenchant commentary; despite its intriguing title and the fulsome praise on its dust jacket, it is nothing more than a collection of ____.

   (A) reinforces. . pronouncements
   (B) belies. . platitudes
   (C) prejudices. . insights
   (D) advances. . aphorisms
   (E) undermines. . judgments

SECTION 64 解答

1.【正确答案】D

【中文释义】对于动物保护区里的猴子而言最重要的是它们是一个团体,之所以这样,是因为灵长目动物根深蒂固地具有群居性并且在一起生活。

【解题分析】由空格所处的小连接结构可知空格应填"build their lives around each other",即"群居"的之义。正确答案为D。

【重点词条】sanctuary *n*. ①神殿(the most sacred part of a religious building such as the part of a Christian church in which the altar is placed)
②礼拜堂(the room in which general worship services are held)
③避难所(a place of refuge and protection)
④禁猎区,鸟兽保护区(a refuge for wildlife where predators are controlled and hunting is illegal)

inveterate *adj*. ①根深蒂固的(firmly established by long persistence) 例 the ~tendency to overlook the obvious
②积习难改的(confirmed in a habit, habitual) 例 an~liar

2.【正确答案】C

【中文释义】通常,在公众眼中成长的困难性会导致少年天才在成年之前逃避这个充满了成就的世界;令人欣慰的是他们之后某时又会回到竞争中去并且取得辉煌的成功。

【解题分析】由before 和later 这一组反义词可知,空格中应填"return to"的反义词,正确答案为C。

【重点词条】prodigy *n*. ①奇迹,奇事(an extraordinary, marvelous, or unusual accomplishment, deed, or event)
②奇才,天才(a highly talented child or youth)

retire *v*. ①撤退(to withdraw from action or danger, retreat)
②隐居(to withdraw esp. for privacy)

③后退(to move back, recede)

④退休(to withdraw from one's position or occupation, conclude one's working or professional career)

⑤就寝(to go to bed)

3.【正确答案】C

【中文释义】在科学研究中,支持的证据比否定性的假设汇报起来更让人满意,但是,事实上,发现错误是比支持一个可能的真理更加有用的。

【解题分析】全句中出现了两次比较结构,故根据比较句的解题规律:"一套比较结构中比较双方相反;两套比较结构中比较双方不变"可知,下句中的 establishment of probable truth 重复上文的 supporting evidence 一段,而 discredited hypotheses 一段则应对应于下文的第一个空格。若想否定别人的学说,需要做的动作为 C 的 detection errors,故正确答案为 C。

【重点词条】agreeable adj. ①令人愉快的,惬意的

②欣然同意的,愿意的

③适合的,一致的

4.【正确答案】D

【中文释义】职业摄影家通常认为作品中偶尔出现的超现实主义是一种诅咒而不是祝福;杂志摄影家尤其认为自己幸运到了这种程度以至于可以尽量减少它们在作品中的存在。

【解题分析】分号句上下句为重复关系,该句上下句的主语为上下义关系,因为 magazine photographer 属于一种 professional photographer。上句表明职业的摄影家认为偶尔出现的超现实主义是坏的事物,因为下句的杂志摄影家应采取相同的观点。由此可知第二个空格为 B 和 D 中的一个,而 B 选项的第一个词又出现了失误,句意正好相反了,认为"自己减少了偶尔的超现实主义是一种无能"。正确答案为 D。

【重点词条】inadequate adj. ①不充分的,不适当的,不够格的(not adequate, insufficient; not capable)

②有缺点的

inadvertent adj. ①漫不经心的(not focusing the mind on a matter, inattentive)

②非故意的(unintentional)

5.【正确答案】E

【中文释义】麦里森是一个具有非同寻常的洞察力和想象力的科学家,他在比大多数人普遍认识之前先发现新基础原则方面具有令人叹为观止的成功。

【解题分析】第二个空格中应为麦里森成功的某个动作,当然比别人更早才是一种成功,所以空格中应为更早地"recognize",从而可选 A 和 E,而比别人更早地认识到基本规律体现的正是 E 的 insight,故正确答案为 E。

【重点词条】**startling** *adj*. 令人震惊的(causing momentary fright, surprise, or astonishment)

　　　　　　restiveness *n*. ①焦躁不安

　　　　　　　　　　　　　　②倔强，不受管束

6.【正确答案】B

　【中文释义】愚昧的集权主义的经理很少能够认识到一个关键的原因——为何以民主方式运作的工作小组中只有很少的严重冲突：一些对不同政见者的容忍态度通常会阻止分裂对抗。

　【解题分析】文中显然有两个主体词汇 authoritarian 和 democratically，解题时应牢牢抓住主体词汇。冒号后的"a modicum of tolerance for dissent"实际上就是民主的方式，因而空格里只能填 B。因为民主不会阻止其他四个选项，读者可自行判断。当然，冒号前后表示解释，空格中填的实际上就是上文的 serious conflict，由于民主容忍不同的政见，所以持不同政见者就不会分裂对抗，而是采取更温和的方式。

　【重点词条】**demur** *v*. ①顾虑，迟疑(delay, hesitate)

　　　　　　　　　　　　②反对，异议(to take exception, object)

　　　　　　schism *n*. ①分裂(division, separation; discord, disharmony)

　　　　　　　　　　　　②教会分裂(formal division in or separation from a church or religious body)

　　　　　　　　　　　　③分歧，不和

7.【正确答案】B

　【中文释义】卡罗莎最新的文学评论辜负了她具有深刻批评能力的声誉；除了吸引人的标题和防尘封皮上的过誉之辞之外，这本书只不过是一个陈词滥调的文集而已。

　【解题分析】由分号下半句的转折结构可以轻松地知道第二个空格应为贬义词。当然 nothing more than 也很清楚地提示第二个空格应为贬义词，故答案为 B。

　【重点词条】**trenchant** *adj*. ①锐利的，尖锐的(keen, sharp)

　　　　　　　　　　　　　②有力的，中肯的(vigorously effective and articulate) 例 a～analysis

　　　　　　　　　　　　　③尖刻的(caustic) 例 ～remarks

　　　　　　fulsome *adj*. ①大量的(characterized by abundance, copious) 例 describes in ～detail/～bird life; The feeder overcrowded.

　　　　　　　　　　　　②丰富的(generous in amount, extent, or spirit) 例 The passengers were～in praise of the plane's crew/a～victory for the far left/the greetings have been～, the farewells tender.

　　　　　　　　　　　　③成熟的，丰满的(being full and well developed) 例 She was in generally～, limpid voice.

　　　　　　　　　　　　④令人不快的(aesthetically, morally, or generally offensive) 例 ～lies and nauseous flattery/The devil take thee for a～rogue.

⑤使人作恶的(exceeding the bounds of good taste, overdone)
例 The ～ chromium glitter of the escalators dominating the central hall.

⑥过分恭维的,虚伪的(excessively complimentary or flattering, effusive) 例 An admiration whose extent I did not express, lest I be thought～.

SECTION 65

1. If those large publishers that respond solely to popular literary trends continue to dominate the publishing market, the initial publication of new writers will depend on the writers' willingness to ____ popular tastes.
   (A) struggle against
   (B) cater to
   (C) admire
   (D) flout
   (E) elude

2. Candidates who oppose the present state income tax must be able to propose ____ ways to ____ the financing of state operations.
   (A) intelligent. . initiate
   (B) individual. . diversify
   (C) innovative. . alleviate
   (D) arbitrary. . maintain
   (E) alternate. . continue

3. Although strong legal remedies for nonpayment of child support are ____, the delay and expense associated with these remedies make it ____ to develop other options.
   (A) unpopular. . useful
   (B) required. . impossible
   (C) available. . imperative
   (D) unavailing. . impractical
   (E) nonexistent. . ridiculous

4. Calculus, though still indispensable to science and technology, is no longer ____; it has an equal partner called discrete mathematics.
   (A) preeminent
   (B) pertinent
   (C) beneficial
   (D) essential
   (E) pragmatic

5. Demonstrating a mastery of innuendo, he issued several ____ insults in the course of the evening's conversation.
   (A) blunt
   (B) boisterous
   (C) fallacious
   (D) veiled
   (E) embellished

6. The ____ of gamblers' unsuccessful decision strategies is one ____ of the illusions built into games of chance in order to misguide players and take their money.
   (A) distortion. . outcome
   (B) restriction. . result
   (C) maintenance. . function
   (D) prediction. . accomplishment
   (E) demonstration. . prerequisite

7. The natures of social history and lyric poetry

are ___ , social history always recounting the ___ and lyric poetry speaking for un-changing human nature, that timeless essence beyond fashion and economics.

(A) predetermined. . bygone

(B) antithetical. . evanescent

(C) interdependent. . unnoticed

(D) irreconcilable. . unalterable

(E) indistinguishable. . transitory

SECTION 65 解答

1.【正确答案】B

【中文释义】如果那些只对通俗文字潮流做出回应的出版商继续控制出版市场,那么新作家的处女作的出版与否将取决于作者是否愿意迎合通俗口味。

【解题分析】文中的 popular literary trends 为对 popular tastes 的重复,既然出版商只迎合大众潮流,而作家新作的出版又取决于出版家,所以作者只能迎合大众潮流。正确答案为 B。

【重点词条】cater *v*. 满足…的需要,迎合,投合(to supply what is required or desired)

例 ~ing to middle-class tastes

2.【正确答案】E

【中文释义】反对目前政府收入调节税的候选人必须能够提出不同的方法来继续为州政府的运作募集资金。

【解题分析】此句误读的人甚多,finance 作名词为"财政,金融"之意,而此句中作动词,意为"募集,筹集资金"之意。不少同学将此句中的 financing 理解成"花销,费用"从而误选 C。州政府的运作必须有资金支持,以前是通过收入调节税来筹集这批资金,而候选人为了取悦民众而反对收入调节税,问题是如何继续募集这批资金。所以此句中的第二个空格只能填 D 和 E 两个选项。D 和 E 的第一词中显然是 alternate 正确,故正确答案为 E。

【重点词条】finance *v*. ①资助(to raise or provide funds or capital for) 例 ~ a new house

②筹措资金(to furnish with necessary funds) 例 ~ a son through college

initiate *v*. ①发起(to cause or facilitate the beginning of, set going) 例 ~ a program of reform/enzymes that~fermentation

②接纳新成员(to induct into membership by or as if by special rites)

③使初步了解(to instruct in the rudiments or principles of something, introduce)

3.【正确答案】C

【中文释义】尽管针对拒付小孩抚养费行为的强有力的法律措施存在,但是与这些方法密切联系在一起的延误以及过高的费用都使得发展其他方案成为必然。

【解题分析】下半句中强调了与法律方案密不可分的种种缺点,故一眼可判知作者欲否定法律的方案。而这种丑恶的行为又不能不制裁,所以发展其他方案就显得必要或是有用。第二空格可以候选 A 或 C。而 A 的第一个词填入后构成了因果关系,而不是转折关系,C 为正确答案。

【重点词条】imperative *adj*. ①祈使的(of, relating to, or constituting the grammatical mood that expresses the will to influence the behavior of another)

②强迫的(having power to restrain, control, and direct)

③必需的(not to be avoided or evaded, necessary) 例 an~ duty

　　　　　　unavailing *adj*. 徒劳的,一事无成的,无效的(not availing, futile, useless)

4.【正确答案】A

【中文释义】代数,尽管对于科学和技术而言仍然是必不可缺的,但不再独占鳌头;它有一个平起平坐的伙伴——离散数学。

【解题分析】空格在 longer 之后,故应填代数过去的状况。而分号句的下半句告之了现在的状况为"有一个平起平坐的伙伴",也就是说明,过去没有哪一个学科可以与代数平等,故过去的代数是独占鳌头的,答案为 A。

【重点词条】preeminent *adj*. 卓越的,杰出的(having paramount rank, dignity, or importance, outstanding)

5.【正确答案】D

【中文释义】展示出了暗中讽刺的精湛技巧,在夜晚谈话的过程中,他说出了好几句暗中侮辱人的话。

【解题分析】句首状语提供了答案。正确答案为 D,有一些同学误选 E,事实上 embellished 是指"装饰过的",它的目的是为了引人注目,而不是隐藏。

【重点词条】blunt *adj*. ①迟钝的(slow or deficient in feeling, insensitive, obtuse in understanding or discernment, dull)

②钝的(having an edge or point that is not sharp)

③粗鲁的(abrupt in speech or manner)

④率直的(being straight to the point, direct)

　　　　　　veiled *adj*. ①有遮蔽的(having or wearing a veil or a concealing cover) 例 a~ hat

②不明言的(characterized by a softening tonal distortion)

③隐藏的(obscured as if by a veil, disguised) 例 ~threats

6.【正确答案】C

【中文释义】保持赌徒的不成功决策策略是幻觉的一个功能,这个幻觉被植根于赌博游戏中,目的是为了误导赌徒并且骗取他们的金钱。

【解题分析】此句是一难句,事实上主干非常简单"The ＿＿ is one ＿＿ of the illusion"。文中有两点是常规的解题点。其一是 gamblers' unsuccessful decision strategies,由于出现了物主代词加特征动作的结构,所以要引起高度重视,由此结构可知赌徒的特征动作就是输。第二个常规解题点就是 in order to,因为它表示了明确的逻辑关系。这两个常规解题点一旦明确,问题就迎刃而解。目的是为了误导赌徒,而赌徒的特征动作又总是不成功的决策策略。由此可知目的得逞了。故第二个空格中可候选 A、B、C、D。而第一个空格的选择仍应按照这个简单的目的结果关系来判断,答案为 C。因为 distortion, prediction 或 restriction 都不是 in order to 之后的目的,当然也就不可能成为其结果。有不少同学将文中的 illusion 理解成庄家所做的迷惑性动作或欺骗局面,实际上题中根本未涉及庄家。句中的 illusion 是指赌博游戏本身所具有的欺骗性,如似有实无的规律性等。这种似有实无的规律性在各种赌博游戏中都有体现。它可以误导赌徒,让其依照此虚幻规律去思考和下注,而实际上一切又落入了设计好的结局里。设计赌博游戏规则的人都是智商超群的人,能在其中设计规律已十分不易,再能在其中设计似是而非的规律就更不容易了,老虎机的设计就是一个高深的任务,非一般人所能及。

【重点词条】**maintenance** *n*. ①维持,保持(the act of maintaining, the state of being maintained, support)

②维修,保养(the upkeep of property or equipment)

③坚持,主张(an officious or unlawful intermeddling in a legal suit by assisting either party with means to carry it on)

7.【正确答案】B

【中文释义】社会史和抒情诗歌的本质是截然相反的,社会史总是描述短暂之物,而抒情诗歌却表达永恒人性的主题,这个永恒的精华远远超越了时尚和经济现象。

【解题分析】上句主语为联合主语,故其判断词只能分为两大类:相同或是不同,这个小规律我们曾在 SECTION 3 的第 6 题中讲述过,请参阅。而下半句中分别论述社会史和抒情诗歌内容,显然是强调两者的不同。因而第一个空格应表达出两者本性不同这一概念,可选 B 或者 D,D 的第二选项却使得社会史和抒情诗歌都描述永恒事物,故不正确。B 的第二个词表现出了两者的不同,故 B 为正确答案。另外一种解法是:下半句中显然是分别论述社会史和抒情诗歌,而句末的分隔中的 beyond 体现了比较的概念,比较双方有一方为抒情诗歌描述的人性,另一方为社会史所描述的经济现象和社会时尚,故可推知社会史所描述的为时间短暂之物,从而第二个空格可以选 B 和 E,而 E 的第一词却认为抒情诗歌和社会史描述的内容是相同的,上下文矛盾,故 B 为正确答案。

【重点词条】**recount** *v*. 详细叙述,描述,列举(to relate in detail, narrate)

fashion *n*. ①时髦 (a distinctive or peculiar and often habitual manner or way)

例 He will, after his sour~, tell you.

②流行式样(the prevailing style such as in dress during a particular time)

③上流社会(social standing or prominence esp. as signalized by

dress or conduct）例 men and women of～

bygone *adj*. 消逝的,往昔的(gone by, past; outmoded)

SECTION 66

1. Exposure to low-intensity gamma radiation slows the rate of growth of the spoilage microorganisms in food in much the same way that the low heat used in pasteurization ____ the spoilage action of the microorganisms in milk.
   (A) precludes
   (B) initiates
   (C) inhibits
   (D) isolates
   (E) purifies

2. In today's world, manufacturers' innovations are easily copied and thus differences between products are usually ____; advertisers, therefore, are forced to ____ these differences in order to suggest the uniqueness of their clients' products.
   (A) crucial. . downplay
   (B) minimal. . reduce
   (C) slight. . exaggerate
   (D) common. . emphasize
   (E) intrinsic. . create

3. To avoid annihilation by parasites, some caterpillars are able to ____ periods of active growth by prematurely entering a dormant state, which is characterized by the ____ of feeding.
   (A) curtail. . suspension
   (B) foster. . continuation
   (C) prevent. . stimulation
   (D) mediate. . synthesis
   (E) invert. . simulation

4. Prior to the work of Heckel, illustrations of fish were often beautiful but rarely ____; this fact, combined with the ____ nature of most nineteenth-century taxonomic descriptions, often kept scientists from recognizing differences between species.
   (A) impressive. . inaccurate
   (B) realistic. . detailed
   (C) traditional. . progressive
   (D) precise. . inexact
   (E) distinctive. . sophisticated

5. Experienced and proficient, Susan is a good, ____ trumpeter her music is often more satisfying than Carol's brilliant but ____ playing.
   (A) virtuoso. . inimitable
   (B) mediocre. . eccentric
   (C) competent. . influential
   (D) amateur. . renowned
   (E) reliable. . erratic

6. In the midst of so many evasive comments, this forthright statement, whatever its intrinsic merit, plainly stands out as ____.
   (A) a paradigm
   (B) a misnomer
   (C) a profundity
   (D) an inaccuracy.
   (E) an anomaly

7. Marshall's confrontational style could alienate almost anyone: he even antagonized a board of directors that included a number of

his supporters and that had a reputation for
not being easily ____.
(A) intimidated
(B) mollified

(C) reconciled
(D) provoked
(E) motivated

SECTION 66 解答

1.【正确答案】C

【中文释义】暴露在低密度的伽玛射线中可降低食品中腐败微生物的生长速度,这种方式与下一种方式相同,即巴斯德消毒法中所使用的低热抑制了牛奶中微生物的腐败作用。

【解题分析】句中的 in much the same way 点明了逻辑关系,所以,空格中的词应该与上句中的 slows the rate of growth 同义,A 是不少同学所选的答案,A 的含义是"阻止,使…不发生",但上文只是减慢了微生物的生长速度,却没有停止它的生长,故 A 并不正确,C 为正确答案。

【重点词条】**preclude** v. 排除,杜绝(to make impossible by necessary consequence, rule out in advance)

purify v. ①使纯化(to make pure, to clear from material defilement or imperfection)

②洗除罪恶(to free from guilt or moral or ceremonial blemish)

③使洁净(to free from undesirable elements)

2.【正确答案】C

【中文释义】在当今世界上,制造商的发明创造很容易被复制,因此,产品之间的差别通常是很小的;广告商们因而被迫来夸大这些差异来说明他们顾客产品的独特性。

【解题分析】由上半句的 and 并列关系可知第一空格可候选 B 和 C,而 B 和 C 的第二个词中能在下半句构成正确语义的是 C,因为 theses differences 就是其后不远的 uniqueness。正确答案为 C。

【重点词条】**downplay** v. 对…轻描淡写,贬低(play down, de-emphasize)

play down 不重视(to attach little importance to, minimize)

de-emphasize v. 贬低(to reduce in relative importance; play down)

intrinsic adj. ①固有的,本质的(belonging to the essential nature or constitution of a thing) 例 the～worth of a gem/the～brightness of a star

②内部的(originating and included wholly within an organ or part) 例 ～muscles

3.【正确答案】A

【中文释义】为了避免被寄生虫消灭,有些毛毛虫能够通过提前成熟进入休眠期而减短生长期,休眠期被停止进食标志出来。

【解题分析】由第一个空格后 by 所揭示的手段与结果关系可轻易推出第一空格应为减短，因为提前成熟的含义就是生长期变短，从而可选出 A，或者由分隔成分的第二个空格入手，休眠期的特征是不进食，这是一个常识，也可直接得出答案 A。

【重点词条】**characterize** *v.* ①描写，叙说（to describe the character or quality of）　例 ~ s him as ambitious

　　　　　　　　　　②以…为特征（to be a characteristic of, distinguish）　例 an era characterized by greed

　　　　　mediate *v.* ①居中（occupying a middle position）

　　　　　　　　　　②调解，起中介作用（acting through an intervening agency）

　　　　　　　　　　③促成（exhibiting indirect causation, connection, or relation）

　　　　　invert *v.* ①使反向（to reverse in position, order, or relationship）

　　　　　　　　　　②使倒置（to turn inside out or upside down）

　　　　　　　　　　③求倒数（to find the mathematical reciprocal of）　例 to divide using fractions, ~ the divisor and multiply

4.【正确答案】D

　【中文释义】在哈尔克的著作之前，鱼的插图通常很美丽但不精确；这个事实，与 19 世纪绝大部分的分类描述的不精确的性质结合在一起就导致科学家不能辨别鱼的各品种之间的差异。

　【解题分析】分号句的下半句指明插图和文字描述都使得科学家分不清品种之间的差异，可见生物学著作中的分类描述和插图都是很糟糕的，第二个空格应填贬义，第一空格由于在 rarely 之后，故应填褒义。第二个空格可候选 A 和 D。在 impressive 和 precise 之间作取舍时，实际上只需考虑哪一属性会导致对鱼这个品种更清楚的认识即可，显然为 D。仅仅是给人留下深刻印象并不能导致清醒的认识，比如可设想鱼的插图全部是漫画，都很生动夸张，给人留下深刻印象，但对于精确描绘鱼的外形却于事无补。

　【重点词条】**illustration** *n.* 插图，图表（something that serves to illustrate, an example or instance that helps make something clear, a picture or diagram that helps make something clear or attractive）

　　　　　taxonomic *adj.* ①分类学的（the study of the general principles of scientific classification, systematics）

　　　　　　　　　　②分类的（classification; orderly classification of plants and animals according to their presumed natural relationships）

5.【正确答案】E

　【中文释义】很有经验并且很熟练，苏珊是一个优秀的，稳定的喇叭手；她的音乐通常比卡罗尔的富有灵感但却极不稳定的表演更加让人满意。

　【解题分析】显然第一空格为褒义，第二空格为贬义，据此就可得答案 E。当然，细加分析会发现两种音乐其一为 reliable，第一个为 erratic，存在着一个尖锐的对比，这正是一套比较结构的要求。

【重点词条】inimitable *adj*. 不能模仿的,无与伦比的(not capable of being imitated, matchless)

influential *adj*. 有权力的,有势力的(exerting or possessing influence)

renowned *adj*. 著名的,有声誉的(having renown, celebrated)

6.【正确答案】E

【中文释义】在如此多支支吾吾的评论之中,这个直率的言论,不管它的本身的价值多少,非常明确地表现为一个反常之物。

【解题分析】文中强调了 evasive 和 forthright 这两个词的对比,并且强调在周围都 evasive 的情况下,他的语言是 forthright,这显然是为了凸现他与别人的迥然不同。故 E 为正确答案。有部分同学误选了 A 的 paradigm,事实上这个思路中就包含了一个没有根据的思路跳跃。并且文中强调他直率的言论本身的价值仍有待疑问,也即这直率的言论有可能是一个错误的言论,此时怎么可能成为一个模范"paradigm"呢? 故正确答案为 E。

【重点词条】evasive *adj*. ①逃避的,回避的,难以捉摸的(tending or intended to evade, equivocal) 例 ~answers

②易消失的

forthright *adj*. ①直率的(without hesitation, frankly)

②立刻的(at once)

③明确的(free from ambiguity or evasiveness, going straight to the point) 例 a~critic/was~in appraising the problem

plain *adj*. ①平坦的(even, level)

②朴素的(lacking ornament, undecorated)

③纯洁的(free of extraneous matter, pure)

④坦白的,清楚的(free of impediments to view, unobstructed)

⑤平易的(characterized by simplicity, not complicated) 例 ~home-cooked meals

misnomer *n*. 错误或使用不当的名称,术语误用(the misnaming of a person in a legal instrument, a use of a wrong name, a wrong name or designation)

7.【正确答案】D

【中文释义】马歇尔对抗性的风格能疏远任何人;他甚至使得整个委员会都成为他的仇敌,这其中包括了一些他的支持者,并且这些委员有不易被激怒的声誉。

【解题分析】文中的 directors 有两个后置的定语从句,构成了一个特殊并列句题型,故这两个定语从句所起的修饰作用应是相同的。第一个定语从句显然是为了强调他对抗的风格过于强烈——甚至他当初的支持者也反对他! 第二个定语从句应有同样的修饰功能,由此可知"这些委员本来有不易与别人成为仇敌的声誉"才是最好的强调方式。五个选项中能表达此意项的为 D。故正确答案为 D。

【重点词条】antagonize *v*. ①使对抗(to act in opposition to, counteract)

②引起…的敌意(to incur or provoke the hostility of)

confrontation n. ①对抗,冲突(the clashing of forces or ideas, conflict)
②比较(comparison) 例 the flashbacks bring into meaning-ful~present and past, near and far

motivate v. 使有动机,激起(to provide with a motive, impel) 例 questions that excite and~youth

SECTION 67

1. Paradoxically, England's colonization of North America was ____ by its success: the increasing prosperity of the colonies diminished their dependence upon, and hence their loyalty to, their home country.

(A) demonstrated

(B) determined

(C) altered

(D) undermined

(E) distinguished

2. Although Harry Stack Sullivan is one of the most influential social scientists of this century, his ideas are now so ____ in our society that they seem almost ____.

(A) novel. . antiquated

(B) revolutionary. . fundamental

(C) commonplace. . banal

(D) disputed. . esoteric

(E) obscure. . familiar

3. Her first concert appearance was disappointingly perfunctory and derivative, rather than the ____ performance in the ____ style we had anticipated.

(A) talented. . tenuous

(B) prosaic. . classic

(C) artistic. . mechanical

(D) inspired. . innovative

(E) literal. . enlightened

4. As is often the case with collections of lectures by ____ authors, the book as a whole is ____, although the individual contributions are outstanding in themselves.

(A) different. . disconnected

(B) incompetent. . abysmal

(C) famous. . systematic

(D) mediocre. . unexciting

(E) various. . coherent

5. Although some consider forcefulness and ____ to be two traits desirable to the same degree, I think that making a violent effort is much less useful than maintaining a steady one.

(A) promptness

(B) persistence

(C) aggression

(D) skillfulness

(E) lucidity

6. The popularity of pseudoscience and quack medicines in the nineteenth century suggests that people were very ____, but the gullibility of the public today makes citizens of yesterday look like hard-nosed ____.

(A) cautious. . educators

(B) sophisticated. . realists

(C) rational. . pragmatists

(D) naive. . idealists

(E) credulous. . skeptics

7. Though extremely _____ about his own plans, the man allowed his associates no such privacy and was constantly _____ information about what they intended to do

next.

(A) idiosyncratic. . altering

(B) guarded. . eschewing

(C) candid. . uncovering

(D) reticent. . soliciting

(E) fastidious. . ruining

SECTION 67 解答

1.【正确答案】D

【中文释义】自相矛盾的是,英国在北美的殖民被它的成功破坏了,殖民地持续的繁荣减少了他们对祖国的依赖性,以及由此而减少了忠诚性。

【解题分析】由 paradoxically 可知下文会出现反义词,故第一个空格应为被成功导致"不成功",五个选项中能表达此含义的为D,故正确答案为D。

【重点词条】**paradoxically** *adv*. ①似非而是地
②自相矛盾地
③悖理地,反常地

2.【正确答案】C

【中文释义】尽管哈雷·史塔克·苏利文是本世纪最有影响的社会科学家之一,但是他的思想在当今社会是如此平凡以至于看上去几乎显得陈腐了。

【解题分析】由转折句可知空格应填贬义词,由于两个空格处于因果句中,故应同为贬义词,符合的选项为C和D,而D的两个选项不能构成因果关系,故答案为C。

【重点词条】**esoteric** *adj*. ①秘传的,只有内行才懂的(designed for or understood by the specially initiated alone) 例 a body of～legal doctrine
②限于小圈子的(of or relating to knowledge that is restricted to a small group, limited to a small circle) 例 ～pursuits
③秘密的(private, confidential) 例 an～purpose

3.【正确答案】D

【中文释义】她的第一次音乐会的表现令人失望地草率并且无新意,而非我们所期待的创新风格的具有灵感的表演。

【解题分析】由 rather than 构成的小连接可轻松推知第一空格应为"有灵感的",而第二空格后的分隔也提供了线索,因为我们失望的是"表演无新意",所以我们期待的必然是"表演有新意",所以第二个空格也应为"有新意的",正确答案为D。

【重点词条】**prosaic** *adj*. ①散文的(characteristic of prose as distinguished from poetry, factual)
②乏味的(dull, unimaginative)
③日常的,平凡的(everyday, ordinary)

derivative *adj.* ①派生的,衍生的(formed by derivation, made up of or marked by derived elements)

②缺乏独创性的,模仿他人的(lacking originality, banal)

enlightened *adj.* ①开明的,文明的(freed from ignorance and misinformation)

例 an~people

②有知识的(based on full comprehension of the problems involved) 例 issued an~ruling

4. 【正确答案】A

【中文释义】正如由不同作者的文章所构成的文集的通常情形那样,本书整体风格是不统一的,尽管个人的作品就自身而言都是很杰出的。

【解题分析】由转折句可知第二空格为贬义词,可候选 A、B 和 D,而一组反义词 as a whole 与 individual 为第一个空格的解题提供了线索,B 和 D 的第一个词肯定不对,因为平庸的作者的文集不管是从整体上看,还是从单篇文章看都会是平庸的,正确答案为 A。

【重点词条】**abysmal** *adj.* ①深不可测的(having immense or fathomless extension downward, backward, or inward) 例 an~cliff

②极度的(immeasurably great, profound) 例 ~ignorance

5. 【正确答案】B

【中文释义】尽管有些人认为强有力的努力和持之以恒是两个同样值得喜爱的品格,但我认为做出激烈的努力没有维持稳定的努力有用。

【解题分析】上下句为两次比较句,只不过上半句的比较句为一个同级比较而已。因而比较双方不应发生变化,下句中的 making a violent effort 重复上文的 forcefulness,故空格应该重复 maintaining a steady one。正确答案为 B。

【重点词条】**promptness** *adj.* ①迅速的,果断的(being ready and quick to act as occasion demands)

②敏捷的,立即的(performed readily or immediately) 例 ~assistance

persistence *n.* 坚持不懈,执意(the action or fact of persisting, the quality or state of being persistent)

6. 【正确答案】E

【中文释义】伪科学和庸医药物在 19 世纪的流行就说明那时候人们是非常容易上当受骗的,但是今天公众轻易上当受骗的性格使昨天的臣民看上去好像精明的怀疑主义者。

【解题分析】由上句可知昨天的臣民至少也不是一个 hard-nosed 的人,而下句却认为今天的人的 fallibility 使得他们看上去 hard-nosed,显然是用了一种反衬的手法。上文的臣民也是非常 gullibility,只不过今天的更加明显而已。故第一空格应填"易上当受骗的",正确答案为 E。

【重点词条】**pragmatist** *n*. ①实用主义(a practical approach to problems and affairs)

例 tried to strike a balance between principles and～

②实践主义(An American movement in philosophy founded by C. S. Peirce and William James and marked by the doctrines that the meaning of conceptions is to be sought in their practical bearings, that the function of thought is to guide action, and that truth is preeminently to be tested by the practical consequences of belief.)

7.【正确答案】D

【中文释义】尽管对自己的计划极端地沉默,但这个男人却不让他的下属有相同的隐私权,并且不断地公开询问他们下一步想干什么的信息。

【解题分析】文中的 such privacy 说明上文已经出现过一次 privacy,只有可能是第一个空格表现出这个男人对自己的计划极端的保密,这样才会出现一个 privacy 的概念。五个选项中符合这一选择的只有 D,故正确答案为 D。

【重点词条】**idiosyncratic** *adj*. 具有个人特质的,个人特性的

guarded *adj*. 谨慎的,小心提防着的,有保留的(cautious, circumspect)

solicit *v*. ①请求(to make petition to, entreat)

②恳求(to approach with a request or plea)

③强烈要求(to urge such as one's cause strongly)

④教唆(to entice or lure esp. into evil)

⑤征求(to try to obtain by usu. urgent requests or pleas)

SECTION 68

1. Having sufficient income of her own constituted for Alice ____ independence that made possible a degreeof ____ in her emotional life as well.

   (A) a material. . security
   (B) a profound. . conformity
   (C) a financial. . economy
   (D) a psychological. . extravagance
   (E) an unexpected. . uncertainty

   tors are paid for creative work, so it would be ____ if expanded protection under these laws discouraged entrepreneurial innovation by increasing fears of lawsuits.

   (A) desirable
   (B) coincidental
   (C) ironic
   (D) natural
   (E) sensible

2. Copyright and patent laws attempt to encourage innovation by ensuring that inven-

3. Unfortunately, since courses in nutrition are often ____ medical school curriculums. a

family physician is,＿＿ to be an enlighten-
ing source of general information about diet.

(A) questioned by. . encouraged

(B) encountered among. . unable

(C) unappreciated by. . expected

(D) neglected in. . unlikely

(E) squeezed into. . intended

4. The success of science is due in great part to
its emphasis on ＿＿: the reliance on evidence rather than ＿＿ and the willingness
to draw conclusions even when they conflict
with traditional beliefs.

(A) causality. . experimentation

(B) empiricism. . facts

(C) objectivity. . preconceptions

(D) creativity. . observation

(E) conservatism. . assumptions

5. James had idolized the professor so much for
so long that even after lunching with her
several times he remained quite ＿＿ in her
presence, and as a result, he could not really
be himself.

(A) pleased

(B) disregarded

(C) heartened

(D) relaxed

(E) inhibited

6. However ＿＿ they might be, Roman poets
were bound to have some favorite earlier author whom they would ＿＿.

(A) subservient. . imitate

(B) independent. . inspire

(C) original. . emulate

(D) creative. . admire

(E) talented. . neglect

7. Human nature and long distances have made
exceeding the speed limit a ＿＿ tradition in
the state, so the legislators surprised no one
when, acceding to public practice, they
＿＿ increased penalties for speeding.

(A) disquieting. . endorsed

(B) long-standing. . considered

(C) controversial. . suggested

(D) cherished. . rejected

(E) hallowed. . investigated

SECTION 68 解答

1.【正确答案】A

【中文释义】有足够多的个人收入构成了艾丽丝物质上的独立性,这就使得情感生活上有
一定程度的保障同样成为可能。

【解题分析】由句首状语可知第一空格可候选 A 和 C,而下文的 as well 则明确表明"情感生
活也具有独立性"这一概念,故选 A。

【重点词条】**security** *n*. ①安全(freedom from danger, safety, freedom from fear or anxiety, freedom from the prospect of being laid off) 例 job~

②保证(something given, deposited, or pledged to make certain
the fulfillment of an obligation)

③公债(an evidence of debt or of ownership such as a stock certifi-
cate or bond)

conformity *n*. ①一致(correspondence in form, manner, or character, agreement) 例 behaved in～with her beliefs

②遵从,顺从(action in accordance with some specified standard or authority) 例 ～to social custom

2.【正确答案】C

【中文释义】版权和专利法企图通过保障发明者能够因他们创造性的工作而得到报酬这种方式来鼓励发明创造,这将会是非常具有讽刺意味的,如果这些法律的保护反而因增加了对诉讼的恐惧而打击了企业的发明创造的热情。

【解题分析】由文中的一组反义词 encourage 和 discouraged 可知专利法的目的和结果恰好相反,因此这是一件非常奇怪,并且可笑的事情,正确答案为 C。

【重点词条】coincidental *adj*. ①巧合的(resulting from a coincidence)

②同时发生的(occurring or existing at the same time)

sensible *adj*. ①明智的,合情理的

②知道的,认识的

③明显的

④可觉察的

3.【正确答案】D

【中文释义】非常不幸的是,既然营养学的课程通常会在医学院的课程中被忽略掉,因此一个家庭医生不可能成为一个食谱常识的启蒙源头。

【解题分析】句首状语 unfortunately 修辞全文,也即主句,故可直接得知第二个空格为医生"不能"提供知识帮助,可选 B 和 D,而 B 和 D 符合因果关系的为 D。故正确答案为 D。

【重点词条】squeeze *v*. ①挤压(to exert pressure esp. on opposite sides of, compress, to extract or emit under pressure, to force or thrust by compression)

②勒索,压榨(to get by extortion, to deprive by extortion, to cause economic hardship to, to reduce the amount of) 例 ～s profits

③挤塞(to crowd into a limited area)

④勉强通过(to gain or win by a narrow margin)

encounter *v*. ①不期而遇(to meet as an adversary or enemy, to engage in conflict with)

②遇上(to come upon face-to-face)

③碰见(to come upon esp. unexpectedly)

4.【正确答案】C

【中文释义】科学的成功很大程度上归功于其强调客观事实:依赖客观证据而不是先入为主的概念,并且愿意得出一些哪怕与传统观点相反的结论。

【解题分析】冒号后表示对前文的重复,reliance on 即是对前文 emphasis on 的重复,所以第一个空格应填 evidence 的同义词,答案为 C。当然也可由 rather than 知第二空

格应为 evidence 的反义词。

【重点词条】preconception *n*. ①先入之见(a preconceived idea)

②成见(prejudice)

causality *n*. ①起因(a causal quality or agency)

②因果关系(the relation between a cause and its effect or between regularly correlated events or phenomena)

5.【正确答案】E

【中文释义】詹姆斯已经崇拜这位教授如此强烈如此长久,以致即使与她几次共进晚餐后,他在她在场时仍然保持非常拘谨,因而他就不能真正地大方起来。

【解题分析】由 and as a result 可推知空格应为 E,即由"拘谨"导致"行为的不自然"。

【重点词条】inhibit *v*. ①制止(to prohibit from doing something)

②抑制(to hold in check, restrain, to discourage from free or spontaneous activity esp. through the operation of inner psychological impediments or of social controls)

idolize *v*. 把…当偶像崇拜,极度崇拜(to worship as a god; to love or admire to excess) 例 the common people whom he so idolized

6.【正确答案】C

【中文释义】不管他们多么具有独创性,罗马的诗人注定会有一些他们所模仿并企图超越的他们所喜爱的早期的作家。

【解题分析】第二空格填上对自己所喜爱的早期作家的态度,故只能选 A、C 和 D,能够构成转折的为 C。尽管 C 和 D 的第一个词是同义词,但 C 的 emulate 具有"模仿"的含义,因而可以与 original 构成转折,正确答案为 C。

【重点词条】subservient *adj*. ①从属的,有帮助的(useful in an inferior capacity, subordinate)

②屈从的,阿谀的(obsequiously submissive, truckling)

7.【正确答案】D

【中文释义】人的本性和长途距离使得超速成为该州受人喜爱的习惯做法;所以当立法者们顺从了公众的实践而拒绝增加对超速的惩罚之时,立法者们没有引起任何人的惊奇。

【解题分析】由上半句可知人们会愿意超速,而下半句中的 acceding to public practice 表明了立法者的态度会认可超速,所以第二空格就不应该增加对超速的惩罚,可直接得答案 D。此句并不难,但有些同学由于思维定势认为超速就应该罚款,而误解句意,事实上美国各州在制定各自的交通法时,措施是非常灵活的,比如佛蒙特州中的沙漠高速公路上就没有速度限制,因而道路指示牌上写着"请司机在你自己认为安全的速度范围内行驶"。

【重点词条】disquieting *adj*. 使人不安的,使人忧虑的(to take away the peace or tranquillity of, disturb, alarm)

hallowed *adj*. 被尊为神圣的,受人崇敬的(holy, consecrated, sacred, revered) 例 ~customs

SECTION 69

1. Though environmentalists have targeted some herbicides as potentially dangerous, the manufacturers, to the environmentalists' dismay,____ the use of these herbicides on lawns.
   (A) defy
   (B) defer
   (C) defend
   (D) assail
   (E) disparage

2. To believe that a culture's achievement can be measured by the ____ of its written material requires one to accept that a page of junk mail is as ____ as a page of great literature.
   (A) nature. . readable
   (B) quality. . prevalent
   (C) timelessness. . understandable
   (D) applicability. . eloquent
   (E) volume. . valuable

3. Given the failure of independent laboratories to replicate the results of Dr. Johnson's experiment, only the most ____ supporters of her hypothesis would be foolish enough to claim that it had been adequately ____.
   (A) fastidious. . defined
   (B) partisan. . verified
   (C) vigilant. . publicized
   (D) enlightened. . researched
   (E) fervent. . undermined

4. Roman historians who study the period 30 B.C. to A.D. 180 can ____ the "Augustan peace" only by failing to recognize that this peace in many respects resembled that of death.
   (A) decry
   (B) applaud
   (C) ridicule
   (D) demand
   (E) disprove

5. Although Tom was aware that it would be ____ to display annoyance publicly at the sales conference, he could not ____ his irritation with the client's unreasonable demands.
   (A) inadvisable. . evince
   (B) efficacious. . suppress
   (C) pragmatic. . counter
   (D) captious. . express
   (E) impolitic. . hide

6. It is no accident that most people find Davis' book disturbing, for it is ____ to undermine a number beliefs they have long ____.
   (A) calculated. . cherished
   (B) annotated. . assimilated
   (C) intended. . denied
   (D) anxious. . misunderstood
   (E) reputed. . anticipated

7. One virus strain that may help gene therapists cure genetic brain diseases can enter the peripheral nervous system and travel to the brain, ____ the need to inject the thera-

peutic virus directly into the brain.

(A)suggesting

(B)intensifying

(C)elucidating

(D)satisfying

(E)obviating

SECTION 69 解答

1.【正确答案】C

【中文释义】尽管环境保护主义者攻击某些除草剂,认为其潜在地非常危险,但制造商们令环境保护主义者们失望,他们支持在草坪上使用这些除草剂。

【解题分析】由 to the environmentalists dismay 可知答案为 C。

【重点词条】**target** *v.* 以…为攻击目标

defy *v.* ①向…挑战(to challenge to combat)

②违抗,反抗(to challenge to do something considered impossible, dare)

③蔑视(to confront with assured power of resistance, disregard) 例 ~ public opinion

④经受得住(to resist attempts at, withstand) 例 The paintings~classification.

2.【正确答案】E

【中文释义】若要相信一种文化的成就可以由其书面材料的数量来衡量,这就要求一个人接受这个观点,即一页纸的三等邮件与一页纸的伟大的文学作品同样具有价值。

【解题分析】第一空格中要求填入书面材料的某种属性,这属性应由下文提供答案,下文提及两种书面材料:伟大的文学作品和三等邮件;涉及两种属性,文字数量和文字质量。故第一个空格应填文字数量或文字质量。若填文字数量则下文的两种文字材料显然是相同的,可以用原句的 as...as 结构来表达;若填文字质量,不管第二个空格填何形容词也不可能正确,都不可能用 as...as 来表达。因为三等邮件的文字质量永远不可能和伟大文学作品的文字质量相等,故空格只能填文字数量。答案为 E。本题的句子采用了反证的手法,这是历年填空考题中惟一的一道。

【重点词条】**junk mail**   三级邮件,(成批大量发出的)邮寄广告宣传品

3.【正确答案】B

【中文释义】考虑到独立实验室不能复制琼森博士的实验,只有对他的假设的最固执的支持者才会愚蠢地宣称她的假设已经被足够多地证明了。

【解题分析】请注意这样的常识,一个实验结果若不能被其他独立的实验室所复制就等同于宣判了这个实验结果的死刑,replicate 或 duplicate 用于科学家复制实验的场合中实际上指的是校验。此句中琼森博士的实验显然是错的,从而她的支持者会愚蠢地称这个实验是"正确的",从而可知第二个空格应选 B 或 E。第一个空格当然应选贬义词,因为这些支持做出了愚蠢的动作。所以答案为 B。

【重点词条】**partisan** *n.* ①坚决支持者(a firm adherent to a party, faction, cause, or person; one exhibiting blind, prejudiced, and unreasoning allegiance)

②帮伙(a member of a body of detached light troops making forays and harassing an enemy)

③游击队员(a member of a guerrilla band operating within enemy lines)

vigilant *adj*. 警戒的,警觉的(alertly watchful esp. to avoid danger)

publicize *v*. 引起公众对…的注意,宣传(to bring to the attention of the public, advertise)

4.【正确答案】B

【中文释义】研究公元前30年到公元180年的罗马史学家们只有在没有认识到这段太平时期在许多方面等同于死亡的条件下才会赞美"奥古斯都太平盛世"。

【解题分析】文中的 only by failing to recognize 提供我们推理的思路,此句为一强调原因的句型,有其独特的推理方式。详细的句型解释请参阅 SECTION 54 的第1题的解答,由"这段太平盛世等同于死亡"可知作者对此时期持批判态度,而主句中反应表现出赞美态度,故答案为B。

【重点词条】**disprove** *v*. 证明…不能成立,证明…虚假(或不正确),反驳(to prove to be false or wrong, refute)

5.【正确答案】E

【中文释义】尽管汤姆清楚知道在产品交易会上公开地表现出愤怒是非常不明智的,但是他不能隐藏自己对顾客的无理要求的愤怒。

【解题分析】第二个空格很好推理,因为文中的 with 表示了一种因果关系,所以可知第二人格可填B、C和E。这样可知下句的含义为他没有隐藏、压抑或控制自己的愤怒,与上句转折后,上句应为他知道公开表现愤怒是不好的行为,因而第一空格为贬义词,B、C和E中应选E的 impolitic。

【重点词条】**inadvisable** *adj*. 不可取的,不妥当的,失策的(not advisable)

counter *v*. ①反对,反击(to act in opposition to, oppose)

②抵消(offset, nullify) 例 tried to～the trend toward depersonalization

③抗辩(to adduce in answer) 例 we～ed that our warnings had been ignored

captious *adj*. ①吹毛求疵的(marked by an often ill-natured inclination to stress faults and raise objections)

②诡辩的(calculated to confuse, entrap, or entangle in argument)

impolitic *adj*. 失策的,不当的,不审慎的(not politic, rash)

6.【正确答案】A

【中文释义】一点都不让人感到意外的是人们觉得戴维斯的书非常讨厌,因为这本书故意破坏一些他们长期喜爱的信仰。

【解题分析】既然戴维斯的书是讨厌的,因此可推知第二个空格中他所破坏的信仰为读者所支持的信仰,故可选 A、B 和 E,而 A、B、E 的第一个词中令人讨厌的态度当然是 A 的 calculated,故正确答案为 A。

【重点词条】**calculated** *adj*. 精心计划的,蓄意的

assimilate *v*. ①吸收消化(to take in and appropriate as nourishment, absorb into the system, to take into the mind and thoroughly comprehend)

②使同化,使趋于一致(to make similar, to alter by assimilation, to absorb into the culture or mores of a population or group)

reputed *adj*. ①驰名的(having a good repute, reputable)

②被一般认定的,普遍认为的(being such according to reputation or popular belief)

7.【正确答案】E

【中文释义】一种可以帮助基因治疗专家治愈脑部遗传疾病的病毒种类可以进入到周围神经系统,然后进入大脑,从而排除了直接注射治疗用的病毒到大脑中的需求。

【解题分析】空格实际上是一分隔结构,只要能重复上文的信息即可。上文宣称病毒可以进入到大脑中,这样就无必要再注射病毒入大脑,故可直接选 E。

【重点词条】**peripheral** *adj*. ①外围的,周边的(of, relating to, involving, or forming a periphery or surface part)

②表面的,周围的(of, relating to, or being part of the peripheral nervous system) 例 ~nerves

③辅助性的(auxiliary, supplementary) 例 ~equipment

inject *v*. ①注射(to introduce into something forcefully) 例 ~fuel into an engine

②注入(to force a fluid into such as for medical purposes)

③引入,插入(to introduce as an element or factor in or into some situation or subject) 例 condemning any attempt to~religious bigotry into the campaign

SECTION 70

1. Artificial light ____ the respiratory activity of some microorganisms in the winter but not in the summer, in part because in the summer their respiration is already at its peak and thus cannot be ____.

(A)stimulates. . lessened

(B)inhibits. . quickened

(C)reflects. . expanded

(D)elevates. . measured

(E)enhances. . increased

2. Doreen justifiably felt she deserved recognition for the fact that the research institute had been ____ a position of preeminence, since it was she who had ____ the transformation.

(A)reduced to. . controlled

(B)raised to. . observed

(C)mired in. . imagined

(D)maintained in. . created

(E)returned to. . directed

3. The prospects of discovering new aspects of the life of a painter as thoroughly studied as Vermeer are not, on the surface,____ .

(A)unpromising

(B)daunting

(C)encouraging

(D)superficial

(E)challenging

4. Even those siblings whose childhood was ____ familial feuding and intense rivalry for their parents' affection can nevertheless develop congenial and even ____ relationships with each other in their adult lives.

(A)scarred by. . vitriolic

(B)dominated by. . intimate

(C)filled with. . truculent

(D)replete with. . competitive

(E)devoid of. . tolerant

5. Because they have been so dazzled by the calendars and the knowledge of astronomy possessed by the Mayan civilization, some anthropologists have ____ achievements like the sophisticated carved calendar sticks of the Winnebago people.

(A)described

(B)acknowledged

(C)overlooked

(D)defended

(E)authenticated

6. Aptly enough, this work so imbued with the notion of changing times and styles has been constantly ____ over the years, thereby reflecting its own mutability.

(A)appreciated

(B)emulated

(C)criticized

(D)revised

(E)reprinted

7. The sea was not an ____ the ____ of the windmill; on the contrary, while the concept of the new invention passed quickly from seaport to seaport, it made little headway inland.

(A)element in. . evolution

(B)issue in. . acceptance

(C)aid to. . designers

(D)obstacle to. . diffusion

(E)impediment to. . creation

SECTION 70 解答

1.【正确答案】E

【中文释义】人造光在冬天,而不能在夏天,增加某些微生物的呼吸作用,部分原因是在夏天它们的呼吸作用早就处于顶峰因而不能再被增加了。

【解题分析】第二个空格处于 and 小连接中,可知 B、C 和 E 候选,又由上下句时间状语的对比,可知第一个空格应为"增加",故答案为 E。

【重点词条】**artificial** *adj.* ①人造的(humanly contrived often on a natural model, man-made) 例 an～limb/～diamonds

②人为的(having existence in legal, economic, or political theory, caused or produced by a human and esp. social or political agency) 例 an～price advantage/～barriers of discrimination

③虚伪的(artful, cunning)

④矫揉造作的(lacking in natural or spontaneous quality) 例 an～smile/an～excitement

elevate *v.* ①提高(to lift up, raise)

②提升(to raise in rank or status, exalt)

③改善(to improve morally, intellectually, or culturally)

④使情绪高昂(to raise the spirits of, elate)

2.【正确答案】E

【中文释义】道林合情合理地觉得她值得表扬,因为这样的事实——这个研究所已经回到了一个杰出的地位,因为是她而不是别人指导了这场转变。

【解题分析】请注意文中的 for the fact 与下句的 since 原因从句都是在对主句做出解释。因而翻译时特意保留了原貌。所以这两个原因实际上就是重复,下句中的 the transformation 应在上文中重复。只有第一个空格可能重复 the transformation,可候选 B 或 E。而 B 选项的 observe 体现不出道林为何应受表扬,E 选项的 direct 却是一个有功劳,值得表扬的动作,故选 E。

【重点词条】**reduce to** ①数量减少

②状态变差

③身分下降

④归结为某种类型

mire *v.* ①使陷入泥潭(to cause to stick fast in or as if in mire)

②使陷入困境(to hamper or hold back as if by mire, entangle)

3.【正确答案】C

【中文释义】发现一个像弗美尔一样被彻底研究过的画家的生活的新的方面的前景是并不让人欢欣鼓舞的,至少表面上看如此。

【解题分析】全句简化后即为"The prospects are not ____"。发现一个被彻底研究过的事物的新的方面当然是不容易的,前途比较渺茫,因此选答案 C。On the surface 在此句中的含义为"从表面上看,从感觉看来"的意思,上文对 prospects 的判断当然指的是感觉上的判断。如果我们是画家,做深入的调查和研究后很可能会得出迥异的结论。

【重点词条】**daunt** *v.* 恐吓,使气馁 (to lessen the courage of, cow, subdue)

prospect *n.* ①预期,展望,指望

②景象,视野

③机会,前景,前程,前途

4.【正确答案】B

【中文释义】即使是那些童年生活中充满了家庭内的仇恨以及为了获得父母亲的爱而导致的强烈竞争的兄弟姐妹也能最终在成年生活中发展出亲切友好甚至是亲密无间的关系。

【解题分析】由第二个空格前的 and 即可判断出第二个空格应为比 congenial 递进的词,答案为 B。

【重点词条】scare $v.$ 使惊吓(to frighten esp. suddenly, alarm)

vitriolic $adj.$ 辛辣的,尖刻的(something felt to resemble vitriol esp. in caustic quality; virulence of feeling or of speech)

intimate $v.$ ①宣布,声明(to make known esp. publicly or formally, announce)

②暗示(to communicate delicately and indirectly, hint)

truculent $adj.$ ①凶残的(feeling or displaying ferocity, cruel, savage)

②致命的(deadly, destructive)

③刻毒的(scathingly harsh, vitriolic)

④好战的(aggressively self-assertive, belligerent)

replete $adj.$ ①充满的(fully or abundantly provided or filled) 例 a book ~ with...delicious details

②肥胖的,强壮的(abundantly fed, fat, stout)

③完备的(complete)

5.【正确答案】C

【中文释义】因为那些古人类学家已经被玛雅文明所拥有的日历和天文学知识如此强烈地惊呆了,他们就忽略了威诺巴林人复杂的雕刻而成的日历棍这样的成就。

【解题分析】此句理解的关键为 dazzled,本意是指"强光眩目而看不清别的事物",比喻义为"因过于痴迷某物而对其他事物漠不关心"。可据此选答案 C。

【重点词条】dazzle $v.$ ①使目眩(to lose clear vision esp. from looking at bright light)

②使倾倒(to arouse admiration by an impressive display)

authenticate $v.$ 证明…是确实可信的(to prove or serve to prove the authenticity of)

6.【正确答案】D

【中文释义】非常恰当的是,这部如此充满了时代与风格变化概念的作品这些年来一直被不停地改编,从而反映出它自身的可变性。

【解题分析】由句首状语可知,这本书所遭受的动作应该与自己所宣称的观点相吻合,即"不停地变化",或由句末的分隔也可知空格中应填"自身的变化"。五个选项中只有 D 的 revise 表示了自身的变化,故正确答案为 D。

【重点词条】apt $adj.$ ①恰当的,适宜的(unusually fitted or qualified, ready) 例 proved an

~tool in the hands of the conspirators

　　②有…倾向的(having a tendency, likely) 例 plants~to suffer from drought

　　③贴切的(suited to a purpose; being to the point) 例 an~quotation

　　④反应敏捷的(keenly intelligent and responsive)

imbue v. ①感染,弥漫(to permeate or influence as if by dyeing) 例 the spirit that~s the new constitution

　　②浸透(to tinge or dye deeply)

7.【正确答案】D

【中文释义】海洋并不是风车传播的阻碍;相反,这个新发明的概念从一个海港快速传播到另外一个海港,但却很少向内陆传播。

【解题分析】此句又为一分号句,上下句应重复。上句中仅出现海洋和风车这两个概念,故下句应重复这两者。显然 the new invention 只能指风车,而 from seaport to seaport 显然是指沿着海港传播。尤其是下句的对比更是揭示了海洋成为风车的传播的途径,而陆地却无法完成风车这个概念传播的任务。上句的第二个空格是最易判断的,因为风车在下半句中只有一个动作发生,那就是 pass,对应于答案 D 的 diffusion,表示风车这个概念的传播。B 的 acceptance 也可勉强接受。而 A、C 和 E 则明显都不是指"传播"这个动作。B 和 D 的第一个词显然是 D 的 obstacle 说明了下句中重复的信息。事实上,本句中的风车是当时人类的一大发明,是一种先进的生产工具。先进的生产工具和方式往往都是沿海洋传播的,这就是为何沿海地区和国家往往比内陆要发达的原因所在。

【重点词条】**headway** n. ①进展,进步(motion or rate of motion in a forward direction, advance, progress)

　　②同向而行的车船距离(the time interval between two vehicles traveling in the same direction on the same route)

diffusion n. ①扩散(the process whereby particles of liquids, gases, or solids intermingle as the result of their spontaneous movement caused by thermal agitation and in dissolved substances move from a region of higher to one of lower concentration)

　　②散射(reflection of light by a rough reflecting surface, transmission of light through a translucent material, scattering)

　　③传播(the spread of cultural elements from one area or group of people to others by contact)

SECTION 71

1. A computer program can provide information in ways that force students to ____ learning instead of being merely ____ of knowledge.

(A) shore up. . reservoirs

(B) accede to. . consumers

(C) participate in. . recipients

(D) compensate for. . custodians

(E) profit from. . beneficiaries

2. The form and physiology of leaves vary according to the _____ in which they develop: for example, leaves display a wide range of adaptations to different degrees of light and moisture.

(A) relationship

(B) species

(C) sequence

(D) patterns

(E) environment

3. One theory about intelligence sees _____ as the logical structure underlying thinking and insists that since animals are mute, they must be _____ as well.

(A) behavior. . inactive

(B) instinct. . cooperative

(C) heredity. . thoughtful

(D) adaptation. . brutal

(E) language. . mindless

4. Though _____ in her personal life, Edna St. Vincent Millay was nonetheless _____ about her work, usually producing several pages of complicated rhyme in a day.

(A) jaded. . feckless

(B) verbose. . ascetic

(C) vain. . humble

(D) impulsive. . disciplined

(E) self-assured. . sanguine

5. The children's _____ natures were in sharp contrast to the even-tempered dispositions of their parents.

(A) mercurial

(B) blithe

(C) phlegmatic

(D) introverted

(E) artless

6. By _____ scientific rigor with a quantitative approach, researchers in the social sciences zmay often have _____ their scope to those narrowly circumscribed topics that are well suited to quantitative methods.

(A) undermining. . diminished

(B) equating. . enlarged

(C) vitiating. . expanded

(D) identifying. . limited

(E) imbuing. . broadened

7. As early as the seventeenth century, philosophers called attention to the _____ character of the issue, and their twentieth-century counterparts still approach it with _____.

(A) absorbing. . indifference

(B) unusual. . composure

(C) complex. . antipathy

(D) auspicious. . caution

(E) problematic. . uneasiness

SECTION 71 解答

1.【正确答案】C

【中文释义】电脑程序提供信息的方式可以强迫学生们参与到学习过程中,而不仅仅是知识的接受者。

【解题分析】分隔结构 instead of being 就提示应与前文反义重复,从而选出正确答案。分隔一般都是同义重复,但当分隔由 whatever, instead of, yet, but 或 very(表转折)引导时,分隔为反义重复前文。

【重点词条】**shore up** ①用支柱支撑(to support by a shore, prop)
②支持(to give support to, brace)

custodian *n.* 看管者,监护人(one that guards and protects or maintains; esp. one entrusted with guarding and keeping property or records or with custody or guardianship of prisoners or inmates)

2. 【正确答案】E

【中文释义】叶子的形态和生理状况会根据其所处的环境的变化而发生变化:比如说,叶子对不同的光照和湿度程度会表现出很多不同的适应性变化。

【解题分析】冒号后是对前文的重复,当然这种重复可以是同义重复、反义重复或上下义重复。此句下文中用了光照和湿度这些词表示决定叶子形态变化的因素,所以上文的空格或者填光照和湿度,或者填能包含它们的上义词,答案 E 和光照湿度构成上下义关系。

【重点词条】**sequence** *n.* ①连续系列(a continuous or connected series)
②次序(order of succession)
③结果,连续性进展(consequence, result; a subsequent development)
④过程的连续(continuity of progression)
v. 连续排列(to arrange in a sequence)

3. 【正确答案】E

【中文释义】一种关于智慧的理论将语言看成思维的最底层的逻辑结构,并且坚持认为,既然动物是没有语言的,它们必然也没有思维。

【解题分析】And 前后为并列关系,and 之前谈到了某物为思维的底层逻辑结构,and 之后继续谈到了两个事物之间的关系,即没有语言就导致空格的发生,所以前后两个事物就应为相同的两个事物,这样才能构成 GRE 填空所特有的重复式的并列句。所以第一空格应和 mute 相关,第二空格应和 thinking 相关,符合该判断的只有 E。

【重点词条】**underlying** (**underly**) *adj.* ①下方的(lying beneath or below) 例 The~rock is shale.;基本的(basic, fundamental)/an investigation of the~issues
②隐含的(evident only on close inspection, implicit)
③优先的(anterior and prior in claim) 例 ~mortgage

thoughtful *adj.* ①思想中的,冥思的(absorbed in thought: meditative; characterized by careful reasoned thinking)

②有思想的（having thoughts; heedful 例 became～about religion; given to or chosen or made with heedful anticipation of the needs and wants of others）

4.【正确答案】D

【中文释义】尽管埃德娜·圣·米利在她个人情感生活中容易冲动,但她对工作却仍然非常有自控能力,总是每天都完成好几页纸的复杂的押韵诗。

【解题分析】一道典型的老题目,某人对工作的态度与日常的态度截然不同,前后两个空格反义即可。而第二空格又由分隔结构提供了答案,能每天都完成好几页的诗歌,这种对工作的态度只有 D 能概括。

【重点词条】jaded adj. ①筋疲力尽的（fatigued by overwork, exhausted）
②厌倦的（dulled by experience or by surfeit）

feckless adj. ①虚弱的（weak, ineffective）
②无意义的（worthless, irresponsible）

ascetic adj. ①苦行的（practicing strict self-denial as a measure of personal and esp. spiritual discipline）
②严谨的,严肃的（austere in appearance, manner, or attitude）

impulsive adj. ①冲动的（having the power of or actually driving or impelling）
②推动的（actuated by or prone to act on impulse）
③突发的（acting momentarily）

discipline n. ①惩罚（punishment）
②学习领域（a field of study）
③纪律,法规（a rule or system of rules governing conduct or activity）

5.【正确答案】A

【中文释义】这小孩喜怒无常的性情和他的父母亲的平和的性情构成了强烈的对比。

【解题分析】In sharp contrast to 前后找反义词即可。

【重点词条】mercurial adj. ①水星特征的（having qualities of eloquence, ingenuity, or thievishness attributed to the god Mercury or to the influence of the planet Mercury）
②多变的（characterized by rapid and unpredictable changeableness of mood）

phlegmatic adj. 懒散的,迟钝的,冷漠的 having or showing a slow and stolid temperament）

6.【正确答案】D

【中文释义】由于认定科学的严谨等同于数量分析方法,社会科学的研究者们经常限制他们的课题到那些非常狭隘的方面,这些方面的课题往往非常适合数量分析方法。

【解题分析】第二个空格的动词与其后的 to 构成搭配,也就是说动词的结果是那些狭隘的课题,所以动词本身就不可能是 B、C、E 的"加大加宽"的意思,只能在 A 和 D 当中选择,而 A 的 undermining 显然不会是它的逻辑主语 researcher 的动作,所以答案选 D。

【重点词条】identify v．①统一化（to cause to be or become identical；to conceive as united）
　　　　　　　　②一致（to be or become the same；to practice psychological identi-fication）例 ～with the hero of a novel

　　　　　　equate v．等同,使相似,使相关（to make equal, equalize）例 ～s disagree-ment with disloyalty

7. 【正确答案】E

【中文释义】早在 17 世纪,哲学家们就提醒人们注意该问题过于困难而不可知的性质,而 20 世纪的哲学家们仍然不能轻松解决这个问题。

【解题分析】And 前后并列,并且 counterparts 这个词实际上就是在提示前后的哲学家们都以相同的态度对待这个问题,所以前后态度相同,应该选同义词。问题是前面是形容词,而后面的空格是名词。这种情况近几年的考卷当中频繁出现,既有词性不同的同义词,也有词性不同的反义词。这种情况下我们需要将它们全部转化为形容词去考虑。比如说该题中,A 选项的 difference 可转化成形容词,即然哲学家们用冷漠、无动于衷的态度对待这个问题,说明这个问题不吸引人,那么第一空格的同义词就应该是不吸引人的,而 A 的第一空格为吸引人的,所以 A 不对。同样由 B 的第二个词 composure,可知该问题不让人感到惊奇,否则就不会 composure(冷静)了,而 B 的第一选项恰恰是非同一般、非同小可的,正好是反义词,同样的思路方式可知 C 和 D 也不对,故选 E。E 前后正好构成了反义词。

【重点词条】problematic adj．棘手的,难以得出最终答案的(so full of difficulty as to make only uncertain solutions possible)

SECTION 72

1. Since most if not all learning occurs through ____, relating one observation to another, it would be strange indeed if the study of other cultures did not also illuminate the study of our own.

(A) assumptions
(B) experiments
(C) comparisons
(D) repetitions
(E) impressions

2. The new ____ of knowledge has created ____ people: everyone believes that his or her subject cannot and possibly should not be understood by others.

(A) specialization. . barriers between
(B) decline. . associations among
(C) redundancy. . complacency in
(D) disrepute. . concern for
(E) promulgation. . ignorance among

3. If a species of parasite is to survive, the host organisms must live long enough for the parasite to ____ ; if the host species becomes ____ , so do its parasites.

   (A) atrophy. . healthy
   (B) reproduce. . extinct
   (C) disappear. . widespread
   (D) succumb. . nonviable
   (E) mate. . infertile

4. The author argues for serious treatment of such arts as crochet and needlework, finding in too many art historians a cultural blindness ____ to their ____ textiles as a medium in which women artists predominate.

   (A) traceable. . prejudice against
   (B) opposed. . distrust of
   (C) referring. . need for
   (D) reduced. . respect for
   (E) corresponding. . expertise in

5. Those who fear the influence of television deliberately ____ its persuasive power, hoping that they might keep knowledge of its potential to effect social change from being widely disseminated.

   (A) promote
   (B) underplay
   (C) excuse
   (D) laud
   (E) suspect

6. Because the high seriousness of their narratives resulted in part from their metaphysics, Southern writers were praised for their ____ bent.

   (A) technical
   (B) discursive
   (C) hedonistic
   (D) philosophical
   (E) scientific

7. Far from being ____ , Pat was always ____ to appear acquiescent.

   (A) unctuous. . loath
   (B) brazen. . reluctant
   (C) ignoble. . concerned
   (D) obsequious. . eager
   (E) gregarious. . willing

SECTION 72 解答

1.【正确答案】C

【中文释义】即使不是全部那也是大多数的学习认识发生在比较当中,也就是将一种观察与另一个观察联系起来考虑,那么这将是非常奇怪的,即如果对其他文化的研究不能同样启迪我们自身文化的研究。

【解题分析】第一空格后紧接着就是一个分隔(分词短语),给空格提供答。五个选项当中表示出将两个事物联系起来考虑的只有 C 答案。

【重点词条】illuminate v. ①启蒙(to enlighten spiritually or intellectually)

②照亮((to supply or brighten with light)

③解释,澄清(to make clear, elucidate)

④用金银或亮丽的色彩或精致的小物品装饰物装饰(to decorate with gold or silver or brilliant colors or with often elaborate designs or miniature picture)

impression *n*. ①影响，印象（a characteristic，trait，or feature resulting from some influence）例 the～on behavior produced by the social milieu

②演员身上的耀眼而俗气的小装饰物

2.【正确答案】A

【中文释义】知识的新专业化分工创造出了人和人之间的障碍：每个人都认为他的或她的专业不可能也不应该被别的人理解。

【解题分析】冒号后表示对前文的重复，冒号后谈到了人和人之间的相互不能理解，由此可以选出 A 和 E，而 E 答案的 promulgation 不但含义是错的——知识的传播导致人的无知，而且 promulgation 在冒号后也没有重复的对应词，而 A 的 specialization 却和下文的 subject 高度相关，且含义正确，故选 A。

【重点词条】**decline** *v*. ①下滑，下降（to slope downward，descend）

②规避（avert，avoid）

③下滑（to cause to bend or bow downward）

④拒绝（to refuse to undertake，undergo，engage in，or comply with）

promulgate *n*. ①公开宣布（to make known by open declaration，proclaim）

②实施（法律），推广宣传（法律）（to make known the terms of laws，to put laws into action）

3.【正确答案】B

【中文释义】如果一种寄生虫的种类要存活下去，寄主生物就必须活得足够的长来让寄生虫繁殖；如果寄主生物绝种的话，寄生虫同样会绝种。

【解题分析】If 条件句出现 to survive 表示目的，而主句中用 for 这个短语表示目的，所以实际上就是重复表达，第一空格可填与 survive 同义的词。另外一个思路是分号句的思路。既然分号句上下句必须同义或反义重复，所以第二空格的动词只有可能填上句中的 live 的同义或反义词。看五个选项即可知，满足条件的只有 B。

【重点词条】**atrophy** *v*. ①萎缩（decrease in size or wasting away of a body part or tissue；

②消耗，消退（a wasting away or progressive decline，degeneration）

例 the～of freedom/was not a solitude of～，of negation，but of perpetual flowering

succumb *v*. ①屈服（to yield to superior strength or force or overpowering appeal or desire）

②被征服，压垮；死于（to be brought to death by the effect of destructive or disruptive forces）

nonviable *adj*. 不能生存的，不可行的

4.【正确答案】A

【中文释义】这位作者支持严肃地对待诸如编织和刺绣这些艺术形式,他发现在大多数艺术史学家当中存在一个文化上的错误见解,这种错误见解可追溯到他们对编织物这种艺术媒介的偏见,即在编织物这一领域女艺术家占据着无与伦比的优势地位。

【解题分析】Finding 所引导的这一分隔当中的文化误解(culture blindness)显然是和上文的正确见解(serious treatment)相反,故大多数艺术史学家的错误之处就在于他们不严肃认真地对待编织物。第二个空格前为 their 这个物主代词,根据我们总结的规律,物主代词后填该人物的特征动作或特征性格,故第二个空格应填大多数艺术史学家的特征动作,在此句中,当然就是指不严肃认真的对待编织物。此时,可以候选的答案为 A 和 B,B 的第一个词 opposed 错误,因为前后并没有反对、对立的意思,相反却应为相同,而 A 的第一个词正好表达了大多数艺术史学家的错误见解也就是他们的偏见这个意思。

【重点词条】argue v. ①理论,推理(to give reasons for or against something, reason)

②争辩(to contend or disagree in words, dispute)

predominate v. ①占绝大多数 (to hold advantage in numbers or quantity)

②占主导地位的(to exert controlling power or influence, pre-vail)

5.【正确答案】B

【中文释义】那些害怕电视影响力的人故意地削弱电视的说教能力,希望这样可以使得电视具有潜能来影响社会改变的事实不能被广为传播。

【解题分析】Hoping 所引导的分隔重复前文,分隔中的关键词组是"keep...from..."。由分隔可知他们是在有意识地隐瞒电视的这种潜能,正确答案为 B。答案 E 是有些同学误选的答案。事实上,这些人并不是怀疑电视有没有这种能力,而是非常清楚地认识到了这一点,并由此而产生了恐惧并希望努力消除电视的影响。

【重点词条】underplay v. 对…轻描淡写,贬低…的重要性(downplay)

disseminate v. 散播,传播,散布 (to spread abroad as though sowing seed)

6.【正确答案】D

【中文释义】由于南方作家们高度严肃认真的叙述,这种严肃认真部分上是由他们的形而上学导致的,所以南方作家们由于他们的哲学倾向而受到了一致好评。

【解题分析】如果熟悉填空句的答案必然会在原文当中重复的特点的话,这个句子读完后就应知道空格里或者填 serious 或者填 metaphysic,这时候符合条件的选项只剩下一个答案 D。

【重点词条】discursive adj. ①离题的(moving from topic to topic without order, rambling)

②推论的(marked by analytical reasoning)

philosophical adj. ①哲学的(of or relating to philosophers or philosophy)

②镇定自若的,超然的 (characterized by the attitude of a philosopher; calm or unflinching in face of trouble, defeat, or loss)

transcendental *adj*. ①超越的,卓越的(transcendent)

②超自然的(supernatural)

③抽象的,玄奥的(abstruse, abstract)

④先验的,超验的(of or relating to transcendentalism)

metaphysic *n*. 形而上学

7.【正确答案】A

【中文释义】并不愿意逆来顺受,帕特不愿意表现出逆来顺受的姿态。

【解题分析】Far from 就提示我们前后应为反义词,而第二空格的五个选项中,或者是愿意,或者是不愿意,答案 C 的 concerned 与前后构成一个词组 be concerned to do sth,意思是"非常愿意、很有兴趣地做某事",仍然是愿意的意思。所以第一个空格和下文构成反义,那么或者是 acquiescent 的同义,或者是反义。表示出这两个含义之一的词只有 A 和 D,并且都是不愿意 acquiescent 的意思,A 和 D 的第二个选项一个为 loath,一个为 eager,能构成上下句反义的当然是 A。该句的解题中,句子结构和逻辑关系都很好判断,但选词却很难,需要对词义有较精确的了解,这也是新题的一个明显倾向。

【重点词条】**unctuous** *adj*. ①甜言蜜语的,虚情假意的(marked by ingratiating and false earnetness)

②逆来顺受的,无可奈何地接受的(comply tacitly or passively)

obsequious *adj*. 奉承拍马的(marked by or exhibiting a fawning attentiveness)

gregarious *adj*. ①合群的(tending to associate with others of one's kind, social)

②群居的(growing in a cluster or a colony; living in contiguous nests but not forming a true colony)

acquiescent *adj*. 默许的,无可奈何地接受的(inclined to acquiesce)

acquiesce *v*. 默许,无可奈何地接受(to accept or comply tacitly or passively, accept as inheritable or inhdisputable) 例 ~ political sociologists today are often relunctant to ~ to Michels' law

SECTION 73

1. Though ____ to some degree, telling a small lie sometimes enables one to avoid ____ another's feelings.

   (A) necessary. . mollifying

   (B) regrettable. . harming

   (C) unfortunate. . exaggerating

   (D) attractive. . considering

   (E) difficult. . resisting

2. Perhaps because scientists have been so intrigued by dogs' superior senses of smell and hearing, researchers have long ____ their eyesight, assuming that they inhabit a drab, black-and-white world, devoid of color.

(A) studied

(B) coveted

(C) appreciated

(D) resented

(E) underestimated

3. Despite a string of dismal earnings reports, the two-year-old strategy to return the company to profitability is beginning to ____.

(A) falter

(B) disappoint

(C) compete

(D) work

(E) circulate

4. The President reached a decision only after lengthy ____, painstakingly weighing the ____ opinions expressed by cabinet members.

(A) deliberation. . divergent

(B) confrontation. . unanimous

(C) relegation. . consistent

(D) speculation. . conciliatory

(E) canvassing. . arbitrary

5. Although just barely ____ as a writer of lucid prose, Jones was an extremely ____ editor who worked superbly with other writers in

helping them improve the clarity of their writing.

(A) deficient. . muddling

(B) proficient. . contentious

(C) adequate. . capable

(D) appalling. . competent

(E) engaging. . inept

6. The accusations we bring against others should be ____ ourselves; they should not ____ complacency and easy judgments on our part concerning our own moral conduct.

(A) definitions of. . produce

(B) instructions to. . equate

(C) denigrations of. . exclude

(D) warnings to. . justify

(E) parodies of. . satirize

7. Although the meanings of words may necessarily be liable to change, it does not follow that the lexicographer is therefore unable to render spelling, in a great measure,____.

(A) arbitrary

(B) superfluous

(C) interesting

(D) flexible

(E) constant

SECTION 73 解答

1.【正确答案】B

【中文释义】尽管某种程度上让人后悔,但有时撒个小谎却使人能够避免伤害别人的感情。

【解题分析】Enable one to avoid 这种语言表达就充分提示第二空格是贬义词,因为我们要避免的当然是坏的情况,这时可以候选的是 B 和 E,而又能构成上下句转折的是 B。

【重点词条】**resist** *vt*. ①抵抗,反抗(to exert oneself so as to counteract or defeat)

②忍耐(to withstand the force or effect of)

2.【正确答案】E

【中文释义】可能是由于科学家已经如此地痴迷于狗的超级的嗅觉和听觉能力,研究者们长期以来低估了狗的视觉,认为狗生活在一个单调的、黑白的、缺乏色彩的世界里。

【解题分析】分隔结构重复前文,分隔中认为狗辨别不出色彩,所以空格的动词当然是认为狗的视觉能力不好的一个判断,符合这一要求的只有 E。

【重点词条】**covet** *v.* 贪求,垂涎（wish for enviously）

3. 【正确答案】D

【中文释义】尽管有一长串的令人沮丧的收入报告,这个两年期的扭亏为盈的计划已经开始起作用。

【解题分析】有一些同学被主语 strategy to 后的一长串单词所迷惑,事实上,诸如 fascination with, plan of, book about, idea of 等等结构中,具体的计划内容、具体的思想内容等都不重要,重要的是对这个思想或这本书的判断。该句中只有一个简单的转折关系,空格的词显然应和 dismal 构成对比,正确答案不言而喻选 D。

【重点词条】**circulate** *v.* ①绕圈,循环（to move in a circle, circuit, or orbit） 例 blood～s through the body

                  ②传递,传播（to pass from person to person or place to place） 例 rumors circulated through the town

4. 【正确答案】A

【中文释义】这位总统在长时间的深思熟虑后才会得出决定,(他)总是煞费苦心地反复权衡由内阁成员所表达的不同观点。

【解题分析】第一个空格后紧接一个分隔成分,第一个空格显然应填 weighing"反复权衡思考"的意思。答案 A 和 D 候选,而 D 的 speculation 更强调哲学家的思索,而不是政治家的思考,并且 D 的第二个词也不对,需要反复权衡的应该是不同的观点。

【重点词条】**weigh** *v.* ①称重（to ascertain the heaviness of by or as if by a balance）

                  ②衡量,比较（to consider carefully by balancing opposing factors or aspects in order to reach a choice or conclusion: evaluate）

         relegate *v.* ①放逐（to send into exile: banish）

                  ②降职（to assign to a place of insignificance or of oblivion, put out of sight or mind）

         conciliatory *adj.* ①讨好的（to gain goodwill by pleasing acts）

                  ②抚慰的（to make compatible, reconcile）

5. 【正确答案】C

【中文释义】尽管只是一个勉强合格的文句清晰的作家,但琼斯却是一个极为胜任的编辑,在帮助其他作家提高他们语句的清晰程度时,他工作得极为出色。

【解题分析】第二个空格为形容词,修饰 editor,而 editor 后又来了一个定语从句作分隔,故第一个空格应与定语从句同义,可以选 C 和 D,再根据上下文的转折关系可知答案为 C。

【重点词条】muddling v. ①使浑浊（to make turbid or muddy）

②使迷惑（to befog or stupefy with liquor）

③使混乱（to mix confusedly；to make a mess of, bungle）

contentious adj. ①有异议的（likely to cause contention）例 a～argument

②好争吵的（exhibiting an often perverse and wearisome tendency to quarrels and disputes）例 a man of a most～nature

adequate adj. ①足够的（sufficient for a specific requirement）例 Her first performance was merely～.

②充分的（lawfully and reasonably sufficient）

appalling adj. 令人震惊的，骇人听闻的（inspiring horror, dismay, or disgust）例 living under～conditions

6.【正确答案】D

【中文释义】我们对别人的指责非难应该成为对我们自己的警醒；这些指责非难不应该用于开脱我们自己德行操守中的自身的自高自大和草率判断等错误。

【解题分析】分号句上下句重复，当然这种重复同样是可以有三种方式：同义、反义、上下义。上下句的主语相同，谓语分别由 should 和 should not 引导，可见相应的动词应为一组反义词。

【重点词条】warning n. ①警告（the act of warning, the state of being warned）例 he had ～of his illness

②警示物（something that warns or serves to warn）

justify v. ①证明是正确的（to prove or show to be just, right, or reasonable）

②证明无罪，开释。

7.【正确答案】E

【中文释义】尽管单词的意义必然会变化，但这并不意味着词典的编写者们就不能将单词的拼写大致保持不变。

【解题分析】前后转折，上文为 change，故下文的拼写应保持不变。下半句只不过用了双重否定句来加大这一题的难度而已。It does not follow that 是一个学术文章中常见的句式，表否定的意思。与之类似的是 It does not require that，也表示否定，require 的意思是"必然产生，必然导致"。

【重点词条】render v. ①传递（to transmit to another, deliver）

②放弃，屈服（give up, yield）

③归还（to give in return or retribution）

④致使（to cause to be or become, make）例 enough rainfall...to～irrigation unnecessary

liable adj. ①有责任的，有义务的（obligated according to law or equity, responsible）

②容易导致,倾向于(being in a position to incur) 例 ～ to a fine

be liable to sth　易遭受
be liable for sth　为…负责

SECTION 74

1. Some activists believe that because the health-care system has become increasingly ____ to those it serves, individuals must ____ bureaucratic impediments in order to develop and promote new therapies.
   (A) attuned. . avoid
   (B) inimical. . utilize
   (C) unresponsive. . circumvent
   (D) indifferent. . supplement
   (E) sensitized. . forsake

2. The acts of vandalism that these pranksters had actually ____ were insignificant compared with those they had ____ but had not attempted.
   (A) hidden. . renounced
   (B) advocated. . meditated
   (C) inflicted. . dismissed
   (D) committed. . effected
   (E) perpetrated. . contemplated

3. Though one cannot say that Michelangelo was an impractical designer, he was, of all nonprofessional architects known, the most ____ in that he was the least constrained by tradition or precedent.
   (A) pragmatic
   (B) adventurous
   (C) empirical
   (D) skilled
   (E) learned

4. Before adapting to changes in values, many prefer to ____, to ____ the universally a-greed-on principles that have been upheld for centuries.
   (A) innovate. . protect
   (B) resist. . defend
   (C) ponder. . subvert
   (D) vacillate. . publicize
   (E) revert. . ignore

5. Although the records of colonial New England are ____ in comparison with those available in France or England, the records of other English colonies in America are even more ____.
   (A) sporadic. . irrefutable
   (B) sparse. . incontrovertible
   (C) ambiguous. . authoritative
   (D) sketchy. . fragmentary
   (E) puzzling. . unquestionable

6. High software prices are frequently said to ____ widespread illegal copying, although the opposite—that high prices are the cause of the copying—is equally plausible.
   (A) contribute to
   (B) result from
   (C) correlate with
   (D) explain
   (E) precede

7. Because early United States writers thought that the mark of great literature was grandiosity and elegance not to be found in

common speech, they ____ the vernacular.

(A) dissected
(B) avoided
(C) misunderstood
(D) investigated
(E) exploited

SECTION 74 解答

1.【正确答案】C

【中文释义】某些行动家认为,既然健康保健体系越来越对它所服务的病人冷淡,人们就必须规避官僚的阻碍来发展和促进新的治疗体系。

【解题分析】后文的目的短语表示出要发展新的方案,所以可知旧的保健体系是为大家抛弃的体系,由此可知第一空格应描述该健康体系的为人所厌恶的性质。这时可选答案 B、C 和 D,而这三个答案的第二个选项动词中只有 C 正确。

【重点词条】**attune** *v*. ①使和谐(to bring into harmony, tune)

②使警觉,调节(to make aware or responsive) 例 ~ businesses to changing trends

responsive *adj*. ①做出反应的(giving response, constituting a response, answering) 例 a~glance/~aggression

②反应敏捷的(quick to respond or react appropriately or sympathetically, sensitive)

forsake *v*. 放弃,抛弃(to renounce or turn away from entirely) 例 Friends have forsaken her/forsook the theater for politics.

2.【正确答案】E

【中文释义】这些恶作剧的人所真正做出的蓄意破坏行为,与他们曾谋划过但又没有实施的行为相比实在是微不足道的。

【解题分析】请注重词组 compared with,它表示了一种比较。在句子填空当中,凡是一套比较结构都意味着比较双方两个事物是相反的,两套比较结构时比较双方应该上下句重复。这几年的新考题中这个规律得到了反复的映证。当然现在考题的比较结构有了更多的方式,不仅仅有 more...than...,还有 as...as...,to the same degree 等同级比较,或 beyond 等不显眼的词或词组表现出的差级比较。大家需要注意辨认。该句中由前后比较可知应将 attempt 填到第一空中,也就是说真正做了的动作和没有做过的动作对比。符合这一要求的有 D 和 E,而 D 的第二个词完全不能和 but 之后构成正确的转折,故正确答案为 E。

【重点词条】**renounce** *v*. ①声明放弃(to give up, refuse, or resign usu. by formal declaration) 例 ~ his errors

②反对,批判(to refuse to follow, obey, or recognize any further, repudiate) 例 ~ the authority of the church

inflict *v*. ①冲突,使痛苦(afflict)

②使遭受,强加(to give by or as if by striking) 例 ~ pain/~ heavy losses

> **committee** *v.* ①任命(to put into charge or trust, entrust)
> ②实施,施行(to carry into action deliberately, perpetrate)
> 例 ~a crime
> ③有义务做(obligate, to pledge or assign to some particular course or use) 例 all available troops were committed to the attack
>
> **contemplate** *v.* ①沉思(to view or consider with continued attention, meditate on)
> ②预期(to view as contingent or probable or as an end or intention)
>
> **perpetrate** *v.* 犯罪(commit)

3. 【正确答案】B

　【中文释义】尽管不能称米开朗基罗是一个不切实际的设计家,但是他在所有已知的非职业的建筑家当中却是最具有创新精神的,因为他最不局限于传统或先例。

　【解题分析】空格和后面的 in that 构成一个最直接的因果关系,符合这一因果关系的只有 B,我们解题时往往只需要抓住与空格直接相关的那个逻辑关系去思考,因为最直接的也就是最准确,最简单的。

　【重点词条】**adventurous** *adj.* ①喜欢冒险的(disposed to seek adventure or to cope with the new and unknown) 例 an~explorer
> ② 充满危险的(characterized by unknown dangers and risks) 例 an~journey
>
> **learned** *adj.* ①有学问的(characterized by or associated with learning: erudite)
> ②学术上的(acquired by learning) 例 ~behavior

4. 【正确答案】B

　【中文释义】在接受价值观的改变之前,很多人倾向于抵制,反而是支持已经被信奉了几个世纪的广为接受的原则。

　【解题分析】Before 引出一个时间对比型,所以第一空格应填 adapt 的反义词,而第二个空格是重复前文,所以也仍然是不接受新价值观的意思,双重否定的说法就是支持老的价值观,可以选 A 和 B,再结合第一个空填 adapt 反义词的判断可得正确答案 B。

　【重点词条】**ponder** *v.* ①评价(to weigh in the mind, appraise) 例 ~ed their chances of success
> ②考虑(to think about, reflect on) 例 ~ed the events of the day
>
> **vacillate** *v.* ①摇摆不定的(to sway through lack of equilibrium, fluctuate, oscillate)
> ②犹豫不定(to waver in mind, will, or feeling, hesitate in choice of opinions or courses)

revert *v.* ①回复（to come or go back to a former condition, period, or subject）

②回归（to return to the proprietor or his heirs at the end of a reversion）

5. 【正确答案】D

【中文释义】尽管新英格兰殖民地的档案与在法国和英国可获得的档案相比是非常粗略的,但在美洲的其他英国殖民地的档案更加支离破碎。

【解题分析】前后都是简单的判断句,两个判断词之间的关系由 even more 表现了出来,应为递进关系,满足的选项为 D。

【重点词条】**sketchy** *adj.* ①粗线条的(of the nature of a sketch, roughly outlined)

②粗略的（wanting in completeness, clearness, or substance, slight, superficial）

fragmentary *adj.* 由碎片组成的,断断续续的(consisting of fragments, incomplete)

6. 【正确答案】B

【中文释义】高的软件价格总是被称为广泛的盗版的结果,尽管相反的说法——高价格是盗版的原因——同样合情合理。

【解题分析】The opposite 提示出了上下句的关系为对立面反义,所以空格里填下句 cause 的反义词即可。

【重点词条】**correlate** *n.* ①相关物,互补物(either of two things so related that one directly implies or is complementary to the other)

②相关,关联

7. 【正确答案】B

【中文释义】因为早期的美国作家认为伟大文学作品的标记是华丽和优雅,这两者都不可能在日常方言口语中找到,所以他们避免方言口语。

【解题分析】Vernacular 和 common speech 同义,上文否定了 common speech,认为其不优雅、不精致,所以第二空格应继续否定 vernacular,B 答案正确。C 答案的 misunderstood 并不表示作家们主动否定方言土语,同时也不是上文原因句所能得出的结果。

【重点词条】**dissect** *v.* ①把～切成碎片,解剖(to separate into pieces, expose the several parts for scientific examination)

②仔细研究,分析(to analyze and interpret minutely)

exploit *v.* ①开发,开采(to make productive use of, utilize) 例 ～ing your talents／～your opponent's weakness

②剥削（to make use of meanly or unjustly for one's own advantage）

例 ～ing migrant farm workers

SECTION 75

1. While scientists dismiss as fanciful the idea of sudden changes in a genetic code (spontaneous mutation), it is possible that nature, like some master musician,＿＿ on occasion, departing from the expected or predictable.
   (A) repeats
   (B) improvises
   (C) ornaments
   (D) corrects
   (E) harmonizes

2. Despite the ＿＿＿ of time, space, and history, human societies the world over have confronted the same existential problems and have come to remarkably ＿＿＿ solutions, differing only in superficial details.
   (A) continuity. . identical
   (B) uniformity. . diverse
   (C) actualities. . varied
   (D) contingencies. . similar
   E) exigencies. . unique

3. Although he was known to be extremely ＿＿＿ in his public behavior, scholars have discovered that his diaries were written with uncommon ＿＿＿.
   (A) reserved. . frankness
   (B) polite. . tenderness
   (C) modest. . lucidity
   (D) reticent. . vagueness
   (E) withdrawn. . subtlety

4. With the ＿＿＿ of scientific knowledge, work on the new edition of a textbook begins soon after completion of the original.

   (A) limitation
   (B) culmination
   (C) veneration
   (D) certainty
   (E) burgeoning

5. She is most frugal in matters of business, but in her private life she reveals a streak of ＿＿＿.
   (A) antipathy
   (B) misanthropy
   (C) virtuosity
   (D) equanimity
   (E) prodigality

6. If the state government's latest budget problems were ＿＿＿, it would not be useful to employ them as ＿＿＿ examples in the effort to avoid the inevitable effects of short-sighted fiscal planning in the future.
   (A) typical. . representative
   (B) exceptional. . aberrant
   (C) anomalous. . illuminating
   (D) predictable. . helpful
   (E) solvable. . insignificant

7. Just as some writers have ＿＿＿ the capacity of language to express meaning, Giacometti ＿＿＿ the failure of art to convey reality.
   (A) scoffed at. . adjured
   (B) demonstrated. . exemplified
   (C) denied. . refuted
   (D) proclaimed. . affirmed
   (E) despaired of. . bewailed

SECTION 75 解答

1.【正确答案】B

【中文释义】尽管科学家轻视这种思想——遗传代码的突发变异,即自发变异——为奇思异想,但是有可能大自然会像某些音乐大师一样偶尔即兴演奏,远非所期待的,或可预料得到的。

【解题分析】空格之后出现的一段分隔"departing from the expected or predictable"显然是给空格提供答案的,五个选项中能表达出这个分隔的为 B 的 improvises。故正确答案为 B。

【重点词条】spontaneous *adj.* ①自发的(proceeding from natural feeling or native tendency without external constraint)

②突发的(arising from a momentary impulse)

③内控的 (controlled and directed internally, self-acting)

例 ~movement characteristic of living things

④自然生成的(produced without being planted or without human labor, indigenous)

⑤非外力影响的(developing without apparent external influence, force, cause, or treatment)

⑥自然的(not apparently contrived or manipulated, natural)

improvise *v.* ①即兴创作(to compose, recite, play, or sing extemporaneously; to make, invent, or arrange offhand)

②临时准备 (to fabricate out of what is conveniently on hand)

harmonize *v.* 协调(to play or sing in harmony; to be in harmony)

2.【正确答案】D

【中文释义】尽管时间,空间,历史和各种人类社会形态具有偶然性,但以上种种世界却面临着相同的问题,并且得出了高度类似的解决方案,差别只是存在于琐碎的细节之中。

【解题分析】由第二个空格之后的分隔"differing only in superficial details"可知第二空格只能选 A 和 D,并且 D 更好,因为分隔中指明仍存在一些细微的差异,而并非完全 identical。由 A 和 D 的第一个词来看,构成转折的也为 D,故正确答案为 D。

【重点词条】contingency *n.* ①偶然性(the quality or state of being contingent)

②偶然事件(a contingent event or condition)

identical *adj.* ①同一的(being the same, selfsame) 例 the~place we stopped before

②一致的(having such close resemblance as to be essentially the same) 例 ~hats

③同源的,同因的(having the same cause or origin) 例 ~infec-
tions

exigency n. ①苛求(that which is required in a particular situation usu. used in
pl.)

②紧急性,紧急事件(the quality or state of being exigent;a state
of affairs that makes urgent demands) 例 A leader must act in
any sudden ~.

3.【正确答案】A

【中文释义】尽管他广为人知的是在他的公开行动中极端地拘谨沉默,但学者们发现他的
日记却是以非同一般的坦率态度而写就的。

【解题分析】由转折关系可轻松得知两个空格应为一组反义词,分别表示他在公开行为中和个
人日记中的相反态度,五个选项构成一组反义词的选项为 A,故 A 为正确答案。

【重点词条】withdrawn adj. ①孤立的,孤独的(removed from immediate contact or easy
approach, isolated)

②性格孤僻的(socially detached and unresponsive, exhibiting withdrawal, introverted)

subtlety n. 微妙,精明,敏感(the quality or state of being subtle;something
subtle)

4.【正确答案】E

【中文释义】由于科学知识日新月异的发展,教科书新版本的编辑工作在原作之后不久就
开始了。

【解题分析】句中的 with 是填空中一再出现的表示因果或条件关系的连词,此文中的 with
表因果,因此我们阅读时要注意寻找上下句的关系,事实上本句中除了将 scientific knowledge 和下句的 textbook 联系起来之外,上下句几乎无法找到任何
相关联之处,所以思路中应将 scientific knowledge 和 textbook 等同起来,事实
上教科书就是记述科学知识的,所以教科书的不停更新就代表着科学知识的
不断更新,故空格应填科学的"更新",正确答案为 E。

【重点词条】burgeon v. ①萌芽(sprout)

②迅速成长(to grow and expand rapidly, flourish)

culmination n. ①终极行为(the action of culminating)

②顶点(culminating position, climax)

5.【正确答案】E

【中文释义】她在商业事务中非常节省,但在她的个人生活中却展示出一系列的挥霍行为。

【解题分析】文中的 in mattes of business 与 in her private life 显然是一组反义的状语,相应
地,空格应与上文的 frugal 相反义,故正确答案为 E。

【重点词条】streak n. ①条纹(a line or mark of a different color or texture from the ground,
stripe)

②细小的光线(a narrow band of light, a lightning bolt)

③痕迹(a slight admixture, trace) 例 had a mean～in him

    misanthropy *n*. 厌恶人类 (a hatred or distrust of mankind)

    equanimity *n*. ①镇定,平静(evenness of mind esp. under stress)

        ②平衡(right disposition,balance)

6.【正确答案】C

【中文释义】如果政府最新的预算问题是反常的,这样做,即避免在未来岁月中目光短浅的财政计划会出现的必然后果的努力中,利用它们作为启迪性的例子,是无益的。

【解题分析】全句为一条件结果句结构,好的条件导致好的结果,坏的条件导致坏的结果。该句中的结果已经明确指明为"not useful",故第一个空格应为贬义词,可以候选的只有C,故C为正确答案。

【重点词条】**solvable** *adj*. 可溶解的,可解释的(susceptible of solution or of being solved, resolved, or explained)

    illuminate *v*. ①启蒙(to enlighten spiritually or intellectually)

        ②照亮(to supply or brighten with light)

        ③解释,澄清(to make clear, elucidate)

        ④用金银或亮丽的色彩或精致的小物品来装饰物来装饰(to decorate with gold or silver or brilliant colors or with often elaborate designs or miniature pictures)

7.【正确答案】E

【中文释义】正如一些作家对于语言的表达能力感到绝望一样,Giacometti 为艺术表达现实的失败而痛苦不堪。

【解题分析】该句所讲述的观点与 SECTION 18 中的第7题的观点是一模一样的,大家可以将这个观点记忆到脑海中,这是 ETS 的另外一个固定观点。在解题时应注意到两个常见的解题点,其一是 just as 表示了上下句的同义重复,其二是上半句中的 express 与下半句中的 convey 为同义重复,从而可知"艺术表达现实"也即上句"语言表达现实",从而知上半句中的"语言表达现实"也应该是失败的,故可选C和E或A,第二个词应继续完成上下文的这个同义重复含义,故E为正确答案。

【重点词条】**abjure** *v*. ①发誓放弃(to renounce upon oath)

        ②郑重放弃(to reject solemnly)

    exemplify *v*. ①用例子来展示(to show or illustrate by example)

        ②公证(to make an attested copy or transcript of a document under seal)

        ③证明(to be an instance of or serve as an example, embody)

        ④成为典型(to be typical of)

    bewail *v*. ①痛哭(to wail over)

②通过痛哭来表示深深的悲痛(to express deep sorrow by wailing and lamentation) 例 wringing her hands and～ing her fate

SECTION 76

1. In spite of the fact that it is convenient to divide the life span of animals into separate stages such as prenatal, adolescent, and senescent, these periods are not really ____.
   (A) advanced
   (B) variable
   (C) repeatable
   (D) connected
   (E) distinct

2. Although the number of reported volcanic eruptions has risen exponentially since 1850, this indicates not ____ volcanic activity but rather more widespread and ____ record keeping.
   (A) abating. . detailed
   (B) increasing. . systematic
   (C) substantial. . erratic
   (D) stable. . superficial
   (E) consistent. . meticulous

3. The challenge of interpreting fictional works written under politically repressive regimes lies in distinguishing what is ____ to an author's beliefs, as opposed to what is ____ by political coercion.
   (A) innate. . understood
   (B) organic. . imposed
   (C) contradictory. . conveyed
   (D) oblique. . captured
   (E) peripheral. . demanded

4. I am often impressed by my own ____ other

people's idiocies: what is harder to ____ is that they, in their folly, are equally engaged in putting up with mine.
   (A) analysis of. . justify
   (B) forbearance toward. . underestimate
   (C) exasperation with. . credit
   (D) involvement in. . allow
   (E) tolerance of. . appreciate

5. Despite vigorous protestations, the grin on the teenager's face ____ her denial that she had known about the practical joke before it was played on her parents.
   (A) belied
   (B) illustrated
   (C) reinforced
   (D) exacerbated
   (E) trivialized

6. Far from undermining the impression of permanent decline, the ____ statue, seemed emblematic of its ____ surroundings.
   (A) indecorous. . opulent
   (B) grandiose. . ramshackle
   (C) pretentious. . simple
   (D) ungainly. . elegant
   (E) tawdry. . blighted

7. Despite the fact that it is almost universally ____, the practice of indentured servitude still ____ in many parts of the world.
   (A) condemned. . abates
   (B) tolerated. . survives

(C) proscribed. . persists   (E) disdained. . intervenes

(D) mandated. . lingers

SECTION 76 解答

1. 【正确答案】E

   【中文释义】尽管事实上将动物的生命周期分为诸如幼年期,青壮期和衰老期这样的离散的阶段是很方便的,但这些时段并不是真正的截然分开的。

   【解题分析】下句中的 periods 重复上句中的 stages,上句中用 separate 修饰 stages,下句转折后应否定 separate,故正确答案为 E。

   【重点词条】prenatal *adj*. ①出生前的(occurring, existing, or performed before birth)

              例 ～care/the～period

              ②胎前护理的(providing or receiving prenatal medical care)

              例 a～clinic/～patients

          senescent *n*. ①衰老(the state of being old; the process of becoming old)

              ②植物由完全成熟到死亡期(the growth phase in a plant or plant part 〔as a leaf〕 from full maturity to death)

2. 【正确答案】B

   【中文释义】尽管自从 1850 年以来被汇报的火山爆发的数目呈指数上升,但这并不表示火山活动增加,相反却表明了更加广泛和系统化的记录手段。

   【解题分析】第二个空格的形容词与 widespread 并列,表示一种好的记录方法,故可选 A、B。而第一个空格又与后文构成转折,故选 B。

   【重点词条】exponential *adj*. ①含有指数的,含有幂的(of or relating to an exponent)

              ②指数增加的(characterized by or being an extremely rapid increase as in size or extent) 例 an～growth rate

          abate *v*. ①终结(to put an end to) 例 ～a nuisance

              ②使无效(nullify) 例 ～a writ

              ③下降,缓和(to reduce in degree or intensity, moderate)

              ④贬值(to reduce in value or amount, make less by way of relief)

              例 ～a tax

          meticulous *adj*. 极端仔细的(marked by extreme or excessive care in the consideration or treatment of details)

3. 【正确答案】B

   【中文释义】诠释在政治压迫政体下写成的小说的挑战在于区分哪些是作者的信仰本身固有的部分,与之对立的是哪些是由政治压力所强加的部分。

   【解题分析】由第二个空格后的 by 短语可轻松得知空格的动词应为 coerce。五个选项中与 coerce 同义的是 B。答案 E 的 demanded 也可勉强入选。再结合第一个空格判断,organic 和 peripheral 为反义词,正确的为 organic,因为两个 what 从句之间又为对比关系。B 正确地表达了这个关系,故正确答案为 B。

【重点词条】**innate** *adj.* ①与生俱来的(existing in, belonging to, or determined by factors present in an individual from birth, native, inborn) 例 ～behavior

②本性的(belonging to the essential nature of something, inherent)

oblique *adj.* ①歪的,斜的(neither perpendicular nor parallel, inclined)

②斜角的(having no right angle) 例 an～triangle

③间接的,模糊的(not straightforward, indirect, obscure)

peripheral *adj.* ①外围的,表尺的(of, relating to, involving, or forming a periphery or surface part)

②周围神经的(of, relating to, or being part of the peripheral nervous system) 例 ～nerves

③附加的,补充的(auxiliary, supplementary) 例 ～equipment

④计算机外设的(of or relating to computer peripherals)

4.【正确答案】E

【中文释义】我总是为自己本身对别人的愚蠢行为的容忍态度而吃惊;更难于理解的是他们也非常愚蠢地同样致力于认同我的愚蠢行为。

【解题分析】由文中的 equally 可知上下句的动作是相同的,故第一个空格应填上 put up with 的同义词,答案为 E。而第二个空格又应当与 impress 为同义词。

【重点词条】**idiocy** *n.* ①白痴(extreme mental retardation commonly due to incomplete or abnormal development of the brain)

②愚笨(something notably stupid or foolish)

put up with *v.* 毫无怨言地忍受(to endure or tolerate without complaint or attempt at reprisal)

exasperation *n.* 激怒

5.【正确答案】A

【中文释义】尽管有强劲的狡辩,这十多岁小孩脸上露齿一笑的表情揭穿了她的否认,即她在这个恶作剧实施在她的父母亲身上之前已经知道了这个恶作剧。

【解题分析】很有趣的句子。Despite 表明全句为转折句。上句的 protestation 就是下句的 denial 的同义词,故下句应否定 denial 以构成转折"尽管一再辩解,但脸上的表情却揭穿了辩解"。空格中应填上一个否定 denial 的词,故正确答案为 A。

【重点词条】**trivialize** *v.* 使…变得不重要(to make trivial, reduce to triviality)

6.【正确答案】E

【中文释义】并没有消除掉永恒衰落的形象,这个俗丽的雕像看上去反而成了它凋零的周围景观的象征。

【解题分析】由句首状语即可知,这个雕像未起到好的作用,故此雕像为一"不好"的雕像,第一个空格应为贬义词,相应地第二个空格也应为贬义词,据此即可知 E 为正确答案。

【重点词条】 **indecorous** *adj*. 不优雅的(not decorous, conflicting with accepted standards of good conduct or good taste)

　　　　　　opulent *adj*. ①充足的(exhibiting or characterized by opulence, as having a large estate or property, wealthy) 例 hoping to marry an～widow

　　　　　　②行为或语言过于华丽的,过于时髦的(amply or plentifully provided or fashioned often to the point of ostentation) 例 living in～comfort

　　　　　　ramshackle *adj*. ①堕落的,腐朽的(appearing ready to collapse, rickety)

　　　　　　②建筑物摇摇欲坠的(carelessly or loosely constructed)

　　　　　　ungainly *adv*. ①笨拙地(lacking in smoothness or dexterity, clumsy)

　　　　　　②难于控制地(hard to handle, unwieldy)

　　　　　　③外观丑陋地(having an awkward appearance, ugly)

　　　　　　blighte *n*. ①植物的枯萎病(a disease or injury of plants resulting in withering, cessation of growth, and death of parts without rotting)

　　　　　　②被破坏的景象(a deteriorated condition) 例 urban～

　　　　　　tawdry *adj*. 俗气而亮丽的(cheap and gaudy in appearance or quality, ignoble)

7.【正确答案】C

【中文释义】尽管几乎已经是广为禁止,但契约苦役的行为仍然在世界的许多地区存在。

【解题分析】文中的 it 即指代下句中的 the practice。由转折关系可知第一空与第二空为一组反义词,故正确答案为 C。

【重点词条】 **abate** *v*. ①终结(to put an end to) 例 ～a nuisance

　　　　　　②使无效(nullify) 例 ～a writ

　　　　　　③下降,缓和(to reduce in degree or intensity, moderate)

　　　　　　④贬值(to reduce in value or amount; make less by way of relief) 例 ～a tax

　　　　　　proscribe *v*. ①禁止(to condemn or forbid as harmful or unlawful, prohibit)

　　　　　　②抄家充公(to publish the name of as condemned to death with the property of the condemned, forfeited to the state)

SECTION 75(2)

1. It is assumed that scientists will avoid making ＿＿＿ claims about the results of their experiments because of the likelihood that they will be exposed when other researchers can- not ＿＿＿ their findings.

(A) hypothetical. . evaluate

(B) fraudulent. . duplicate

(C) verifiable. . contradict

(D) radical. . contest

(E) extravagant. . dispute

2. As long as the nuclear family is _____ a larger kinship group through contiguous residence on undivided land, the pressure to _____ and thus to get along with relatives is strong.

(A) nurtured among. . abstain

(B) excluded from. . compromise

(C) embedded in. . share

(D) scattered throughout. . reject

(E) accepted by. . lead

3. In contrast to the substantial muscular activity required for inhalation, exhalation is usually a _____ process.

(A) slow

(B) passive

(C) precise

(D) complex

(E) conscious

4. The documentary film about high school life was so realistic and _____ that feelings of nostalgia flooded over the college-age audience.

(A) logical

(B) pitiful

(C) evocative

(D) critical

(E) clinical

5. Although Georgia O' Keeffe is best known for her affinity with the desert landscape, her paintings of urban subjects _____ her longtime residency in New York City.

(A) condemn

(B) obfuscate

(C) attest to

(D) conflict with

(E) contend with

6. Even though the survey was designated as an interdisciplinary course, it involved no real _____ of subject matter.

(A) encapsulation

(B) organization

(C) synthesis

(D) discussion

(E) verification

7. The failure of many psychotherapists to _____ the results of pioneering research could be due in part to the specialized nature of such findings: even _____ findings may not be useful.

(A) understand. . baffling

(B) envision. . accessible

(C) utilize. . momentous

(D) reproduce. . duplicated

(E) affirm. . controversial

SECTION 75(2)解答

1.【正确答案】B

【中文释义】据称,科学家们会避免作欺骗性的实验结果报告,因为存在这种可能,当其他的研究者们不能得出与他们相同的实验结果时,他们就会被揭露出来。

【解题分析】这一句的基本含义在第三套 SECTION 29 的第三题就有过重复,在 92 年的考卷中也重复了。科学家们 replicate 或是 duplicate 相互的实验结果就是为了检验结果的真伪,原句中的 be exposed 显然是由 cannot duplicate their findings 所导致的。

【重点词条】**fraudulent** *adj*. 欺骗的(characterized by, based on, or done by fraud, deceitful)

　　　　　　radical *adj*. ①根的,根部的

　　　　　　②词根的(of, relating to, or constituting a linguistic root)

　　　　　　③方程的根(of or relating to a mathematical root)

　　　　　　④根治的(designed to remove the root of a disease or all diseased tissue) 例 ~surgery

　　　　　　⑤根本的(of or relating to the origin, fundamental)

　　　　　　⑥极端的(marked by a considerable departure from the usual or traditional, extreme)

　　　　　　⑦激进的(tending or disposed to make extreme changes in existing views, habits, conditions, or institutions)

　　　　　extravagant *adj*. ①奇异的(strange, curious, wandering)

　　　　　　②超出常规的(exceeding the limits of reason or necessity) 例 ~claims

　　　　　　③夸张的,夸大的(extremely or excessively elaborate)

　　　　　　④挥霍浪费的(spending much more than necessary, profuse, lavish)

　　　　　　⑤价格过高的(unreasonably high in price, excessive)

2.【正确答案】C

　【中文释义】通过户挨户地居住在一块未分开的土地上,核心家庭被包含在了一个更大的亲戚群当中,这就使得共同相处及与亲戚处理好关系的压力非常强大。

　【解题分析】第二个空格处于 and 的小连接当中,and 之后表示与别人共处,所以 and 前同样应有这方面的含义。五个选项中能表示出与别人处好关系的词只有一个答案 C。

　【重点词条】**embed** *v*. ①镶嵌(to enclose closely in or as if in a matrix) 例 fossils embedded in stone

　　　　　　②嵌入(to make something an integral part of) 例 the prejudices embedded in our language

3.【正确答案】B

　【中文释义】和吸气所需要的大量肌肉活动相比,呼气通常是一个消极被动的过程。

　【解题分析】前后对立面转折,所以下文的呼气应该不需要肌肉的活动,强调了不需要自身肌肉参与的形容词为 B,尽管有人感觉 A 也可以,但实际上,如果下文要强调呼气是个缓慢的过程,则和下文相对比的应该是大量肌肉活动就造成了吸气很快,而上文强调的是肌肉的参与,所以下文应对称地强调肌肉不参与。这样答案只有可能是 B。

　【重点词条】**substantial** *adj*. ①物质的(consisting of or relating to substance)

②真实的(not imaginary or illusory, real, true)

③重要的(important, essential)

④丰富的,充足的(ample to satisfy and nourish, full) 例 a~ meal

⑤结实的,牢固的(firmly constructed, sturdy)

⑥绝大部分的(being largely but not wholly that which is specified) 例 a~lie

4.【正确答案】C

【中文释义】关于高中生活的纪录片是如此的真实和扣人心弦,以至于怀旧的情绪淹没了大学年龄的观众。

【解题分析】So...that...结构的结果是大学年龄的观众被激发出了怀旧的情绪,所以可得答案 C,答案 B 的 pitiful 的含义是"令人同情的",如果选 B,那么结果就应该是产生同情心,而原文中是产生了怀旧的情绪,所以 B 并不正确。

【重点词条】**evocative** *adj*. 扣人心弦的(evoking or tending to evoke an emotional response) 例 settings so~that they bring tears to the eyes

clinical *adj*. ①门诊的(of, relating to, or conducted in or as if in a clinic, as involving direct observation of the patient)

②客观的,冷静的(analytical or coolly dispassionate) 例 a~attitude

5.【正确答案】C

【中文释义】尽管乔治·奥凯夫以她对沙漠风光的熟悉而闻名,但她的城市主题作品证实了她长期居住在纽约。

【解题分析】前后转折,上句是对沙漠的熟悉,所以下句应该肯定她在纽约的居住,这样就构成了"尽管住在大都市,却对沙漠风光很熟悉"这样的转折句。

【重点词条】**obfuscate** *v*. ①使黑暗(darken)

②使模糊(to make obscure)

③使糊涂(confuse)

6.【正确答案】C

【中文释义】尽管这个研究被定性为交叉课程,它实际上并不存在对课题的综合。

【解题分析】前后转折,后文应该否定 disciplinary 这个词。

【重点词条】**encapsulate** *v*. ①包裹起来(to enclose in or as if in a capsule) 例 a pilot encapsulated in the cockpit

②概括,典型化(epitomize, summarize) 例 ~ an era in an aphorism

designate *v*. ①指定,指派(to indicate and set apart for a specific purpose, office, or duty) 例 ~a group to prepare a plan

②指明标题或主题为(to call by a distinctive title, term, or expression）例 a particle designated the neutron

7.【正确答案】C

　【中文释义】很多精神治疗医生不能利用最前沿的研究结果,这可能应归因于这些发现结果过于专业化的性质:即使是重要的发现结果也可能是没有用的。

　【解题分析】冒号后表示重复,冒号后表达出这些结果没有用,而第一个空格要求填上治疗医生对这些结果没有做什么动作,事实上这些结果没有作用,当然就是指这些结果没有被治疗专家们用上,所以第一空格直接填使用就可以了。

　【重点词条】**baffle** *v*. 难倒,使困惑（to defeat or check a person by confusing or puzzling, disconcert）

　　　　　　envision *v*. 想象,思考（to picture to oneself）例 ~s a career dedicated to promoting peace

SECTION 76(2)

1. In the nineteenth century, novelists and unsympathetic travelers portrayed the American West as a land of ＿＿ adversity, whereas promoters and idealists created ＿＿ image of a land of infinite promise.

   (A) lurid. . a mundane
   (B) incredible. . an underplayed
   (C) dispiriting. . an identical
   (D) intriguing. . a luxuriant
   (E) unremitting. . a compelling

2. Honeybees tend to be more ＿＿ than earth bees: the former, unlike the latter, search for food together and signal their individual findings to one another.

   (A) insular
   (B) aggressive
   (C) differentiated
   (D) mobile
   (E) social

3. Joe spoke of superfluous and ＿＿ matters with exactly the same degree of intensity, as though for him serious issues mattered

neither more nor less than did ＿＿.

   (A) vital. . trivialities
   (B) redundant. . superficialities
   (C) important. . necessities
   (D) impractical. . outcomes
   (E) humdrum. . essentials

4. The value of Davis' sociological research is compromised by his unscrupulous tendency to use materials ＿＿ in order to substantiate his own claims, while ＿＿ information that points to other possible conclusions.

   (A) haphazardly. . deploying
   (B) selectively. . disregarding
   (C) cleverly. . weighing
   (D) modestly. . refuting
   (E) arbitrarily. . emphasizing

5. Once Renaissance painters discovered how to ＿＿ volume and depth, they were able to replace the medieval convention of symbolic, two-dimensional space with the more ＿＿ illusion of actual space.

   (A) reverse. . conventional

(B) portray..abstract

(C) deny..concrete

(D) adumbrate..fragmented

(E) render..realistic

6. He had expected gratitude for his disclosure, but instead he encountered ____ bordering on hostility.

(A) patience

(B) discretion

(C) openness

(D) ineptitude

(E) indifference

7. The diplomat, selected for her demonstrated patience and skill in conducting such delicate negotiations, ____ to make a decision during the talks because any sudden commitment at that time would have been ____.

(A) resolved..detrimental

(B) refused..apropos

(C) declined..inopportune

(D) struggled..unconscionable

(E) hesitated..warranted

SECTION 76(2) 解答

1.【正确答案】E

　【中文释义】在 19 世纪,小说家和没有同情心的旅行者将美国西部描绘成一块永远多灾多难的土地,而开发商和理想主义者们却创造出了极为吸引人的具有无穷无尽希望的土地的形象。

　【解题分析】上下句分别是两种截然不同的人,所以尽管 whereas 不能表达对立面转折,但这两种相反的人都显然提示我们应挑选反义词。下句支持美国西部,认为其是一个充满无尽希望的土地,所以上句应为一个对等的反义词,即无穷灾难的土地。所以正确答案选 E。

　【重点词条】unremitting *adj*. 永不停息的,不间断的(not remitting, constant, incessant)

2.【正确答案】E

　【中文释义】蜜蜂比土蜂更有群居性:和后者不一样的是,前者一起寻找食物并且将它们各自的发现发信号给另外一个蜜蜂。

　【解题分析】冒号后表示重复解释,后文的 together 等词汇显然是一再提示蜜蜂的群居性格。

　【重点词条】insular *adj*. ①岛的(of, relating to, or constituting an island; dwelling or situated on an island) 例 ~residents

　　　　　　　②岛国寡民的,心肠狭隘的(being, having, or reflecting a narrow provincial viewpoint)

3.【正确答案】A

　【中文释义】乔以完全相同的力度谈及肤浅琐碎和生死攸关的事件,好像对他而言,严重的问题和琐碎的问题没有什么区别。

　【解题分析】请注意这一句的比较结构。上句用 to the same degree 来表示同级比较,下句用 mattered neither more or less than 来表示同级比较,所以就表现出了两套比较结构这种基本题型。此时比较双方不应发生变化,故第一个空格应填下文出现过的 serious issues,第二个空格应填上文的 superfluous。

【重点词条】**superficiality** *n*. ①浅薄（the quality or state of being superficial）

②肤浅的事物（something superficial）

　　　　　 humdrum *adj*. 单调的（monotonous, dull）

4.【正确答案】B

【中文释义】戴维斯的社会学研究的价值被他毫无顾忌地挑选材料的做法破坏了,他之所以这样做是为了证实自己的观点,同时忽略那些可得出别的结论的事实。

【解题分析】While 的前后为对比关系,通常我们又会主动地在 while 前后找反义词,这样就可以将不明确的对比关系进一步深化为对立面转折关系,此句的 while 前后出现了一组反义词,his own claims 和 other possible conclusions。所以解题思路顿时就明快了,while 之前是 use 了那些支持 his own claims 的材料,那么 while 之后就应该不使用那些支持 other possible conclusions 的材料,所以第二个空格应与 use 反义,可得答案 B。

【重点词条】**unscrupulous** *adj*. 肆无忌惮的,不谨慎的（not scrupulous, unprincipled）

　　　　　 deploy *v*. ①布置军队（to extend〔a military unit〕esp. in width）

②展开,配置（to spread out, utilize, or arrange strategically）

5.【正确答案】E

【中文释义】一旦文艺复兴时期的画家们学会了如何表现深度和体积,他们就能够用更加真实可信的三维空间的图像来代替中世纪的象征的、二维空间的约定俗成的表现方法。

【解题分析】主句的动词为 replace A with B,显然 A 和 B 应该是反义词,故第二个空格应与 symbolic 构成反义词,事实上 two-dimensional space 已经与 actual space 构成了一个明显的反义,与 symbolic 构成反义的有 C 和 E 两个答案,C 答案导致前后文矛盾。

【重点词条】**convention** *n*. ①协议（agreement, contract）

②集会号召（the summoning or convening of an assembly）

③习俗,习惯（usage or custom esp. in social matters）

　　　　　 adumbrate *v*. ①预示（to foreshadow vaguely, intimate）

②画轮廓（to give a sketchy representation or outline of）

③使模糊（overshadow, obscure）

6.【正确答案】E

【中文释义】他满以为自己会因为告密而受到感激,但实际上他遇到的是近似于敌意的冷漠。

【解题分析】由 but instead 可以得出结论空格与 gratitude 构成反义词;或者由空格后的分隔结构可知空格中的词应与敌意的态度接近（bordering）,与敌意态度最接近的当然是答案 E 的 difference。

【重点词条】border *n*. ①边缘（an outer part or edge）

②边饰（an ornamental design at the edge of a fabric or rug）

openness *n*. 开放，大方（characterized by ready accessibility and usu. generous attitude）

7.【正确答案】C

【中文释义】这位外交官,因为她在处理这种细微的谈判所表现出的耐心和技巧而被选拔出来,在谈判中拒绝做出任何决策,因为在那时候的任何突然的承诺都是不恰当的。

【解题分析】这位外交官的特征性格已经在 her demonstrated patience and skill 中充分表现出来,对于一个有足够耐心的人而言 sudden commitment 当然是一个不好的做法,所以第二空格可以选 A、C、D,再根据 because 的因果关系可得答案 C。

【重点词条】unconscienable *adj*. ①不受良心制约的（not guided or controlled by conscience, unscrupulous）

②过度的,不合理的（excessive, unreasonable） 例 found an~number of defects in the car

SECTION 77

1. Because the monkeys under study are ____ the presence of human beings, they typically ____ human observers and go about their business

   (A) ambivalent about. . welcome

   (B) habituated to. . disregard

   (C) pleased with. . snub

   (D) inhibited by. . seek

   (E) unaware of. . avoid

2. Given her previously expressed interest and the ambitious tone of her recent speeches, the senator's attempt to convince the public that she is not interested in running for a second term is ____.

   (A) laudable

   (B) likely

   (C) authentic

   (D) futile

   (E) sincere

3. Many of her followers remain ____ to her, and even those who have rejected her leadership are unconvinced of the ____ of replacing her during the current turmoil.

   (A) opposed. . urgency

   (B) friendly. . harm

   (C) loyal. . wisdom

   (D) cool. . usefulness

   (E) sympathetic. . disadvantage

4. Unlike many recent interpretations of Beethoven's piano sonatas, the recitalist's performance was a delightfully free and introspective one; nevertheless, it was also, seemingly paradoxically, quite ____.

   (A) appealing

   (B) exuberant

   (C) idiosyncratic

   (D) unskilled

(E) controlled

5. Species with relatively ____ metabolic rates, including hibernators, generally live longer than those whose metabolic rates are more rapid.

(A) prolific

(B) sedentary

(C) sluggish

(D) measured

(E) restive

6. Belying his earlier reputation for ____ as a negotiator, Morgan had recently assumed a more ____ stance for which many of his erstwhile critics praised him.

(A) intransigence. . conciliatory

(B) impropriety. . intolerant

(C) inflexibility. . unreasonable

(D) success. . authoritative

(E) incompetence. . combative

7. Although Irish literature continued to flourish after the sixteenth century, a ____ tradition is ____ in the visual arts: we think about Irish culture in terms of the word, not in terms of pictorial images.

(A) rich. . superfluous

(B) lively. . found

(C) comparable. . absent

(D) forgotten. . apparent

(E) lost. . extant

SECTION 77 解答

1.【正确答案】B
　【中文释义】由于被研究的猴子习惯了人的存在,所以它们通常会忽略人的观察而我行我素。
　【解题分析】第二个空格后第三个单词 and 是个小连接,and 后的 go about their business 是"旁若无人,我行我素"的意思,所以 and 前应为同样的含义,答案 B 为 disregard human observers, 即为旁若无人之意。
　【重点词条】**ambivalence** *n*.①矛盾情绪或态度(simultaneous and contradictory attitudes or feelings such as attraction and repulsion toward an object, person, or action)
　　　　　　　②摇摆,举棋不定(continual fluctuation such as between one thing and its opposite)

2.【正确答案】D
　【中文释义】考虑到她以前表达过的兴趣以及最近演讲中的雄心勃勃的语调,这位议员试图使公众确信她对第二届连任不感兴趣的企图就徒劳无功。
　【解题分析】Given 在句首表原因,此句的因果关系非常的明显。如果 given 在句尾,则往往表示条件,请参照 SECTION 62 的第 2 题。
　【重点词条】**ambitious** *adj*.雄心壮志的(having a desire to achieve a particular goal, aspiring)
　　　　　　　futile *adj*.①无益的,无效的(serving no useful purpose, completely ineffective) 例 efforts to convince him were~
　　　　　　　②不重要的(occupied with trifles, frivolous)

③缺乏目的的

④愚蠢的

3.【正确答案】C

【中文释义】很多她的支持者继续忠实于她,即使是那些反对她的领导的人也不敢肯定在现在的混乱中替换她是否正确。

【解题分析】Remain 是主体词,该题是 remain 两种考法中的第二种,在 remain 前找一词填到其后即可,在其前面的四个单词 many, of, her, followers 中当然选 followers。此处只不过需要词性变化一下而已。与支持者 followers 最吻合的形容词是 C 的 loyal。

4.【正确答案】E

【中文释义】和许多最近对贝多芬钢琴奏鸣曲的演绎不一样,这位独奏家的表演是欢快自由和内省的风格;但是,看起来似乎矛盾的是,他的演绎却一点没有失控。

【解题分析】分号上半句中很明显判断词 free and introspective 是主体词,所以下半句转折就应针对 free and introspective 来进行。Free 的反义词为 E 的 controlled。解题时不必拘泥于 introspective 这个音乐专业词汇,既然 introspective 和 free 为并列的小连接,那么只需找 Free 的反义词即可。事实上 introspective 的专业词义即为内心独白的,自由奔放的,即兴发挥的。需要强调的是 B 的 exuberant 也有类似的专业词义。

【重点词条】**introspective** *adj*. 内省的(a reflective looking inward, an examination of one's own thoughts and feelings)

　　　　　appeal *n*. ①呼吁,请求(an earnest plea, entreaty)

　　　　　　　　②吸引力(the power of arousing a sympathetic response, attraction)

　　　　　　　　[例] Movies had a great ~ for him.

　　　　　　v. ①上诉(to take proceedings to have a lower court's decision reviewed in a higher court)

　　　　　　　　②请求裁判员裁决(to call upon another for corroboration, vindication, or decision)

　　　　　　　　③请求(to make an earnest request)

　　　　　　　　④激发同情心(to arouse a sympathetic response)

　　　　　exuberant *adj*. ①大量的(extreme or excessive in degree, size, or extent)

　　　　　　　　　②极为热情的(joyously unrestrained and enthusiastic, unrestrained or elaborate in style, flamboyant) [例] ~ architecture

　　　　　　　　　③极为丰富的(produced in extreme abundance, plentiful)

5.【正确答案】C

【中文释义】代谢速度相对比较慢的物种,包括有冬眠习性的动物,通常会比那些代谢速度更快的物种长寿。

【解题分析】显然是一套比较结构的题目。比较双方应互相对比,with relatively 加空格这一段和 whose metabolic rates are more rapid 对比。和 rapid 对比的是 C 的 sluggish。

【重点词条】**prolific** *adj*. ①丰富的(producing young or fruit esp. freely, fruitful)
②富于创造力的(causing abundant growth, generation, or reproduction)
③多产的(marked by abundant inventiveness or productivity)
例 a～composer

sedentary *adj*. ①非迁徙的(not migratory, settled) 例 ～birds
②久坐不动的(doing or requiring much sitting)
③永远附着的(permanently attached) 例 ～barnacles

sluggish *adj*. ①不动的(averse to activity or exertion, indolent, torpid)
②迟滞的(slow to respond to stimulation or treatment)
③行动缓慢的(markedly slow in movement, flow, or growth)
④经济疲软的(economically inactive or slow)

measured *adj*. ①比例恰当的(marked by due proportion)
②协调的,有韵律的(marked by rhythm, regularly recurrent)
例 a～gait
③深思熟虑的(deliberate, calculated) 例 a～response

restive *adj*. ①不安分守己的(stubbornly resisting control, balky)
②好动的,不安的(marked by impatience, fidgety)

6.【正确答案】A

【中文释义】与他早期的毫不妥协的谈判者的声誉截然相反,摩根现在采取了一种更利于和解的态度,他的早期的批评者们因此而赞扬他。

【解题分析】Earlier reputation 与后文的 recently 显然在提示时间对比。并且同时又是一个空对空的题型(虽然知道两个空格之间的逻辑关系,但是由于两个均为空格,无法一步推断答案,但这种情况下通常句中会在第二空格后有进一步的提示),在第二个空格后有限定,由这两点可以知道两空格为反义词,并且后面的空格为褒义,前面为贬义,满足这两个条件的为 A。

【重点词条】**conciliatory** *adj*. ①讨好的(to gain goodwill by pleasing acts)
②调和的(to make compatible, reconcile)
③抚慰的(appease)

impropriety *n*. ①不恰当的行为(an improper or indecorous act or remark)
②措辞不当(an unacceptable use of a word or of language)

7.【正确答案】C

【中文释义】尽管爱尔兰口头文学在 16 世纪后继续兴旺,但一个类似的流传却没有在视图艺术领域发生:所以我们现在是通过(他们的)语言文字而不是用视觉图像来认识爱尔兰文化。

【解题分析】冒号表示重复,该句的冒号后出现的 words 即重复前文的 literature,而 pictorial imagines 显然是重复 visual arts。所以冒号后肯定了 words，对应的前文应肯定 literature，那么由冒号后否定了 pictorial images 可以推断出前文应否定 visual arts，第二空格可选的表示否定的词只有 absent。

【重点词条】tradition *n*. ①传统

②民众的习惯做法

comparable *adj*. ①可相互比较的 (capable of or suitable for comparison)

②类似的（similar, like）例 fabrics of～quality

SECTION 78

1. Although sales have continued to increase since last April, unfortunately the rate of increase has ＿＿.

   (A) resurged

   (B) capitulated

   (C) retaliated

   (D) persevered

   (E) decelerated

2. Although the mental process that creates a fresh and original poem or drama is doubtless ＿＿ that which originates and elaborates scientific discoveries, there is clearly a discernible difference between the creators.

   (A) peripheral to

   (B) contiguous with

   (C) opposed to

   (D) analogous to

   (E) inconsistent with

3. It is disappointing to note that the latest edition of the bibliography belies its long-standing reputation for ＿＿ by ＿＿ some significant references to recent publications.

   (A) imprecision. . appropriating

   (B) relevance. . adding

   (C) timeliness. . updating

   (D) meticulousness. . revising

   (E) exhaustiveness. . omitting

4. Although Simpson was ingenious at ＿＿ to appear innovative and spontaneous, beneath the ruse he remained uninspired and rigid in his approach to problem-solving.

   (A) intending

   (B) contriving

   (C) forbearing

   (D) declining

   (E) deserving

5. She was criticized by her fellow lawyers not because she was not ＿＿, but because she so ＿＿ prepared her cases that she failed to bring the expected number to trial.

   (A) well versed. . knowledgeably

   (B) well trained. . enthusiastically

   (C) congenial. . rapidly

   (D) hardworking. . minutely

   (E) astute. . efficiently

6. Schlesinger has recently assumed a conciliatory attitude that is not ＿＿ by his colleagues, who continue to ＿＿ compromise.

   (A) eschewed. . dread

   (B) shared. . defend

   (C) questioned. . reject

   (D) understood. . advocate

   (E) commended. . disparage

7. The National Archives contain information so ____ that researchers have been known never to publish because they cannot bear to bring their studies to an end.

(A) divisive

(B) seductive

(C) selective

(D) repetitive

(E) resourceful

SECTION 78 解答

1.【正确答案】E

【中文释义】尽管销售自从去年开始一直持续增长,使人遗憾的是,增长速度放慢了。

【重点词条】capitulate v. ①投降(to surrender often after negotiation of terms)

②屈从,停止抵抗(to cease resisting, acquiesce)

retaliate v. 报仇(to get revenge, usu. implies a paying back of injury in exact kind, often vengefully) 例 The enemy retaliated by executing their prisoners.

2.【正确答案】D

【中文释义】尽管创作有新意并且独特的诗和戏剧的思维与创建和解释科学发明的思维毫无疑问地类似,但是在它们的创造者之间却有显著的差异。

【解题分析】很巧妙的比较结构,请注意短语 a discernible difference between,它表明的是差级比较;而上半句是同样的比较双方,因为下半句中的 the creators 显然就是 the mental process's creators,这是一种常见的重复方式。根据两套比较结构的出题规律"比较双方不变,比较结果一定改变"可以得出结论:上半句的比较结果应为没有 difference。D 的 analogous 吻合。ETS 越来越倾向于用隐含的比较结构(beyond, different, compared with)和同级比较(to the same degree, as...as, similar to, analogous)来出题,请记住这几个短语。请参阅 SECTION 65 的第 7 题,SECTION 67 的第 5 题,SECTION 74 的第 2 题。

【重点词条】peripheral adj. ①外围的,周边的(of, relating to, involving, or forming a periphery or surface part)

②表面的,周围的(of, relating to, or being part of the peripheral nervous system) 例 ~nerves

③辅助性的(auxiliary, supplementary) 例 ~equipment

analogous adj. 相似的,可比拟的(showing an analogy or a likeness that permits one to draw an analogy)

inconsistency n. ①前后矛盾,不一致(an instance of being inconsistent)

②易变,反复无常(the quality or state of being inconsistent)

3.【正确答案】E

【中文释义】令人失望的是,这个最新版的文献目录辜负了它长期(具有)的大而全的声誉,因为它遗漏了一些有关最新出版物的条目。

【解题分析】又是一道现在的动作证明了过去的某声誉为假的老题,类似的题目出现在科学
            家身上(SECTION 29 的第 3 题),出现在文学评论家身上(SECTION 64 第 7
            题),现在又到了文献目录学身上。我很同情 ETS,它已经很难玩出什么新花样
            了。本题中第二空格为现在的动作,应是伤害过去声誉的动作,必为贬义的动
            作,A 和 E 候选。第一空格为过去的声誉,应与第二空格的动作相反,故 E 正确。

【重点词条】relevance *n*. ①切题(relation to the matter at hand)
                    ②关联(pertinence)

             timely *adj*. 及时的,恰当的(in time, opportunely) 例 The question was
                not. . . ~ raised in the state court.

             meticulousness *n*. 极端小心的(marked by extreme or excessive care in the
                consideration or treatment of details)

             exhaustiveness *n*. 穷尽各种可能性(testing all possibilities or considering all
                elements, be thorough)

4.【正确答案】B

【中文释义】尽管辛普森擅长于以做戏来表现机灵勃发而富有创造力,但在这骗术的背后,
            他对问题的解决方案却是僵化无灵气的。

【解题分析】能大致构成转折的只有 A 和 B,如果知道 contrive 的词义的话,没有人会做错。
            而 contrive 与 spontaneous 这两个词居然就是刚刚考过的 1993 年 4 月 SEC-
            TION 3 第 3 题的主考词,请参阅 SECTION 63 的第 3 题。

【重点词条】spontaneous *adj*. ①自然的,天真率直的(proceeding from natural feeling or
                native tendency without external constraint)
                ②自发的,不由自主的(arising from a momentary impulse,
                controlled and directed internally, self-acting) 例 ~
                movement characteristic of living things

             contrived *adj*. 人工制成的,不自然的,非即兴而发的(to form or create in an
                artistic or ingenious manner) 例 contrived household utensils
                from stone

5.【正确答案】D

【中文释义】她被律师同行们批评,并不是因为她不勤奋,而是因为她如此详尽地准备案例
            以至于她不能将大家期待的数量的案例提交法庭审理。

【解题分析】最有效的推理总是最直接的那个推理,此句中的 so. . . that 结构中包含了一个
            空格,所以这一个逻辑关系最直接,可由此逻辑直接推理得 minutely。D 正确。

【重点词条】minute *adj*. ①细小的
                    ②详细的
                    ③琐碎的

             versed *adj*. 熟悉的,熟练的(to familiarize by close association, study, or expe-
                rience) 例 well versed in the theater

             knowledgeable *adj*. 富有知识和智慧的(having or exhibiting knowledge or intelligence, keen)

congenial *adj*. ①和谐一致的(having the same nature, disposition, or tastes, kindred, or existing or associated together harmoniously)

②高兴的，相宜的(pleasant; agreeably suited to one's nature, tastes, or outlook)

astute *adj*. 敏锐精明的(having or showing shrewdness and perspicacity)

例 an～observer/～remarks

6.【正确答案】E

【中文释义】史莱辛格最近采取了一种更加有利于和解的态度,这种态度不被他的同僚们所称赞,他们继续贬低妥协的态度。

【解题分析】有 continue to 这个短语时应该寻找过去的动作或状态,而上文又有一明显的提示 recently, 故过去的状态应和 conciliatory 相反,则应为拒绝妥协和解,这时第二空格可选 C 和 E, C 的两个空格相 矛盾,E 正确。

【重点词条】**eschew** *v*. 避开,逃避(to avoid habitually esp. on moral or practical grounds, shun)

share *v*. ①共享(a portion belonging to, due to, or contributed by an individual or group)

②同时具有(the same thing or idea possessed by several people) 例 ～ an opinion

7.【正确答案】A

【中文释义】国家档案馆贮存信息如此容易制造分裂,以至于众所周知,研究人员们永远都不会公开发布,因为他们不能承受研究终止的结局。

【解题分析】此句中 so...that 为因果结构,由因果结构的同褒同贬的规律可知研究人员之所以不发表这些信息是由于这些信息具有负面影响,五个选项中只有 A 为贬义词,故选 A。

【重点词条】**divisive** *adj*. 造成分裂的,不和的(creating disunity or dissension)

publish *v*. ①发表(to put out an edition)

②公布(to have one's work circulate)

seductive *adj*. 诱人的,有吸引力的(tending to seduce, having alluring or tempting qualities) 例 a～, sometimes disingenuous man /a～ spring morning

SECTION 79

1. We first become aware that her support for the new program was less than ____ when she refused to make a speech in its favor.

(A) qualified

(B) haphazard

(C) fleeting

(D) unwarranted

(E) wholehearted

2. When a person suddenly lose consciousness a by stander is not expected to _____ the problem but to attempt to _____ its effects by starting vital functions if they are absent.

(A) cure. . precipitate

(B) minimize. . predict

(C) determine. . detect

(D) diagnose. . counter

(E) magnify. . evaluate

3. The remark was only slightly _____, inviting a chuckle, perhaps, but certainly not a _____.

(A) audible. . reward

(B) hostile. . shrug

(C) amusing. . rebuke

(D) coherent. . reaction

(E) humorous. . guffaw

4. Doors were closing on our past, and soon the values we had lived by would become so obsolete that we would seem to people of the new age as _____ as travelers from an ancient land.

(A) elegant

(B) ambitious

(C) interesting

(D) comfortable

(E) quaint

5. Ability to _____ is the test of the perceptive historian; a history, after all, consist not only of what the historian had included, but also, in some sense, of what has been left out.

(A) defer

(B) select

(C) confer

(D) devise

(E) reflect

6. Some artists immodestly idealize or exaggerate the significance of their work; yet others, _____ to exalt the role of the artist, reject a transcendent view of art.

(A) appearing

(B) disdaining

(C) seeking

(D) failing

(E) tending

7. Estimating the risks of radiation escaping from a nuclear plant is _____ question, but one whose answer then becomes part of value-laden, emotionally charged policy debate about whether to construct such a plant.

(A) an incomprehensible

(B) an undefined

(C) an irresponsible

(D) a divisive

(E) a technical

SECTION 79 解答

1. 【正确答案】E

【中文释义】当她拒绝为这个项目做一个有益的演讲时,我们第一次清楚地认识到她对这个新项目的支持并不是全心全意的。

【解题分析】Less than 表否定,anything more than 表"不仅仅是",nothing more than 和 little more than 表"只不过是"。

【重点词条】**fleeting** *adj*. 快速的,短暂的(passing swiftly, transitory)

       qualify *v*. ①限定(to reduce from a general to a particular or restricted form)

           ②缓和(to make less harsh or strict, moderate)

           ③修正(to limit or modify the meaning of)

           ④使胜任(to fit by training, skill, or ability for a special purpose)

           ⑤证明合格(to declare competent or adequate, certify)

      qualified *adj*. ①有限制的

           ②合格的

   unqualified *adj*. ①无限制的,无条件的 例 ～acceptance

           ②不合格的

2.【正确答案】D

【中文释义】当一个人突然失去知觉时,旁观者并不需要诊断问题,而应试图去消减该问题的后果——如果致命的生理功能停止了的话,应激活它们。

【解题分析】By 前后进行推理,starting vital function 和 its effect(lose consciousness)是相反方向的事件,A:precipitate 反而是促进,B,C,E 都没有表现出相反的概念。答案 D。

【重点词条】**counter** *adj*. ①相反的(contrary, opposite) 例 counterclockwise/counter-march

           ②对立的(opposing, retaliatory) 例 counterforce/counteroffensive

           ③相应的(complementary, corresponding) 例 counterweight/counterpart

    magnify *v*. ①表扬(extol, laud)

           ②使敬重(to cause to be held in greater esteem or respect)

           ③使重要(to increase in significance, intensify)

           ④夸大(exaggerate)

           ⑤扩大,增大(to enlarge in fact or in appearance)

3.【正确答案】E

【中文释义】这些话只是少许幽默,可能会引发轻轻一笑,但绝对不会是大笑。

【解题分析】Inviting a chuckle 为分隔,可推断 C 或 E,再由第二空得 E。

【重点词条】**chuckle** *v*. ①轻笑(to laugh inwardly or quietly)

           ②发出类似于轻笑的连续的声音(to make a continuous gentle sound resembling suppressed mirth) 例 The clear bright water chuckled over gravel.

     rebuke *v*. ①猛烈地批评(to criticize sharply, reprimand)

           ②抑制,压制(to turn back or keep down, check)

    guffaw *v*. 暴笑(a loud or boisterous burst of laughter)

4. 【正确答案】E

【中文释义】大门关闭了过去的岁月,而我们曾赖以生存的价值观也会很快变得如此陈旧,以致我们将会被新时代的人看成像来自于外星球的旅行者一样古怪。

【解题分析】So…that 结构为同褒同贬的因果结构,与 obsolete 同褒贬的只有 E。

【重点词条】quaint *adj*. ①专业的,熟练的(expert, skilled)

②精致的,优美的(marked by beauty or elegance)

③非同寻常的,古怪的(unusual or different in character or appearance, odd) 例 figures of fun, ~people

④过时的,古老得滑稽的(pleasingly or strikingly old-fashioned or unfamiliar)

5. 【正确答案】B

【中文释义】选择的能力是对具有洞察力的历史学家的考验;毕竟历史不只由历史学家们包括的那部分,而且从某种意义上来说,也由被省略的那部分构成。

【解题分析】分号下半句的结构由 consist ont only of…but also of… 构成。同样是分号句的基本解题规律,上下句重复。上句要填一个动词,动词的逻辑主语是 historian,所以到下句找 historian 做过的动作,include 与 left out,既包括一些东西又省略一些东西,这个动作由哪个动词来表达? 在五个选择中无疑是 B。该句没有一个难词,只需要有分析的思路。

【重点词条】confer *v*. ①授予,给予(to bestow from or as if from a position of superiority)

例 conferred an honorary degree on her/Knowing how to read was a gift conferred with manhood.

②商量(to compare views or take counsel, consult)

perceptive *adj*. ①感官的(responsive to sensory stimuli, discerning) 例 a~eye

②有洞察力的(capable of or exhibiting keen perception, observant) 例 a~scholar

③有理性认识的(characterized by sympathetic understanding or insight)

6. 【正确答案】B

【中文释义】有些艺术家不恰当地理想化或夸大了他们工作的重要性;但是另外一些艺术家,反感夸大艺术家的重要性,因而反对超越物质的玄虚的艺术观。

【解题分析】分号句,上句主语为 some artists 下句为 others, 所以上下句应该相反。上句的动词为 exaggerate,下句为空格接 exalt, exalt 即为 exaggerate 的重复,故空格里应填表否定的动词,B 正确,D 并不是主动否定,而表示主观上想否定但结果却失败的意思。

【重点词条】transcendental *adj*. ①超越的,卓越的(transcendent)

②超自然的(supernatural)

③抽象的,玄奥的(abstruse, abstract)

④先验的,超验的(of or relating to transcendentalism)

7.【正确答案】E

【中文释义】估计从核电站泄露的辐射的危险是技术问题,但同时它的答案是特定价值取向的一部分,非常情绪化地决定着是否该建立这种核工厂的政策讨论。

【解题分析】正如 continue, remain 前后会同义一样,become 的转变在填空的两极思维中会反义,该题中 become 后的"one",也就是 question 的重复,会 emotionally charged,可见 become 前应该是非 emotionally 的方式,强调这种对比的答案是 E。

【重点词条】charge v. ①强加任务或责任(to impose a task or responsibility on) 例 ~ him with the job of finding a new meeting place

②命令,责令(to command, instruct, or exhort with authority) 例 I ~ you not to go.

③裁决(of a judge, to give a charge to a jury)

④指控(to make an assertion against by ascribing guilt or blame) 例 ~ s him with armed robbery／They were charged as being instigators.

SECTION 80

1. Because modern scientist find the ancient Greek view about cosmos outdated and irrelevant, they now perceive it as only of ____ interest.

   (A) historical

   (B) intrinsic

   (C) astronomical

   (D) experimental

   (E) superfluous

2. Religious philosopher that he is, Henry More derived his conception of his infinite universe from the infinite God in whom he believed, a benevolent God of ____ whose nature was to create ____.

   (A) plentitude. . abundance

   (B) vengeance. . justice

   (C) indifference. . suffering

   (D) indulgence. . temperance

   (E) rectitude. . havoc

3. While some argue that imposing tolls on highway users circumvents the need to raise public taxes for road maintenance, the phenomenal expense of maintaining a vast network of roads ____ reliance on those general taxes.

   (A) avoids

   (B) diminish

   (C) necessitate

   (D) discourage

   (E) ameliorate

4. Although they were not direct ____, the new arts of the Classical period were clearly created in the spirit of older Roman models and thus ____ many features of old style.

   (A) impressions. . introduced

   (B) translations. . accentuated

   (C) copies. . maintained

   (D) masterpieces. . depicted

(E) borrowings. . improvised

5. In spite of the increasing _____ of their opinions, the group knew they had to arrive at a consensus so that the award could be presented.
   (A) impartiality
   (B) consistency
   (C) judiciousness
   (D) incisiveness
   (E) polarity

6. By forcing our surrender to the authority of the clock, systematic timekeeping has a form of _____ on society.
   (A) anarchy

(B) permanence
(C) provincialism
(D) tyranny
(E) autonomy

7. Our highly _____ vocabulary for street crime contrasted sharply with our _____ vocabulary for corporate crime, a fact that corresponds the general public's unawareness of the extent of corporate crime.
   (A) nuanced. . subtle
   (B) uninformative. . misleading
   (C) euphemistic. . abstract
   (D) differentiated. . limited
   (E) technical. . jargon-laden

SECTION 80 解答

1.【正确答案】A
  【中文释义】因为现代科学家发现古代希腊的宇宙观过时而且无关紧要,他们现在只是出于历史的兴趣而看待它。
  【解题分析】该题的内容和 SECTION 21 的第 4 题的内容类似。
  【重点词条】**relevant** *adj*. ①相关的,重要的(having significant and demonstrable bearing on the matter at hand)
                   ②社会现实性(having social relevance)

2.【正确答案】A
  【中文释义】作为一个宗教哲学家,亨利·摩尔从他信仰的无限的上帝那推断出了他的无限的宇宙的概念,这位无穷丰富的上帝的本质是来创造无尽的丰富。
  【解题分析】分析结构可知:a benevolent God 是 the infinite God 的同位语重复,故 a benevolent God 的后置定语应为 inifite 的同义词。A 正确。
  【重点词条】**plenitude** *n*. ①完整(the quality or state of being full, completeness)
                   ②极为丰富(a great sufficiency, abundance)
        infinite *adj*. ①无限的(extending indefinitely, endless) 例 ~space
                   ②无有穷尽的(immeasurably or inconceivably great or extensive, inexhaustible) 例 ~patience
        vengeance *n*. 复仇(punishment inflicted in retaliation for an injury or offense, retribution)
        temperance *n*. ①节制(moderation in action, thought, or feeling, restraint)

②饮酒有度(moderation in or abstinence from the use of intox-
icating drink)

havoc *n*. ①摧毁(wide and general destruction, devastation)
②混乱不堪(great confusion and disorder) 例 Children can create～
in a house.

3.【正确答案】C
　【中文释义】尽管有人认为征收高速公路使用者的过路费会消除加收公路维护税的必要,但维护一个巨大的公路网所需的巨额费用必须依赖公路维护税这样的公众税。
　【解题分析】下句的 these general taxes 即照应上句的 public taxes,上句为消除对 public taxes 的需求,所以下句转折后应为必然需求 these general taxes。
　【重点词条】**phenomenal** *adj*. ①现象的(relating to or being a phenomenon, as known through the senses rather than through thought or intuition)
②能知觉的(concerned with phenomena rather than with hypotheses)
③非凡的(extraordinary, remarkable)

4.【正确答案】C
　【中文释义】尽管它们并不是直接的复制品,古典时期的新艺术很明显地是在更古老的罗马模式的精神下创造出来的,因此保存了很多古老风格的特征。
　【解题分析】第三行的 and 为小连接,可直接推理得 C。
　【重点词条】**impression** *n*. ①影响,印象(a characteristic, trait, or feature resulting from some influence) 例 the～on behavior produced by the social milieu
②演员身上的耀眼而俗气的小装饰物
accentuate *v*. 重要,强调(accent, emphasize, intensify) 例 ～s the feeling of despair
depict *v*. ①描绘(to represent by or as if by a picture)
②描写(describe)
improvise *v*. ①即兴创作(to compose, recite, play, or sing extemporaneously; to make, invent, or arrange offhand)
②临时准备 (to fabricate out of what is conveniently on hand)

5.【正确答案】E
　【中文释义】尽管他们的观点越来越对立,但这个小组知道他们必须达成一致意见,以便颁发奖励。
　【解题分析】In spite of, far from, not like 都意味着对立面反义词的出现。
　【重点词条】**incisiveness** *n*. 有决断力(impressively direct and decisive in manner or presentation)

6.【正确答案】D

【中文释义】通过强迫我们向时钟的权威屈从，系统时间保存法强加给了我们的社会某种形式的专制。

【解题分析】Force 和 impose 同义,答案应和 authority 同义,D 正确。

【重点词条】**anarchy** *n*. ①无政府(absence of government)

　　　　　　　②无法律,无政治秩序(a state of lawlessness or political disorder due to the absence of governmental authority)

　　　　　autonomy *n*. ①自治,独立(the quality or state of being self-governing; the right of self-government)

　　　　　　　②自由(self-directing freedom and moral independence)

　　　　　　　③自治州(a self-governing state)

7.【正确答案】D

【中文释义】我们关于街头犯罪的高度详细明晰的词汇与我们对集体犯罪的少量的词汇构成了强烈的对比,这个事实和公众对集体犯罪程度的普遍无知相一致。

【解题分析】Contrasts sharply 提示两空格应为反义词,A,E 为同义词, B,C 不构成反义词。可得答案 D。或由 unwareness of the extent of corporate crime 可知:公众对 corporate crime 的词汇量同样是很少的。

【重点词条】**corporate** *adj*. ①法人的(formed into an association and endowed by law with the rights and liabilities of an individual, incorporated)

　　　　　　　②公司的(of or relating to a corporation) 例 a plan to reorganize the～structure

　　　　　nuance *n*. ①细微的差别(a subtle distinction or variation)

　　　　　　　②微妙的(a subtle quality, nicety)

　　　　　　　③敏感(sensibility to, awareness of, or ability to express delicate shadings of meaning, feeling, or value)

SECTION 81

1. What these people were waiting for would not have been apparent to others and was perhaps not very ____ their own minds.

(A) obscure to

(B) intimate to

(C) illusory to

(D) difficult for

(E) definite in

2. The attempt to breed suitable varieties of jojoba by using hybridization to ____ favorable traits was finally abandoned in favor of a simpler and much faster: the domestication of flourishing wild strains.

(A) eliminate. . alternative

(B) reinforce. . method

(C) allow. . creation

(D) reduce. . idea

(E) concentrate. . theory

3. According to one political theorist, a regime that has as its goal absolute ____, without any ____ law or principle, has declared war on justice.

   (A) respectability. . codification of
   (B) supremacy. . suppression of
   (C) autonomy. . accountability to
   (D) fairness. . deviation from
   (E) responsibility. . prioritization of

4. Despite its ____, the book deals ____ with a number of crucial issues.

   (A) optimism. . cursorily
   (B) importance. . needlessly
   (C) virtues. . inadequately
   (D) novelty. . strangely
   (E) completeness. . thoroughly

5. Although frequent air travelers remain unconvinced, researchers have found that, paradoxically, the ____ disorientation inherent in jet lag also may yield some mental health ____.

   (A) temporal. . benefits
   (B) acquired. . hazards

   (C) somatic. . disorders
   (D) random. . deficiencies
   (E) typical. . standards

6. Ironically, the proper use of figurative language must be based on the denotative meaning of the words, because it is the failure to recognize this ____ meaning that leads to mixed metaphors and their attendant incongruity.

   (A) esoteric
   (B) literal
   (C) latent
   (D) allusive
   (E) symbolic

7. Although it seems ____ that there would be a greater risk of serious automobile accidents in densely populated areas, such accidents are more likely to occur in sparsely populated regions.

   (A) paradoxical
   (B) axiomatic
   (C) anomalous
   (D) irrelevant
   (E) portentous

SECTION 81 解答

1.【正确答案】E
   【中文释义】这些人所期待的事物对别人不会是已经清楚的,并且可能在他们自己的思想中也不是很明确的。
   【解题分析】And 为小连接,空格填 apparent 的同义词。
   【重点词条】definite *adj*. ①明确的(having distinct or certain limits) 例 set～standards for pupils to meet
   ②确切的(free of all ambiguity, uncertainty, or obscurity)
   例 demanded a～answer
   ③毫无疑问的(unquestionable, decided) 例 The quarterback was a～hero today.

2.【正确答案】B

【中文释义】通过杂交的方法来加强好的生物特征以便培养适宜的加洲希蒙得木新品种，这种尝试最终被人们摒弃,转而采用一种更简单和更快的方法:将繁茂的野生品种驯化。

【解题分析】Attempt to 表目的,by 短语中的 to 仍然表达目的,并且两个宾语 suitable varieties 与 favorable traits 同义,故相应的动词应同义,与 breed 构成同义词的为 B 的 reinforce。

【重点词条】in favor of　①相一致(in accord or sympathy with)
　　　　　　　　　②支持(in support of)
　　　　　　　　　③优先选择(in order to choose, out of preference for) 例 turned down the scholarship in favor of a pro career

3.【正确答案】B

【中文释义】根据某位政治理论家的理论,一个将绝对的权威当成自己目标的政权,如果不愿意屈服于法律和准则,就已经在向正义宣战。

【解题分析】A regime has declared war on justice 是该句的主干。Without 在此表示条件,结果是 has declared war on justice,故条件相吻合的为 C。

【重点词条】supreme adj. ①权威的(highest in rank or authority) 例 the~commander
　　　　　　　　　②最高级的(highest in degree or quality) 例 ~endurance in war and in labour
　　　　　　　　　③最后的,最终的(ultimate, final) 例 the~sacrifice

accountibility n. 责任心,责任感(the quality or state of being accountable; an obligation or willingness to accept responsibility or to account for one's actions) 例 public officials lacking~

prioritization n. 划分优先级(to list or rate in order of priority usage)

autonomy n. ①自治,独立(the quality or state of being self-governing; the right of self-government)
　　　　　　　　　②自由(self-directing freedom and moral independence)
　　　　　　　　　③自治州(a self-governing state)

4.【正确答案】C

【中文释义】尽管它有很多优点,但是这本书解决许多重要问题却很不充分。

【解题分析】前后构成转折,名词和形容词需要构成反义词,将名词转化为形容词考虑,C 正确。

【重点词条】cursorily adv. 快速地,草率地(rapidly and often superficially performed or produced, hasty) 例 a~glance

5.【正确答案】A

【中文释义】尽管频繁的空中旅行者保持怀疑态度,但确已发现,非常反常的是,时差所固有的暂时方向迷失症也会对精神健康产生益处。

【解题分析】Paradoxically 修饰 disoriention may yield 加空格这一句,所以空格当然是产生好事物,否则无法 paradoxically。A 是惟一的好词。

【重点词条】hazard *n*. ①一种赌博游戏(a game of chance like craps played with two dice)

②危险(a source of danger)

③机会,冒险(chance, risk)

somatic *adj*. 肉体的(of, relating to, or affecting the body esp. as distinguished from the germ plasm or the psyche)

disorder *v*. ①打乱顺序(to disturb the order of)

②使功能紊乱(to disturb the regular or normal functions of)

6. 【正确答案】B

【中文释义】具有滑稽意义的是,能否正确使用比喻句依赖于词汇的本体义,因为正是不能辨认这个本体义,才导致交叉纠缠的暗喻和意义的谬误。

【解题分析】由 ironically 可知 denotative 与 figurative 为反义词,由空格前的 this 可知空格应填 denotative 的同义词,因而是 figurative 的反义词,为 literal。这个词考过很多次了。

【重点词条】denote *v*. ①注解(to serve as an indication of, betoken) 例 the swollen bellies that～starvation

②标志(to serve as an arbitrary mark for) 例 red flares denoting danger

③宣告(to make known, announce) 例 His crestfallen look denoted his distress.

esoteric *adj*. ①秘密的(designed for or understood by the specially initiated alone) 例 a body of～legal doctrine

②秘不外传的(of or relating to knowledge that is restricted to a small group)

③私人的,保密的(private, confidential) 例 an～purpose

latent *adj*. 潜伏的(present and capable of becoming though not now visible, obvious, or active) 例 a～infection

incongruous *adj*. ①不和谐的(not harmonious, incompatible) 例 ～colors

②不一致的(not conforming, disagreeing) 例 conduct～with principle

③自相矛盾的(inconsistent within itself) 例 an～story

7. 【正确答案】B

【中文释义】尽管似乎天经地义的是在人口稠密的地区会有更严重的交通事故的风险,但是这样的事故更有可能发生在人口稀少的地区。

【解题分析】上下句转折,上下句已存在 densely populated areas 和 sparsely populated regions 的对比,故空格应填 most likely 的同义词,B 正确。

【重点词条】axiomatic *adj*. ①不证自明的(taken for granted, self-evident)

      ②公理的(based on or involving an axiom or system of axioms)

     例 ~ set theory

portentous adj. ①预兆的,凶兆的(of, relating to, or constituting a portent)

     ②不寻常的,令人难以置信的(eliciting amazement or wonder; prodigious)

     ③自负的(self-consciously solemn or important;pompous)

SECTION 82

1. If the theory is self-evidently true, as its proponents assert, then why does _____ it still exist among well-informed people?
   (A) support for
   (B) excitement about
   (C) regret for
   (D) resignation about
   (E) opposition to

2. Although the _____ of cases of measles has _____, researchers fear that eradication of the disease, once believed to be imminent, may not come soon.
   (A) occurrence. . continued
   (B) incidence. . declined
   (C) prediction. . resumed
   (D) number. . increased
   (E) study. . begun

3. Nothing _____ his irresponsibility better than his _____ delay in sending us the items he promised weeks ago.
   (A) justifies. . conspicuous
   (B) characterizes. . timely
   (C) epitomizes. . unnecessary
   (D) reveals. . conscientious
   (E) conceals. . inexplicable

4. The author did not see the _____ inherent in her scathing criticism of a writing style so similar to her own.
   (A) disinterest
   (B) incongruity
   (C) pessimism
   (D) compliment
   (E) symbolism

5. Whereas the Elizabethans struggled with the transition from medieval _____ experience to modern individualism, we confront an electronic technology that seems likely to reverse the trend, rendering individualism obsolete and interdependence mandatory.
   (A) literary
   (B) intuitive
   (C) corporate
   (D) heroic
   (E) spiritual

6. Our biological uniqueness requires that the effects of a substance must be _____ verified byexperiments, even after thousands of tests of the effects of that substance on animals.
   (A) controlled
   (B) random
   (C) replicated
   (D) human
   (E) evolutionary

7. Today water is more _____ in landscape architecture than ever before, because technological advances have made it easy, in some instances even _____ to install water features in public places.

(A) conspicuous. . prohibitive
(B) sporadic. . effortless
(C) indispensable. . intricate
(D) ubiquitous. . obligatory
(E) controversial. . unnecessary

SECTION 82 解答

1.【正确答案】E
　【中文释义】假如该理论正如它的支持者所声称的是不证自明的正确,那么,为什么在受过良好教育的人们当中仍存在着对它的反对意见呢?
　【解题分析】上下句转折,上句称理论是 self-evidently true,故下句会反对它,认为它是 false 而非 true,故选 E 。
　【重点词条】**resignation** n. ①听任,顺从(an act or instance of resigning something, surrender)
　　　　　　　　②辞职(a formal notification of resigning)

2.【正确答案】B
　【中文释义】尽管麻疹的发病率已经下降了 ,但研究者担心,这种疾病的彻底消除——过去认为很快就能实现——可能并不会马上实现。
　【解题分析】上下句转折,下句主干意为消除麻疹不会很快实现,是一种不好的情况,上句该讲好的情况,只有 B 正确。
　【重点词条】**decline** v. ①下降(to slope downward, descend; to bend down, droop)
　　　　　　　②降价(to become less in amount) 例 prices declined
　　　　　　　③衰减(to draw toward a close, wane) 例 the day declined
　　　　　　　④变坏,变差(to tend toward an inferior state or weaker condition) 例 His health declined.
　　　　resume v. ①恢复(to return to or begin again after interruption) 例 resumed her work
　　　　　　　②概括(reiterate, summarize)

3.【正确答案】C
　【中文释义】没有什么能比他毫无必要地拖延运送他几个星期前就承诺的货物这件事更好地体现他的不负责任。
　【解题分析】Nothing. . . better than 为最高级结构,better than 前后并不是对比,而是相同,后部分为耽误了寄送,所以前半部分应表现出不负责任,可选 B、C、D,再看 B、C、D 的第二格选项,只有 C 是正确的。
　【重点词条】**conscientious** adj. ①有道德感的(governed by or conforming to the dictates of conscience, scrupulous) 例 a~public servant

②细心的(meticulous, careful) 例 a~listener

inexplicable *adj*. 不可解释的,不可知的(incapable of being explained, interpreted, or accounted for)

timely *adj*. 及时的,恰当的(in time, opportunely) 例 The question was not~raised in the state court.

4.【正确答案】B

【中文释义】该作者没有意识到在她对与她自己的文风是如此相似地某种文风的严厉批评中所内含的那种冲突。

【解题分析】So simlar to her own 修饰 a writing style,简化的理解就是批评自己的风格,可得答案 B。

【重点词条】**incongruity** *n*. ①不调和(the quality or state of being incongruous)

②不和谐的事物(something that is incongruous)

compliment *n*. ①恭维,赞扬(an expression of esteem, respect, affection, or admiration,an admiring remark,formal and respectful recognition, honor)

②祝福(best wishes, regards) 例 accept my ~s/~s of the season

5.【正确答案】C

【中文释义】尽管伊丽莎白时代的人们通过奋斗才实现了由中世纪集体的生存经验向现代个人主义的转折,然而,我们却面临着一种似乎有可能逆转这一潮流的电子技术,这会导致个人主义过时,而使得相互依赖成为绝对必要。

【解题分析】Transition from...to 这个短语也曾经考过,from...to 前后连接反义词,与 individualism 反义的是 C 选项的 corporarate。

【重点词条】**render** *v*. ①致使,造成(to cause to be or become, make) 例 enough rainfall to ~irrigation unnecessary /~ed him helpless

②演出

③给予

spiritual *adj*. ①精神的(of, relating to, consisting of, or affecting the spirit, incorporeal) 例 man's~needs

②圣灵的(of or relating to sacred matters) 例 ~songs

③宗教的(concerned with religious values)

6.【正确答案】D

【中文释义】我们自身生理的特殊性必然要求每一种物质的效果必须通过对人体的实验来验证,尽管那种物质在动物身上已经经过了数以千计的测试。

【解题分析】Even 前后对比,even 后为"在动物身上检测过的效果",even 前当然填"在人身上检测过的效果",即答案 D。

【重点词条】**controlled** *adj*. ①压抑的(restrained)

②受控的(regulated by law with regard to possession and use)

例 ~drugs

7. 【正确答案】D

   【中文释义】今天,水在园林建筑中要比以往任何时候都来得普遍,因为技术的进步使得这种做法很容易实现,在某种情形中,几乎是强迫性地必须在公共场所中安装水的景观。

   【解题分析】Because 连接一个因果关系,因为今天实现起来比过去容易,所以就会怎么样了呢? 显然填 D。

   【重点词条】 indispensable *adj*. ①不能忽略的(not subject to being set aside or neglected)

   例 an~obligation

   ②必不可缺的(absolutely necessary, essential) 例 an~ member of the staff

   ubiquitous *adj*. 无处不在的(existing or being everywhere at the same time, constantly encountered, widespread)

SECTION 83

1. While many Russian composers of the nine-teenth century contributed to an emerging national style, other composers did not ____ idiomatic Russian musical elements, ____ in-stead the traditional musical vocabulary of Western European Romanticism.

   (A) utilize. . rejecting

   (B) incorporate. . preferring

   (C) exclude. . avoiding

   (D) repudiate. . expanding

   (E) esteem. . disdaining

2. Because the painter Albert Pinkham Ryder was obsessed with his ____ perfection, he was rarely ____ a painting, creating endless variations of a scene on one canvas, one on top of another.

   (A) quest for. . satisfied with

   (B) insistence on. . displeased with

   (C) contempt for. . disconcerted by

   (D) alienation from. . immersed in

   (E) need for. . concerned with

3. Objectively set standards can serve as a ____ for physicians, providing them ____ unjusti-fied malpractice claims.

   (A) trial. . evidence of

   (B) model. . experience with

   (C) criterion. . reasons for

   (D) test. . questions about

   (E) safeguard. . protection from

4. In spite of ____ reviews in the press, the production of her play was ____ almost cer-tain oblivion by enthusiastic audiences whose acumen was greater than that of the critics.

   (A) lukewarm. . condemned to

   (B) scathing. . exposed to

   (C) lackluster. . rescued from

(D) sensitive. . reduced to

(E) admiring. . insured against

5. The passions of love and pride are often found in the same individual, but having little in common, they mutually ____, not to say destroy, each other.

　(A) reinforce

　(B) annihilate

　(C) enhance

　(D) weaken

　(E) embrace

6. The necessity of establishing discrete categories for observations frequently leads to attempts to makeabsolute ____ when there are in reality only ____ .

(A) analyses. . hypotheses

(B) correlations. . digressions

(C) distinctions. . gradations

(D) complications. . ambiguities

(E) conjectures. . approximations

7. A unique clay disk found at the Minoan site of Phaistos is often ____ as the earliest example of printing by scholars who have defended its claim to this status despite equivalent claims put forward for other printing artifacts.

　(A) questioned

　(B) overlooked

　(C) adduced

　(D) conceded

　(E) dismissed

SECTION 83 解答

1.【正确答案】D

　【中文释义】尽管很多19世纪的俄罗斯作曲家支持新出现的民族风格,但其他作曲家并不放弃传统的俄罗斯音乐风格,相反扩增了传统西欧浪漫音乐语言的数量。

　【解题分析】Many Russian composers 和 other composers 构成对比,故上句为 contributed to emerging national style 简单理解为"支持新事物",而下句为 idiomatic Russian musical elements 简单理解为"传统的老的事物",与上句对比,可以选 C、D。第二空格是分隔结构,重复前文的"不反对老事物",又由于它的宾语是"traditional musical vocabulary"故应该填"支持老事物"以重复前文,答案选 D。请注意原文中的 emerging,idiomatic,traditional 的三次转换。

　【重点词条】idiomatic adj. ①成语的,俗语的(of, relating to, or conforming to idiom)

　　　　　　emerging adj. ①出现,表现(to become manifest)

　　　　　　　　　　　②浮现(to rise from or as if from an enveloping fluid,come out into view)

　　　　　　　　　　　③恢复(to rise from an obscure or inferior position or condition)

2.【正确答案】A

　【中文释义】因为画家阿尔伯特·皮郝姆·雷达沉浸在他对完美的追求中,所以他很少对一幅画满意,总是在同一张画布上创作出同一个场景的无休无止的不同表达,一个覆盖着另外一个。

　【解题分析】第二空格后为分隔结构,重复第二空格的内容,意为一次又一次地重新画一个场景,可以得出他对刚完成的画立刻不满意,又重新画一遍这个推论,故选 A。

【重点词条】**obsess** v. 着迷(to haunt or excessively preoccupy the mind of) 例 was ~ ed with the idea

3.【正确答案】E

【中文释义】客观公正的标准可以起到对医生的保护伞的作用,为他们提供当遭受不公正的误诊控告时的保护措施。

【解题分析】Providing 是分隔结构,重复前文它的逻辑主语是 objectively set standards 故可以理解为"客观的衡量标准为医生提供了一个"。请注意空格动词的宾语是 unjustified malpractice。正好出现了"unjustified"这个 objective 的反义词。故问题迎刃而解,客观公正的标准当然反对不公正的指控,故选 E。

【重点词条】**safeguard** v. 保护(to make safe, protect)

4.【正确答案】C

【中文释义】尽管报纸的评论无精打采,这次戏剧演出却被热情的观众们从被遗忘中拯救出来,这些观众的洞察力总是强于那些评论家。

【解题分析】第二个空格的 by 短语是一个常见的解题点,热情的听众永远热情,当然不会淡忘这部分作品,故可选 A、C、E。后半句的比较结构实际上就在提示着评论家和观众是对立的,所以第一空格填评论家们的态度,当然应该填不好的态度,C正确。

【重点词条】**acumen** n. 敏锐(keenness and depth of perception, discernment, or discrimination in practical matters, shrewdness)

lukewarm adj. ①温热的(moderately warm, tepid)
②缺乏坚定的,半心半意的(lacking conviction, halfhearted)

lackluster adj. 愚笨平庸的(lacking in sheen, brilliance, or vitality, dull, mediocre)

5.【正确答案】D

【中文释义】爱和傲慢的情绪通常会在同一人身上发现,但却毫无共同之处,即使不是相互摧毁,它们通常也是相互削弱的。

【解题分析】Having little in common 是其后句子的句首状语,应该修饰谓语动词,故选 D,答案 B 错在和紧随其后的分隔相冲突。

【重点词条】**embrace** v. ①拥抱(to clasp in the arms, hug)
②喜爱(cherish, love)
③包括(encircle, enclose)
④欢迎(to avail oneself of, welcome) 例 embraced the opportunity to study further
⑤等同于(to be equal or equivalent to) 例 his assets embraced $10

passion n. ①耶稣受难受苦(the sufferings of Christ between the night of the

Last Supper and his death)

②激情(the emotions as distinguished from reason)

③强烈的情绪(intense, driving, or overmastering feeling or conviction)

④暴怒(an outbreak of anger)

⑤酷爱(a strong liking or desire for or devotion to some activity, object, or concept)

annihilate *v*. ①使失效(to cause to be of no effect, nullify)

②消灭,摧毁(to destroy the substance or force of)

③严重地伤害(to destroy a considerable part of) 例 bombs annihilated the city

---

6.【正确答案】C

【中文释义】建立观察时所需的分类目录的必然性往往会导致一个企图来做绝对的分类,而现实中往往只是渐变现象。

【解题分析】Leads to 这个短语在 SECTION 19 的第 6 题就出现过,与这一题的考法完全一致,continue, remain, lead to 都会产生同义词; become, transition, change 都会导致反义词。应该将 discrete 填到第一空格,答案为 C。

【重点词条】**discrete** *adj*. ①离散的(constituting a separate entity, individually distinct)

②分散的(consisting of distinct or unconnected elements, noncontinuous)

③有限的(taking on or having a finite or countably infinite number of values) 例 ～probabilities/a～random variable

digression *n*. 游离主题(the act or an instance of digressing in a discourse or other usu. organized literary work)

gradation *n*. ①序列(a series forming successive stages)

②逐渐的转移(a gradual passing from one tint or shade to another)

ambiguity *n*. ①模糊(the quality or state of being ambiguous esp. in meaning)

②模糊语(an ambiguous word or expression)

7.【正确答案】C

【中文释义】在 Phaistos 的 Minoan 遗址所发现的独特的泥板通常被学者们举证为最早的印刷的例子,这些学者支持这泥板(第一块印刷品)的历史地位,尽管有很多同等的观点支持其他印刷的人工制品。

【解题分析】By 的解题方法又一次出现,by 前要填学者的动作,而 by 后告诉这个动作"defened its claim to this status"。Its 指代的是 clay disk, claim 的意思是"特性", this status 指上文的"as the earliest example",故下句明确说明学者们 defend 即支持 clay disk 具有这种特征。所以上句仍应为学者们认可支持这种看法。事实上 despite 之后说得更明确,转折之后支持 other printing artifacts, 所以上文的学者当然是支持上文的 clay disk 为 earliest example,正确答案为 C。

【重点词条】adduce *v*. ①引用为证据(to offer as example, reason, or proof in discussion or analysis)

concede *v*. ①接受(to grant as a right or privilege)

②认为正确(to accept as true, valid, or accurate) 例 The right of the state to tax is generally conceded.

③勉强接受(to acknowledge grudgingly or hesitantly)

SECTION 84

1. Punishment for violating moral rules is much more common than reward for following them; thus,____ the rules goes almost ____ in society.

   (A) association with. . undefended

   (B) adherence to. . unnoticed

   (C) affiliation of. . uncorrected

   (D) opposition to. . unchecked

   (E) ignorance of. . unresolved

2. Compassion is a great respecter of justice: we pity those who suffer ____.

   (A) shamelessly

   (B) unwittingly

   (C) vicariously

   (D) intensively

   (E) undeservedly

3. No work illustrated his disdain for a systematic approach to research better than his dissertation, which was rejected primarily because his bibliography constituted, at best, ____ survey of the major texts in his field.

   (A) an unimaginative

   (B) an orthodox

   (C) a meticulous

   (D) a comprehensive

   (E) a haphazard

4. In contrast to the ____ with which the acquisition of language by young children was once regarded, the process by which such learning occurs has now become the object of ____.

   (A) intensity. . fascination

   (B) incuriosity. . scrutiny

   (C) anxiety. . criticism

   (D) reverence. . admiration

   (E) impatience. . training

5. The senator's remark that she is ambivalent about running for a second term is ____ given the extremely ____ fund-raising activities of her campaign committee.

   (A) disingenuous. . reluctant

   (B) futile. . clandestine

   (C) sincere. . visible

   (D) persuasive. . apathetic

   (E) straightforward. . energetic

6. Until quite recently research on diabetes had, as a kind of holding action, attempted to refine the ____ of the disease, primarily because no preventive strategy seemed at all likely to be ____.

   (A) definition. . necessary

   (B) anticipation. . acceptable

   (C) understanding. . costly

    (D) treatment. . practicable

    (E) symptoms. . feasible

7. Most plant species exhibit ____ in their geographical distribution: often, a given species
is found over a large geographical area, but
individual populations within that range are

widely ____ .

    (A) discontinuity. . separated

    (B) density. . dispersed

    (C) symmetry. . observed

    (D) uniformity. . scattered

    (E) concentration. . adaptable

SECTION 84 解答

1.【正确答案】B

  【中文释义】违反道德准则的惩罚比遵守道德准则的奖励更普遍,因此,遵守准则在社会中总是不被人注意。

  【解题分析】分号句上句谈到了破坏和遵守道德准则两种行为,所以分号句下半句重复时,只有这两种可能性,可选 B、D、E;D 和 E 这两个选项都是讲破坏道德准则,所以应该遭受到惩罚,而第二个选项都未能表达出这个意思,B 选项表达只遵守准则但却不受到表扬,也就是 unnoticed。正确答案是 B。

2.【正确答案】E

  【中文释义】同情心是对正义的一个巨大的关怀:我们往往同情那些遭受无辜苦难的人。

  【解题分析】冒号后表示重复,pity 即重复上文的 compassion,空格应该针对 justise 这个概念,故选 E。

  【重点词条】**unwitting** *adj*. ①不聪明的(not knowing, unaware) 例 kept the truth from
their~friends

          ②没有预料到的(not intended, inadvertent) 例 an~mistake

      vicarious *adj*. ①替代的(serving instead of someone or something else)

          ②已降级的(that has been delegated) 例 ~authority

          ③替罪羊的(performed or suffered by one person as a substitute
for another or to the benefit or advantage of another, substitu-
tionary) 例 a~sacrifice

          ④通过…感受到的(experienced or realized through imaginative
or sympathetic participation in the experience of another)

3.【正确答案】E

  【中文释义】他的论文最好地展示了他对系统研究方法的鄙夷不屑,他的论文被广为反对,主要就是因为他的参考书籍最多只是表明了对这个领域的主要著作的随机的研究。

  【解题分析】分析主干可知空格应和 disdain for a systematic approach 吻合,答案为 E。

  【重点词条】**meticulous** *adj*. 极端挑剔的(marked by extreme or excessive care in the consideration or treatment of details)

haphazard *adj*. 毫无计划的,缺乏顺序的(marked by lack of plan, order, or direction)

4.【正确答案】B

【中文释义】与人们过去对待儿童学习语言行为的漠不关心构成了强烈的对比,这种学习发生的过程现在已经成为仔细研究的对象。

【解题分析】第一空格后的 with 和 regard 构成词组 regard with,故第一空格填某种态度,第二空格填一种相反态度。构成一组相反态度的为 B。

【重点词条】acquisition *n*. ①获取(the act of acquiring)
　　　　　　　　　　②获取物(something acquired or gained)

　　　　　　scrutiny *n*. ①检查,审查(a searching study, inquiry, or inspection, examination)
　　　　　　　　　　②审查的眼神(a searching look)
　　　　　　　　　　③仔细地看(close watch, surveillance)

5.【正确答案】D

【中文释义】这位议员的声明——她对是否参加第二届连任竞选仍未下决心——是很可信的,考虑到她的竞选委员会的极为冷淡的集资活动。

【解题分析】Given 表示因果关系,答案为 D。

【重点词条】clandestine *adj*. ①隐秘的(marked by, held in, or conducted with secrecy, surreptitious)

　　　　　　apathetic *adj*. ①冷淡的(having or showing little or no feeling or emotion, spiritless)
　　　　　　　　　　②不感兴趣的(having little or no interest or concern, indifferent)

　　　　　　straightforward *adj*. ①坦白的,精确的,清楚的(free from evasiveness or obscurity, exact, candid) 例 a～account
　　　　　　　　　　②概念清晰的(clear-cut, precise)
　　　　　　　　　　③直截了当的(proceeding in a straight course or manner, direct, undeviating)

6.【正确答案】D

【中文释义】直到最近,对糖尿病的研究一直作为一种抑制疾病的手段,尝试改进治疗效果,主要因为根本没有预防性的方案看上去是可行的。

【解题分析】As a kind of holding action 修饰下文,holding action 为抑制作用的意思。与下文的 preventive strategy 相比:一个是疾病发生前的预防措施,另一个则应为疾病发生后的抑制疾病危害的治疗手段。答案为 D。

【重点词条】hold back ①抑制(to hinder the progress or achievement of, restrain)
　　　　　　　　　　②强忍住(to refrain from revealing or parting with)

hold-down ①用于固定物品在原地的器具(something used to fasten an object in place)

②控制(an act of holding down)

③限制(limit) 例 agreed to wage-rate～s

hold down ①控制在许可范围内(to keep within limits) 例 hold the noise down

②承担责任(to assume the responsibility for) 例 holding down two jobs

hold off ①耽误(to block from an objective, delay)

②拖延,推迟(to defer action on, postpone)

③对抗,抵制(to fight to a standoff, withstand)

hold up ①阻止(delay, impede)

②吸引注意力(to call attention to, single out) 例 his work was held up to ridicule/hold this up as perfection

③继续有效(to continue in the same condition without failing or losing effectiveness or force) 例 You seem to be holding up under the strain.

hold on ①坚持(to maintain a condition or position, persist)

②保持在接通状态(to await a telephone connection or similar things desired or requested)

hold out ①继续发挥作用(to remain unsubdued or operative, continue to cope or function)

②出局,离群(to refuse to go along with others in a concerted action or to come to an agreement) 例 holding out for a shorter workweek

③提供,展示(to present as something realizable, proffer)

7.【正确答案】A

　【中文释义】大多数植物在地理分布上展示了不连续性:通常一个物种可以在很大的地理区域中找到,但是在那个地域范围内,一个个植物群落却是非常分散的。

　【解题分析】第一空格后的介词短语为 in their geographical distribution,故空格中所填的词为某种分布特征,进一步可知冒号后应从分布特征的角度去阅读。冒号前后表达的分布特征相同的是答案 A。

　【重点词条】 uniformity *n*. 统一(the quality or state of being uniform)

SECTION 85

1. There is hardly a generalization that can be made about people's social behavior and the values informing it that can not be ____ from one or another point of view, or even ____ as

simplistic or vapid.

(A) accepted. . praised

(B) intuited. . exposed

(C) harangued. . retracted

(D) defended. . glorified

(E) challenged. . dismissed

2. Although any destruction of vitamins caused by food irradiation could be ____ the use of dietsupplement, there may be no protection from carcinogens that some fear might be introduced into foods by the process.

(A) counterbalanced by

(B) attributed to

(C) inferred from

(D) augmented with

(E) stimulated by

3. Though he refused any responsibility for the failure of the negotiations, Stevenson had no right ____ himself; it was his ____ that had caused the debacle.

(A) blame. . skill

(B) congratulate. . modesty

(C) berate. . largesse

(D) accuse. . obstinacy

(E) absolve. . acrimony

4. The prevailing union of passionate interest in detailed facts with equal devotion to abstract ____ is a hallmark of our present society; in the past this union appeared, at best, ____ and as if by chance.

(A) data. . extensively

(B) philosophy. . cyclically

(C) generalization. . sporadically

(D) evaluation. . opportunely

(E) intuition. . selectively

5. A century ago the physician's word was ____; to doubt it was considered almost sacrilegious.

(A) inevitable

(B) intractable

(C) incontrovertible

(D) objective

(E) respectively

6. So much of modern fiction in the United States is autobiographical, and so much of the autobiography fictionalized, that the ____ sometimes seem largely ____.

(A) authors. . ignored

(B) needs. . unrecognized

(C) genres. . interchangeable

(D) intentions. . misunderstood

(E)misapprehensions. . uncorrected

7. Robin's words were not without emotions; they retained their level tone only by a careful ____ imminent extremes.

(A) equipoise between

(B) embrace of

(C) oscillation between

(D) limitation to

(E) subjection to

SECTION 85 解答

1.【正确答案】E

【中文释义】很难有一个这样的综合概括,这个概括能够对人们的社会行为及指导这一行为的各种价值观做出归纳,这个概括同时从其他的各种角度来看又能不被动摇,或者不会被指责为思维简单或毫无意义。

【解题分析】两个从句同时修饰 generalization,所以这两个特殊并列的从句应该同义重复,
　　　　　　第一个从句的观点是能够建立这样的概括,第二个从句重复的方式是以双重否
　　　　　　定来表示对这种概括的肯定。事实上全句讲述的就是中国古老的观点"仁者见
　　　　　　仁,智者见智",也就是对任何社会行为和价值观都无法做出一个综合的最终的
　　　　　　概括。

【重点词条】generalization *n*. ①概括,归纳(the act or process of generalizing)
　　　　　　　　　　　　　　②总则(a general statement, law, principle, or proposition)
　　　　　　　　　　　　　　③类似(the act or process whereby a response is made to a
　　　　　　　　　　　　　　　　stimulus similar to but not identical with a reference stimu-
　　　　　　　　　　　　　　　　lus)

　　　　　　inform *v*. ①赋予内涵(to give character or essence to) 例 the principles which
　　　　　　　　　　　　　~modern teaching
　　　　　　　　　　　②指导,导引(guide, direct)
　　　　　　　　　　　③通知,告诉(to make known)

　　　　　　simplistic *adj*. ①简单的(simple)
　　　　　　　　　　　　　②简化主义的(of, relating to, or characterized by simplism,
　　　　　　　　　　　　　　oversimple) 例 adequate, if occasionally~, historical back-
　　　　　　　　　　　　　　ground

2. 【正确答案】A

　　【中文释义】尽管食品的放射性处理所导致的维他命的损失可以由使用食品添加剂来弥
　　　　　　　补,但是也可能缺乏对致癌物的防范,这种致癌物是由(使用食品添加剂)这个
　　　　　　　过程所导致的,从而产生了对食品的某种恐慌心理。

　　【解题分析】上下句转折,下句为 no protection, 是一种坏的情况,所以上句应为好的情况,
　　　　　　　上句结构简化即为 destruction could be counterbalanced(A),只有这一选择才能
　　　　　　　表示一种好的情况。

　　【重点词条】destruction *n*. ①被破坏的状态(the state or fact of being destroyed,ruin)
　　　　　　　　　　　　　　②破坏(the action or process of destroying something)

　　　　　　counterbalance *n*. ①均衡(a weight that balances another)
　　　　　　　　　　　　　　②反向均衡力(a force or influence that offsets or checks an
　　　　　　　　　　　　　　　opposing force)
　　　　　　　　　　　v. 相抗衡(to oppose or balance with an equal weight or force)

3. 【正确答案】E

　　【中文释义】尽管他拒绝承担任何谈判失败的责任,但是史蒂文自己也没有推托的理由;的
　　　　　　　确是由于他的尖刻才导致了这场彻底的失败。

　　【解题分析】分号上下句重复,上句的主句与从句转折,即使不填答案也应知道上句主句的
　　　　　　　意思为:他该承担责任,所以分号下半句重复这个意思,表示他有责任,可选 D
　　　　　　　或者 E,而 D 的第一个单词不正确,故选择 E。

　　【重点词条】berate *v*. ①训斥(to scold or condemn vehemently and at length,scold,accuse)

②污蔑(to charge with a fault or offense,blame)

③公诉(to charge with an offense judicially or by a public process)

4.【正确答案】C

【中文释义】这种占绝对主导地位的将对细节事实的强烈兴趣与对抽象概括的同样的专注结合的做法是我们当今社会的特点;在过去,这种结合最多只是零星地出现,并且显得是偶然出现的。

【解题分析】简化句结构即为:union is a hallmark of our present society; in the past, this union appeared sporadically。一个常见的时间对比型。句子最为复杂的部分为 union 后的介词短语,但这个介词短语的分隔纯属 ETS 设置的陷阱,根本不需要理会。

【重点词条】devotion *n*.①虔诚(religious fervor, piety)

②宗教的献身(a religious exercise or practice other than the regular corporate worship of a congregation)

③奉献(the act of devoting)

hallmark *n*.①金银的纯度标记(an official mark stamped on gold and silver articles in England to attest their purity)

②商标,铭牌(a mark or device placed or stamped on an article of trade to indicate origin, purity, or genuineness)

③特征,特点(a distinguishing characteristic, trait, or feature)

例 the dramatic flourishes which are the~of the trial lawyer

cyclic *adj*.①圆的 (of, relating to, or being a cycle)

②周而复始的,循环的(moving in cycles) 例 ~time

5.【正确答案】A

【中文释义】一个世纪以前医生的话是无可驳斥的,怀疑它几乎被看成是亵渎神灵的。

【解题分析】冒号表示重复和解释,既然医生的话被认为是亵渎神灵,当然就会遭到怀疑。

【重点词条】inevitable *adj*.不可避免的

incontrovertible *adj*.无可驳斥的(unexceptionable)

sacrilegious *adj*.亵渎神灵的

6.【正确答案】C

【中文释义】如此多的美国现代小说是自传体的,并且又有如此多的自传体作品小说化了,以至于文体之间有时看上去很大程度上是可以互换的。

【解题分析】整句是一个 so...that 的因果结构,原因句中频繁出现小说和自传,并且是两者的相互表达,所以结果句中选 C 答案是显而易见的。

【重点词条】interchangeable *adj*.可相互代替的(capable of being interchanged;permitting mutual substitution)

misapprehension *n*.误解(to apprehend wrongly,misunderstand)

7.【正确答案】A

【中文释义】鲁宾的话并不缺乏情绪,它们只是通过小心翼翼地平衡各种突发的极端情绪来保持平稳的语调。

【解题分析】By 前后是手段和因果的关系,若要保持平稳的语调则应尽量减少极端情绪,答案为 A。

【重点词条】**equipoise** *n*. ①平静,宁静(a state of equilibrium)

②平衡(counterbalance)

level *adj*. ①稳定的,不犹豫的(steady, unwavering) 例 gave him a～look

②平静的,不兴奋的(calm, unexcited) 例 spoke in～tones

③合情合理的(reasonable, balanced) 例 arrive at a justly proportional and～judgment on this affair

SECTION 86

1. That she seemed to prefer ____ to concentrated efforts is undeniable; nevertheless the impressive quantity of her finished painting suggests that her actual relationship to her art was anything but ____.

(A) preparation. . passionate

(B) artfulness. . disengaged

(C) dabbling. . superficial

(D) caprice. . considered

(E) indecision. . lighthearted

2. Because of the excellent preservation of the fossil, anatomical details of early horseshoe crab were ____ for the first time, enabling experts to ____ the evolution of the horseshoe crab.

(A) scrutinized. . ensure

(B) verified. . advance

(C) identified. . distort

(D) obscured. . illustrate

(E) clarified. . reassess

3. The philosopher claimed that a person who must consciously ____ his or her own indifference before helping another is behaving more nobly than one whose basic disposition allows such an act to be performed without ____.

(A) feign. . enthusiasm

(B) censure. . comment

(C) embrace. . duplicity

(D) suffer. . effort

(E) overcome. . deliberation

4. The senator's attempt to convince the public that he is not interested in running for a second term is ____ given the extremely ____ fund raising activities of his campaign committee.

(A) futile. . clandestine

(B) sincere. . visible

(C) specious. . apathetic

(D) disingenuous. . public

(E) straightforward. . dubious

5. Although a change in management may appear to ____ shift in a company's fortunes, more often than not is its impact is ____.

(A)hinder. . measurable

(B) promote. . demonstrable

(C) accelerate. . Profound

(D) betray. . fundamental

(E) augur. . inconsiderable

6. The skeleton of _____ bird that was recently discovered indicated that this ancient creature _____ today's birds in that, unlike earlier birds and unlike reptilian ancestors, it had not a tooth in its head.

   (A) a primeval. . obscured

   (B) a unique. . preempted

   (C) a primitive. . anticipated

(D) a contemporary. . foreshadowed

(E) an advanced. . differed from

7. While many unitize homeopathic remedies to treat health problems, other people not _____ such alternate treatment, _____ conventional medical treatments instead.

   (A) distrust. . employing

   (B) embrace. . eschewing

   (C) reject. . envisioning

   (D) countenance. . relying on

   (E) recommend. . turning from

SECTION 86 解答

1. 【正确答案】C

   【中文释义】她看上去更喜爱时断时续的而不是集中突击式的努力,这种做法是无可否认的;况且,她完成的作品惊人的品质说明了,她和她的艺术之间真正的关系绝对不是浅尝辄止的。

   【解题分析】分号句上下句重复。上句讲她的做法是 undeniable 的,所以下句应对她和艺术的关系做褒扬,而 anything but 表示否定,故第二空格应为贬义词,B、C、候选,但 B 的 disengaged 不能作 relationship 的表语,故选 C。

   【重点词条】**dabbling** *n*. 漫不经心,随随便便的态度(a superficial or intermittent interest, investigation, or experiment) 例 his~s in philosophy and art

          indecision *n*. 犹豫不决(a wavering between two or more possible courses of action, irresolution)

          considered *adj*. ①深思熟虑的(matured by extended deliberative thought)

                    例 a~opinion

                  ②认真严肃的(viewed with respect or esteem)

          disengage *v*. ①解开,分离(to release from something that engages or involves)

                  ②脱离,撤退(to release or detach oneself,withdraw)

2. 【正确答案】E

   【中文释义】因为化石的完美保存,早期马蹄蟹的解剖体细节才第一次得以澄清,使得科学家能够重新衡量马蹄蟹的演变。

   【解题分析】由因果关系可得 B、C、E,由分隔结构可得 E。

   【重点词条】**identify** *v*. ①使相同(to cause to be or become identical)

              ②认为相同(to conceive as united as in spirit, outlook, or principle) 例 groups that are identified with conservation

          obscure *v*. ①使暗淡无光(dark, dim,shrouded in or hidden by darkness)

②模糊,看不清(not clearly seen or easily distinguished, faint)

③不易理解或表达的(not readily understood or clearly expressed; also: mysterious)

④没有名气(not prominent or famous) 例 an～poet

clarify v. ①过滤,澄清(to make a liquid clear or pure usu. by freeing from suspended matter)

②澄清事实(to free of confusion)

③解释清楚(to make understandable)

3.【正确答案】E

【中文释义】哲学家们认为一个必须在帮助别人之前非常清醒地克服自己的冷漠的人是比另外一种人做得更高尚的,另外那种人是指那些自身的基本性格导致这些助人行为发生而不需要事先深思熟虑的人。

【解题分析】一套比较好的题型,第一种人需要 must consciously 做一件事。故一对比即可知道后文的 without 后应填上 consciously 对应的同义词。答案选 E。

【重点词条】duplicity n. ①欺骗,诈骗(contradictory doubleness of thought, speech, or action; the belying of one's true intentions by deceptive words or action)

②两面性(the quality or state of being double or twofold)

4.【正确答案】D

【中文释义】这议员试图来使公众相信他对参加第二届连任不感兴趣是不真诚的,考虑到他的竞选委员会的极为公开的募集资金活动。

【解题分析】该题题干与 SECTION 84 的第 5 题几乎完全一样,逻辑结构也一样,只不过 4 月份的考卷中议员说了真话,而 11 月份中又说了假话而已。

【重点词条】straightforward adj. ①坦白的,精确的,清楚的(free from evasiveness or obscurity, exact, candid) 例 a～account

②概念清晰的(clear-cut, precise)

③直截了当的(proceeding in a straight course or manner, direct, undeviating)

5.【正确答案】E

【中文释义】尽管管理的变化可能显得预示了公司命运的转变,更多的可能是它的影响微不足道。

【解题分析】上下句转折,上句谈这种转变可能会有作用,下句的主语是 its impact,下句应对上句提出否定,答案 E 的 inconsiderable 指影响力微不足道,表否定,成为正确答案。

【重点词条】betray v. ①误导,欺骗(to lead astray, seduce)

②背叛(to deliver to an enemy by treachery)

③不自觉中流露(to reveal unintentionally)

④揭示,展示(show, indicate)

⑤泄密(to disclose in violation of confidence)

augur *n*. ①古罗马的占卜官(an official diviner of ancient Rome)

②占卜师(one held to foretell events by omens)

v. ①占卜 (to foretell esp. from omens)

②预示,展示(to give promise of, presage) 例 Higher pay ~s a better future.

inconsiderable *adj*. 不重要的(not considerable, trivial)

6.【正确答案】C

【中文释义】最近发现的一种古老的鸟的骨骼表明,这个古代动物不像更早的鸟和爬行动物的祖先,它的头部没有牙齿,在这方面它比今天的鸟类提前了。

【解题分析】This ancient creature 指代上文的 bird,所以第一空格填 ancient 的同义词,可选 A 和 C,下文中又有了一次比较,可得知这个古代的鸟没有牙齿,而它和今天的鸟在有没有牙齿这个问题上是相同还是不同呢? 当然,今天的鸟也没有牙齿,所以答案选 C。

【重点词条】**foreshadow** *vt*. 预示(to represent, indicate, or typify beforehand, prefigure)

7.【正确答案】D

【中文释义】尽管很多人使用顺势治疗法来解决健康问题,但其他人不支持这样的另类治疗法,反而依赖传统的医药治疗。

【解题分析】第二空格为分隔结构,重复前文,alternate treatment 与 traditional medical treatments 又显然是反义词,故两空格应为同义词,可直接选择得答案 C。

【重点词条】**homeopathic** *adj*. ①同种疗法的,顺势疗法的(of or relating to homeopathy)

②性情平淡的(of a diluted or insipid nature) 例 a ~ abolitionist

employ *v*. ①使用(to make use of someone or something inactive) 例 ~ a pen for sketching

②雇用(to provide with a job that pays wages or a salary)

③奉献(to devote to or direct toward a particular activity or person) 例 ~ed all her energies to help the poor

eschew *v*. 避开,逃避(to avoid habitually esp. on moral or practical grounds, shun)

envision *v*. 构思,构图(to picture to oneself) 例 ~s a career dedicated to promoting peace

countenance *n*. ①平静的表情,安详(calm expression, mental composure)

②表情,面庞(look, expression)

v. 支持,赞助 (to offer approval or sanction, moral support)

SECTION 87

1. As business become aware that their adver-
   tising must ＿＿ the everyday concerns of
   cinsumers, their commercials will be charac-
   terized by a greater degree of ＿＿.
   (A) allay. . pessimism
   (B) address. . realism
   (C) evade. . verisimilitude
   (D) engage. . fancy
   (E) change. . sincerity

2. Because the lawyer's methods were found to
   be ＿＿, the disciplinary committee ＿＿ his
   privileges.
   (A) unimpeachable. . suspended
   (B) ingenious. . withdrew
   (C) questionable. . expanded
   (D) unscrupulous. . revoked
   (E) reprehensible. . augmented

3. People of intelligence and achievement can
   nonetheless be so ＿＿ and lacking in ＿＿
   that they gamble their reputations by break-
   ing the law to further their own ends.
   (A) devious. . propensity
   (B) culpable. . propensity
   (C) obsequious. . deference
   (D) truculent. . independence
   (E) greedy. . integrity

4. A number of scientists have published articles ＿＿ global warming, stating ＿＿ that
   there is no solid scientific evidence to support the theory that the earth is warming
   because of increases in greenhouse gases.
   (A) debunking. . categorically

   (B) rejecting. . paradoxically
   (C) deploring. . optimistically
   (D) dismissing. . hesitantly
   (E) proving. . candidly

5. The senator's attempt to convince the public
   that she is not interested in running for a
   second term is as ＿＿ as her opponent's at-
   tempt to disguise his intention to run against
   her.
   (A) biased
   (B) unsuccessful
   (C) inadvertent
   (D) indecisive
   (E) remote

6. MacCrory's conversation was ＿＿; she
   could never tell a story, chiefly because she
   always forgot it, and she was never guilty
   of a witticism, unless by accident.
   (A) scintillating
   (B) unambiguous
   (C) perspicuous
   (D) stultifying
   (E) facetious

7. Despite its many ＿＿, the whole-language
   philosophy of teaching reading continues to
   gain ＿＿ among educators.
   (A) detractors. . notoriety
   (B) adherents. . prevalence
   (C) critics. . currency
   (D) enthusiasts. . popularity
   (E) practitioners. . credibility

SECTION 87 解答

1.【正确答案】B

【中文释义】因为商界已清醒地意识到他们的广告必须着眼于消费者日常关心之物,所以他们的商业广告将会有更多的现实主义的特征。

【解题分析】As 引导一个简单的因果关系,第二空格应与上文的 everyday concerns 相关,同义或反义取决于第一个空格,但在五个选项中, everyday concerns 的同义词或反义词只出现一个 B 的 realism, 故直接选 B 即可。

【重点词条】**allay** *v*. ①减轻,缓和(to subdue or reduce in intensity or severity, alleviate)

例 expect a breeze to~the heat

②使平静(to make quiet, calm)

address *n*. 地址,致辞,演讲,说话的技巧

v. 向…致辞,演讲,从事于,忙于某事

2.【正确答案】D

【中文释义】因为这个律师的方法被查明是很无耻的,所以纪律委员会废除了他的特权。

【重点词条】**unscrupulous** *adj*. 肆无忌惮的(not scrupulous, unprincipled)

revoke *v*. ①撤消,废除(to annul by recalling or taking back, rescind) 例 ~a will

②回退(to bring or call back)

reprehensible *adj*. 应该谴责的(worthy of or deserving reprehension, culpable)

3.【正确答案】E

【中文释义】如此具有智慧和成就的人们居然会如此贪婪并且缺乏正直感,以至于他们不惜违反法律,以他们的声誉为赌注来进一步推进他们自己最终成就。

【解题分析】Nonetheless 表转折,所以第一空格应填贬义,第二空格填褒义,再由 so...that 结构,可得答案 E。

【重点词条】**devious** *adj*. ①遥远的(out-of-the-way, remote)

②不正的,歪斜的(wandering, roundabout) 例 a~path

③随意的(moving without a fixed course, errant) 例 ~breezes

④不正直的,邪恶的(deviating from a right, accepted, or common course, not straightforward, cunning)

integrity *n*. ①正直(firm adherence to a code of esp. moral or artistic values, incorruptibility)

②完整(the quality or state of being complete or undivided, completeness)

4.【正确答案】A

【中文释义】一些科学家发表文章来揭示全球变暖的真相,断然指出并没有充分的科学论据支持这个理论——由于温室气体的增加,地球正在变暖。

【解题分析】第二空格填副词,可以不予考虑,直接由这一段文字知学者们认为温室效应并无根据,这一段分隔就是对前文的重复,可选出 A、B、D,而 B、D 第二个副词又不对,故选 A。

【重点词条】**debunk** *v*. 揭穿(to expose the sham or falseness of) 例 ~a legend

    categorical *adj*. ①绝对的,无条件的(absolute, unqualified) 例 a~denial
        ②分类的,类属的

    deplore *v*. ①忏悔(to feel or express grief for)
        ②懊悔(to consider unfortunate or deserving of deprecation)

5.【正确答案】B

【中文释义】这个议员企图使公众确信她对参加第二届连任竞选毫无兴趣,这种企图与她的对手希望掩盖自己与她竞选的企图一样不成功。

【解题分析】这个句子已经是第三次出现了,又少许变了点花样,句子简化后为 the attempt is as unsuccessful as her opponent's attempt。事实上只要挑一个能修饰主语 attempt 的形容词就可以了,答案 B。

【重点词条】**inadvertent** *adj*. ①未预料到的(not focusing the mind on a matter, inattentive)
        ②无目的的(unintentional)

    remote *adj*. ①遥远的
        ②与世隔离的
        ③遥控的

6.【正确答案】D

【中文释义】默克莱里的谈话展示着自己的愚蠢:她从来不能讲一个故事,主要因为她总是忘记,并且,除非是意外情况,她从来都没有能力理解一个俏皮话。

【解题分析】冒号前后表示解释,冒号后显然是在展示她的各种愚蠢的表现。Be guilty of 的含义在这一句子中是"理解了或意识到了…"。

【重点词条】**stultify** *v*. ①宣布无效(to allege or prove to be of unsound mind and hence not responsible)
        ②愚弄(to cause to appear or be stupid, foolish, or absurdly illogical)
        ③破坏,使失效(to impair, invalidate, or make ineffective, negate)

    guilty *adj*. 清醒地认识或认知(conscious, cognizant);此义项比较特殊,依据 Page 1010 Webster's Third New International Dictionary

7.【正确答案】C

【中文释义】不管不顾对它的许多批评,阅读教学法的纯文本宗旨继续在教育家中获得主流地位。

【解题分析】两个空格应为反义词,正确答案 C。

【重点词条】**detractor** *v.* ①贬低(to speak ill of)

②分散注意力(divert) 例 ~attention

③降低重要性(to diminish the importance, value, or effective-

ness of something)

notoriety *n.* ①臭名昭彰(the quality or state of being notorious)

②声誉极差的人(a notorious person)

prevalence *n.* ①普遍流行(the quality or state of being prevalent)

②流行的程度,尤指传染病人口密度(the degree to which some-

thing is prevalent; the percentage of a population that is affect-

ed with a particular disease at a given time)

credibility *n.* ①信誉(the quality or power of inspiring belief) 例 an account

lacking in~

②信心(capacity for belief) 例 strains her reader's~

SECTION 88

1. That she was _____ rock climbing did not diminish her _____ to join her friends on rock
climbing expenditure.

(A) attracted to. . eagerness

(B) timid about. . reluctance

(C) fearful of. . determination

(D) curious about. . aspiration

(E) knowledgeable about. . hope

2. Data concerning the effects on a small population of high concentrations of a potentially
hazardous chemical are frequently used to
_____ the effects on a large population of
lower amounts of the same chemical.

(A) verify

(B) redress

(C) predict

(D) realize

(E) augment

3. Conceptually, it's hard to reconcile a defense attorney's _____ to ensure that false

testimony is not knowingly put forward
with the attorney's mandate to mount the
most _____ defense conceivable for the client.

(A) efforts. . cautious

(B) duty. . powerful

(C) inability. . eloquent

(D) failure. . diversified

(E) promise. . informed

4. The term "modern" has always been used
broadly by historians, and recent reports indicate that its meaning has become more
_____ than ever.

(A) precise

(B) pejorative

(C) revisionist

(D) acceptable

(E) amorphous

5. He would _____ no arguments, and to this
end he enjoined us to _____.

(A) brook. . silence

(B) acknowledge. . neglect

(C) broach. . abstinence

(D) fathom. . secrecy

(E) tolerate. . defiance

6. Originally, most intellectual criticism of mass culture was ＿＿＿ in character, being based on the assumption that the wider the appeal, the more ＿＿＿ the product.

(A) unpredictable. . undesirable

(B) ironic. . popular

(C) extreme. . outlandish

(D) frivolous. . superfluous

(E) negative. . shoddy

7. Surprisingly, given the dearth of rain that fell on the corn crop, the yield of the harvest was ＿＿＿; consequently, the corn reserves of the country have not been ＿＿＿.

(A) inadequate. . replenished

(B) encouraging. . depleted

(C) compromised. . salvaged

(D) abundant. . extended

(E) disappointing. . harmed

SECTION 88 解答

1. 【正确答案】C

【中文释义】她对攀岩很害怕,这并没有动摇她去参加朋友们攀岩历险的决心。

【重点词条】**aspiration** *n*. ①呼吸声(the pronunciation or addition of an aspiration)

②呼吸(a drawing of something in, out, up, or through by or as if by suction)

③雄心壮志(a strong desire to achieve something high or great)

knowledgeable *adj*. 富有智慧的,知识广博的(having or exhibiting knowledge or intelligence, keen)

2. 【正确答案】C

【中文释义】关于高浓度的具有潜在危险的化学物对少量人口的影响的数据总是频繁地被用来预测更低的同种化学物在更大数量人口中的影响。

【解题分析】句子主干为 data are used to predict (C) the effects 能和 data 构成搭配的是 C。

【重点词条】**augment** *v*. ①增大,加大密度(to make greater, more numerous, larger, or more intense) 例 The impact of the report was～ed by its timing.

②使…增大(to add an augment to)

③补充(supplement) 例 ～ed her scholarship by working nights

3. 【正确答案】B

【中文释义】从概念上来看,很难调和这两个概念:其一是辩护律师的责任来确保不会故意地提供虚假证词,其二是律师的被授予的权利来为当事人准备令人信服的最有力的辩护词。

【解题分析】只要分清主干 reconcile a defense attorney's (duty) with the attorney's mandate 即可知空格应填 mandate 的反义词。

【重点词条】**mandate** *n.* ①权威的命令(an authoritative command; a formal order from a superior court or official to an inferior one)

②赋予代表的行动的权利(an authorization to act given to a representative) 例 accepted the~of the people

mount *n.* ①高山(a high hill, mountain)

v. ①上升(rise, ascend)

②增加(to increase in amount or extent) 例 expenses began to~

4.【正确答案】E

【中文释义】"现代"这个词汇被历史学家们用得非常广泛,最近的汇报表明,它的含义已经变得比以往任何时候都更不确定。

【解题分析】由 be used broadly 可推断"modern"的含义现在变得"不确定"。

【重点词条】**pejorative** *adj.* 贬义的,轻蔑的(having negative connotations, tending to disparage or belittle, depreciatory)

n. 贬义词

amorphous *adj.* ①变形的,无定形的(having no definite form, shapeless)

例 an~cloud mass

②不明确的,无定则的(being without definite character or nature, unclassifiable) 例 an~segment of society

③散漫的(lacking organization or unity) 例 an~style

④非结晶态的(having no real or apparent crystalline form, uncrystallized) 例 an~mineral

5.【正确答案】A

【中文释义】他不会容忍任何讨论,最终他命令我们沉默。

【解题分析】And 前后表因果,符合因果关系得只有 A。

【重点词条】**fathom** *n.* ①英寸(a unit of length equal to six feet or 1.83 meters used for measuring the depth of water)

②理解领会(comprehension)

vi. ①探测(probe)

②揣摩,推测(to penetrate and come to understand) 例 couldn't~the problem

6.【正确答案】B

【中文释义】从本质上说,大多数对通俗文化的理性批判在其内涵上是可笑的,它们建立在这样的假设之上,即吸引力越广泛,作品越受欢迎。

【解题分析】后半句的假设实际上就是通俗文化的精神实质,所以理性批判的前提假设实际上与通俗文化一致,故理性批判对通俗文化的批判就变成了对自己的根本前提的批判,所以非常可笑。

【重点词条】appeal *n*. ①呼吁,请求(an earnest plea, entreaty)

②吸引力(the power of arousing a sympathetic response, attraction)

例 Movies had a great～for him.

v. ①上诉(to take proceedings to have a lower court's decision reviewed in a higher court)

②请求裁判员裁决(to call upon another for corroboration, vindication, or decision)

③请求(to make an earnest request)

④激发同情心(to arouse a sympathetic response)

outlandish *adj*. ①国外的(of or relating to another country, foreign)

②奇异古怪的(strikingly out of the ordinary, bizarre) 例 an ～costume

③离经叛道的(exceeding proper or reasonable limits or standards)

shoddy *adj*. ①低级趣味的,浮夸的(inferior, imitative, or pretentious articles or matter)

②庸俗而华丽的(pretentious vulgarity)

7.【正确答案】B

【中文释义】让人吃惊的是,考虑到稻谷只承受了如此少的降雨,收成是相当令人欢欣鼓舞的;随之而来的是这个国家的稻谷储量并没有减少。

【解题分析】由 given 因果关系可得 B、D,再由 consequently 可得 B。

【重点词条】replenish *v*. ①充满,装满(to fill with persons or animals, stock)

②激励,鼓舞(to fill with inspiration or power, nourish)

③再充满(to fill or build up again) 例 ～ed his glass

读者反馈表

尊敬的读者：

　　您好！非常感谢您对**新东方大愚图书**的信赖与支持,希望您抽出宝贵的时间填写这份反馈表,以便帮助我们改进工作,今后能为您提供更优秀的图书。谢谢！

　　为了答谢您对我们的支持,我们将对反馈的信息进行随机抽奖活动,当月将有 20 位幸运读者可获赠**《新东方英语》**期刊一份。我们将定期在新东方大愚图书网站 www.dogwood.com.cn 公布获奖者名单并及时寄出奖品,敬请关注。

来信请寄：　　北京市海淀区海淀中街 6 号新东方大厦 750 室　　北京新东方大愚文化传播有限公司
　　　　　　　　　　　　　　　　图书部收

　　　　邮编：100080　　　　　　　　　　　　　　E-mail：club@dogwood.com.cn

姓名：＿＿＿＿＿＿　年龄：＿＿＿＿＿＿　职业：＿＿＿＿＿＿　教育背景：＿＿＿＿＿＿　邮编：＿＿＿＿＿＿

通讯地址：＿＿＿＿＿＿＿＿＿＿＿＿＿＿＿＿＿＿＿＿＿＿＿＿　联系电话：＿＿＿＿＿＿＿＿＿

E-mail：＿＿＿＿＿＿＿＿＿＿＿＿＿　您所购买的书籍的名称是：＿＿＿＿＿＿＿＿＿＿＿＿＿

1. 您是通过何种渠道得知本书的（可多选）：
　 □书店　□新东方网站　□大愚网站　□朋友推荐　□老师推荐　□其他＿＿＿＿＿＿＿＿＿＿

2. 您是从何处购买到此书的？　　□书店　□邮购　□图书销售网站　□其他＿＿＿＿＿＿＿＿

3. 影响您购买此书的原因（可多选）：
　 □封面设计　□书评广告　□正文内容　□图书价格　□新东方品牌　□新东方名师　□其他＿＿＿＿＿＿

4. 您对本书的封面设计满意程度：□很满意　□比较满意　□一般　□不满意　□改进建议＿＿＿＿＿＿

5. 本书配哪种音像资料更适合您？　□磁带　□光盘　□MP3　□其他＿＿＿＿＿＿＿＿

6. 您认为本书的内文在哪些方面还需改进？　□结构编排　□难易程度　□内容丰富性　□内文版式

7. 本书最令您满意的地方：□内文　□封面　□价格　□纸张

8. 您对本书的推荐率：□没有　□1 人　□1—3 人　□3—5 人　□5 人以上

9. 您更希望我们为您提供哪些方面的英语类图书？
　 □四六级类　　□考研类　□雅思考试类　□GRE、GMAT 类　□NEW SAT 类　□实用商务类
　 □休闲欣赏类　□初高中英语类　□其他＿＿＿＿＿＿＿＿＿＿＿＿
　 您目前最希望我们为您出版的图书名称是：＿＿＿＿＿＿＿＿＿＿＿＿＿

10. 您在学习英语过程中最需要哪些方面的帮助？（可多选）
　　□词汇　□听力　□口语　□阅读　□写作　□翻译　□其他

11. 您最喜欢的英语图书品牌：＿＿＿＿＿＿＿＿＿＿＿＿＿＿＿＿＿＿＿
　　理由如下（可多选）：□版式漂亮　□内容实用　□难度适宜　□价格适中　□对考试有帮助　□其他＿＿＿＿＿＿＿＿

12. 看到"新东方"三个字,您首先想到什么？＿＿＿＿＿＿＿＿＿＿＿＿＿＿＿

13. 您的其他意见和建议（可附在本页背面）：＿＿＿＿＿＿＿＿＿＿＿＿＿＿＿＿＿
　　＿＿＿＿＿＿＿＿＿＿＿＿＿＿＿＿＿＿＿＿＿＿＿＿＿＿＿＿＿＿＿＿＿＿＿

14. 填表时间：＿＿＿＿＿＿ 年 ＿＿＿＿ 月 ＿＿＿ 日